BURT FRANKLIN: RESEARCH & SOURCE WORKS SERIES 686

THE HISTORY OF
AMERICAN MUSIC

THE HISTORY OF

AMERICAN MUSIC

BY

LOUIS C. ELSON

*WITH TWELVE FULL-PAGE PHOTOGRAVURES AND ONE HUN-
DRED AND SIX ILLUSTRATIONS IN THE TEXT*

BURT FRANKLIN
NEW YORK

Published by LENOX HILL Pub. & Dist. Co. (Burt Franklin)
235 East 44th St., New York, N.Y. 10017
Originally Published: 1925
Reprinted: 1971
Printed in the U.S.A.

S.B.N.: 8337-10559
Library of Congress Card Catalog No.:79-132809
Burt Franklin: Research and Source Works Series 686

Reprinted from the original edition in the University of Arizona
Library.

EDITOR'S NOTE

THIS series of books brings together for the first time the materials for a history of American art. Heretofore there have been attempts to narrate some special period or feature of our artistic development, but the narrative has never been consecutive or conclusive. The present volumes begin with colonial times, and carry the record down to the year 1904. They are intended to cover the graphic, the plastic, the illustrative, the architectural, the musical, and the dramatic arts, and to recite the results in each department historically and critically. That the opinions ventured should be authoritative, the preparation of each volume has been placed in the hands of an expert, — one who practises the craft whereof he writes. The series is therefore a history of American art written from the artist's point of view, and should have special value for that reason.

In this "History of American Music," the second of the series, the author has told of the beginnings, the foreign influences, the changes, the methods, the personal endeavors, that have gone to the making of our present music. Many of the events here narrated occurred but yesterday or are happening to-day, and hence have little perspective for the historian. It has not always been possible to say a final word, even if that were desirable. In its stead the widely scattered facts have been brought together and arranged sequentially that they might tell their own story and point their own conclusion.

CONTENTS

PHOTOGRAVURES

ILLUSTRATIONS IN TEXT

THE HISTORY OF AMERICAN MUSIC

CHAPTER I

THE RELIGIOUS BEGINNINGS OF AMERICAN MUSIC

In presenting a history of the development of American music, one ought, if following chronological sequence, to speak first of the songs of the Aborigines; but although these were, as a matter of course, the earliest melodies that can be traced on this continent, it will be found, when the subject is alluded to in a later chapter, that the music of the North American Indians is responsible for very little of the composition of later times, and seems to have been almost as absolutely "no thoroughfare" as the ancient chants of China.

The true beginnings of American music — seeds that finally grew into a harvest of native compositions — must be sought in a field almost as unpromising as that of the Indian music itself, — the rigid, narrow, and often commonplace psalm-singing of New England. It may be admitted that there was a civilized music on these shores that antedated even these psalm-tunes. There were Englishmen in Virginia almost a generation before the Pilgrims reached their cisatlantic destination; but these adventurers sang their home-songs with absolutely no attempt to alter or to modify them to their new surroundings; they made no effort to establish any new school of music, either vocal or instrumental; and although they gave concerts long before the Pilgrims or Puritans (who would have deemed "concerts" a very heterodox thing) lifted their voices in holy strains in New England, these were merely a reproduction of similar events as they took place in England. They were exotics — abnormal things that took no root in American soil and brought forth no fruit of any kind.

The far less artistic music that was developed in Puritan Boston and Pilgrim Plymouth was something that, although it had its origin overseas, soon became indigenous to the soil, and altered gradually from the style of its prototype as, in the Middle Ages, the Gregorian chant altered in France and became the *Cantus Gallicanus.*

At the very start, both Pilgrims and Puritans, although differing on many points of doctrine, united in a distrust of music. Calvin's views as regards the "divine art" (he had grave doubts about its divinity) tinctured the earliest music of New England. The Pilgrims would have abolished it all but for the fact that the ancient Hebrews had undoubtedly employed psalm-singing in their religious services. They therefore, while rejecting hymns and other sacred music, allowed Psalms to be sung during their devotions.

FIG. I. — ST. MARY'S TUNE.

From Dr. Thomas Walter's "Grounds and Rules of Musick Explained." Boston, 1721.

It is recorded that at the first they used but five tunes for their psalmody. What these tunes were has not been clearly proven. "Old Hundred" was one of them; "York" was another; "Hackney," "Windsor," and "Martyrs" were probably the other three. "Hackney" was sometimes called "St. Mary's" (Fig. 1).

The version used in singing the Psalms, both in Boston, among the Puritans, and in Plymouth, among the Pilgrims, was that arranged by Rev. Henry Ainsworth. As was the case with all the old Puritan versions of the Psalms, it followed the original with painstaking fidelity. The following example of the One Hundredth Psalm may clearly illustrate this: —

" Showt to Jehovah, all the earth
  Serve ye Jehovah with gladnes:
  before him come with singing-mirth
  Know that Jehovah he God is.

" Its he that made us, and not wee;
  his folk and sheep of his feeding.
  O with confession enter yee
  his gates, his courtyards with praising.

" Confesse to him, blesse ye his name.
  Because Jehovah he good is:
  his mercy ever is the same:
  and his faith unto all ages."

The book used by the Pilgrims was a neat duodecimo, a copy of which is preserved in the Public Library of Boston. It has a few tunes, wretchedly printed in very small notes, but the five tunes chosen by the early singers were probably sung without reference to the notation. Another version of the Psalms, by Sternhold and Hopkins, was used in Ipswich, but in Boston all versions were soon superseded by the "Bay Psalm Book,"[1] published in 1640 at Cambridge, Massachusetts, the first book (except a trivial Almanac) printed in the colonies (Fig. 2). Its heading ran —

" The Psalmes in Metre: Faithfully translated for the Use, Edification, and Comfort of the Saints in publick and private, especially in New England."

In the translation and setting to metre of these Psalms many of the most scholarly of the divines of the colony assisted; Eliot and Welds of Roxbury, Mather of Dorchester, and many others

---

[1] The "Bay Psalm Book" exerted a wide and long-continued influence; by 1750 it had reached its twenty-seventh American edition; altogether it must have passed through more than seventy editions. Many editions were published in England and in Scotland. Prince says, in his preface to the version of 1758: "I found in England it was by some eminent Congregations prefer'd to all Others in their Publick Worship, even down to 1717, when I last left that Part of the British Kingdom."

coöperated to make this a valuable and reliable work. Although the style of the poetry may occasionally provoke a smile, one is compelled to pay tribute to the fidelity to the sacred text in every line (Fig. 3). The following version of the Twenty-third Psalm may serve to show this: —

> " The Lord to mee a shepheard is,
> want therefore shall not I
> He in the folds of tender grasse,
> Doth cause me down to lie.

> " To waters calm mee gently leads
> Restore my soule doth hee :
> he doth in paths of righteousnes :
> for his name's sake leade mee.

> " Yea though in valley of deaths shade
> I walk, none ill I'll feare :
> Because thou art with mee, thy rod,
> and staffe my comfort are.

> " Fore me a table thou hast spread,
> in presence of my foes :
> thou dost anoynt my head with oyle,
> my cup it overflowes.

> " Goodnes and mercy surely shall
> all my dayes follow mee :
> and in the Lord's house I shall dwelle
> so long as dayes shall bee."

"Spiritual Songs," that is, hymns, were not as yet admitted into either Pilgrim or Puritan service, but a few appeared in the 1647 edition of the "Bay Psalm Book." The musical repertoire had now extended far beyond the original "five tunes," and more than fifty melodies were suggested, in this edition, for the singing of the Psalms. The setting was the excellent one of Ravenscroft,[1] first published in England in 1621. The tunes were undoubtedly sung in unison, for the harmonization in Ravenscroft was out of the reach of non-musicians. In accordance with the habit of his day

---

[1] Besides the Ravenscroft settings it is probable that the weaker arrangements of John Playford were known to many Americans in the seventeenth century.

he carried his melody in the tenor part, as the following setting
of "Old Hundred," by John Dowland, in Ravenscroft's volume,
may show:—

There was considerable difference of opinion about vocal matters in the church in New England during the seventeenth century.
Some believed that only the elect, those that had found grace,
should sing, while the body of the congregation joined in the final
"Amen"; on the other hand, a few were liberal enough to countenance the addition of an accompaniment when the singing was done
in private; "so that attention to the instrument does not divert the
heart from attention of the matter of song,"—as good John Cotton
put it in his tract, "Singing of Psalms a Gospel Ordinance."

It was but natural that New England should at once accept the
custom of "lining-out" the Psalms and Hymns, for, barbarous as
this habit was, it had its foundation in the scarcity of books in the
early days of the colony. The "lining" consisted in the minister
or the deacon reading the text that was to be sung, line by line, the
congregation pausing in their singing, at the end of each phrase,

sufficiently long to allow this piece-meal recitation. A clear statement of this fact is found in Samuel Sewall's Diary, as follows:—

"Feb. 26, 1723. Now about, Cousin Sewall and others sung, 'Once more our God.' I gave every one a booke, so the singing was continued without reading between whiles. Gave 15 or 16."

Judge Sewall was evidently opposed to this reading "between whiles." He was precentor of his church until 1718. His diary is full of contemporaneous comment on the tunes sung, and their execution. As will be seen by some subsequent notes, the congregation could not always catch the tune readily; this finally led to his resigning the office of precentor. He speaks of this, also, in his diary:—

"Lord's Day, Feb. 23 [1718]. Mr. Foxcroft preaches. I set York tune, and the congregation went out of it into St. David's in the very 2nd going over. They did the same 3 weeks before. This is the 2nd sign.[1]

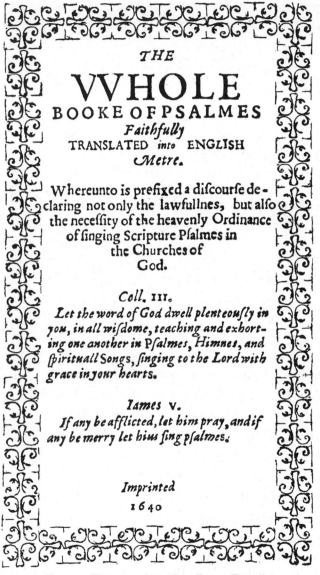

THE
VVHOLE
BOOKE OF PSALMES
Faithfully
TRANSLATED *into* ENGLISH
Metre.

Whereunto is prefixed a difcourfe declaring not only the lawfullnes, but alfo the neceffity of the heavenly Ordinance of finging Scripture Pfalmes in the Churches of God.

Coll. III.
Let the word of God dwell plenteoufly in you, in all wifdome, teaching and exhorting one another in Pfalmes, Himnes, and ffirituall Songs, finging to the Lord with grace in your hearts.

Iames V.
If any be afflicted, let him pray, and if any be merry let him fing pfalmes.

Imprinted
1640

FIG. 2.—TITLE-PAGE OF "BAY PSALM BOOK."

---

[1] It was his second break within a few weeks.

I think they began in the last line of the first going over. This seems to me an intimation and call for me to resign the Præcentor's place to a better voice. I have, through the divine Long-suffering and Favour done it for 24 years, and now God by his Providence seems to call me off; my voice being enfeebled. I spoke to Mr. White earnestly to set it in the afternoon; but he declin'd it.

"After the exercises . . . laid this matter before them, told them how long I had set the Tune; Mr. Prince said, Do it six years longer. I persisted and said that Mr. White or Mr. Franklin[1] might do it very well. . . .

"Feb. 27. I told Mr. White, Next Sabbath was in a Spring Moneth, he must then set the Tune. I set now Litchfield to a good Key. . . .

"March 2. I told Mr. White the elders desired him, he must set the tune, he disabled himself, as if he had a Cold. But when the Psalm was appointed, I forbore to do it, and rose up and turn'd to him, and he set York tune to a very good Key. I thanked him for restoring York Tune to its Station with so much Authority and Honor: I saw 'twas

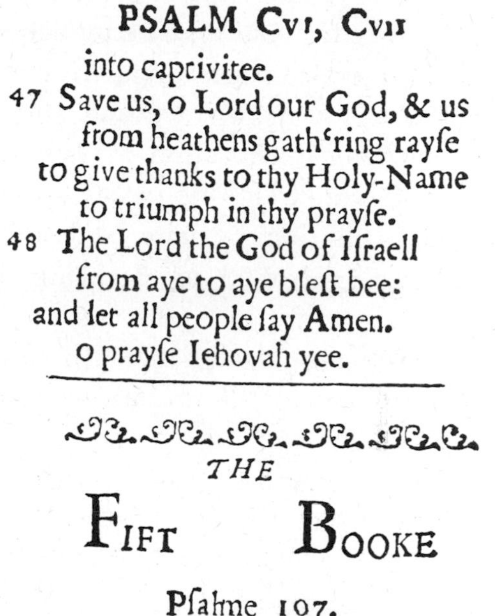

PSALM Cvi, Cvii

into captivitee.

47 Save us, o Lord our God, & us
from heathens gath'ring rayfe
to give thanks to thy Holy-Name
to triumph in thy prayfe.
48 The Lord the God of Ifraell
from aye to aye bleft bee:
and let all people fay Amen.
o prayfe Iehovah yee.

THE

FIFT BOOKE

Pfalme 107.

O Give yee thanks unto the Lord,
because that good is hee:
because his loving kindenes lafts
to perpetuitee.
2 So let the Lords redeem'd fay: whom
hee freed from th'enemies hands:
3 And gathred them from Eaft, & *Weft*,
from South, & Northerne lands
4 I'th defart, in a defart way
they wandred: no towne finde,
5 to dwell in. Hungry & thirfty:
their foule within them pinde.
6 Then did they to Iehovah cry
when they were in diftreffe:
who did them fet at liberty

FIG. 3.—PAGE OF "BAY PSALM BOOK."

---

[1] The father of Benjamin Franklin.

Convenient that I had resigned, being for the benefit of the Congregation."

Fortunately, even when musical matters were at the lowest ebb,
there were some cultured men among the clergy who worked
assiduously to build up a better school of singing in divine service,
and Mather, Symmes, Walter, Prince, Eliot, Dwight, and others,
labored by sermon, tract, and singing-book to elevate this part of
the Puritanical education. There was, however, strong opposition
among the rank and file to any special attention being paid to this
branch. Singing by note, and anything that savored of skill in
music, was regarded as decidedly heterodox. A book published
in London, entitled "Observations made by the Curious in New
England" (1673), states that "In Boston there are no musicians by
trade," and speaks of the attempt to found a dancing-school being
swiftly put down.[1]

There were plenty of "scruples" regarding the church music,
some of which may be cited: —

"Whether one be to sing for all the rest, the rest joyning onely
in spirit, and saying Amen; or the whole Congregation?

"Whether women, as well as men; or men alone?

"Whether carnall men and Pagans may be permitted to sing
with us, or Christians alone, and Church-Members?

"Whether it be lawfull to sing Psalmes in Meeter devised by
men?

"Whether in Tunes invented?

"Whether it be lawfull in Order unto Singing, to reade the
Psalme?"

Among the especial objections to the tunes we find the following: —

"They are inspired.

"To sing man's melody is only a vain show of art.

"God cannot take delight in praises where the man of sin has
had a hand in making the melody."[2]

There were also plenty of attacks upon the attempts to turn the
Psalms into metre, the objectors urging that no metre could be

---

[1] Mr. Stepney, the dancing-master, was fined £100.
[2] Quoted in Rev. John Cotton's tract, "Singing of Psalms a Gospel Ordinance," 1647.

as exact as the prose, and attacking the changes made necessary by the dictates of poetry. One commentator urges, with more zeal than Hebraic knowledge, that

" They sometimes breake the Attributes of God, and for the verse sake put *Jah* for *Jehovah*: which is a mangling of the word."

Many went so far as to consider skilful singing a direct sin. Nevertheless, the leaven was in the meal, and out of the desire to sing the Psalms properly there came the earliest New England singing-schools. A singing-school existed in Boston as early as 1717, and about this time we find a number of psalm-books published, which were in fact primitive vocal methods. Works by the Rev. Mr. Tufts, Dr. Mather, and the Rev. Mr. Walter (Fig. 4) were the earliest of these, and contained rules of music and a few instructions as to vocalization. Nothing of any intricacy was attempted, the methods confining themselves chiefly to the explanation of singing simple melodies by note. No attempt seems to have been made to employ the fine harmonization of Ravenscroft, or to go beyond unison work. Such was the chief manner of singing until the first American composers came upon the scene.

Even this slight training was naturally deemed quite unnecessary by those who had memorized a tune for each Psalm and reverenced the melody quite as much as the words. One or two Psalms were sung each Sunday in church, and, in pious families, two were sung each week-day and eight on the Sabbath. As the Psalms were sung in rotation, this gave the zealous singer a chance to go through each number about six times per annum. With such singers to make a science or an amusement of the tunes certainly meant trifling with holy things; they thought that vocalization, like Salvation, ought to come by Grace, and they asked such questions as : —

" Whether you do believe that the singing in the worship of God ought to be done skilfully ?

" Whether you do believe that skilfulness in singing may ordinarily be gained in the use of outward means by the blessing of God ? "

And, naturally enough, some of the elders in the Faith put the plaintive question : —

"Is it possible for Fathers of forty years old and upward to learn to sing by rule? And ought they to attempt at that age to learn?"

Nevertheless, music was taking root in the crevices and crannies of these granite rocks, and was growing fairly well in the unpromising soil. The entrance of a church organ into Boston, although fought against fiercely by the Puritans, and its placing in the Episcopalian church of Boston (King's Chapel), must have exerted some influence in the city. A full account of this instrument (Fig. 7) and the contention regarding it may be found in the present writer's "National Music of America," to which account may be added that this same organ, an instrument of one manual and possessed of an obliging appliance which makes it possible to play it either by the foot of the organist or by an assistant's pumping, was exhibited in Boston in 1902, by Chickering & Sons, by permission of the vestry of St. John's Church of Portsmouth, New Hampshire, its present owner. It was imported from London by Mr. Thomas Brattle, of Boston, in 1713.[1]

Choir-singing began to take the place of the crude congregational psalm-singing as early as the middle of the eighteenth century. This advance was made so gradually that even the conservative adherents of "the old style" were not aroused to opposition. It was a natural consequence of the singing-schools (Fig. 5) that some of the congregation should be much more advanced in music than others,[2] and it was equally a matter of course that the musical members should gather together as much as possible, in order to obtain the best vocal results. Thus the choir began to exist before the opposing faction became aware of

---

[1] The distrust of the organ in divine service by the Puritans is not only shown by its curt rejection by the Puritan church in 1713, but by many allusions to the instrument in the writings and sermons of the clergy of the epoch. Even the judicial Dr. Samuel Sewall had his doubts regarding organ-playing in service, as may be seen by a letter addressed to Mr. Burbank, July 22, 1695, in which he describes an experience in Oxford, England. It runs: —

"The next Sabbath day after the Coronation I heard a service at St. Mary's. I am a lover of Musick to a fault, yet I was uneasy there; and the justling out of the Institution of Singing Psalms, by the boisterous Organ, is that which can never be justified before the great Master of Religious Ceremonies."

[2] Some congregations must have had very poor singing. Sewall writes in his diary, — "Feb. 6, 1715. This day I set Windsor tune, and the people at the second going over into Oxford, do what I could."

it.[1] It was an easy transition from this informal gathering of the musical forces to an assignment of special seats to those most active in church-singing. We find many records of this step being taken in different New England churches, and no trace of any active dissent.

The singing-school and the choir having established a degree of interest in the study and practice of music, the next step was an advance to a larger musical repertoire. Vocal collections began to become numerous. But most of these were wholly devoted to Psalms and Hymns, during the last half of the eighteenth century.

for Singing by N O T E.   3

us in the right and true finging of the Tunes that are already inUfe in ourChurches; which, when they firft came out of the Hands of the Compofers of them, were fung according to the Rules of the *Scale of Mufick*, but are now miferably tortured, and twifted, and quavered, in fome Churches, into an horrid Medly of confufed and diforderly Noifes. This muft neceffarily create a moft difagreeable Jar in the Ears of all that can judge better of Singing than thefe Men, who pleafe themfelves with their own ill-founding *Echoes.* For to compare fmall Things with Great, our *Pfalmody* has fuffered the like Inconveniencies which our *Faith* had laboured under, in cafe it had been committed and trufted to the uncertain and doubtful Conveyance of *Oral Tradition*. Our Tunes are, for Want of a Standard to appeal to in all our Singing, left to the Mercy of every

unfkilful Throat to chop and alter, twift and change, according to their infinitely divers and no lefs odd Humours and Fancies. That this is moft true, I appeal to the Experience of thofe who have happened to be prefent in many of our Congregations, who will grant me, that there are no twoChurches that fing alike. Yea, I have my felf heard (for Inftance) *Oxford* Tune fung in *three*Churches (which I purpofely forbear to mention) with as muchDifference as there can poffibly be between *York* and *Oxford*, or any two other different Tunes. Therefore any Manıthat pleads with me for what they call the *Old Way*, I can confute him only by making this Demand, *What is the* OLD WAY? Which I am fure they cannot tell. For, one town fays, their's is the true *Old Way*, another Town thinks the fame of their's, and fo does a Third of their Way of tuning it. But let fuch.

B
Men

FIG. 4. — PAGE FROM DR. THOMAS WALTER'S SINGING-BOOK.

A few native composers now appear upon the scene.[2] That careful musical historian, Oscar G. Sonneck, gives a full account of the work of Rev. James Lyon (1735–1794) in sacred composition, and of Francis Hopkinson (1737–1791) in the secular field. These were the two earliest of American composers. The song " My Days have been so wondrous Free," given in the appendix, was probably the

[1] The faithful chronicler Sewall records the result of the singing-schools; the singing at divine service suddenly became better. In his diary, under date of March 16, 1721, he says: "At night Dr. Mather preaches in the School-House to the young musicians, from Rev. 14. 3. — No man could learn that song. — House was full and the singing extraordinarily excellent, such as had hardly been heard before in Boston. Sung four times out of Tate and Brady." Tate and Brady were two English poets (the former born in Ireland) who published their " book of Psalms in Metre " before 1696. It is probable, therefore, that an English edition was used by the singers, for we find no record of a colonial edition until nearly a score of years later.

[2] George Hood, in his " History of Music in New England," p. 170 *et seq.*, gives quite a detailed list of these.

first secular song composed by an American. But both Lyon and Hopkinson took up music merely as an avocation. Lyon published a collection of psalms about 1762, entitled "Urania." Some of these psalm-tunes were his own composition. Hopkinson's song above alluded to was composed in 1759, and this gives him the claim to have been the first American composer. But these two amateurs were soon followed by a man who was in some degree a professional; a man who devoted his life to music and was the first American who actually lived by the art.

This first of the native composers was William Billings. He was born in Boston, October 7, 1746, and died there, September 29, 1800. He was a self-taught musician; an apprentice to a tanner, he seems to have neglected his regular work, in some degree, for the avocation of composition. He wrote his earliest attempts at harmony with chalk upon the sides of leather in the tannery. He was an eccentric character who found many ready to laugh at him, but his earnest love of music and unswerving honesty of purpose won him some influential friends. Among these were Governor Samuel Adams and Dr. Pierce, who encouraged his earliest ventures into the field of publication. The first of his publications was "The New England Psalm Singer, or American Chorister," which was published in 1770. The time was opportune for the presentation of a book of this kind; the "Bay Psalm Book" was beginning to be superseded by Watts's "Hymns" and other works; a taste for variety in music had been cultivated by the singing-schools, yet the musical collections had not struck into new paths but, at this time, still held to the old selections that were familiar to the New Englander. Billings was a believer in the effects of florid counterpoint (of its rules, however, he was entirely ignorant), and early began to introduce into his work "fugue-tunes," which were really not fugues at all. In such pieces the different parts naturally presented more of contrast than was possible in choral-like harmony, and this diversity seems to have charmed Billings, who thus rhapsodizes over its beauties: —

"It has more than twenty times the power of the old slow tunes, each part straining for mastery and victory, the audience entertained and delighted, their minds surpassingly agitated and extremely fluctuated, sometimes declaring for one part, and sometimes for another. Now the solemn bass demands their attention, next the manly tenor; now the lofty counter, now the volatile treble. Now here, now there; now here again, — O ecstatic! Rush on, you sons of harmony!"

The above not only gives a fair description of imitative counter-point, but affords an index of the enthusiasm of this first Ameri-can composer, whose zeal in choir-singing was so great that his sturdy voice gener-ally drowned out all the others in his vicinity during the musical part of the ser-vice.

There were, however, other opinions about "fugue tunes" and their use in sacred music, as the follow-ing words of Samuel Hol-yoke, used as preface to

Samuel Wadfworth

BEGS leave to inform the Publick, but the Female Sex in particular, that he has opened a SINGING-SCHOOL for their Ufe, at his Dwelling-Houfe near the Town-Houfe, to be kept on Tuefday and Friday Evenings, from 6 to 9 o'Clock. If any of the Sex are defirous of being inftructed in this beautiful Science, they fhall be inftructed in the neweft Method.

Ye Female Sex, I pray draw near,
To Mufic fweet pray lend an Ear;
Young Virgins all with beauteous Voice,
Make mufic Harmony your Choice.
Philo Mufico.

FIG. 5. — ADVERTISEMENT FROM OLD SALEM NEWSPAPER.

his "Harmonia Americana" (published in 1791), may show:—

"Perhaps some may be disappointed that fuguing pieces are in general omitted. But the principal reason why few were inserted was the trifling effect produced by that sort of music; for the parts, falling in, one after another, each conveying a different idea, con-found the sense, and render the performance a mere jargon of words."

To return to William Billings: the first of his books spoken of above contained 108 pages, and presented 120 tunes as well as 22 pages of elementary instruction and an "Essay on the Nature and Properties of Musical Sound." It boldly bore as a motto:—

"Out of the mouths of babes and sucklings
Hast Thou perfected praise."

This motto was peculiarly fitted to the composer who was entirely innocent of musical laws, at least as regarded composition. Billings acknowledged this with childlike frankness in his preface:—

" Perhaps it may be expected by some, that I should say something concerning Rules for Composition; to these I answer that
Nature is the best dictator, for all the hard dry studied rules that
ever were prescribed, will not enable any person to form an Air, any
more than the bare Knowledge of the four and twenty letters, and
strict Grammatical Rules will qualify a Scholar for composing a
piece of Poetry, or properly adjusting a Tragedy without a Genius.
It must be Nature, Nature must lay the foundation, Nature must
inspire the Thought. . . . For my own part, as I don't think
myself confined to any Rules for Composition laid down by any
that went before me, neither should I think (were I to pretend to
lay down rules) that any who come after me were any ways obligated
to adhere to them any further than they should think proper; so in
fact I think it is best for every Composer to be his own Carver.
Therefore, upon this consideration, for me to dictate, or pretend to
prescribe Rules of this Nature for others, would not only be very
unnecessary but also a very great piece of Vanity."

CHESTER. L. M.

BILLINGS. 1770.

Let the high heav'n your songs invite, Those spacious fields of brilliant light, Where sun and moon and plan-ets   roll, And stars that glow from   pole   to pole.

FIG. 6. — BILLINGS'S " CHESTER."

In 1778 Billings brought out a revision of the above work (102
pages) which he now called " The Singing Master's Assistant," and
his recantation of his former audacity was as naïve as his original
defiance.   It ran as follows: —

" Kind Reader, no doubt you remember that about ten years
ago I published a book entitled ' The New England Psalm Singer ';
and truly a most masterly performance I then thought it to be.
How lavish was I of encomiums on this my infant production!
Said I, Thou art my Reuben, my first born, the beginning of my
strength; but to my great mortification I soon discovered that
it was Reuben in the sequel, and Reuben all over.   I have

discovered that many pieces were not worth my printing or your inspection."

The second book soon received the name of "Billings's Best," and became very popular throughout New England.   Many of Billings's tunes were heard around the camp-fires of the Revolutionary army, and "Chester," the best known of them all, was often played by the fifers in the Continental ranks (Fig. 6).

Billings frequently wrote his own text, and his ringing verse to the last-named tune was an admirable outburst of patriotism:—

> " Let tyrants shake their iron rod
>   And Slavery clank her galling chains,
>   We'll fear them not ; we trust in God,
>   New England's God forever reigns."

Billings was a fiery patriot, as may well be conjectured from the above.   In his first volume he was still a British subject, as may be seen by his opening verse:—

> " O, praise the Lord with one consent,
>   And in this grand design,
>   Let Britain and the Colonies
>   Unanimously join."

But when the Revolution began, his muse was turned against " Britain " with a vengeance.   In his " Lamentation over Boston " (because of its being occupied by English soldiers) he employed the metaphor of the One Hundred and Thirty-seventh Psalm, and wailed:—

> " By the rivers of Watertown, we sat down ;
>   Yea we wept as we remembered Boston."

And he continued by calling down frightful imprecations upon himself, — "if I forget thee, O Boston!"

No man is ridiculous who is thoroughly in earnest.[1]   One can forgive Billings his hundreds of errors of harmonic construction because of his devotion to his chosen art and to his country.   He was handicapped in many ways; his lack of musical education was but slightly amended by a study of Tans'ur's faulty " Musical Grammar " (Fig. 8), and his general education was of the slightest.   When he left

---

[1] John Eliot alludes to Billings as "an original genius," and speaks of him as the editor of the *Boston Magazine*.

the tannery and launched upon a musical career he suffered poverty almost constantly; he was very untidy in personal habit, he was physically deformed, and his sight was defective. Such a man was likely to become the butt of many coarse natures, and practical jokes were often played upon the unfortunate son of the Muses. He had a sign over the door of his house, near the White Horse Tavern, with " Billings' Music " inscribed upon it. One night two cats were found suspended from this, by their tails, giving vocal illustrations that roused the entire neighborhood. On another occasion a wag sought him out, and after much flattery besought him to answer an important musical question. The important point turned out to be a query as to whether snoring was to be classed as vocal or instrumental music.

After his second volume Billings issued four others as follows: " Music in Miniature," 32 pages, 12 mo, published in 1779 (this little volume was intended for insertion in the psalm-books of the time); " The Psalm-singer's Amusement," 103 pages, 1781 ; " The Suffolk Harmony," 56 pages, 1786, and " The Continental Harmony," 199 pages, published in 1794 (Fig. 9). He also issued some separate compositions, chiefly anthems.

Billings is said to have introduced the use of the pitch-pipe into the choir, an important improvement when one considers the ludicrous mishaps that often occurred when the tune was pitched by ear,[1]

[1] These mishaps may be surmised by the following extract from the Diary of Judge Samuel Sewall : —

" 1705. Sixth-day, Decr 28. Mr. Pemberton prays excellently, and Mr. Willard preaches from Ps. 66. 20. very excellently. Spoke to me to set the tune ; I intended Windsor, and fell into High Dutch [this was another name for 'Canterbury'], and then, essaying to set another tune, went into a Key much too high. So I prayed Mr. White to set it ; which he did well, Litchf. [Litchfield] Tune. The Lord humble me and instruct me, that I should be the occasion of any interruption in the Worship of God."

Yet this slip did not deter the musical enthusiast from trying again, for later in the diary we read : —

" July 5, 1713. Mr. Stoddard preaches P.M. . . . At the close appoint 1½ staff in the first part 40th Ps. I try'd to set Low Dutch tune and failed. Tried again and fell into the tune of 119th Psalm, so Capt. Williams read the whole first part, that he might have psalm to the tune."

Nor did this second mishap daunt the zealous psalm-singer, and subsequently his efforts seem to have met with better success, for the Diary states (regarding a wedding ceremony) : —

" Oct. 22, 1713. Sung the 45th psalm from the 8th verse to the end. five staves. I set it to Windsor tune. I had a very good Turky-Leather Psalm-Book, which I looked in while Mr. Noyes read : and then I gave it to the Bride-groom saying, 'I give you this Psalm-Book in order to your perpetuating this song : and I would have you pray that it may be an introduction to our Singing with the Choir above.' "

FIG. 7. — THE BRATTLE ORGAN.

Reproduced by courtesy of the Rev. Henry Emerson, Rector of
St. John's Church, Portsmouth.

and it is said that he was the first to use the violoncello in church music in New England.   That he was the first to introduce concerts in the colony (for which he is often given the credit)[1] must be regarded as improbable, for he was born in 1746, and Mr. Dipper gave two concerts in Boston in 1761 (Fig. 10), at which time the young Billings was perhaps still chalking his first compositions on the sides of sole leather in the tannery.   That he continued poor to the end of his days is clearly indicated by an advertisement in the *Massachusetts Magazine* for August, 1792, regarding his last volume, which concludes with the following: —

" The distressed situation of Mr. Billings's family has so sensibly operated on the minds of the committee as to induce their assistance in the intended publication."[2]

We have stated that Billings committed many harmonic and contrapuntal errors.   In spite of these his music deserved preservation from oblivion; it was melodic and cheerful; it was strongly rhythmic and, for all its "fuguing," was easily memorized; it was not above the heads of his public.   A Beethoven could have obtained no hearing in America in the eighteenth century, but

TANS'UR'S
Royal   Melody   Compleat,
the laſt and beſt Edition, with Additions, on Copper Plate, may be had at JOHN PERKINS's Shop in Union-Street, Boſton, next Door to Mr. *Frederick William Geyer*'s.   N. B. At the ſame Place may be had a large Aſſortment of Paper Hangings for Rooms.

FIG. 8. — ADVERTISEMENT FROM *BOSTON GAZETTE*, 1767.

Billings found a willing audience and cheered many a fireside and camp where higher art would not have been understood.

Although Billings's publication of 1770 was the earliest example of native composition of part music, a few melodies were probably evolved before this time.   The chief contemporary of Billings was Oliver Holden, whose " Coronation "[3] has held its own much better than Billings's masterpiece, " Chester," and is as popular to-day as it was a century ago.   Holden was no better educated musically than

---

[1] Ritter's " Music in America " states this erroneously.

[2] Another proof of his ending his days in poverty is found in the fact that his grave was not marked by any stone or monument.   It is known that he was buried somewhere in the cemetery on Boston Common.   The cemetery still exists, but it seems impossible, at this late date, to discover the spot where the first American composer was laid to rest.

[3] The words of this famous hymn were written by the Rev. Edward Perronet, son of Vincent Perronet, vicar of Shoreham, England.

Billings.   He was born in Shirley, September 18, 1765, and moved
to Charlestown, Massachusetts, in 1788, where he followed the trade
of a carpenter.   He finally became a music-teacher.   The *Salem
Gazette*, in October, 1792, printed the following advertisement: —

"THE AMERICAN HARMONY,
containing a select number of Odes, Anthems and Plain Tunes,
composed for performance on Thanksgivings, Ordinations, Christmas, Fasts,
Funeral and other occasions : the whole entirely new,
By Oliver Holden,
Teacher of Musick in Charlestown "—

which shows that at that time Holden had left the carpenter's bench.
Also in the sixth edition of " Laus Deo " (first edition, 1786, sixth
edition, 1797) we read in the preface, written by Isaiah Thomas: —

" The subscriber informs his musical friends who have so liber-
ally encouraged the five former editions of the Worcester Collection,
that he has contracted with Mr. Oliver Holden, to compile and correct the present and future editions, which he presumes will be
pleasing to its patrons."

And Mr. Holden edited three editions of the book, a fact which
shows that he had attained considerable popularity in the state
as a composer.   He was of about the Billings quality of musician,
earnest, melodic, but seldom correct in passages of any intricacy.
He died September 4, 1844.

Much higher, from a musical standpoint, than either of the two
preceding writers, was Andrew Law, whose collections of Tunes
and Anthems, published in 1779, followed closely upon the heels
of the first volume of his predecessor.   Law was born in Cheshire,
Connecticut, in 1748, and had the advantage of a much better education than either Holden or Billings.   Yet in music Law was
also a self-taught man.   His taste, however, seems to have been
more evenly balanced and more refined than any of the early New
England singing-teachers.   He seems not to have cared much for
the imitative counterpoint which was miscalled "fuguing."   In
his song-books we generally find good discrimination and careful
judgment displayed throughout.

Naturally such a man was not very popular in a country almost
destitute of artistic taste, and Law was voted slow and tiresome.

Yet he wrote one tune that rivalled in popularity even Billings's "Chester," or Holden's "Coronation," the hymn known as "Archdale." He made several innovations in the singing-school of his time, even inventing a special system of notation. His giving of the melody of his tunes to the soprano voice was not a new matter, considering that this had been done in Germany for more than two centuries before Law's time (Hassler and Osiander were the founders of this system), but it was at least novel in New England where the singing was either in unison, or with a distribution of parts like that shown in Dowland's setting of "Old Hundred" printed in the first part of this chapter. Law's chief works were the collection alluded to above; the "Rudiments of Musick" published in 1783 and running through four editions during the next ten years; "Musical Primer on a New Plan," 1803 (an attempt to do away with the musical staff); *The Musical Magazine*, 1804; and a "Harmonic Companion" published in Philadelphia without date. Law died in Cheshire in 1821.

To the PUBLICK.

A large Committee having been felected by the feveral Mufical Societies in Bofton and its vicinity, beg leave to folicit the attention of the publick to the following

PROPOSALS

For Publifhing a Volume of Original

AMERICAN MUSICK,

COMPOSED BY

WILLIAM BILLINGS, *of Bofton*.

THE intended Publication will confift of a number of Anthems, Fuges, and Pfalm Tunes, calculated for publick focical Worfhip, or private Mufical Societies. — A Dialogue between MASTER and SCHOLAR will preface the book, in which the Theory of Harmony, grounded on Queftion and Anfwer, is adapted to the moft moderate capacity. — Alfo an elegant FRONTISPIECE, reprefenting the ARETINIAN ARMS, engraved on Copperplate.

FIG. 9. — ADVERTISEMENT FROM *MASSACHUSETTS MAGAZINE*, August, 1792.

Jacob Kimball, Jr., who produced a volume called "Rural Harmony," was less rustic than such a title might indicate. He was born at Topsfield, Massachusetts, in February, 1761, and was a lawyer by profession. His desertion of the legal fold seems to have brought him a little honor but no worldly advancement, for we find that his poems were held in esteem (especially when set to music by Billings), that he was allowed to sit in the elder's seat in the Topsfield meeting-house and lead the singing, and that he eventually died in the poor-house, in 1826. After his "Rural Harmony" Kimball produced another volume, entitled "The Essex Harmony," which did not equal the other in popularity. How much this unfortunate son of the Muses loved his art may be judged by the impassioned lines with which he prefaced this latter work: —

> "Music's bright influence, thrilling thro' the breast,
> Can lull e'en raging anguish into rest;
> And oft its wildly sweet enchanting lay
> To Fancy's magic heaven steals the rapt thought away."

Of Samuel Holyoke we have already spoken. He was a more versatile musician than most of his contemporaries, but he scarcely possessed as much natural talent as Billings, Law, or Kimball. As was the case with many of the old composers, his name is associated chiefly with a single tune, "Arnheim," which he composed when only fourteen years of age. He was the son of the Rev. Dr. Holyoke, was born in Boxford, Massachusetts, in 1771, and died at Concord, New Hampshire, in 1816. He was for some time active in the musical matters of Salem, Massachusetts, and sometimes attempted rather ambitious feats, as the following advertisement from the *Salem Gazette* (September, 1808) may show: —

"CONCERT.

"The subscriber, by the encouragement of his friends in this town, proposes to give a Concert of Sacred, Vocal, and Instrumental Music, in which the *Celebrated Hallelujah Chorus* by Mr. Handel will be performed."

The concert was repeated with the same chorus the next year, and Mr. Holyoke gave many other musical entertainments in Salem. The director's voice became so harsh in his later years that he used a clarinet in leading his singing-classes.

Among the lesser composers, who came in the wake of William Billings, were Daniel Read, who combined comb-manufacturing and music at Hartford, Connecticut, and Timothy Swan (born at Suffield, Connecticut, July 23, 1757),[1] the composer of the well-known

---

[1] Baker, "Biographical Dictionary of Musicians," gives Worcester, Massachusetts, as his birthplace.

tunes, " China," " Poland," " Ocean," and " Pownal."   Some of these men would pass quite unnoticed in the musical activity of the present; their names are, however, worthy of record as pioneers at a time when to become a musician meant much self-sacrifice.   It will be noticed that almost all their works were in the sacred field; but there were a few general collections of music published in which the secular side was presented, chiefly by reprints of favorite English songs, and sometimes by rather bold plagiarisms.

It was an epoch when the ascetic character of the Puritan church was relaxing; the Congregationalist kept the forms bequeathed him by his forefathers, but their spirit was less severe.   Yet it was deemed necessary to cloak innocent amusement under the garb of religion, and the study of music was still held to be a dubious proceeding unless it were sanctified by being devoted to religious ends.   Of the instrumental side of music at this time we shall speak in connection with the early orchestras, but it may be readily understood that it was impossible to cover some of this with the religious cloak. Even here some such attempt was made by using arrangements from the Handelian oratorios.   Toward the end of the eighteenth century plays were occasionally smuggled into popular acceptance under the title of " Moral Lectures." [1]   The ice was gradually breaking, and the beginning of the nineteenth century found matters free for the advance of American music.

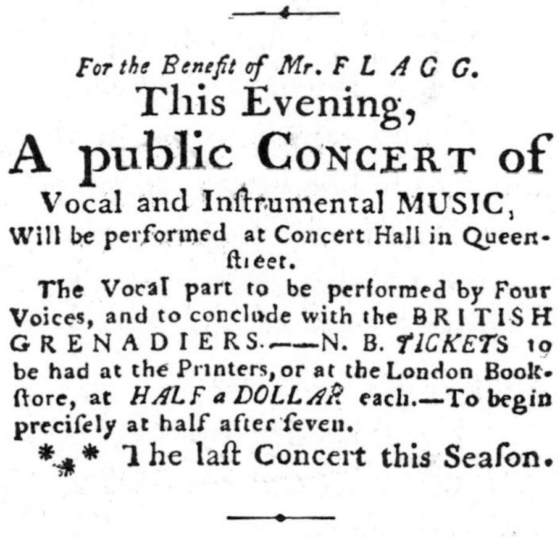

For the Benefit of Mr. F L A G G.
This Evening,
A public CONCERT of
Vocal and Inftrumental MUSIC,
Will be performed at Concert Hall in Queen-ftreet.
The Vocal part to be performed by Four Voices, and to conclude with the B R I T I S H G R E N A D I E R S.———N. B. *TICKETS* to be had at the Printers, or at the London Book-ftore, at *HALF a DOLLAR* each.—To begin precifely at half after feven.
*** The laft Concert this Seafon.

FIG. 10. — ADVERTISEMENT FROM *BOSTON CHRONICLE*, 1769.

[1] The following advertisement in the *Salem Gazette*, July 10, 1792, illustrates this custom : —

> "At Concert Hall
> This evening, will be performed
> A Concert of Vocal and Instrumental Music,
> between the parts of which will be delivered
> the *Tragic* and *Moral Lecture* called
> DOUGLAS
> With various songs, as will be expressed
> In the hand-bills."

Although thus far we have spoken almost entirely of the music of New England, because this was the seed whence grew the earliest "American School" of composition, it must not be supposed that other parts of the country neglected the divine art. Philadelphia was the art-centre of America during the latter part of the eighteenth century, its culture being almost European in its advancement. In 1741 Benjamin Franklin published Dr. Watts's hymns in that city; Raynor Taylor and Benjamin Carr, both cultivated Englishmen and excellent organists, were very active in advancing the taste of the people, and concerts and musical gatherings were not infrequent. The first really ambitious concert given in this country took place in Philadelphia on May 4, 1786. The following account of it is taken from a contemporary newspaper [1]: —

"On Thursday, the 4th of May, at the Reformed German Church, in Race Street, was performed a Grand Concert of vocal and instrumental musick, in the presence of a numerous and polite audience. The whole band consisted of 230 vocal and 50 instrumental performers, which, we are fully justified in pronouncing, was the most complete, both with respect to number and accuracy of execution, ever, on any occasion, combined in this city, and, perhaps, throughout America.

" The first idea of this concert was suggested to the trustees of the musical institution by the Commemoration of Handel in London, and the Sacred Concert in Boston.[2] It was planned in January last, and a series of preparatory measures pursued until its accomplishment.

" Nearly one thousand tickets were sold at two-thirds of a dollar each, and the net proceeds, after deducting for necessary expences, have been delivered to the managers of the Pennsylvania Hospital, Philadelphia Dispensary, and overseers of the Poor, to be applied by them for the use of said institutions and unprovided poor."

Philadelphia had listened to public musical performances before this time. The " Beggar's Opera " had been presented at the New Theatre, on Society Hill, in 1759. In 1787 General Washington

---

[1] *Salem Gazette*, Philadelphia correspondence.

[2] A large charitable concert (combined with religious services) given in King's Chapel, January 10, 1786, but much less ambitious than the Philadelphia affair.

attended the performance of a "Puppet Opera," in Philadelphia, entitled "The Poor Soldier." A performance of part of Handel's "Messiah" took place in the hall of the University of Pennsylvania (then on Ninth Street, north of Chestnut Street) in 1801, the performers being recruited from the Chestnut Street Theatre. In 1810 a classical concert was given in the city, at which parts of Handel's "Messiah" and of Haydn's "Creation" were given.

Philadelphia had, indeed, a Musical Association as early as 1740, but there is no record of its doings. It was probably unimportant, for the Quaker city was more opposed to music than even the Puritans were, and the real musical activity there did not begin until the first part of the nineteenth century. Yet Philadelphia had an organ, in Christ Church, soon after 1700, and a few teachers of music found a home in that city at an early date. In 1749, "John Beals, music-master from London," advertised himself as "teacher of violin, hautboy, flute, and dulcimer," and professed himself ready to play for balls and entertainments. Other teachers soon followed.[1]

In New York we find William Tuckey, one time vicar-choral of Bristol Cathedral in England, teaching singing to the children of his district as early as 1753, and in 1756 he was paid £15 for furnishing the music at the opening of St. Paul's Church in the same city. The chief music of New York was found in the Episcopal churches, and Trinity Church upheld something of the dignity of the English Cathedral music within its walls. Outside of the churches the public did not desire classical music of any kind, and a few musical societies that were founded in the eighteenth century soon died from lack of appreciation. Baltimore and New Orleans possessed some musical activity in these early days, but their concerts exerted no influence in shaping American progress in music; nor can we consider the religious music of the Moravians in northeastern Pennsylvania, taught from books chiefly printed in German, as an important factor in the native development.

[1] See Scharf and Westcott's "History of Philadelphia," Vol. II, p. 864.

PLATE II

PARK STREET CHURCH, BOSTON

CHAPTER II

EARLY MUSICAL ORGANIZATIONS

THE earliest musical organization of importance, in America, was the Stoughton Musical Society, still existing, which formed the link between the old psalm-singing and the later oratorio-singing of Massachusetts. In 1774 William Billings taught a singing-class of forty-eight members in the house of Robert Capen, in Stoughton. Out of this organization, after the Revolution had passed, there eventually grew the larger and more permanent Society. It is pleasant, therefore, to state that the influence of William Billings was not lost, but gradually merged into something greater than he himself could have conceived. He builded better than he knew.

The list of Billings's class still exists, and illustrates the wretched custom of uniting male and female voices in the tenor part, — the part which at that time carried the tune. The list runs: —

Singers of Tenor

Geo. Monk.
Jno. Wadsworth, Jr.
Lazarus Pope.
Dr. Peter Adams.
Jacob French (afterwards a prominent composer).
Robt. Swan, Jr.
Jos. Wadsworth.
Hannah Wadsworth.
Abigail Wadsworth.
Andrew Capen.
Susanna Capen.
Ruth Tilden.
Abigail Jones.
Eliz. Toleman.
Jerusha Dickerman.
Eliz. Dickerman.
Mehitable Talbot.

Esther Talbot.
The Fenno Girls.
Lydia Gay.

Singers of Treble

Lucy Swan.
Melatiah Swan.
Jerusha Pope.
Patience Drake.
Waitstill Capen.
Bertha Capen.
Hannah Capen.
Rachel Capen.
Hannah Holmes.
Eunice Holmes.
Chloe Bird.
Kesiah Bird.
Mendevill Bird.
Hannah Briggs.

Irene Briggs.
Mary French.
Eliz. Cummings.
Sarah Tolman.

Singers of Counter

David Wadsworth.
Theodore Capen, A.M.
Thomas Tolman.
Isaac Morton.
Eliphalet Johnson.

Singers of Bass

Jonathan Belcher.
Samuel Tolman.
William Tilden.
Geo. Wadsworth.
John Capen.

48 in all.

Deacon Samuel Tolman has left a manuscript which states that:—

"In the year 1786, Nov. 7th., we set up a large Singing Society in Canton, Stoughton and Sharon; we have followed meetings from that time to the present day [The paper is dated April 13th, 1826], the Society has, always been under good discipline. We have a good Constitution. The officers are a President, Vice President, Secretary, and other officers; the Society is large and respectable; Attended with spirit."

About the year 1790 a singing contest took place, which was probably the first ever instituted in America. It may serve to show that there was an intensity of musical feeling existing in Massachusetts at that time, and suggests that the harvest of the unpromising seed of psalm-singing was good. Many clergymen, in following the good old fashion of "exchanging pulpits," had become familiar with the excellent church music of Stoughton, and sounded its praises abroad. The singers of the First Parish of Dorchester, Massachusetts, took umbrage at this, and challenged the Stoughton vocalists to a trial of skill. The gauntlet was at once taken up, and the contest took place in a large hall in Dorchester, many of the leading Bostonians coming out to witness it. The Dorchester choristers were male and female, and had the assistance of a bass viol. The Stoughton party consisted of twenty selected male voices, without instruments, led by the president of the Stoughton Musical Society, Elijah Dunbar, a man of dignified presence and of excellent voice. The Dorchester singers began with a new anthem. The Stoughtonians commenced with Jacob French's "Heavenly Vision," the author of which was their fellow-townsman. When they finally sang, without books, Handel's "Hallelujah Chorus" the Dorchestrians gave up the contest, and gracefully acknowledged defeat.

The Handel and Haydn Society has been, and is, of infinitely greater influence than the Stoughton Society, with its right of primo-geniture.[1] This great society had its inception in the choir of the Park Street Church, a religious association which still worships in

---

[1] The Massachusetts Musical Society, born in 1807, had a brief and unimportant existence of three years. The Boston Musical Institute which, in 1837, was formed by seceders from the Handel and Haydn also lived three years without any important results.

its original edifice, at the corner of Park and Tremont streets in Boston (Pl. II). In spite of its conservative tenets, so severe at the beginning of the nineteenth century that it refused to use an organ,[1] the music of the society was of a very high order, and there were many enthusiastic amateurs in the ranks of its choir. General H. K. Oliver, the composer of "Federal Street," thus writes about the early stages of the choir in Park Street Church: —

"From 1810 to 1814, the writer, a Boston lad, having a high soprano voice, was a singing-boy, with two or three others, in the choir of the Park Street Church, a choir consisting of some fifty singers, and deservedly renowned for its admirable rendering of church music, ignoring the prevalent fugue-tunes of the day, and giving the more appropriate and correct hymn-tunes and anthems of the best English composers.

A Concert of ſacred
Muſick, Vocal and Inſtrumental, will be performed in ST. PETER'S CHURCH, on the 25th inſtant (being Thankſgiving day), for the purpoſe of raiſing money for repairing the Organ in ſaid Church.
  Mr. SELBY on the Organ, with the BAND from Boſton.
  Doors to be opened at 5 o'clock in the evening, and ſhut at 6 preciſely.
  Tickets for the ground floor at 1/6, and for the gallery at 9d., may be had of John Dabney, Daniel Saunders, James King, Benjamin Carpenter, or Joſeph Cabot.

FIG. II. — ADVERTISEMENT FROM *SALEM GAZETTE*, 1790.

Out of this choir came many of the original members of the Handel and Haydn Society. There was then no organ at Park Street, the accompaniment of their singing being given by a flute, a bassoon, and a violoncello. At that remote date very few musical instruments of any sort were to be found in private houses. In the entire population of Boston, of some six thousand families, not fifty pianofortes could be found." The accompaniment described above was the one generally used (thanks to Billings) in those churches which declined to employ an organ, although a clarinet frequently took the place of the flute.

A fortuitous circumstance aided in bringing into existence the Handel and Haydn Society. The War of 1812 was concluded by the Peace signed at Ghent on Christmas Eve, 1814, and less than two months later, on Washington's birthday, February 22, 1815, Boston held a great musical jubilee in honor of the event. It took place in King's Chapel (corner of School and Tremont streets), an edifice

---

[1] It was nicknamed " Brimstone Corner " by the liberals.

still in use as a church (Pl. IX). There had been many good concerts given in the "Stone Chapel," as it was then called, chiefly
through the instrumentality of Dr. G. K. Jackson, an Englishman,
who had been an organist at several Boston churches and was
now director of music at this chapel, but this concert in honor of
the new Peace was probably the greatest ever attempted, up to that
time, in the New England metropolis. In speaking of its results,
the Hon. Robert C. Winthrop says: —

"Its echoes had hardly died away — four weeks, indeed, had
scarcely elapsed since it was held — before a notice was issued by

FIG. 12. — SYMPHONY HALL, BOSTON.

Gottlieb Graupner, Thomas Smith Webb and Asa Peabody, for a
meeting of those interested in the subject 'of cultivating and improving a correct taste in the performance of sacred music.' In that
meeting, held on the 30th of March, 1815, the Handel and Haydn
Society originated. On the 20th of April their constitution was
adopted. The following Mayday witnessed their first private practising from the old Locke Hospital Collection; and on the succeeding
Christmas evening at the same consecrated chapel where Washington attended that memorable public concert a quarter of a century
before, and where that solemn Jubilee of Peace had been so recently

celebrated, their first grand Oratorio was given to a delighted audience of nine hundred and forty-five persons, with the Russian consul, the well-remembered Mr. Eustaphieve, assisting as one of the performers in the orchestra."

With the exception of the great concert in Philadelphia, already spoken of, this was the largest musical event that had yet occurred in America, and it was by all odds the most ambitious, the most classical, and the most important. The chorus numbered nearly one hundred, and of these but ten were female voices. The orchestra, of which we shall speak hereafter, consisted of less than a dozen performers, and the organ assisted in most of the numbers.

All Boston was in sympathy with the event, the *Columbian Centinel*, two days before the concert, had published a eulogy of the society, and the fashionables of the town were interested, many of them as performers. Boston at this time possessed many musical enthusiasts and, at last, some thoroughly trained European musicians. Dr. Jackson was probably the most skilful of these, but he held aloof from the doings of the Handel and Haydn Society during its experimental stages, only heartily coöperating with it after the organization was able to get along without him.

The concert on that memorable Christmas Eve began at 6 P.M., and must have been about four hours in length. We have received a description of it from an actual auditor, General Oliver, who spoke of it as an occasion of great dignity and impressiveness rather than of fervid applause, although occasionally the plaudits would burst forth with much spontaneity. Part I was wholly devoted to numbers from Haydn's "Creation"; Parts II and III were Handelian. Tickets were $1 each, with a reduction on taking a quantity, — four or six. The officers of the society at its beginning were: —

President, — Thomas S. Webb.

Vice-President, — Amasa Winchester.

Treasurer, — Nathaniel Tucker.

Secretary, — Matthew S. Parker.

Trustees, — Elnathan Duren, Benjamin Holt, Joseph Bailey, Charles Nolan, Ebenezer Withington, John Dodd, Jacob Guild, W. K. Phillips, and S. H. Parker.

Almost all the singers in the first dozen concerts of the society were native Americans, but European soloists were soon sought for in the more and more elaborate concerts given by the association. The ambitious character of the society is indicated by the fact that, in 1823, it wrote to Beethoven offering him a commission to write an oratorio especially for its use. The commission is not mentioned in the society records, and Thayer, the chief biographer of Beethoven, thinks that it was given unofficially by Richardson and a few other members. That an order was sent is quite certain. Schindler, a friend and biographer of Beethoven, informed Mr. Thayer that, in 1823, a Boston banker, whose name he did not recall, had occasion to write to a Viennese banker named Geymüller, and had enclosed an order for Beethoven to compose an oratorio for somebody or some society in Boston, and Schindler adds that this order was received by Beethoven. At that time Beethoven was about to begin a work to be entitled "The Victory of the Cross" for a Viennese society, and he determined to send this work (which he afterwards abandoned) to Boston. He was delighted with this commission from across the ocean.

In one of Beethoven's note-books (in Berlin) Thayer found this memorandum : —

"Bühler writes — 'The Oratorio for Boston ;' — I cannot write what I should best like to write, but that which the pressing need of money obliges me to write. This is not saying that I write only for money."[1]

There was also a notice of the work in the *Morgenblatt für gebildete Leser*, November 5, 1823, in an article on Beethoven, which alludes to an oratorio with English text, for Boston, as a projected work. Fortunately it remained only a project; one shudders to think of the fate of a work of perhaps the caliber of Beethoven's great Mass, or "The Mount of Olives," or the finale of the "Ninth Symphony," handed over to the tender mercies of an American orchestra and chorus in 1823.

Much more legitimate was the appeal of the society, in later years, to Robert Franz, to finish the additional accompaniments to Handel's "Messiah." The complete version of the great old masterpiece was first given by the Handel and Haydn Society, and its achievement is due to the assistance of its officials and their

[1] "History of the Handel and Haydn Society," by C. C. Perkins, Vol. I, No. 2, p. 87.

commission to Franz. Incledon, Phillips, and other English soloists engaged by the society soon taught it the true Handelian
interpretation of the " Messiah," and some of them speak in terms
of praise of the work accomplished in Boston even before 1820.

In the early days of the Handel and Haydn Society, the president of the association was supposed to act as the conductor, but
as a matter of fact the chorus and orchestra followed the time indicated by the leading violinist, who was, for a considerable time,
Signor Ostinelli, one of the foreign musicians who so thoroughly
advanced the music of Boston and of America.

FIG. 13. — HOME OF HANDEL AND HAYDN SOCIETY IN 1850.
From an old print.

It is interesting and almost an historical study to watch the
advancing programmes of the society from its inception. Up to
1818 the concerts were made up of sacred selections, but on December 25 of that year comes the " Messiah " *complete*, perhaps the first
entire oratorio performed in America ; the next year the " Creation," also complete ;[1] then followed the " Dettingen Te Deum."

[1] There are, however, other claims which must be mentioned in connection with the first
complete oratorio given in America. The Moravians at Bethlehem, Pennsylvania, in 1811, gave
a performance of the " Creation " ; the " Messiah " was performed in Trinity Church, New
York, January 9, 1770, and repeated in 1771, and again in 1772 Whether these were complete
performances cannot be ascertained, but they certainly deserve mention as possibly the earliest
oratorio performances on American soil. See further account of Moravian music, Chap. XVII.

D

These were probably the only complete works for many years. A Haydn and a Mozart Mass appeared in 1829; in 1834 the larger part of Beethoven's "Mount of Olives" was presented; then followed a period of Neukomm, and that composer's "David" (not a great work and very seldom heard at present) was repeated an incredible number of times from 1836 to 1845. In 1836 "David" was performed twelve times; in 1839 it received fourteen performances; in 1840 the same composer's "Mount Sinai" began to be performed by the society, but, although it received many representations, it by no means equalled "David" in the frequency of its repetitions. In 1845 fourteen performances of "Samson" lifted a heavy load of debt from the society; in 1849–50 the society won considerable success with an opera. Donizetti's "Martyrs" was performed seven times.

The concerts took place, at first, in King's Chapel, afterwards in Boylston Hall, then in the Melodeon, then in Music Hall, and finally in Symphony Hall (Fig. 12), where they now occur. A picture of the Melodeon as it appeared in 1850 is shown herewith (Fig. 13). The building with the flag at the window is the old home of the Handel and Haydn Society; the one with lanterns at its entrance is the Boston Theatre, where many of the early operas were given. The Handel and Haydn concerts are chiefly given on Sunday evenings. The first president was Thomas Smith Webb, two years; then came Amasa Winchester (a most tactful and gentle leader), seven years; Robert Rogerson; Lowell Mason, five years; Samuel Richardson, two years; Charles W. Lovett, two years; Bartholomew Brown; George J. Webb, three years; Charles Zeuner; James Clark; I. S. Withington, and Jonas Chickering. The subsequent presidents were not so important, for, in 1847, the president ceased to be the conductor, a regular leader being engaged by the society. Charles E. Horn was the first of these conductors. In 1850 the posts of president and director were again temporarily united in the person of Charles C. Perkins,[1] but after that they were permanently separated, and the following conductors were appointed: J. E. Goodson, 1851; G. J. Webb, 1852; Carl Berg-

---

[1] Too much praise cannot be given to this cultured gentleman; he aided music in many ways, and his "History of the Handel and Haydn Society" (whence many of the above facts are taken) would have been a monumental work, had it not been abruptly ended by the death of the author, in 1886. The work was subsequently continued by John S. Dwight.

mann, in the same year. Carl Zerrahn (the most prominent conductor of the list), who was appointed in 1854, held the position of
conductor of this society for more than forty years (to 1895). Benjamin J. Lang followed him. After this there came a thorough
renovation of the society. There were in its ranks many veterans
who had done loyal service during the days "when Music, heavenly
maid, was young" in Boston; their voices had grown thin with
years, their vocal method had become antiquated now that Boston
was a musical centre with many thorough instructors. It was a
sad task to bid these depart, but necessity forced such a course.
A new examination of voices was ordered, the numbers of the
choristers were reduced, new members were admitted, and a
thorough musical reorganization began under the direction of Mr.
Emil Mollenhauer, who is at present the conductor of the society.

As Carl Zerrahn (Fig. 14), prominent in various fields of music, did
most of his service in connection
with the Handel and Haydn Society, it is fitting that we should here
speak of the influence that he exerted upon American music. He
was born in Malchow, in Mecklen-
burg, July 28, 1826. Coming to
America in 1848, he was for a time
the first flute-player of the Germania Orchestra (Fig. 26). In 1854
he began his career as conductor
by assuming the leadership of the
Handel and Haydn Society, and
inaugurated many instrumental
concerts in Boston at his own risk.

FIG. 14. — CARL ZERRAHN.

In 1865 he became conductor of the Harvard Symphony Concerts,
in addition to his other duties. The leadership of the Worcester
festivals also became his charge, and he likewise conducted the
Salem Oratorio Society. The great triennial festivals of the Handel
and Haydn, and the still vaster Peace Jubilee in Boston, were led
by him. In 1872 he led the chorus of twenty thousand voices, at

the second jubilee.   He conducted in other cities, even in the far West.

When he completed his fortieth year of service with the Handel and Haydn Society he was given a benefit, which was a triumph such as few musicians are ever accorded.   Thousands of dollars poured in at the box-office; a gold medal studded with diamonds was given him by the society; floral offerings in incredible profusion came from the public.   It was New England's outpouring of gratitude for nearly a half-century of loyal service to art.   " Elijah " was the oratorio given at this concert.

Mr. Zerrahn was exactly the man for his time and place; he was not of the rank of a Thomas or a Seidl, but his sure and decisive beat was firm as a rock, and bred confidence even in the amateur singer.   His unfailing good humor, his painstaking explanations, made him the idol of all his choruses.   He was the best possible leader for the transition period of American chorus and orchestral music.   He died at Milton, Mass., December 29, 1909.

The great service to American music rendered by this society has not been limited to the mere performance of large classical works during a period when America was yet semi-barbaric in the art; it has also published oratorios and collections of music that were far in advance of the music described in our first chapter.   The best of the collections was made by Dr. Lowell Mason (Fig. 15), a man who stands as the chief link between the early American composers and the school of the present — if it can be called a school.

Dr. Lowell Mason (the degree was conferred by the University of New York) was born at Medfield,[1] Massachusetts, January 8, 1792. His youth was spent in Savannah, Georgia, where he became a clerk in a banking house.   He pursued music as an avocation, and found a good instructor in the person of F. L. Abel, who opened to him the field of original composition.   The first results of this were revealed in a compilation of sacred music, which contained many of his own works.   The manuscript was offered unavailingly to publishers in Philadelphia and in Boston.   Fortunately for our musical advancement it finally secured the attention of the great musical society of America, and by its committee was submitted to

[1] Baker, " Biographical Dictionary of Musicians," misstates the birthplace as " Boston."

FIG. 15.—DR. LOWELL MASON.

Dr. G. K. Jackson, the severest critic in Boston. Dr. Jackson approved most heartily of the work, and added a few of his own compositions to it. Thus enlarged, it was issued as " The Handel and Haydn Society Collection of Church Music, harmonized for Three or Four Voices, with figured Bass, for Organ and Pianoforte."

Mason's name was omitted from the publication at his own request, which he thus explains: —

" I was then a bank officer in Savannah, and did not wish to be known as a musical man, as I had not the least thought of ever making music a profession."

President Winchester, of the Handel and Haydn, sold the copyright for the young man. Mason went back to Savannah with probably $500 in his pocket as the preliminary result of his Boston visit. Edition followed edition, and at the end of five years the book had yielded a profit of more than $4000. On realizing this success Mason determined to accept an invitation to come to Boston and enter upon a musical career. This was in 1826. He was made an honorary member of the Handel and Haydn, but declined to accept this, and entered the ranks as an active member. He had been invited to come to Boston by President Winchester and other musical friends and was guaranteed an income of $2000 a year. He was also appointed, by the influence of these friends, director of music at the Hanover, Green, and Park Street churches, to alternate six months with each congregation. Finally he made a permanent arrangement with the Bowdoin Street Church, and gave up the guarantee, but again friendly influence stepped in and procured for him the position of teller at the American Bank.

It has been already stated that in 1827 Lowell Mason became president and conductor of the Handel and Haydn Society. It was the beginning of a career that was to win for him the title of " the father of American church music." Although this may seem rather a bold claim it is not too much under the circumstances. Mason might have been in the average ranks of musicianship had he lived in Europe; in America he was well in advance of his surroundings. It was not too high praise (in spite of Mason's very simple style) when Dr. Jackson wrote of his song collection: " It is much the best book I have seen published in this country, and I do not hesitate to give it my most decided approbation," or that the great contrapuntist, Hauptmann, should say that the harmonies of the tunes were dignified and church-like, and that the counterpoint was good, plain, singable, and melodious. Charles C. Perkins gives a few of the reasons why Lowell Mason was the very man to lead American music as it then existed. He says: —

" First and foremost, he was not so very much superior to the members as to be unreasonably impatient at their shortcomings. Second, he was a born teacher, who, by hard work, had fitted himself to give instruction in singing. Third, he was one of themselves, a plain, self-made man, who could understand them and be understood of them." [1]

Dr. Mason resided in Boston from 1826 until 1851, when he removed to New York. Not only Boston benefited directly by this enthusiastic teacher's instruction, but he was constantly travelling to other societies in distant cities, and helping their work. He had a notable class at North Reading, Massachusetts; and he went, in his later years, as far as Rochester, New York, where he trained a chorus of five hundred voices, many of them teachers, and some of them coming long distances to study under him. Before 1840 he had developed his idea of " Teachers' Conventions " and, as in these he had representatives from many different states, he made musical missionaries for almost the entire country. He left behind him no less than fifty volumes of musical collections, instruction books, and manuals.

Dr. Mason married Miss Abigail Gregory in 1817, and had four sons, all of whom became prominent in American musical life. Two were founders of the American organ manufactory of Mason & Hamlin, and one of the quartette was Dr. William Mason, of whom more hereafter. Lowell Mason died at " Silverspring " (his residence at Orange, New Jersey), August 11, 1872, bequeathing his great musical library, much of which had been collected abroad, to Yale College.

[1] " History of the Handel and Haydn Society," Vol. I, No. 2, p. 95.

PLATE III

HENRY L. HIGGINSON

CHAPTER III

INSTRUMENTAL MUSIC AND AMERICAN ORCHESTRAS

In the seventeenth and eighteenth centuries instrumental music was by no means so common as vocal music. It was much oftener heard in Baltimore, New Orleans, Philadelphia, and New York than it was in any part of New England, for in the last-named locality there was still a prejudice against it as being frivolous and allied to immorality. Yet even New England had a few instrumental enthusiasts. Allusion has already been made to the organ-playing that took place in the house of Mr. Brattle. In Judge Sewall's home there was virginal-playing in the seventeenth century. A note in the famous Sewall Diary (December 1, 1699) shows that a " Mr. Hiller" either sold or repaired these instruments, in Boston, at that time.

Regarding the class of compositions performed in America upon spinets and virginals, perhaps the less said the better. In the last half of the seventeenth century there was a ceaseless succession of marches and " battle-pieces " written for the spinets.[1] The taste of London, rather than that of France or Germany, was followed by the colonies, and even the fingering used in England (" x, 1, 2, 3, 4," for the five fingers) was so thoroughly assimilated, that it to-day bears the name of " American fingering."

In the eighteenth century we find many advertisements of horns, flutes, clarinets, violins, and trombones, a proof that band-playing

---

[1] The virginals and spinets were of much less compass than the piano (only from three to four octaves), and differed from that instrument in having jacks instead of hammers. Instead of the string being struck, as it is in the piano, the jack was provided with a little spur of goose-quill which plucked the thin wire almost as a mandolin-player plucks his string with his " pick." There was, therefore, a constant staccato effect produced upon these instruments. No shading was possible, all notes having the same power and quality. The harpsichord (also used in America at this time) was a larger and more powerful instrument of the same general mechanism.

was beginning to be popular,[1] and in 1773 J. Flagg established a band in Boston.

Mr. Henry M. Brooks, a reliable antiquarian, in his "Olden-Time Music," states that the earliest reference to music that he has been able to discover in the advertisements of the American newspapers, is in the *Newport* (Rhode Island) *Mercury* of December 19, 1758, which runs: —

"Any person who plays well on a *violin*, on application to the printer hereof, may be informed where he will meet with proper encouragement."

Naturally enough, in the warlike times of the eighteenth century, the fife became a favorite instrument. Music stores did not exist, and an advertisement in the journal above quoted, in 1766, announced that Abraham Remsen "sells sewing-materials, jewelry, dress goods, violins, wash-balls, frying-pans, Liverpool ale, etc."

In the first concert advertised in a Boston paper (*Postboy*, of February 2, 1761) two French horns were used in addition to the harpsichord. By 1792 we find the "Piano Forte" announced in some of the public concerts. Music teachers began advertising for pupils in the eighteenth century. Their terms were not very high; the best received, for lessons given at the residence of their pupils, was an "entrance fee" of $5 and $1 a lesson thereafter. But many were content with half of this fee. That these pioneers in teaching were not extremely prosperous is shown by the fact that they not only tried to teach half a dozen other instruments, but also offered to instruct in drawing, languages, dancing, and (a good proof of the scarcity of instruments) they allowed their pupils, for a slight additional fee, the use of their piano for the purpose of practising. The manufacture of instruments began in America in the last half of the eighteenth century. Philadelphia and New York had instrument-makers and repairers at that time, and Samuel Blyth, in Salem, made several spinets for which he received from £15 to £20 each.

According to the *Boston Gazette*, Mr. John Harris, of Boston, was

---

[1] At the beginning of the nineteenth century the West Point Band was held to be the best in the country. It consisted of five clarinets, two flutes, two horns, one bassoon, one trumpet, one trombone, one bugle, and one drum.

the first spinet-maker in America, a country which now leads the world in the manufacture of pianos. The *Gazette* of September 18, 1769, says: —

"It is with pleasure we inform the public That a few days since was shipped for Newport a very curious Spinnet, being the first ever made in America, the performance of the ingenious Mr. John Harris, of Boston (Son of the late Mr. Joseph Harris, of London, Harpsichord and Spinnet maker) and in every respect does Honour to that Artist, who now carries on Business at his House, a few doors Northward of Dr. Clark's, North end of Boston."

Before this date, however, the first American organ had been built (in 1745) in Boston, by Edward Bromfield, Jr. He had intended giving to this instrument twelve hundred pipes, but died, at the early age of twenty-three, before it was entirely completed. In this case the builder was an amateur, and the organ seems never to have been used in any church. Thomas Johnstone, of Boston, also built practical church organs in 1752 and 1754.

A music store, kept by J. Carr, existed in Baltimore, in 1794. In Boston Gottlieb Graupner had a musical establishment at No. 6 Franklin Street, the two sons of Dr. G. K. Jackson, on Market Street, and there was also the "Franklin Music Warehouse" on Milk Street, No. 2, soon after 1800. At this latter warehouse some of the earliest upright pianos manufactured in this country were made. From 1813 to 1819 this company made over fifty upright pianos and twenty organs, some of large size. Square pianofortes had been made at an earlier time in the United States.

Who made the first American piano? That is still a mooted question. The statement has been made that John Behrent,[1] a native of Philadelphia, constructed one in 1774. New York claims to have had piano-makers as early as 1785. It is a matter of record that Benjamin Crehorne, of Milton, Massachusetts, in 1803, made

---

[1] In Scharf and Westcott's "History of Philadelphia" we read (Vol. II, p. 879) — "The first piano, in all probability, that was built in this country, was made by John Behrent, in Third Street (opposite Coates' burying-ground, below Brown Street). He advertised in 1775 that he had 'just finished an extraordinary instrument by the name of the Pianoforte, made of mahogany, being of the nature of a Harpsichord, with hammers and several changes.'"

The same work further states (Vol. III, p. 2289) that James Julian, in 1785, advertised — "The great American Pianoforte of his own invention."

an instrument which is claimed to have been the first authenticated American piano. In the *Columbian Centinel* of July 30, 1806, there is an advertisement announcing " American Piano Fortes" (as well as English ones) for sale. It is certain that the first piano manufacture of any importance took place in and around Boston.

It may be mentioned, in passing, that the Franklin Music Warehouse published a musical journal, the first of its kind. This was entitled the *Euterpeiad* (Fig. 16), and was begun in 1820. It gives a good insight into the taste, or lack of it, that guided music in America at this time. " The Waterloo March," " Lord Wellington's Grand March," " Lord Wellington's Trumpet March," " The Cobourg Trumpet March," " The Battle of New Orleans," the time-honored " Washington's March," and other bombastic pieces which

EUTERPEIAD

OR, MUSICAL INTELLIGENCER,
& LADIES' GAZETTE.

No. 1.]   BOSTON, SATURDAY, MARCH 31, 1821.   [Vol. 1.

Fig. 16. — Heading of an Early Musical Journal.

gave a maximum of noise with a minimum of difficulty, were in constant demand. Ritter[1] gives an account of the mobbing of a band which attempted to play a movement of a Haydn symphony in New York at the beginning of the nineteenth century. After loud calls for " Washington's March" and " Yankee Doodle" the gallery began bombarding the classical musicians with eggs and vegetables.

It was about this time that the pioneer of American piano-building, Jonas Chickering (Fig. 17), came to Boston. He was born at New Ipswich, New Hampshire, in April, 1798; in this town he worked as apprentice to a cabinet-maker named John Gould. When the single piano of New Ipswich got out of order, young Chickering boldly offered to try and repair it.[2] This he succeeded in doing, and

---

[1] " Music in America," p. 135.

[2] The instrument was a London piano made by Christopher Ganer and originally used by the Princess Amelia, daughter of George III.

his experiments with the instrument aroused that interest in piano construction which ended only with his life.   At about twenty years of age he came to Boston with his mechanical and musical abilities, and very little else.   He joined the Park Street Church, and sang in its choir.   He also joined the Handel and Haydn Society in 1818, and afterwards became its conductor and president.   He was sufficiently advanced in vocal work to sing the solo part of David in Neukomm's oratorio of that name.   Very soon after arriving in Boston the youth obtained employment with Mr. John Osborne, then the only piano-manufacturer in the city, and in five years he had mastered all the details of the business and made many improvements in piano construction.   About 1820 Chickering associated himself with James Stewart, a Scotchman, who, two years later, returned to England.   In 1823 Chickering began business on his own account. The statement that is frequently made, that he manufactured the first American upright pianos, may be doubted on the authority of numerous advertisements in the Boston papers of 1819–20;[1] but it is certain that in 1830 he began the regular manufacture of such instruments, of a much better design and quality than had existed before that time.

Chickering soon associated himself with a sea-faring partner, Captain John Mackay.   This was of great advantage to both parties, for Mackay would often sail to South America with pianos and bring back cargoes of the precious woods used in their construction, thus making a profit on both trips.   The firm of Chickering & Mackay came to an end when the captain, in 1841, having determined that this should be his last sea venture, sailed away from Boston, and never was heard of more.   Chickering subsequently bought out the son, and thereafter kept the business in his own family.

In 1837 Chickering patented the first practical casting of a full iron frame to resist the tremendous tension of the modern piano without constantly allowing the wires to deflect from pitch.   This and other important inventions patented in 1843 and in 1845 made the American piano the most durable in the world.   The maker was

---

[1] In the *Palladium* there is a letter from the Franklin Music Warehouse, dated Feb. 23, 1819, which states that this company had made above fifty upright pianofortes from the year 1813 to that time.

quite unspoiled by his prosperity, and remained to the end of his days a genial and even jovial nature, caring little for formality or for elegance of dress, always ready to go either to the workman's bench or to any meeting that promised advancement for his city. He died December 8, 1853.

Having now traced the beg·nnings of piano music and manufacture in America, it is necessary to turn back a half-century and study the birth of orchestral music. Although the Moravians possessed a small orchestra in 1780, it was entirely devoted to accompanying religious music and did not aim at symphonic work.

In 1787 there was, in a Hanoverian regiment in Germany, a very good oboe-player named Gottlieb Graupner. Leaving his regiment with an honorable discharge, in 1788, this musician settled in London. Three years later Haydn came to that metropolis, and his manager, Salamon, brought together the largest symphony orchestra that the world had possessed up to that time. In this orchestra was the German oboe-player. He seems to have been a rolling stone, for soon after the London experience he came to Prince Edward's Island on this side of the Atlantic. In 1797, he was in Charleston, South Carolina, and married a vocalist there. The next year he settled in a more musical city, — with only a half-dozen professional musicians, — and his remaining years were devoted to carrying the orchestral banner in Boston.

Gottlieb Graupner is the father of American orchestral music. He had scarcely arrived in Boston when he set about forming the first orchestra that this country possessed. He was fortunately a good all-round musician, and could play the contrabass, the piano, and the clarinet, as well as the oboe. Although he found but few professionals in Boston, he was fortunate in discovering a number of musical enthusiasts who worked with more than professional ardor. The Russian consul, Alexi Eustaphieve, entered into the orchestral scheme that Graupner unfolded, most heartily. Filippo Trajetta, who came to Boston in 1799, was probably entirely devoted to the vocal art, and could not assist the new undertaking during the short time that he remained there. Mr. Mallet, although a vocalist, was able to play contrabass; Mr. Schaffer was a performer upon the violoncello; Mr. Granger was a good clarinettist;

FIG. 17. — JONAS CHICKERING.

From the painting in possession of Chickering & Sons.

Signor Ostinelli was an excellent performer, and became first violinist of the orchestra.   These were the professionals, but, as intimated, some amateurs imitated the example of Mr. Eustaphieve, and joined the organization.

In a little hall hired by Graupner, but afterwards in Pythian Hall in Pond (now Bedford) Street, the society met every Saturday night for social and musical purposes.   In 1821 this society was still existing, as witness the following notice from the *Euterpeiad* of October 27 of that year.

"THE PHIL-HARMONIC SOCIETY

"This nursery of Instrumental music opened their season on Saturday evening last at a new Hall lately erected in Orange street, hereafter to be denominated *The Pantheon;* it is commodious in its arrangements, with ante-rooms, &c. and affords a convenience suitable to the objects contemplated by the Phil-harmonic Society; it is 72 feet in length by 22 in width, is well lighted, and is proved to be an eligible Music Hall.

" The Concerts of this Society are chiefly instrumental ; the music is always heard with attention and oft times delight.   The orchestra consists of nearly all the gentlemen of the profession in town, and the members are principally amateurs both vocal and instrumental ; its support is derived from an annual assessment of ten dollars upon its members, who gain admission by ballot.   The public Concerts are always fully attended by a large assemblage of ladies and gentlemen, introduced by members who possess certain privileges of admission on public nights.   The following gentlemen compose the officers of the Society for the year ensuing.

G. GRAUPNER,   *President.*
B. P. TILDEN,   *Vice-President.*
M. S. PARKER,   *Treasurer.*
WM. COFFIN, JR., *Secretary.*
JOHN DODD,
WM. ROWSON,
THOMAS GRANGER,   } *Trustees.*
AMASA WINCHESTER,
EBEN. FROTHINGHAM,

E

Mr. Graupner was president of the society as long as it existed The orchestra was certainly in existence before the Handel and Haydn Society began its career; it was probably founded in 1810 or earlier It numbered from ten to a dozen members, and confined its work to the simpler fields of classical music. The symphonies of Gyrowetz. entirely obsolete to-day, were favorite pabulum for the struggling musicians. Occasionally Graupner would insist upon trying a Haydn symphony; his enthusiasm for that master knew no bounds.

At this early epoch Boston was far in advance of New York in having an oboe. A German musician writes from New York, in 1828 — "only one oboeist exists in North America, and he is said to live in Baltimore" (? Boston). In a review of *Der Freischütz*, printed in New York in 1830, the critic writes : —

"The overture was well played : an addition was made to the orchestra of two horns and a clarinet, the latter to supply the place of an instrument but little known in America, yet essential to the compositions of Weber and Rossini; we allude to the hautboy."

And another reviewer writes, in 1831, regarding an orchestral concert : —

"The band, led by Mr. Hill, contained some individual talents of a high order; but they played by no means together. Mr. Norton performed a concerto on the trumpet with good effect, and Mrs. Thorn on the harp has the caliber of an excellent amateur. We should, however, be inclined to think her a great acquisition to the city as a teacher of that refined and ladylike instrument. The overture to 'Guillaume Tell' we have never heard executed faithfully in this city, owing to the want of instruments — six violoncelli being an impossibility, and a corno inglese with hautboys not having been imported."

The oboe was not permanently in a New York orchestra until 1839. A reviewer speaks of the English horn as a novelty, in May, 1843, saying : —

"Signor Paggi, whose astonishing performances on the oboe created such a sensation at Nagel's concert last week, will, previous to his departure for Europe, afford our citizens an opportunity of hearing him once more on his new and favorite instrument. He will also perform a solo on the English horn — a musical novelty —

never yet attempted in public on this side of the Atlantic. Signor Paggi will be assisted at his concert by Rapetti and other eminent professors."

As Graupner himself played the oboe (sometimes also the contrabass) part, it is natural to suppose that there was no real conducting in our sense of the word. But Boston was not behind London in this matter, for Spohr, at about this time, thus describes the method of leadership in England : —

" This particularly excited my astonishment, for, considering the way in which orchestras are led in England, it must be extremely difficult to carry the whole through correctly. According to old custom (for the English are always loath to relinquish an old custom even when they know a better), the person presiding at the pianoforte accompanies from the score, and takes no part in the direction of the orchestra. On the contrary, the first violin, who may be properly called the leader, has merely the part of the first violin placed before him, and therefore it is impossible that he can either observe the introduction of the wind instruments, or see that the whole be accurately performed. He

FIG. 18. — GEORG HENSCHEL.

does not even mark the time with his bow, a precaution which seems indispensably necessary in an orchestra arranged on so unconnected a plan, but merely executes his part as the rest of the performers do. It is not therefore surprising that failures should occasionally arise, particularly in the forte passages — a circumstance which can never happen when the time is marked visibly, but not audibly."

Such conducting was employed in England with an orchestra of sixty-six performers ! It is therefore extremely probable that our own first orchestra went through its scores almost undirected.[1]

---

[1] Conducting with a *baton* began in Boston in 1843, if we may trust the official report of the Academy of Music, of that year, which congratulates the society upon having its orchestra led, for the first time, by a conductor (George J. Webb) with a baton, who was not obliged to play in the orchestra, but could devote his entire attention to the ensemble effects. It may be added that conducting with a baton cannot be traced, even in Germany, before 1801. Weber first employed it in Dresden in 1817, and Spohr in London in 1820.

Graupner was active in many other musical ways, outside of the Philharmonic Orchestra, for he appeared in miscellaneous concerts, he gave lessons, he had a music store and music-printing establishment on Franklin Street, and seems to have been the most active musical influence in old Boston. It must be noticed that the foreign influence was beginning to tell in our musical affairs, and that a few musicians from abroad now settled, more or less permanently, in Boston. In addition to Graupner one can mention M. Pick, who arrived in 1792, M. Mallet, who was organist of Dr. Kirkland's church and was finally partner of Graupner (he was here as early as 1793), and Hans Gram, who, in 1793, was the organist at the Brattle Church. Several French refugees, with more or less musical ability, were forced to fly to America because of the Revolution in their country. As for Signor Trajetta's influence, it was more exerted in New York than in Boston, as we shall see later.

Mr. John S. Dwight gives the date of the last concert of the Philharmonic Orchestra as November 24, 1824. Sixteen years after this, an orchestra of much larger dimensions was founded in Boston through the instrumentality of the Academy of Music, the first great school of music founded in America. Of the school we shall speak in its proper place; to follow, at present, our orchestral story, we may state that in 1840 the Academy founded a large orchestra which introduced Beethoven's symphonies to a New England audience, the First and the Fifth symphonies being given during the initial year of this orchestra's existence. The orchestra existed for seven years, and repeatedly performed great works by Beethoven and other classical composers. It consisted of from twenty-five to forty performers, and many of these were amateurs. It had an especial predilection for overtures, and these preponderated heavily over the symphonies in its programmes.

Although Boston took the lead in the matter of a permanent orchestra, it is quite possible that sporadic organizations existed in other American cities contemporaneously with Graupner's association. Philadelphia, for example, long ago attracted a German population, among whom were numerous musicians. There is record of several musicians from Hamburg having formed a band in that city as early as 1783, but it seems not to have been anything more than a temporary money-making scheme.

In 1820, however, there was started in Philadelphia an association that ought to have had as great an influence as any in the country, but for lack of public support it remained circumscribed in its influence. This was the Musical Fund Society, which was begun February 20, 1820, to assist indigent professional members and to diffuse a musical knowledge in the city. It was broader in its scope than the Handel and Haydn Society of Boston, for it gave both secular and sacred music, it founded a school, it built a music hall, and it combined instrumental and vocal music in its concerts. At its first concert, given April 24, 1821, not only Handel and Graun choruses were given, but Beethoven's First Symphony was played, probably for the first time in America. It also gave Haydn's "Creation" in 1821, two years after the first performance by the Handel and Haydn Society. The society continued to give concerts until 1857.

New York was not so advanced in orchestral matters. There was an instrumental organization, called the "Euterpean Society," founded in 1799, which gave one concert each year, but it exerted no great influence, although it existed for about thirty years. There were strange instrumental concerts given, in the early part of the nineteenth century, in the metropolis. The following programme [1] may show what kind of "programme-music" our forefathers delighted in.

TUESDAY, MARCH 23, 1802

Concert and Ball at Lowell's Hotel, Broadway

ACT I

Grand sinfonie characteristic of the peace with the French Republic, composed by the celebrated Wranizsky, consisting of ten descriptive movements, viz.: No. 1. The Revolution. 2. March of the English. 3. March of the Austrians and Prussians. 4. Procession and Death of Louis XVI. 5. Funeral March. 6. March of the English. 7. March of the Allies. 8. Tumult of a Battle. 9. Negotiations for Peace. 10. Joyful exclamations for that happy event.

Song . . . . Mr. Fox
Concerto, piano . . . . Mr. Gilfert
(Lately from Europe.)

---

[1] Quoted from the New York *Musical Courier*, National edition, third section.

Song	Mr. Jefferson
Concerto, violin	Mr. Hewitt
Song	Miss Brett

Concerto, clarinet, composed and performed by Mr. Gautier.

ACT II

Overture	Pleyel
Song	Mr. Tyler
Catch, Poor Thomas Day	——

Messrs. Wilson, Jefferson and Tyler.

Song	Mr. Wilson
Concerto, violoncello	Mr. Nicolai, Jr.
Song	Miss Brett

Finale, the celebrated Overture composed by Haydn, in which the performers take their leave of the audience.

At 7 P.M. . . . . One Dollar

"The celebrated Wranizsky" was once esteemed a rival of Haydn in the symphonic field. One might be curious to know just

what instruments conducted the "negotiations for peace," and which ones signed the treaty! In 1842, however, two years later than the Boston Academy Orchestra, there came into existence the most important orchestral society that America had as yet possessed. It was founded in New York, chiefly through the efforts of Uriah C. Hill, a mediocre violinist who had studied in Germany with Louis Spohr. Hill deserves grateful remembrance as one of the pioneers in the musical advance of America. He was born in New York, about 1802, and died, after a life full of

FIG. 19. — WILHELM GERICKE.

disappointments, in 1875. He was the first president of the Philharmonic Society. Its initial concert was given December 7, 1842, and it gave three concerts during the first season. At the beginning its forces were seventeen violins (first and second), five violas, four violoncellos, five contrabasses, three flutes, a piccolo, two oboes, two clarinets, three bassoons, four horns, two trumpets, four trombones, and one pair of kettledrums. Sometimes these forces were augmented, — making an orchestra of between fifty and sixty performers.

If Boston had undoubtedly led in the domain of American vocal music up to this time, in orchestral music, in spite of the precedence of Boston's two orchestras, New York now took the lead, and held it.   The Philharmonic Orchestra still exists, an important factor in the musical life of the present, and the Philharmonic Society was, and is, a strong instance of a musical republic.   The members elect their conductor, give their concerts at their own risk, and the salaries of the musicians consist of a division of whatever profits may result.   The dividends to each artist have not been, however, as large as the salaries that are paid in the permanent orchestras of Chicago or Boston.

What the Handel and Haydn Society had done in the field of oratorio, the Philharmonic Society of New York accomplished in the field of orchestral music.   It began at once with masterworks, and its very first concert presented a Beethoven symphony (the Fifth), a Weber overture (" Oberon "), a scene from " Fidelio," a Mozart aria, and other great works.   Every subsequent concert kept up the standard of these selections; the very best of classical orchestral music was constantly presented.   The execution of such lofty works naturally left much to be desired at first.   The conductors often directed works without having heard any adequate performance of them, without having sufficient clews to their true interpretation. This was, however, only the case with the earliest concerts.

The first conductors were U. C. Hill, H. C. Timm, W. Alpers, G. Loder, L. Wiegers, D. G. Etienne, and A. Boucher.   From 1849 Theodore Eisfeld was conductor, and from 1855 to 1866 this gentleman alternated with Carl Bergmann in the conductorship, after which, for ten years, the latter reigned alone.   Dr. Leopold Damrosch, Theodore Thomas, Adolph Neuendorff, Anton Seidl, Walter Damrosch, and Emil Paur have been conductors of the society since that time, and the standard has been raised enormously.   In 1903–4, with the aid of such wealthy men as Andrew Carnegie, John D. Rockefeller, E. Francis Hyde, Clarence M. Hyde, Grant B. Schley, James Loeb, and Elkan Naumburg, it introduced an innovation that may be regarded as unparalleled, not only in America, but in the

entire world.   It gave a season of orchestral playing that was probably the greatest lesson in conducting that has ever been attempted.
It not only had the services of the excellent Victor Herbert (of whom
more hereafter), but it engaged a number of the best conductors of
Europe, and gave New York an opportunity of comparison of leaders
that was memorable.   Colonne, of France, Weingartner, Richard
Strauss, and Kogel, of Germany, Henry J. Wood, of London, and
Wasili von Safanoff, of Russia, were chosen as competitors in this
contest of conducting, which the musical critic Mr. Henry T. Finck
justly calls " epoch-making."

Boston was not altogether idle after its Academy Orchestra had
become defunct.   Throughout its career the organization had generally numbered from thirty to forty performers, with George J. Webb
for conductor.   After its death in 1847 a genial musician, named
Thomas Comer (they always called him " Tom " Comer, however),
took the orchestral helm for a little while, with an organization
called the " Musical Fund Society," formed, like that of the same
name in Philadelphia, for the combined purposes of charity and
music.   Tom Comer cared more for the popular than the classical
side of music, and, until Mr. George J. Webb took charge of the
orchestra, in its later years, its music was not vastly different from
that of a first-class theatre orchestra of the present time.   The
Musical Fund concerts came to an end in 1855.

Meanwhile a higher plane of orchestral execution had come
about in the United States through the Germania Orchestra.   This
orchestra was formed almost by accident.   Just as the country
derived some benefit by the French Reign of Terror sending
many cultured refugees to our shores, so it again received an impetus in art through the German uprisings of 1848, which forced
many excellent musicians to fly from their native land.   These
had not, in many cases, been active participants in the revolutionary
proceedings ; the unrest that existed throughout continental Europe
caused music to languish to such a degree that many artists were
forced by poverty to emigrate to more peaceful countries.   Thus it
was that a company of some twenty-three young musicians, finding
themselves together in a strange land, founded an orchestra with a
view to filling their empty purses.   The Germania Orchestra was,

as intimated, small in numbers (at first), but each member was a good musician, the leaders, Carl Lenschow and afterwards Carl Bergmann, were thorough musicians, and the programmes were classical.

They gave most of their concerts in Boston, for of the musical cities this presented the freest field, yet they travelled about the country, and Philadelphia and other cities had thus good opportunities for studying a European model — a most necessary thing in those days of untrammelled and often misguided musical enthusiasm.   The Germania Orchestra soon augmented its ranks to fifty musicians.   It performed the most ambitious works, and together with the Handel and Haydn Society, gave Boston its first hearing of Beethoven's Ninth Symphony, which the Philharmonic Orchestra had given in New York a half-dozen years before (in 1846).   The Germania Orchestra was richer in soloists than any other American orchestra of its day.   It had an artist for each instrument.

FIG. 20. — ARTHUR NIKISCH.

Taste in orchestral matters at this time was still in its infancy.   One may read this fact in some of the experiences of the Germania Orchestra.   In Boston their concerts were generally profitable ; in New York, although the Philharmonic concerts were well attended (partly from social reasons), the Germania met with pecuniary loss; [1] in Philadelphia, after going to constantly smaller halls, they wound up their affairs with an attempt to give a concert in a large-sized room, of which the rental was only $10, but the receipts being less even than this small sum, the landlord turned out the gas and the orchestra simultaneously.

Although New York was going steadily on with its orchestral concerts, the Philharmonic Society giving an unbroken series of excellent programmes, Boston had many an interregnum in its orchestral history.   From 1855 to 1863 Mr. Carl Zerrahn, who had come to

---

[1] The Germania Orchestra began its career in New York; one concert, aided by the Philharmonic Society, was quite profitable.

Boston as flute-player of the Germania Orchestra (he may be seen in this character at the extreme left of the picture of the Germania Orchestra, Fig. 26), gave a series of orchestral concerts with an organization which took the title of " Philharmonic Orchestra." The Civil War caused music to languish at this time, and for three years there was not a symphonic orchestra in Boston. In 1866 the Harvard Musical Association (of which more will be said in the next chapter) founded an orchestra of which Mr. Zerrahn was conductor. This orchestra existed until 1882.

It is well to state at this point, that in all the orchestral work in America up to and a little after 1860, there was more of ambition than of true achievement; the performances were generally slipshod and far below any classical standard. We have elsewhere spoken of Gottlieb Graupner as the father of American orchestral music. This is certainly true in a chronological sense, but as regards the establishment of a high standard of execution, the introduction of a true epoch of interpretation, Theodore Thomas (Frontispiece) deserves this honorable title. The beginnings of something akin to European technique and ensemble, the presentation of great musical works with something like their true reading, began with Thomas, and the efforts of other conductors to rival him, of other orchestras to equal his, soon led to much higher attainment in this field than had ever before been thought of in the United States.

Theodore Thomas, who has done more to raise the standard of music in America than any other man, was born in Essen, Hanover, October 11, 1835. He was taught by his father, and so well taught that he played the violin in public at the age of six. The family came to New York in 1845, and the lad soon entered an orchestra there. He inaugurated the first artistic chamber concerts that New York ever listened to, associating William Mason (the eminent pianist), J. Mosenthal, G. Matzka, F. Bergner, and Carl Bergmann in a regular organization. In these Mason-Thomas concerts such composers as Schumann and Brahms were first introduced to America, for although Theodore Eisfeld had started chamber concerts, with Otto Dresel as pianist, four years earlier (in 1851), these were not continued nearly as long as the Mason-Thomas concerts; and as both Eisfeld and Dresel were very conservative, the moderns in chamber music were obliged to wait for a hearing until the two young radicals — Thomas and Mason — gave greater catholicity to the concert repertoire. Of this matter we shall say more in connection with the biography of the last-named musician, — the American leader in early piano music.

In December, 1864, Thomas began a series of orchestral concerts in New York. This led to a wholesome rivalry with the Philharmonic Orchestra, the latter increasing its forces to one hundred men. Thomas, in his endeavor to make his orchestra really permanent, gave a series of summer garden concerts, which were very successful at the outset. He made tours with his orchestra, and thus did missionary work in creating a standard of taste in different cities and, in a slight degree, shaking Boston out of its dull routine of ancient classics. In 1877 and in 1879 Thomas was conductor of the Philharmonic itself, and led that society onward to a higher plane. It must, however, be stated that he never achieved as much with the choral societies with which he was connected as with his orchestras; he had rivals, even superiors, in the vocal field, but in the orchestral domain for a long time he stood alone, and far ahead of his contemporaries.

And now some of the healthy rivalry that had awakened New York in orchestral matters began to appear in belated Boston. The Harvard Musical Association had given the city an orchestra that was a good nursery for its orchestral taste, but Boston had been so thoroughly trained in the old school of Handel, Haydn, and Beethoven, that it looked very much askance at the musicians who were beginning to establish a new order of things. There was a clique of conservatives in control which grudgingly allowed a very little of Berlioz, Wagner, or other musical anarchists, to appear upon the programmes.[1]

But Boston had gradually become the residence of many young European musicians, and these chafed under the restraint put upon

---

[1] A consultation of the files of Dwight's *Journal of Music* will at once show that we are not overstating the case. Prejudice ran rampant at this time. That the prejudice was not always founded on musical judgment may be shown by the fact that this same journal once mistakenly made a bitter attack upon Bach himself, when one of his chorals was given at a Parish Choir Festival with the name of Hassler attached to it as composer. The work was "O Haupt vall Blut und Wunden," of which the melody is by Hassler, the harmonization by Bach.

modern music by the leaders of orchestral matters.   The result was the establishment of a rival to the Harvard Symphony Orchestra. The new orchestra was established as an independent body in 1879, and was organized into a Philharmonic Society in 1880. The conductors of the orchestra were Bernhard Listemann, Louis Maas, and Carl Zerrahn, successively.

The rivalry between the conservatives and the radicals in music became quite bitter, while Boston was going through its transition state.   Both orchestras were inadequate in performance, because of insufficient rehearsals, necessitated by the slight patronage afforded by the public, and both were finally superseded by the establishment of a third and greater institution: an orchestra entirely independent of box-office receipts, an orchestra that was to employ its musicians entirely in the field of classical music, the first really permanent orchestra of America, — the Boston Symphony Orchestra.

FIG. 21. — EMIL PAUR.

Of course such an organization could only be founded by a society or an individual ready to make a large pecuniary sacrifice.   The proper hour was at hand, and so was the man.   Henry L. Higginson (Pl. III), a banker, who had often shown his public spirit and lofty citizenship, founded the orchestra at his own risk, and guaranteed its permanency.

The Boston Symphony Orchestra began its career on Saturday evening, October 22, 1881.   Saturday evening had been, up to that time, almost barren of entertainments (a relic of the Puritan view that the Sabbath began on the eve of the sacred day); it now became the musical evening of the week.   The first conductor was Mr. Georg Henschel (Fig. 18), a man who had not great experience in conducting, but whose general musical education and broad tastes were beyond all question.   The new enterprise began with a species of musical invocation.   Beethoven's " Dedication of the House " was the first number played.   The opening season the orchestra contained sixty-seven members, and gave twenty concerts.   Each concert was preceded by a public rehearsal, after the plan of some foreign orchestras, a proceeding first established in America by the New York Philharmonic.   The rehearsal was actually a concert. The third season the organization gave twenty-six concerts, with rehearsals additional; but after that the number was reduced to twenty-four, which has been the annual quota ever since.

In 1884 Mr. Henschel went abroad, and his place was taken by Mr. Wilhelm Gericke (Fig. 19).   Mr. Gericke, not a musical radical by any means, was a superb drill-master and exactly the man to mould the new organization into a permanent shape.   If America owes its greatest orchestral debt to Mr. Higginson for leading the way to permanency in this field, and to Theodore Thomas for the first revelation of true orchestral interpretation, it also owes much to Mr. Gericke for the firm manner in which he set about forming an orchestra that should be perfect of its kind.   In its first years it had been a pleasant refuge for those musicians who had been prominent in establishing orchestral music, in its larger forms, in the city.   It was a difficult task to turn these veterans out of the ranks, and it was still more unpopular to fill their places with young Europeans who were to form the life-blood of the orchestra for years to come.   Yet this delicate undertaking was brilliantly accomplished under the régime of Mr. Gericke.   The result has been that fewer changes have taken place in the ranks of this orchestra during the last eighteen years than in almost any organization of its kind in the world.

In 1889 there came to the directorship one of the greatest of orchestral virtuosi, — Mr. Arthur Nikisch (Fig. 20).   This eminent conductor found a perfect instrument ready to his hand, and he played upon it as a Liszt might perform upon a keyboard.   He did not make any changes in the band, he could not perhaps have built it up to its perfect organization; but for four years he gave most brilliant interpretations with it, after which he too returned to Europe.   After that, in 1893, there came to the helm a man who combined in himself something of the radical tastes of Nikisch and the firmness of rulership of Gericke. Mr. Emil Paur (Fig. 21) upheld the standard of the work for five years, after which he went to New York, where he was active both in the operatic and symphonic fields. He proved himself a man of broad musical tastes, whose thorough training in the classics by no means prevented the heartiest enthusiasm for the new school of composition. Tschaikowsky, Richard Strauss, Hausegger, and others of the modern band of composers, owe their best New York and Boston interpretations to him — as the West owes them to Theodore Thomas. In 1904, after winning great successes in Europe, Mr. Paur (now in Berlin) was appointed conductor of the Pittsburg orchestra.

Mr. Gericke was again called to the conductorship of the orchestra in 1898. The next year a great Symphony Hall (Fig. 12) was built for the concerts which had become a permanent feature in the musical life of Boston. But the orchestra was by no means a local affair: it made, and still makes, regular tours to New York, Philadelphia, Washington, Providence, and in 1915 it made its appearance in San Francisco. Dr. Karl Muck was the symphonic conductor from 1906 to 1908; Mr. Max Fiedler from 1908 to 1912, and Dr. Muck again from 1912. A pension fund for retired members of the orchestra was established in 1903. Dr. Muck's European contracts were the cause of his absence from 1908 to 1912.

The West has also established an orchestra that has become permanent, and again we find the great instrumental leader in American musical affairs doing yeoman service in his adopted country. Theodore Thomas's first visit to the West occurred in 1869, when he gave three orchestral concerts in Farwell Hall, Chicago. Mr. W. S. B. Mathews, the Chicago critic and pianist, who attended two of these concerts, says that the largest audience did not exceed one thousand people, and the smallest was less than a third of this figure. As an illustration of the progressive character of Thomas's work, it may be mentioned that he performed some of the orchestral excerpts from Wagner's works before they were heard in Europe, Liszt sending these to the American conductor to assist the propaganda here, and finding a willing missionary in the progressive musician.

FIG. 22. — WALTER DAMROSCH.

His subsequent experience (1878–80) as director of the College of Music at Cincinnati will be spoken of in a later chapter.

The Chicago Orchestra came into existence in 1890, fifty business men of that city having sufficient faith in Mr. Thomas to subscribe $1000 each, and pledging themselves to a similar subscription annually for three years, as the nucleus of a fund to support a permanent orchestra that should give twenty or twenty-two concerts each season in Chicago and also do such touring as should be deemed practicable. Mr. Thomas placed at the service of the new organization his private musical library, the largest of its kind in the world, — a collection of orchestral scores such as only a large public society or institution could hope to acquire.

It was an uphill fight, for public taste in Chicago had not received the chances of development that had been afforded Eastern cities, and there was almost a dislike of the bold educational programmes that Thomas put forth. Loss followed loss each season; the first year, even with the advantage of novelty in its favor, the orchestra used up the entire guarantee fund, and was obliged to call for nearly $8000 additional. The second season was a little better, financially, and the third year, in spite of a business panic and generally hard times, the deficit was only $20,000. At the present writing the storm is wholly weathered, and there is a chance of smoother sailing ahead. Theodore Thomas died, in Chicago, January 4, 1905. He directed the Chicago Orchestra up to very nearly the time of his death. Many expected the dispersal of the orchestra after the death of its great founder. But a new general arose to lead the forces, and soon proved that he was competent to take up the burden that Thomas had laid down.

Frederick Stock had been Thomas's assistant conductor from 1899. From 1903 he conducted all the orchestral concerts of this band when on tour. From the time of Thomas's death he became its conductor, and he has more than sustained its greatness. Mr. Stock is also a composer in the large forms, of great and classical merit. His string quartettes and symphony are of especial excellence.

It cannot be said that the material of the Chicago Orchestra is as great as that of its Boston competitor; it is doubtful, for example,

F

if any orchestra in the world possesses such a body of first violins as is found in the Boston Symphony Orchestra.   But in the matter of leadership, of broad and catholic programmes, of musicianly readings on the part of the conductor, the Chicago Orchestra need not fear comparison with any existing organization.   Its concerts in Boston were a revelation to Eastern musicians, and it has won triumphs all through the East, in spite of the standard set up by the older New York and Boston orchestras.   The New York Philharmonic Orchestra in recent years has gained considerably under the conductorship of Josef Stransky, who assumed the direction in 1911.   Mr. Stransky was born in Bohemia, in 1872, and studied at Leipsic under Jadassohn, and at Vienna under Fuchs and Bruckner.   He was conductor at Prague (five years), at Hamburg (seven years), and in Berlin, before he came to America. Mr. Stransky is brilliant and poetic as a leader and his programmes are always interesting and finely made.   The Philharmonic Orchestra has advanced notably under his conductorship.

One must also mention a very successful effort to bring good orchestral music to the masses.   The People's Symphony Concerts, given in Carnegie Hall, New York, were launched as long ago as 1900, by Franz Xavier Arens, who has conducted them ever since.

Mr. Arens was born in Neef, Rhenish-Prussia, in 1856.   His father was cantor and organist, and from him he received his first lessons in singing, piano, organ, and harmony.   At the age of eleven he was taken to America.   When fifteen years old he filled his first position as organist and choir director in a suburb of Cleveland, Ohio.   Later he studied counterpoint, organ, piano, singing, and conducting with John Singenberger, professor of music at the Normal College at St. Francis, Wisconsin, after which he was appointed professor of music at Canisius College, Buffalo, and organist and choir-master at St. Michael's Church.   From 1882 to 1884 he studied at the Royal Conservatory of Music, Munich, under Rheinberger, Abel, Riehl, and others, and in 1884 and 1885 he took a course in composition and conducting under Franz Wüllner at the Royal Conservatory in Dresden, from which institute he graduated with the highest honors.

After a few years spent in Cleveland, Ohio, as conductor of the Philharmonic Orchestra and of a German singing society, he returned to Europe, where from 1890 to 1892 he studied voice with Professor Julius Hey, of Berlin, and introduced American orchestral works of MacDowell, Foote, Paine, Chadwick, Kelly, Huss, Van der Stucken, Victor Herbert, Shelley, Beck, and Busch, at Berlin, Leipsic, Hamburg, Sondershausen, Weimar, Dresden, and Vienna. From 1892 to 1896 he held the positions of conductor of the Indianapolis May music festivals, president of the Indianapolis College of Music, and principal of the vocal department. In 1896 he removed to New York, where he established himself as a vocal teacher. Four years later he founded the People's Symphony Concerts, which are now given at Carnegie Hall, and are intended to educate the masses in orchestral music. The concerts have been very much appreciated by those for whom they were intended; even standing room is often unattainable on some occasions, and the programmes are always of a good class of music.

Another enterprise of similar character in New York is the Young Men's Symphony Orchestra, founded and endowed by the late Alfred Seligman, and for many years under the direction of Arnold Volpe, which gratuitously trains young men in orchestral playing. But the orchestra which now approaches nearest to the permanency of the Boston Symphony Orchestra, as regards endowment and independence of the box office, is the Symphony Society of New York.

The Symphony Society was founded in 1878 by Dr. Leopold Damrosch, the illustrious pioneer of music in America, and conducted by him until his death in 1885. Elected to the position thus left vacant, Walter Damrosch for nearly thirty years has carried on the work begun by his father, so that the destinies of the Society have always remained identified with the name of its founder. The change effected in orchestral conditions during the existence of the Society has been enormous.

At first the orchestra assembled but rarely, giving only twelve concerts yearly. Gradually its activities increased, and for over ten years it has played at least one hundred concerts every year, including extensive tours throughout this country and Canada, and preparing these concerts by daily rehearsals held throughout the entire season.

In 1914 this society entered upon a new and very important phase of its career. In the spring of that year the president of the society, Mr. Harry Harkness Flagler, announced that he would set aside $100,000 annually to defray any deficit in the receipts of the orchestra and to enable it to pursue its highest artistic aims. Thus Mr. Harkness does in New York what Mr. Higginson had done in Boston, and gives to the Symphony Society Orchestra absolute independence.

Mr. Walter Damrosch, of whom we shall find much more in a later chapter, is very broad-minded in his programmes and has labored in almost every field of American music, but probably his conductorship of this orchestra will be the most important under the new conditions, an enviable post for any conductor.

But many other cities are awakening in the field of orchestral music. Philadelphia has a symphony orchestra of the first rank, which was founded in 1900, through the efforts of Dr. Edward I. Keffer and other music-loving citizens. It was put under the conductorship of Fritz Scheel, who was brought from San Francisco for that purpose. Mr. Scheel, one of the most thorough of conductors, gave the most advanced programmes imaginable, secured the coöperation of even Richard Strauss, made tours with the orchestra, and in every way brought it into the front rank. His labors were too conscientious, too severe, for his mind gave way under the task and he died at Philadelphia in 1907.

He was followed in the conductorship by Carl Pohlig, a pupil of Liszt and a Kapellmeister in many European capitals. Mr. Pohlig took charge in 1907, and continued at the head of the orchestra until 1912, when Leopold Stokowski succeeded him. Mr. Stokowski, who had been conductor of the Cincinnati Orchestra until 1912, is now the conductor of the great Philadelphia one. The Philadelphia Orchestra has given works even as great as the Mahler eighth symphony, which demands one thousand performers.

The Cincinnati Orchestra has also shown good signs of permanency. Mr. Van der Stucken (see page 192) was its conductor in 1895, and Leopold Stokowski led it from 1909 to 1912 (then

becoming conductor of the Philadelphia Orchestra), and Ernst Kunwald took up the baton after that. Mr. Kunwald was born in
Vienna, April 14, 1868, and at first studied Law, even taking a
doctor's degree, but soon turned to Music, becoming a pupil of
Grädener, and of Jadassohn, and conducting many European orchestras and operas. Leopold Stokowski was born in London, April
18, 1882, the son of a Polish exile. His musical studies, which
were very thorough and varied, were chiefly taken in England.
He married Olga Samaroff, the famous pianist.

Pittsburg also had an excellent orchestra, but it did not become
permanent as those of Philadelphia and Cincinnati. Under the
direction of the eminent Emil Paur (page 55), long a conductor
of the Boston Symphony Orchestra, it gave most classical and
valuable programmes, and before that Mr. Victor Herbert (page 238)
won great success with the well-equipped band. But Paur went to
Europe in 1910 and the orchestra soon dispersed.

Minneapolis has also an excellent classical orchestra which dates
back to 1902, and shows every sign of permanency. The thanks
for this are due chiefly to Emil Oberhoffer, whose work in this connection cannot be overestimated. He not only gives to Minneapolis a series of Symphony Concerts and a series of more popular
concerts, but has presented every one of Beethoven's nine symphonies and has given several series of young people's concerts at
which his orchestra gives many classical works, and the conductor
explains them and the instruments to his young auditors. There
are many adult auditors at these instructive occasions, for such practical information is craved by all the laity. Minneapolis is, however, a city which is very much in earnest in its art studies. Its
Woman's Club has done most thorough work in this field.

The sister city of St. Paul has been more intermittent in its
orchestral work. From 1908 to 1914 Mr. Walter Henry Rothwell,
an English musician of high attainment, conducted a Symphony
orchestra in that city. It was then discontinued, but there is pros-
pect of its being resuscitated immediately.

St. Louis has a very good symphonic orchestra led by Max
Zach, who was for a long time a member of the Boston Symphony
Orchestra. He has held the position of orchestral conductor in St.

Louis since 1907. Even in the far West the foundation of symphonic orchestras goes on apace. San Francisco has founded an orchestra which is likely to become permanent. It began in 1911, with Henry K. Hadley (page 191) as its conductor. It was a plant of slow growth, for many rehearsals were pecuniarily impossible, and symphonic playing was an avocation rather than a true vocation with the musicians. But Mr. Hadley did loyal work with his handicapped forces until 1915. Then San Francisco determined to put the orchestra upon a real symphonic footing. Alfred Hertz, the world-famous Wagnerian conductor, long connected with the Metropolitan Opera of New York, was engaged as conductor and was given *carte blanche* as to the arrangement and choice of his forces.

San Francisco gained much musically by the Panama Exposition of 1915, for this World's Fair brought great musical attractions to its halls. It is possible that the visit of the Boston Symphony Orchestra, the Kneisel Quartette, etc., may have helped the movement which culminated in the establishment of a great symphony orchestra there.

But Los Angeles, San Diego, Seattle, and other far Western cities are also beginning to stir actively in the advancement of music. Los Angeles, particularly, has shown great enterprise (see supplementary chapter). Of course, there may be a few errors in the headlong rush towards the highest in music, but that will be only a temporary defect, and we may hope soon to see the far West independent of the Eastern centres in its musical development.

In speaking of the advance in conducting in America, we must not omit the name of Emil Mollenhauer, who has done excellent work in the Eastern states in orchestral, oratorio, and choral conducting.

In the field of lighter orchestral music, probably the best of the country is given by the Boston Symphony players during the months of May and June, for then some fifty of the players of the regular Symphony Orchestra combine to give what are colloquially known as "The Pops," a set of popular programmes under the lead of Messrs. Maquarre, Schmidt, Clement Lenom, and other conductors, which are the best of their kind in this country.

Mention must also be made of one of Theodore Thomas's lieutenants who has done good work in conducting since the death of his principal. Mr. Arthur Mees was born in Columbus, Ohio, February 13, 1850, and studied in Europe under Dorn, Weitzmann, and Kullak. He has conducted the Worcester Festival, the Cecilia Society, of Boston, and much choral and orchestral music.

In connection with the orchestral subject a word may be added regarding the influence of foreign orchestras visiting the United States. None of these exerted such an effect upon our art develop- ment as the Germania, whose struggles have already been described- But even before it began its career Gungl came to America with a large and well-equipped orchestra. He met with no success, pecun- iarily, and wrote bitterly of the status of music in America in 1849. Among other sarcastic remarks about the lack of the art instinct in this country, he wrote: —

" How much soever the American, as a business man, perhaps sur- passes most European nations, just so much, perhaps, in all depart- ments of the fine arts — but especially in music — is he behind all, and is therefore not capable of enjoying instrumental music. It is a matter of course, that only the so-called anti-classical music can, in any degree, suit the taste of an American public: such as waltzes, galops, quadrilles, — above all, polkas. That there are exceptions I cannot deny; but only a few — a very few." [1]

But in 1853 Jullien came to America, and met with success. He had an orchestra of forty musicians, and some of these were soloists of the first rank. Lavigne, the best oboeist of the world, Bottesini, the greatest living contrabass player, and others of similar renown, were in this organization. He soon increased his forces to ninety- seven men — the largest orchestra that America had yet heard. Jullien was sufficiently full of eccentricities to become very piquant in American eyes; he had some of the extravagances that modern concert-goers associate with De Pachmann, and, like the latter, was a man of genius in spite of being a *poseur*.[2] He did not fail to

[1] *Neue Berliner Musik-Zeitung*, February 4, 1849. Quoted in Dwight's *Journal of Music*.
[2] The New York *Musical Courier* (National Edition, Part III) thus describes Jullien: —
" His appearance must have been striking. His wealth of black hair, his startling black mustache, his white waistcoat, his elaborately embroidered shirt-front, his wristbands turned back over his sleeves, and his general magnificence gave him an extraordinary individuality. At the last bar he would sink exhausted in his velvet chair. He conducted Beethoven with a jewelled baton and a fresh pair of kid gloves, handed to him at the moment on a silver salver."

seek out some of the native instrumental composers, and movements from the symphonies (for there were American symphonies
existing then) of William H. Fry and George F. Bristow were
performed at some of his concerts. Jullien soon returned to Paris,
and eventually died there in an insane asylum, in 1860.

In recent times, Winderstein, Mascagni, and other great foreign
conductors have led orchestras in America, but, whatever the rank
of the conductors of these orchestras, the latter were not better than
our native bands, often not as good. Even when Nikisch, the most
poetic conductor alive, came to us with the London Symphony
Orchestra, which Richter pompously describes in the Encyclopædia
Britannica as the "greatest orchestra of the world," it was found
that we had some which were certainly as great, on this side of the
water.

Many details concerning the orchestras spoken of in this chapter
can be found in the National editions of "Musical America" and of
the "Musical Courier."

CHAPTER IV

MUSICAL SOCIETIES AND INSTITUTIONS

We have seen that the Philharmonic Society in New York, and the Handel· and Haydn Society in Boston, were the most important beginnings in orchestral and vocal music in America. Nevertheless, outside of these two, and of the other organizations mentioned in the last two chapters, there were many societies at work in different parts of the country that exerted a powerful influence upon the rise of American music. The vocal societies of New York are scarcely to be derived from the New England psalm-singers. H. E. Krehbiel, in his "Notes on Choral Music," says, in speaking of New York musical associations: —

"The seeds that produced our singing societies were brought to New York, not from the older settlements of New England, but from Europe."

One can heartily subscribe to the above statement when one remembers that Trinity Church gave a high class of English music in its services at a time when New England would scarcely tolerate an organ. The record of the earliest New York musical societies is a very vague one. Neither Ritter in his "Music in America," nor Krehbiel in the work above quoted, have been able to find reliable details about the musical clubs or associations of the eighteenth century in the Dutch-English metropolis. About 1820 there existed in New York a Philharmonic Society that was devoted to chorus music, and had no great influence; there was a Handel and Haydn society which had but a brief career; there was the Euterpean Society, alluded to in the preceding chapter; and there was the New York Choral Society. The Handel and Haydn Society grew out of an attempt to raise a fund for the rebuilding of Zion Church. The New York Choral Society, the best of the

73

early vocal societies, was formed in September, 1823, and gave its first concert, April 20, 1824, in St. George's Church, in Beekman Street, with fifty voices and an orchestra of twenty performers. It soon dissolved.

The New York Sacred Music Society now took up the banner of choral music. Just as much of Boston's early chorus music came from one church choir, — that of Park Street Church, — so the early interest in this New York school of art was fostered by the choristers of Zion Church. Out of a quarrel between the choir and the vestry of this church grew the New York Sacred Music Society, which was organized in 1823 by discharged choir-singers in self-defence. It gave its first concert in March, 1824. Very soon this society gave complete oratorios, and to Uriah C. Hill, whose services to the orchestral music of the country have already been recorded, was also due this great step forward in New York's choral music. He was, for a time, director of this society. The organization kept together until 1849. It had a rival in the Academy of Sacred Music, begun in 1832, but this never was able to make much headway against its older competitor.

FIG. 24. — THEODORE THOMAS.
As a young man.

In 1844 came the first great rival to the Sacred Music Society, the Musical Institute, which, directed by Mr. Henry C. Timm, a German musician afterwards very prominent in the Philharmonic Society, gave oratorios and cantatas, both classical and modern, with a chorus of about one hundred and twenty and an orchestra of sixty performers. Mr. Timm's influence may be ranked almost as important at this time as Mr. Hill's, for it was in large degree by his efforts that the chief elements of New York's choral societies were united in 1849, and its greatest choral society (up to that time) was born.

The New York Harmonic Society gave its first concert on May 10, 1850. New York had now a very large hall, well suited for musical festivals. Tripler Hall (it was in Broadway and was burned soon after) could seat nearly five thousand people, and it was in this hall, in June, 1851, that the new society gave Mendelssohn's "Elijah." At the Harmonic Society's concerts some of the greatest European soloists appeared, and the successive conductors were Timm, Eisfeld, Bristow, Bergmann, Morgan, Ritter, and finally Dr. James Peck.

In 1863 some of the members of the Harmonic Society formed another association under the name of the Mendelssohn Union. Bristow, Morgan, Berge, and Theodore Thomas (Fig. 24) were successively its conductors. An examination of its programmes will convince the unbiassed judge that the new society differed much in its aims from the Harmonic Society. Its concerts were more varied and often more ambitious than those of any of its competitors, and it shone especially in its soloists. It came to its end, however, and was succeeded by a still larger organization.

Dr. James Peck, spoken of above as the last conductor of the Harmonic Society, became subsequently the conductor of a new organization called the Church Music Association. Mr. George T. Strong was the chief instigator of this society, which met at his house in 1869 to study masses. The chorus was, from the beginning, of the most select social character, and the "society" element was, from the very first, most prominent in its concerts. It had a strong financial backing at the outset. After Dr. Peck had ended his conductorship, Mr. C. E. Horsley, like his predecessor, an Englishman, took charge of the concerts.

Finally there came a vocal society more earnest and more far-reaching than any of those described above. The New York Oratorio Society came about through the efforts of Dr. Leopold Damrosch (Fig. 25), who desired to found in America a vocal society such as he had directed for many years in Breslau, Germany. Trinity Church, always a great patron of good music, generously gave its chapel for the rehearsals. Subsequently the Knabe piano warerooms were used for this purpose, and in Knabe Hall, December 3, 1873, the first concert of the Oratorio Society took place. Palestrina and Bach, as well as some of the later and, to New York, more familiar classical writers were represented upon the list. The subsequent programmes have ranged from the most ancient to the most modern composers. The directorship descended at the death of Dr. Leopold Damrosch, to his son, Mr. Walter Damrosch, and subsequently to his other son, Mr. Frank Damrosch, who resigned but recently.

Another important influence in New York's musical progress in vocal matters made itself manifest in the great German-American population of that city. Not only was this very prominent in the establishment of the Oratorio Society, but it brought forward other societies that, although only semi-public in their character, have done much in moulding the taste of the entire city. The two male choruses founded in New York by the German residents are both flourishing. The Deutsche Liederkranz is almost as old as the Philharmonic Society itself. It was organized in January, 1847. Two German singing societies had already existed in the city, but this *Maennerchor* was far in advance of its predecessors. While its being, as most German vocal societies are, a male chorus added to its Bohemian character, it circumscribed its repertoire greatly. In 1856, therefore, it changed this feature, and admitted women as active members. This change was at once reflected in its programmes, which have since then embraced selections from almost all of the German composers from Haydn to Richard Strauss, the society wisely avoiding many sacred selections which belonged to the domain of other New York organizations and were scarcely suited to the jovial and social character of the club.

But the dissenters from mixed chorus work soon had a chorus to represent the *Maennerchor*, and the Arion, composed of those who deserted from the Liederkranz ranks in 1854, has become one of the most important choruses of its kind in America, chiefly through the efforts of Dr. Leopold Damrosch, in the days of its infancy.

Every department of vocal music has been covered by the different societies of New York. The glee and madrigal have received (and still receive) excellent interpretation at the hands of the Mendelssohn Glee Club, of which the eminent musician, Joseph Mosenthal, was conductor to the very moment of his death.[1] The old contrapuntal masters have superb rendition at the hands of the Musical Art Society, an organization composed almost wholly of professionals and capable of wonderful *a capella* work, under the lead of Frank Damrosch. The Manuscript Society, of New York, devotes itself to the performance of American compositions, both vocal and instrumental, and has given many concerts from native manuscripts that might otherwise not have been heard in public. There is an excellent French choral society in New York, and many other musical organizations exist whose influence has been less decided than that of the choruses chronicled above.

There were other, and more directly educational, influences beginning to appear in cities outside of New York. We have already alluded to the Musical Fund Society of Philadelphia. Its influence on general musical development in America was especially marked in its earliest days. At a later epoch it yielded too much to popular taste, and became a follower instead of a leader; but by that time its chief mission had been nobly accomplished. Charles P. Hupfeld and Benjamin Carr were the two ruling spirits at the beginning. Hupfeld was a German and an excellent violinist; Carr was an Englishman and a musical enthusiast. Hupfeld had drawn a coterie of music lovers to his side in the early days of the nineteenth century; most of the members of that pleasant circle were Englishmen, with an occasional Scot thrown in. Carr, Cross, Schetky, Loud, and Raynor Taylor were in this coterie, which was not unlike the gatherings which Gottlieb Graupner was holding at the same time in Boston. All of these men became active in the Musical Fund Society soon afterwards founded. Musical meetings and rehearsals were held at the houses of such prominent citizens as Dr. De Wees, Dr. Robert M. Patterson, Peter S. Duponceau, John K. Kane, and Charles A. Poulson. Quartettes by the best composers were studied, and finally a regular place of meeting was found at Earle & Sully's art gallery, near the corner of Fifth and Chestnut streets.

From this nucleus grew the Musical Fund Society. In January, 1820, the Society met in the second story of Elliott's Hotel, near

---

[1] He died at a rehearsal of the society.

the corner of Chestnut and Sixth streets, and from that time on it was the leader of Philadelphia's music.   The Musical Fund Society (Fig. 100) has ·brought a host of famous artists to Philadelphia, among which may be mentioned Malibran (1827), Caradori-Allen, John Braham, Mrs. Seguin, Ole Bull, William Vincent Wallace, Grisi, Lagrange, Mario, Sontag, Alboni, Jennie Lind, Patti.

Among its earliest labors the Musical Fund Society founded the first great music school in America, in May, 1825.   Its academy was opened in September, 1825, with twenty-five pupils only, but with a complete corps of instructors, even the orchestral instruments being represented on its catalogue.   The city was not ripe for such an institution, and, after losing money steadily for six years, the school was closed.   Boston was a much more fruitful soil for such seed. There the foundation of an even more ambitious school led to immediate and very remarkable results.

The Boston Academy of Music was built upon a very liberal plan, and endeavored to guide the growing enthusiasm for music in proper paths.   It founded a large music school, it began normal classes, it gave to Boston its first properly equipped and conducted orchestra, it trained children in vocal work, it established popular and scientific lectures on music in the city, and, at first, it also gave choral concerts, but subsequently abandoned that field as being already well taken care of by the Handel and Haydn Society. Lowell Mason was the chief spirit of the new enterprise, but George J. Webb, Hon. Samuel A. Eliot, and William C. Wood-bridge must also be mentioned with honor in recounting the story of this most advanced step in building up American taste and technical knowledge in music.

The Academy was established in 1833.   William C. Woodbridge had brought back from a trip to Europe the great principles of juvenile training that made Pestalozzi's system so successful, and this American educator had made a convert of Lowell Mason to the new system.   By practice and precept, by translations of the chief works on the subject, by common-sense lectures upon the matter, Mr. Woodbridge gradually succeeded in substituting a practical and artistic method for the bungling and awkward psalm-singing system that had existed in America for more than a century.   The new system would have been introduced into the public schools at once if Mr. Woodbridge could have had his way, but he found public prejudice as yet too strong, and therefore made a place for the new method of musical education, in the Academy of Music. We can therefore regard this academy as the beginner of juvenile work in music in America, and Mr. Wood-bridge and Mr. Mason as the real founders of the system of music in the public schools in our country.

FIG. 25. — DR. LEOPOLD DAMROSCH.

The institution was very successful at first. The normal classes educated missionaries for the new work, who carried the system in every direction. It took three years of very successful experiment to overcome the existing prejudice against music as a part of common school education, but in September, 1836, the school board, on petition of many citizens, allowed Mr. Mason to teach music in the schools, but made no appropriation for the purpose. Financial gain was, however, a secondary matter with such men as Woodbridge and Mason. Books, instruments, and tuition were given free by these ardent teachers. In 1838 the school board was entirely convinced of the success of the experiment, and *music in the public schools* was established for the first time on this continent, as a regular branch of study. The Academy went on with its philanthropic work in almost every branch of music, in spite of financial losses, until 1847, when it wound up its affairs.

The Academy had not only been the founder of American public school music, it had also been the fountainhead of an advanced musical instruction throughout the country. In its third annual report (1835), for example, we read: —

" Letters have been received from persons in Georgia, South Carolina, Virginia, Illinois, Missouri, Tennessee, Ohio, Maryland,

New York, Connecticut, Vermont, New Hampshire, and Maine, besides many individual societies in Massachusetts, asking for information relative to measures which they ought to adopt in order to introduce music as a branch of education into the communities where they live."

It will be seen that nothing less than the noble idea of bringing music to the masses had actuated the founders of the Boston Academy of Music. Although it passed away after fourteen years of existence, it had accomplished its greatest purpose: it had brought music to the schools, and it had founded the Musical Convention, which was for a time to be the conservator of adult musical education in America. It had also given an impetus to orchestral music that was especially valuable at a time when New England was sinking into an oratorio rut.

The *Euterpeiad* (of Boston) of May 12, 1821, has the following item, which may show the general spread of musical societies, in the early part of the nineteenth century, in America: —

" MUSICAL EXCITEMENT

"During the last week we noticed the following Musical Performances that were to take place in the present month of May

"A Concert of Sacred Music, by the Beethoven Society, at Portland, (Me.) a grand Oratorio at Augusta, (Geo.) under the direction of Mr. James Hewitt, formerly of Boston; a select Oratorio at Providence, by The Psallonian Society, under the direction of Mr. O. Shaw; a Grand Concert of Music, for the benefit of the musical fund at Philadelphia; the Grand Oratorio of 'The Creation,' by the Harmonic Society at Baltimore; a performance of Sacred music, by the New-Hampshire Musical Society, at Hanover, (N.H.) and in this town a Concert of Instrumental and Vocal Music for the benefit of Mr. Ostinelli; and the Public Oratorio by the Handel and Haydn Society of this Metropolis, for the benefit of The Howard Benevolent Society."

The colleges in America began to ask for music as a part of a liberal education, at a very early date, but it was still entirely sacred music. There was a Handel society at Dartmouth College very soon after 1800, which had good lectures on music during the

first decade of the nineteenth century, and gave oratorio performances at that time. Harvard College founded an association, August
30, 1837, composed of its alumni, which still exists and has exerted
great influence upon the music of New England, even though it
cannot be considered as having presented anything absolutely
new to the New England metropolis. It was formed at a meeting of the Pierian Sodality, and one sentence of its preliminary
report deserves quotation as presenting a thought in advance of
the time : —

" We that love music feel that it is worthy of its professorship as
well as any other science."

Harvard has since then come to the same conclusion, and
Professor John K. Paine (Pl. XII) was elected to fill almost the first
important musical professorship in a university in America. The
University of Pennsylvania established one, with lesser privileges
and emoluments, at about the same time. At present, Harvard, Yale,
Columbia, Cornell, Brown, Pennsylvania, Ann Arbor (Michigan
State College), Minnesota, and many other universities of America
have their regular professorship in music, or at the least a recognized musical course, of which we shall give details in a succeeding
chapter.

We have said that the Harvard Musical Association gave nothing that was practically new to the country, yet the association of
a set of educated men, of college alumni, for the advancement of
music, was in itself something novel and not without its significance.
The association had annual dinners, began to form a musical
library, and, in 1865, when Boston was without a good orchestra,
it stepped into the breach and furnished a symphonic orchestra
largely at its own expense. The chief mover in the affairs of the
association was John S. Dwight, whose work we shall speak of in
connection with our musical literature. In the early "fifties" the
Germans of Boston took a prominent part in chorus music with
their Orpheus Club, which, with August Kreissman for director,
gave excellent concerts of *Maennerchöre*. The Orpheus Society
went out of existence only a few years ago. In 1871 the Apollo
Club, formed largely of professionals, gave the best male chorus-
singing of the country. Mr. B. J. Lang was the director of this

G

club from its inception until 1901, when he voluntarily relinquished the baton to Mr. Emil Mollenhauer, who is still its director.

Important as the work of the Apollo Club was, it did not do such service as the Cecilia Society, a mixed chorus, which began in 1877. Mr. Lang was also director of this club, retaining the leadership even after leaving the Apollo Club. The Cecilia has given more first performances of great works in its own city than any other Boston musical society, and these have extended all the way from Bach's B minor Mass, to Massenet's " Fall of Jericho " and Wagner's " Parsifal." After this there was also a society (founded in 1901) under the directorship of J. Wallace Goodrich, which devoted itself to ancient music, and did excellent work in unaccompanied vocal numbers of the pure contrapuntal school as well as in the compositions, with orchestra, of later masters. This was called the Choral Art Society. Add to this an orchestral club of amateurs directed by M. Georges Longy (which, however, plays many large works, especially in the French School), a Singer's Society, a series of public singing-classes for working people, and various chamber-music organizations, and it will be seen that in almost every field of music, except opera, Boston is well equipped.

It will be impossible to enumerate each musical society that is at present active in musical performance in America, but a few of the leading ones in the larger cities may be mentioned. Philadelphia alone has about sixty vocal societies ; Milwaukee has a *Musikverein* that has given a series of great compositions in that city since 1851 ; Cincinnati has an Apollo club that, under the direction of Bushrod W. Foley, has also given the greatest choral works with both male and mixed choruses ; even San Francisco felt the influence of the Eastern renascence in music, and its Loring Club, a male chorus, was founded in 1876 in imitation of the Apollo Club of Boston, by one of the members of the latter association. The vocal societies of the United States can scarcely be counted at present.

While the taste for choral music is wide-spread, this cannot be said of chamber-music. The appreciation of the pure school of string quartette music indicates a higher degree of musical culture than can ever be hoped for among the masses. Yet even in

GERMANIA MUSICAL SOCIETY.

C.ZERRAHN   G.KOPPITZ   F.THIEDE   W.MEISEL   W.SALVE.   W.BUCHHEISTER   H.LUHKE.   C.BARTELS.   W.SCHULTZE   OBERGMANN LEADER   H.BAUDT   W.MEYER   W.THOMAI   C.SENTZ   W.PLAGEMANN   H.ALBRECHT   H.ROMER   M.MORITZ   H.GOERINWEGER
                         J.SCHOLZ

FIG. 26. — THE GERMANIA ORCHESTRA, 1850.

From an old print. (Carl Zerrahn, on left, as flute player. Carl Bergmann, centre, conductor.)

this refined field America has been active. New York was the first to enjoy this style of performance, and string quartette music was played there in the second decade of the nineteenth century; these performances were, however, semi-private in character. The first public performances of string quartettes were arranged by that musical agitator and benefactor, U. C. Hill, and were given with a weak quartette in 1843.

The first artistic string chamber-music organization of the United States was founded in Boston, and began its concerts in Chickering Hall in that city, December 14, 1849. This was the Mendelssohn Quintette Club, whose influence in this field was as marked as that of the Germania Orchestra (Fig. 26), of about the same epoch, in orchestral matters. The members of this early organization were August Fries, first violin; Francis Rziha, second; Edward Lehmann, viola and flute; Thomas Ryan, viola and clarinet, and Wulf Fries, violoncello. For nearly fifty years this organization was continued, two of its members, Messrs. Ryan and Wulf Fries, remaining with it to the last. It travelled all over the United States, and, although Boston was its home, it carried classical chamber-music almost everywhere in this country. In 1855 New York founded the Mason and Thomas Quintette (already alluded to), with William Mason, pianist; Theodore Thomas, first violin; Joseph Mosenthal, second; George Matzka, viola, and Carl Bergmann, violoncello (Fig. 27). Since that time almost every city of America has its string quartette or quintette, the leading organizations of this kind being the Kneisel Quartette (Fig. 28) and the Flonzaley Quartette, both of which make extensive tours through the United States, and have achieved the highest possible standard in this pure field. The Kneisel Quartette was founded in 1884.

The educational movement begun in 1833 by Lowell Mason has taken many different directions. The public school movement has spread over the land, and would seem to require a history for itself. The Boston Academy of Music, and the School of the Musical Fund Society of Philadelphia, the first schools of music founded in America for other than commercial purposes, have given rise to other conservatories of the same incorporated character, — the New England Conservatory, the Cincinnati College of

Music, the National Conservatory of New York, — and every city in America has at present one large musical conservatory, and sometimes more. The movement has also brought forth the "Musical Convention," which is a festival that is purely American in its type. It is a combination of the English Choir Festival, the German *Musikfest*, and a brief music school. Thomas Hastings, born at Washington, Connecticut, October 15, 1787, died in New York, May 2, 1872, had an influence in the establishment of these musical

FIG. 27. — THE MASON-THOMAS QUINTETTE.
(William Mason and Theodore Thomas at right.)

conventions, second only to that of Lowell Mason. He was the founder of a great many choirs in different sections of the country.

Nathaniel D. Gould was in the field of juvenile instruction in music even before Mason entered it, although he had not the advantage of the latter's European system. Born at Chelmsford, Massachusetts, in 1781, he died in Boston in 1864. It may be argued from the longevity displayed by Mason, Hastings, and Gould, that the leading of conventions was a very healthful business; it certainly was a prosperous one, and Dyer, Woodbury, Bradbury, L. O. Emerson, and a host of successors reaped good harvests in a field that had sent their predecessors of the "Singing-school" to the poor-house.

The gathering of musical conventions finally led to regular festivals, somewhat after the English pattern. The most notable instance of this improved outcome of the musical convention is the Worcester (Massachusetts) County Musical Association, which began with a convention held in that city in 1858. The present association was formed in 1863, and soon swept up from the simple chorals and sacred cantatas of the usual convention, to the presentation of great compositions. The best solo artists of the world have appeared at the Worcester festivals, and a large chorus and thorough orchestra make an ensemble beyond anything ever attempted by its predecessors. Its festivals take place in September annually.

From the musical convention there sprang another educational and artistic movement that is peculiarly American, the actual democracy of chorus-singing — the training of the working classes in vocal music. Mr. Frank Damrosch, son of Dr. Leopold Damrosch (born at Breslau, June 21, 1859), who has done much for public school music in New York, may be credited with the establishment of such choral classes. The movement soon spread to other cities than New York, and Boston found an enthusiastic leader of the new movement in Samuel W. Cole, who has founded large and successful classes among the wage-earners. The public concerts which are given by such choruses are not of the highest artistic grade, but they are none the less enjoyable both to the auditors and the performers, and they bring musical pleasures into many a humble home, just as the tonic sol-fa classes have done in Great Britain. Of the conservatories of America we shall have more to say in a subsequent chapter.

The most ambitious, or at least the most stupendous, outcome of the convention idea, in America, was the two great Peace Jubilees given by Patrick S. Gilmore, in Boston. These monster festivals were held in 1869 and 1872. Gilmore was born in Ireland, near Dublin, December 25, 1829, and died at St. Louis, Missouri, September 24, 1892. He was connected with military music both before and after the great jubilees. The first jubilee had a chorus of ten thousand, and an orchestra of one thousand; the second exactly doubled these large figures. At the second festival some of the music was punctuated with artillery, and a "bouquet of artists," forty strong, sang some of the solo numbers. Tremendous grand pianos were made to sound in an auditorium that seated about forty thousand people; famous English, German, and French military bands participated; Johann Strauss and Franz Abt led some of their own works; Carl Zerrahn led the large concerted numbers; Peschka-Leutner and other vocalists tried to produce solos in the vast hall; firemen pounded out the rhythm of the "Anvil Chorus" on fifty anvils; one cannot catalogue all the monstrosities of this monster festival.

Of course, this was not art. Groceries or dry-goods may be wholesaled, but not music; yet the second Peace Jubilee was a factor in the advance of music in the eastern part of America. The chorus was made up of innumerable societies from all parts of New England and the Middle states. Many of these societies had been content with practising weak sacred selections and compositions made up of sugary successions of thirds and sixths, and now found themselves launched in the "Peace Jubilee Collection," with generally well-chosen selections from the masterworks. If the Peace Jubilee of 1872 did nothing else, it at least left a better repertoire to the country societies as a legacy.

Musical festivals of higher grade than the convention have been fairly numerous in America in recent years. Unions of German singing societies — *Maennerchöre* — have been held in Cincinnati, Buffalo, Los Angeles, and other cities. The May festivals in Cincinnati have brought large mixed choruses together in the performance of the most ambitious music. Even the little Moravian town of Bethlehem, in Pennsylvania, has added to musical history in America, by being the first to perform the great B minor Mass of Bach in this country; and in 1903, under the leadership of J. Fred. Wolle, a most earnest and enthusiastic musician, the Moravian congregation gave a Bach festival (by no means its first), in which the entire "Christmas Oratorio," the "Magnificat," the "Passion Music" (St. Matthew), and the B minor Mass were performed. Such undertakings prove that, at least in the Eastern states, the

FIG. 28.— THE KNEISEL QUARTETTE.

(At the summer home of Mr. Kneisel, Blue Hill, Maine)

convention has been superseded by something more worthy and more artistic. The Handel and Haydn Society placed the festival permanently in American music by giving a series of triennial occasions that equalled even the English sacred music festivals in importance.

Out of the Cincinnati May festivals there grew a series of operatic carnivals which presented the works of Wagner, Beethoven, Mozart, in better style than had been known in the West before. Chicago followed the lead of Cincinnati in both styles of festival, and gave a most important series of musical performances, especially in 1882 and 1884. In both the Cincinnati and Chicago festivals (outside of the operatic performances) Theodore Thomas was a leading spirit, and the work of Arthur Mees, Otto Singer, and William L. Tomlins was an important factor. This will be alluded to elsewhere in our narrative. Even northern New England has now its orchestral festivals, thanks to the energy of William Rogers Chapman (born at Hanover, Massachusetts, August 4, 1855), who has given fine instrumental and choral performances in Maine, Vermont, and New Hampshire.

Another factor in the rapid advance of music in America, has been the formation of public libraries of musical literature and compositions. We have already intimated that the Harvard Musical Association formed one of the earliest musical libraries on this continent; but this was of a semi-private character. It is only in recent years that the great public libraries of America have begun to form large musical collections. Mr. Allen A. Brown has donated to the Boston Public Library the largest musical library in the country,— a historical collection consisting not only of numerous scores and a tremendous amount of general musical literature, but also of arranged and classified data regarding musical performances, criticisms, notices, covering the last twenty years; in short, a unique collection such as must aid not only the general musician, but the musical historian, at every step (Fig. 52). The Newberry Library of Chicago has also given much attention to the musical side of literature, and has a very fine collection, richer in rarities than any other in the country.

Hand in hand with the advance in musical performance, has progressed the architecture connected with it; almost every American city now possesses a good opera house or large concert hall. The Metropolitan Opera House and Carnegie Hall in New York, the Academy of Music in Philadelphia, Symphony Hall in Boston, the Auditorium in Chicago, are a few of the notable examples.

Public concerts have also done much to elevate the taste of the masses. Each city gives free concerts of more or less excellence, and many of the large cities have recently inaugurated free organ recitals of classical music, naturally of a much higher type than the out-of-door concerts. Pittsburg has been the most prominent city in the last-named field, thanks to the generosity of Andrew Carnegie. This gentleman, who has given many church organs to different American cities, presented Pittsburg with an excellent hall and a notably well-equipped organ. He also established a series of Sunday organ recitals which have gone on regularly for many years. Mr. Frederick Archer was the first organist, and continued in the position until his death in 1902, being succeeded by Edwin H. Lemare.

It will be seen that the spirit of organization has been strong in the musical field in America in almost every direction. Musicians' guilds and protective associations early began to appear, but probably none of these societies reached the importance of the Music Teachers' National Association, which was founded in Delaware, Ohio, in 1876, and has held annual sessions throughout the country ever since that time. Many state organizations of music teachers have been formed in imitation of the plan originally established by the National Society. The Society has done much to foster American composition at a time when the native composer seldom obtained a hearing. At each of its sessions, concerts of American musical works have been given. To-day such protection is no longer necessary (the native composer obtains a hearing without it), yet the recent concerts of the association have not been without interest and value.

In other directions some wholesale agitations have been started by the Music Teachers' National Association; the American copyright laws have been amended; international pitch has been aided; music in the public schools has been assisted; and by essay and debate much good has been accomplished. This was naturally greatest at the time when musical culture was less widely disseminated than it is to-day; yet even now the union of musicians in such a society is productive of good, and can be made an important factor in the musical advancement of the nation. Much of the success of the Music Teachers' National Association has been due to such members as Waldo S. Pratt, Thomas Tapper, and other eminent workers in the cause of American music.

After studying the many efforts which we have recited, many of them public and beneficent, it may be more easy to understand why America has made such rapid progress in music within a generation. The Americans may not be as musically gifted as the Italians, French, or Germans, but in the wide-spread study of the art, in great popular interest, in public festivals, the United States is abreast of some of the most cultivated European nations. It must be confessed, however, that in thoroughness of study, in the art of making haste slowly, and in the establishment of concerted music in the home (probably the greatest factor in Germany's musical greatness), the impatient, energetic American has yet much to learn.

PLATE IV
WILLIAM H FRY

CHAPTER V

OPERA IN AMERICA

IF the story of oratorio in America clusters chiefly around Boston, the story of opera is to be found almost wholly in New York and New Orleans, with New England far in the rear in the development and appreciation of this form of music. The earliest operatic performances in America were derived, not from Italian, but from English sources. The "Beggar's Opera," which caused such a furore in Great Britain, was probably the first entertainment of this kind given in the colonies, being performed in New York as early as December 3, 1750, and innumerable times thereafter. This was followed by a series of other "Ballad Operas," all of them taken from English sources.

To New Orleans belongs the credit of introducing operas of the French and Italian school into America. In 1791 that city possessed a regular troupe of French comedians and singers, who probably gave vaudevilles rather than operas, although it is not improbable that an occasional opera by Grétry or Boieldieu was sung during the first decade of the nineteenth century. In 1810 Paisiello's setting of "The Barber of Seville" was given, and from about this time dates the regular production of standard operas in New Orleans. With a theatre on St. Peter Street, in 1810, a better one (the Theatre St. Philippe) on St. Philip Street, in 1808, and another, the best of the three (the Théâtre d'Orleans), in 1813, New Orleans had plenty of opportunities for theatrical and operatic performances. In the second decade of the century, the growing Southern city had three or four representations each week during the season, and even gave New York a taste of good French opera in 1827.

New York, meanwhile, had gone onward from the conglomerate "Ballad Opera" (often the work of half a dozen composers) to a more unified art-work, and the operas of Arnold, Storace, Shield, and Dibdin were given with some frequency.[1]   During the British occupation, in Revolutionary days, the English regimental bands often assisted in the orchestral parts of the operatic performances. At a later epoch many refugees, driven from France by the Revolution, were to be· found eking out a precarious livelihood by operatic performance, generally in the orchestra.

In 1793 we find Philadelphia imitating New York in operatic performances and in its choice of subjects, Filippo Trajetta being the chief leader after the scheme had become permanent.   Mrs. Oldmixon, Miss Broadhurst, and Miss Brett were the leading singers in the early American performances of English operas.   The two most important conductors were James Hewitt and George Geilfert or Gilfert.   Victor Pellisier, a horn-player in the operatic orchestra, composed what seems to have been one of the earliest American operas, in 1799; it was called " The Vintage," and its libretto was by a Mr. Dunlap, who the next year furnished another book to Mr. Hewitt.

It is somewhat difficult to trace the inception of native opera. According to one writer (W. G. Armstrong), the first American opera was " The Archers, or the Mountaineers of Switzerland," libretto by William Dunlap, music by Benjamin Carr, brother of Sir John Carr, and dealing with the story of William Tell.   It is said to have been performed in New York, April 18, 1796.   In the National Edition of the *Musical Courier* (New York) Miss Singleton states that the first American opera was " Edwin and Angelina," libretto by Smith, music by Pellisier, first performed December 19, 1796. Another opera, entitled " Bourville Castle," by the same composer, was given the next year.   The details of these works are lost, and probably their merits were very small.   The first American opera of any musical worth was " Leonora " by William H. Fry, and this, as well as the subsequent operas of " Rip Van Winkle," by Bristow, " The Scarlet Letter," by Damrosch, and " Azara," by Paine, will be spoken of in their proper places.

At the beginning of the nineteenth century Charleston and Bal-

---

[1] For a most complete list of operas given in New York and details of performances. the reader is referred to " Early Opera in America " by Oscar G. Sonneck.

FIG. 29.—STAGE OF METROPOLITAN OPERA HOUSE, NEW YORK.
"Carmen," Act IV.

timore entered the operatic field, and travelling troupes came into
existence, making short circuits from New York through the three
large cities, but avoiding Boston, which was wholly given over to
Handel, Haydn, and psalms. The advent of two prominent English singers, Incledon and Philips, helped on the performances of
opera in New York and oratorio in Boston. In the latter city
Philips gave a course of lectures on singing — the first musical
lecture course in America.

On November 12, 1823, John Howard Payne's "Clari, the Maid
of Milan," the melodrama containing the song of "Home, Sweet
Home," was produced in New York; and March 3, 1825, New
Yorkers heard a great opera for the first time. "Der Freischütz,"
which had won such a phenomenal success in Germany only a few
years before, came to America by way of England. It was adapted
and arranged with the boldest of alterations and makeshifts. One
can judge of this by the fact that there was no oboe in the orchestra,
and extra dances were introduced to charm the audience. The in-
cantation scene was made the most of, and, with its fireworks, won
public favor at once. It was often given *without singing*, as melodrama, that is, recitation with orchestral accompaniment. The
opera received many performances in New York during the next
five years, and was considered a great favorite.

But the real beginning of opera in New York, and in a certain
sense in America, occurred in the autumn of the same year that saw
the above-mentioned performance. In the fall of 1825 (November
29 was the date of the first representation) there came to the city
a well-equipped opera troupe under the management of Manuel
Garcia, himself a tenor of high rank. Garcia brought with him his
family, each member of which was an important singer, his son
being a bass, his wife a soprano, and his daughter (afterwards Mme.
Malibran) a great vocalist. The younger Crivelli (tenor), Mme.
Barbieri (soprano), and other good singers were with this troupe,
which began its season with "The Barber of Seville."

London had found the troupe rather mediocre, but it was far
and away in advance of anything that America had ever heard.
Well might a critic of that day speak of Manuel Garcia as "our
musical Columbus." The whole season of opera during that

memorable year (1825–26) was a revelation to the new world.   The
orchestra in these performances was a large one for the period, —
seven violins, two violas, three violoncellos, two contrabasses, two
flutes, two clarinets, one bassoon, two horns, two trumpets, and one
pair of kettledrums.   That the orchestral standard was by no means
as high as that of the vocalists may readily be surmised from the
following criticism of one of the earliest performances : —

" The violins might be a little too loud; but one soul seemed to
inspire and a single hand to guide the whole band throughout the
magic mazes of Rossini's most intricate flights, under the direction
of Mr. de Luce ; while M. Etienne presided in an effective manner
at a fine-toned piano, of which every now and then he might be
heard to touch the keynote by those whose attention was turned
that way, and just loud enough to be heard throughout the orchestra,
for whose guidance it was intended."

The use of a piano to keep the orchestra in tune is something
that must strike the modern musician with astonishment.

From November 29, 1825, to September 30, 1826, the troupe,
or part of it, gave operatic performances, seventy-nine in all, at the
Park and Bowery theatres.   The artistic success was great, but
the pecuniary result was also satisfactory, considering the circumstances.   The prices of admission were $2 for box-seats, $1 for
seats in the pit, and twenty-five cents for entrance to the gallery.
The receipts ranged from $1962 on the most successful night to
$250 on the least successful.   The troupe then departed for Mexico,
the daughter, now become Mme. Malibran, remaining in New York,
where she appeared occasionally during the next two years before
beginning her more triumphant career.

Sporadic opera performances up to 1832 gave New York something of Rossini, but far more of Boieldieu, a natural result when we
remember that most of the artists were French residents of the
metropolis.   " Jean de Paris " and " The Caliph of Bagdad " (in an
English translation) seem to have become popular, dividing favor
with the English ballad operas which now had a short renascence.
The most important productions were Auber's " Masaniello,"
Boieldieu's " La Dame Blanche," and Mozart's " Magic Flute,"
all in a more or less " arranged " state, which meant cutting out

whatever was too difficult, interpolating whatever was likely to catch the popular fancy, and leaving strange and hideous gaps in the orchestral score. It was in the last-named matter that the New York operatic performances were most erratic. The wretchedness of the orchestral work in New York, about 1830, cannot be exaggerated.[1]

C. E. Horn executed many of these arrangements. While one may condemn tampering with a work of art, it would be unfair to omit stating that if Horn had not made radical changes in some of the masterpieces, America would have been precluded from hearing them at all. Nor was Horn's work all weak and tawdry. He was an Englishman, born in London, June 21, 1786; a practical musician, director of different English and American theatres, conductor of the Handel and Haydn Society of Boston, and a prolific composer of considerable melodic grace. He died at Boston, October 21, 1849. His practical acquaintance with the orchestra made him an adept in arranging the large works so that they could be attempted by the incompetent American orchestras of his time.

FIG. 30. — BISPHAM AS WOLFRAM, IN "TANNHÄUSER."
(Copyright by Aimé Dupont.)

In 1832 there came a second opera troupe of almost Garcian quality to New York. A change for the better was made, even two oboes appearing for the first time in the ranks of a New York orchestra. Vocally the company was not in advance of that of Garcia, which had been

[1] See Ritter's "Music in America," p. 205, and New York *Musical Courier*, National Edition, Part III, May 10–17, 1899.

heard seven years before. It was under the management of a good tenor, named Montressor, and was brought to America chiefly through the efforts of Lorenzo da Ponte, the poet who had written the libretto of Mozart's "Don Giovanni" (and other of that master's operas), who was now a resident of New York. Da Ponte worked zealously to implant a taste for Italian music and Italian literature in New York. He instigated many operatic performances; he brought his niece, a good soprano singer, to New York, where she frequently appeared in opera, often under the management of her enthusiastic uncle. He had many business reverses, and finally became professor of Italian at Columbia College, dying in New York in 1838. With Da Ponte, in New York, and Trajetta, in Philadelphia, Italian opera had two most earnest, if not entirely successful, propagandists.

The Montressor troupe began its season at the Richmond Hill Theatre, October 6, 1832. It gave Rossini's "La Cenerentola" for its first performance, a wise proceeding, since New York had become quite familiar with the work, but in an adapted, translated, and thoroughly mutilated version. Although some single performances were pecuniarily successful, the season as a whole was disastrous, and the company was dispersed. English opera was, at this time, presented almost continuously, and nothing was too high game for the "adaptors" to fly at; even Meyerbeer's "Robert the Devil" was given in English with an ordinary theatre orchestra.

New York witnessed, November 18, 1833, the opening of a fine opera house, intended exclusively for this form of music, the first building of its kind in America, inaugurated chiefly through the efforts of Lorenzo da Ponte. It was a magnificent auditorium, with many private boxes, and had that species of subscriber's support which has become such a feature in the success of grand opera in New York in recent times. The following quotation from the diary of Philip Hone, one of the wealthy citizens of New York and once its mayor, may indicate this: —

"September 15, 1833. — The drawing for boxes at the Italian Opera House took place this morning. My associates, Mr. Schermerhorn and General Jones, are out of town, and I attended and drew No. 8, with which I am well satisfied. The other boxes will be occupied by the following gentlemen: Gerard H. Coster, G. C. Howland, Rufus Prime, Mr. Panon, Robert Ray, J. F. Moulton, James J. Jones, D. Linch, E. Townsend, John C. Cruger, O. Mauran, Charles Hall, J. G. Pierson, and S. B. Ruggles."

The season opened with Rossini's " La Gazza Ladra." The Italian troupe was a good one, but not equal to the memorable one of Garcia, and it suffered somewhat through the rivalry of English opera, with Mrs. Wood as its prima donna. The battle between the two schools went on for two years, and resulted in the triumph of opera in English. The expensive new opera house was burned to the ground in 1839.

Great artists were, however, now beginning to cast their eyes toward America, and many made trips to this country to try their fortunes in concert tours. Mme. Caradori-Allan, who had sung in the first performance of Mendelssohn's " Elijah " in Birmingham (Mendelssohn did not think much of her art, however), was among the earliest of these foreign invaders. She came in 1837, and in 1838 she gave a short season of opera at the Park Theatre, in English. The orchestral support of opera had been of much more satisfactory character since the Montressor days (1832), but we find in the orchestra of this troupe (the vocal part being made up of resident singers) but one trumpet, one trombone, and not a single oboe — a flute filling in the part of the last-named instrument. This, then, was the situation about the year 1840: opera in a foreign tongue, although considered fashionable, was generally voted a bore; [1] ensemble was a matter scarcely recognized; individual singers were prized above all other points of excellence; the orchestra (in the English performances) was of secondary importance or often not considered at all; mutilations of any famous opera were condoned when the work was given in the vernacular.

In 1837 the Seguins began giving opera in English (as well as English operas) in a somewhat better style than had been customary, and in 1839 a lesser English troop attempted an " arrangement " of Beethoven's " Fidelio," which had a run of fourteen nights. They gave a number of other celebrated foreign operas, French and

---

[1] See " Diary of Mr. Philip Hone," October 31, 1835, or New York *Musical Courier*, May 10–17, 1899.

Italian works, all in English. In 1840 the Woods troupe gave "Fidelio" and the "Beggar's Opera," and the audiences seem to have been as well satisfied with one as with the other. The celebrated Braham attempted a short season of real English operas, but it was not successful, the public evidently preferring the arrangements of more famous German, French, or Italian masterpieces, however maltreated in their revamping for the American market.

In spite of the fact that Italian opera did not pay in New York, there were always, from this time on, some enthusiasts ready to attempt the thorny path of management in this field. To the names of the visionary Da Ponte and the zealous Trajetta (of Philadelphia) there may now be added that of Palmo. He began in New York as a restaurant keeper, and even in this vocation showed his love for the music of his native land by giving many an Italian concert in his café. The fortune that he made in catering he soon lost in music. In 1843 he built an opera house in Chambers Street. It will be remembered that the luxurious opera house previously described had burned down. For a time Niblo's Theatre had been the headquarters of operatic performance, and it may be noted, in passing, that there was a Mlle. Calvé who there captivated New York, more than half a century before the advent of Calvé, the second, and that she came to New York with a French troupe from the home of Gallic opera — New Orleans.

Palmo's new opera house avoided the box system that had almost ruined the preceding one. It had but two private boxes, and the price of seats was the same everywhere throughout the house. The season began February 5, 1844, with "I Puritani," Signorina Borghese being the prima donna. It was the old, old story! Success for the first few performances and neglect after the novelty had worn off. There were very few in New York at that time who understood or enjoyed the Italian opera; it was a fashionable fad for a short time, and then the manager had to pay the bills.

Nevertheless there were some wealthy connoisseurs who missed the opera when it had died of inanition, and there are scarcely any gaps to record in the subsequent history of opera in New York, one troupe following another in constant succession, and often two or three existed, or starved, simultaneously. It is beyond the scope

FIG. 31.—MME. LILLIAN NORDICA.

(Copyright by Aimé Dupont.)

of this work to give a detailed list of every one of these companies; it will suffice to speak briefly of the most important of those having some influence upon the development of American musical taste.

In 1847 a new opera house, seating fifteen hundred people, and backed by a strong subscription list, was opened in Astor Place. The subscribers bound themselves for seventy-five nights each season, for five years; each year found a deficit, and when the subscriptions had expired the enterprise was given up. Many fine operatic companies followed with short seasons. Several of these appeared at Castle Garden, which, about 1850, became the prominent opposition to the Astor Place house. Havana began sending excellent operatic companies to New York as early as 1847, and in 1850 Señor Marty, of that city, brought over one of the finest operatic troupes of the world, decidedly the best and most complete that this country had ever heard.

Boston had by this time decided that Italian opera was not altogether sinful, that music was not entirely limited to Handel, Haydn, Bach, and Beethoven, and the Havanese troupes introduced the new form of art there, at the Howard Athenæum, beginning as early as 1847. Boston had, indeed, heard an occasional opera before the advent of Marty and his people. In 1829 a French troupe gave a short season in that city prior to going to New Orleans, and a year before Thomas Comer had given "Der Freischütz" and "The Barber of Seville," both in English and "arranged" to the needs of the little company that presented them. Comer also gave "La Sonnambula," with the Woods troupe, in Boston, and with such success that it ran twelve nights, with receipts of nearly $700 at each performance. In 1846 the Seguin troupe made a great success in Boston with "The Bohemian Girl" (an opera which Boston still patronizes strongly), and also with the "Postilion of Longjumeau" by Adam. A decade later Adelaide Phillips became Boston's favorite in English opera.

But Boston need not be spoken of in connection with Italian or French opera, for these schools have been only exotics in that city from 1847 almost to the present time. Nor need we speak further of New Orleans, but for exactly the opposite reason; New Orleans was the first city in America to establish opera permanently. It has possessed good French troupes continuously since the early part of the nineteenth century; to describe opera in New Orleans would require a ponderous volume in itself. We may state, however, that the Théâtre d'Orleans, which was erected in 1813, was for the second time destroyed by fire in 1866, while a newer opera house was built in the French quarter (corner of Bourbon and Toulouse streets) in 1859. One may speak in passing of the effort of the Alhaizas to establish Italian opera at this house,—a failure,—of the loss at sea of the Parisian troupe sailing from New York to New Orleans in 1866, and of the reëstablishment of French opera by M. Placide Canonge, afterwards editor of *L'Abeille*, the chief French journal of the city. A slight interregnum is to be noted because of the Civil War and its commercial results, but New Orleans is now again in possession of excellent French opera, and is likely to continue the chief cisatlantic home of this school *in sæculâ sæculorum*. More than once has New Orleans sent operatic companies to New York and to other Northern cities.

Mr. Edward P. Fry, brother of the American composer, had brought a good operatic company to New York in 1848. The most memorable fact connected with this troupe was that it had as its director a young man recently from London, named Max Maretzek. In 1849 Maretzek undertook the management of a company, and from that time became an important factor in American operatic development. Of the group of managers who worked prominently in this field (Strakosch, Ullmann, Grau, Damrosch, Mapleson, Abbey, Ellis), Maretzek was the first.[1]

Although not connected with operatic performances, one may speak here of the concert tour of Jenny Lind, under the management of P. T. Barnum. The advent of this great singer seriously crippled the operatic managers, although she confined herself strictly to concerts. The phenomenal prices received for tickets, the enormous crowds that attended each of her concerts, have probably not been exceeded even by the Patti crazes of more recent times. Jenny Lind first appeared in America at Castle Garden, New York, September 10, 1850, and remained in the United States for two years, making extensive concert tours. Maretzek tried to make headway

---

[1] Maretzek died in New York, September 17, 1897.

against the "Jenny Lind fever" by bringing an excellent singer — Teresa Parodi — to America, but it was impossible to stem the tide.

In 1852 a scheme was begun in New York similar to that described in connection with the Boston Academy of Music in a preceding chapter. The Boston institution devoted itself chiefly to public school and chorus or orchestral work, but the New York Academy was to have opera as its central idea. A large building was erected, costing $335,000, in which it was proposed to give opera at a price within the reach of the masses. It was opened October 2, 1854, with Grisi and Mario among the artists. The enterprise was no more successful than its predecessors had been, one manager after another losing money in the new scheme. Ole Bull was at one time a manager of the Academy, and tried to help along the educational side of the institution (which had been practically *nil* from the beginning) by offering a prize of $1000 for a grand American opera, upon a strictly native subject. This was done in January, 1855; three months later the good-intentioned violinist was obliged to close the Academy, and the New American Opera and the educational beginning of the Academy came to naught. The great building went on as an opera house pure and simple.

In 1855 New York had a short season of German opera, chiefly of the lighter sort, and the year after, Teutonic works of a more ambitious character, with Mme. Johansen in the chief rôles, were given. December 29, 1856, "Fidelio" received its first complete performance in America, being given by this company. A month later Strakosch made his bow as an American manager, competing with Maretzek in the same season. The Pyne and Harrison troupe meanwhile kept the standard of English opera afloat in New York and through the Eastern cities.

In March, 1858, a notable event took place. It was the production of an opera by an American composer. The work, produced under the management of Ullmann and the direction of Carl Anschütz, was called "Leonora," and was composed by William H. Fry, the earliest American composer of real prominence. Fry (Pl. IX) was born in Philadelphia, August 10, 1813, and was the son of the publisher of the *National Gazette*, a prominent weekly of that time.   He received an excellent literary training, but showed an early aptitude for music, teaching himself piano by following the instructions he heard given to his elder brother.   L. Meignen (a graduate of the Paris Conservatoire) taught him harmony and counterpoint.   At twenty years of age he received a gold medal for an overture which was performed by the Philadelphia Philharmonic Society.   He had written an overture when he was but fourteen years of age, and three other compositions before he composed the work which brought him the medal.

" Leonora," the first American opera worthy of record, was composed as an English work, in 1845, and had been performed in Philadelphia by the Seguin troupe thirteen years before it received the honor of performance in Italian by a great opera company.   The numbers of this opera are rather weak copies of the styles of Balfe and Donizetti, but are melodious and pleasing.   The work contains an excellent drinking-song for chorus, which is well harmonized.

When Anschütz produced " Leonora," in 1858, its composer had become a prominent figure in American music.   He had entered journalism, had been European correspondent of the New York *Tribune* for six years, dwelling in London and Paris, and had become intimate with Berlioz and a whole coterie of young French composers.   Then he returned to New York to become editorial writer and musical editor of the *Tribune*.   He had composed symphonies, overtures, cantatas, and lesser works.   In 1863 he completed another opera, " Notre Dame de Paris," the libretto being by his brother, J. R. Fry.   This opera ran for some time in Philadelphia, and was also successful in New York, where it was given later.

It must be confessed that neither his operas nor his symphonies have achieved great success.   He seems to have lacked dramatic power, in spite of his broad culture and earnest work.   How sincere he was in his devotion to art may be judged by the fact that he once gave a series of lectures upon the development of music, intended to teach the public the beauties of the Italian school, and paid for artists, chorus, and orchestra out of his own pocket, simply from a desire to advance the public taste.   But while he will not rank with the world's great composers, he deserves a monument in

FIG. 32.— EMMA EAMES AS JULIET.

America nevertheless, for his criticisms opened a new and high vein of musical literature, his practical efforts in composition unlocked the door to the American, and in every way his life was beneficial to American musical art, stimulating and encouraging it. When one considers his surroundings, the lack of encouragement for the musical pioneer, the few opportunities that he had of hearing the best works worthily performed, and the fact that he was forced to earn his livelihood by other means than music, one can only wonder that Fry achieved so much. In his musical judgments, as in his music, Fry did not take the best possible course. He was something of a partisan also; but in the proper sense of the term he was certainly " the first American opera composer." He did not reach old age, for his death took place in Santa Cruz, in 1864.

The first American opera composer was not long without companionship. In 1855 George F. Bristow composed " Rip Van Winkle." Bristow was of English descent, and was born in Brooklyn, December 19, 1825. He studied at the Royal Academy of Music, London, under Macfarren. He wrote symphonies, overtures, oratorios, and string quartettes, as well as the above-named opera, and also left as a posthumous work an unfinished opera upon the subject of Columbus. He was a good violinist as well as a composer. Bristow came into close contact with Fry, and together they started an anti-German crusade which was an exhibition of ill-judged partisanship. It seems odd to read the diatribes of this pair of early native composers protesting against the "systematized effort for the extinction of American Music," at a time when these two constituted the entire sum and substance of that school, if it could be called a school where one was copying Italian and the other English models.

Some of Bristow's (and also Fry's) instrumental compositions were performed by Jullien in 1853–54, at a time when American music was still in its infancy. The Philharmonic Society had previously played one of Bristow's overtures. He was for a long time the head of the musical department of New York's public schools, and lived to see an entire race of American composers grow up around him and surpass him in the struggle for fame. He died in New York, December 13, 1898. He had the satisfaction of seeing

one of his cantatas — " Niagara " — received with public enthusiasm, when performed by the New York Manuscript Society just
before his death.

To return to our story of opera.   The Italian school still ruled in
its rather impecunious American kingdom.   Occasionally great stars
appeared, but generally there were more artists of sterling merit
in the troupes, than of phenomenal stars, such as are sought for in
the American opera houses to-day.   In spite of the lack of public support of the management, those were halcyon days of opera.
Brignoli, Formes, Susini, Kellogg, Phillips, Cary, Amodio, and a
host of other good artists followed each other in rapid succession.
There was greater variety of cast than is found at present, and much
more equality of performance.

The first taste of Wagner came April 4, 1859, for Carl Bergmann,
with the assistance of the Arion Society, gave a fairly creditable
performance of " Tannhäuser " at that date.   The same year, November 24, a new prima donna, named Adelina Patti, made her
début as Lucia.   Maretzek and Ullmann at this time were in
almost constant rivalry, the result being that New York had frequently two simultaneous opera seasons, and, as these managers
also gave seasons in Philadelphia and Boston, the opportunities for
comparison must have developed American musical judgment to
some extent.

The Civil War caused an interruption of operatic matters, yet
not nearly in as great a degree as might have been imagined.   The
real " hard times " came after the war was over.   There is little need
to chronicle the succession of operatic seasons that followed for the
next dozen years.   Nillson, Tietjens, and other artists of foremost
rank began to come to America.   Italian, French, and German
opera had taken root and become practically permanent, although
the last named had not become as fashionable as the first two
schools.   Mme. Pappenheim was for a time the chief figure in
German opera.   She appeared in " Tannhäuser," and even ventured
as high in Wagnerian flights as " Die Walküre," which, however,
was given with forces that must have made it something of a
burlesque.

To these performances was now added a dash of opera bouffe.

The advent of Offenbach, in 1877, although not entirely successful, gave an impetus to the taste for this musical champagne, which New Orleans had appreciated long before New York.

In 1878 Colonel James Henry Mapleson was called from Her Majesty's Theatre in London, to save the waning fortunes of the Academy of Music in New York. Mapleson, who was an educated musician both in the instrumental and vocal fields, began that "star system" that has almost abolished the comfortable, sterling operatic style of forty years ago, when a good ensemble, enthusiastic performances, and moderate prices were the rule. He came to New York with a troupe of 140 people, with such artists as Gerster, Hauk, Trebelli, Campanini, Galassi, Del Puente, Foli, with Arditi as conductor. In addition to the New York performances, his troupe toured through Chicago, Boston, St. Louis, Cincinnati, Washington, Baltimore, and Philadelphia.

FIG. 33. — LOUISE HOMER AS AMNERIS IN "AÏDA."
(Copyright by Aimé Dupont.)

Strakosch found it impossible to make headway against this "star" combination, and now left the field to Mapleson, who made a contract of several years' duration with the stockholders of the Academy. He continued at this opera house, with varying success, until a new rival drove him from the city. On October 22, 1883, the Metropolitan Opera House (Fig. 29) was opened in New York with a strong company under the management of Henry E. Abbey. This troupe, with Nilsson, Scalchi, Sembrich, and a host of others, was also composed upon the "star" plan, and Mapleson was being fought with his own weapons.

The rivalry was a costly one to both Mapleson and Abbey, for the artists found competition to be an excellent thing for their market, and raised their prices accordingly. The era of tremendous salaries was fairly begun. There was now a perfect shower of operatic meteors; Patti, Sembrich, Nilsson, Gerster, Nordica (Fig. 31), Eames (Fig. 32), and nearly all of the operatic stars of the world were tempted to New York by the lavish salaries offered. It may at once be stated that Boston, Chicago, and Cincinnati had "operatic festivals," which were only reflections of the New York seasons given by Mapleson and Abbey. We shall find, however, in a supplementary chapter, that Philadelphia, Chicago, Boston, and other cities have recently endeavored to establish opera, with more or less success, independent of New York.

We turn from this exciting and somewhat commercial picture to an enterprise that had again the true instincts of art. Abbey had retired from the Metropolitan Opera House after a single season, and Dr. Leopold Damrosch came before the stock-holders with a proposition that they should establish German opera for a change. The Wagner propaganda had made so much progress that he found willing supporters, and on November 17, 1884, the first thorough representations of German opera that had ever taken place in America were begun with "Tannhäuser." In the company were such artists as Materna, Krauss, Hanfstängel, Brandt, Schott, Staudigl. It may be remarked, however, that opera was now no longer restricted to a single school in America. Just as the Italian troupes were obliged to give "Fidelio," "Lohengrin," "Carmen," so the German company presented "La Juive," "The Huguenots," "Rigoletto." But of course the Wagnerian operas formed the field-nights of the Damrosch company.

Dr. Leopold Damrosch (Fig. 25) advanced the musical taste of New York in many ways. Born in Posen, October 22, 1832, he had studied medicine and had taken his degree in Berlin, in 1854. But he turned from this career to music, and through the teaching of Liszt became a devoted adherent of the Wagnerian school. He had conducted many important musical societies in Breslau before he came to New York, in 1871. Here he reorganized the Arion Society, founded the Oratorio Society, conducted the Philharmonic

Orchestra, organized the Symphony Society, and was active in almost every branch of music. He also brought about some large music festivals in New York. The season of German opera, which he had inaugurated, cost him his life, for he caught a severe cold at one of the rehearsals, continued his work with dangerous ardor, and died February 15, 1885. He was succeeded by the most important conductor of German opera that ever became resident in America.

Anton Seidl (Pl. VII) began his American career as conductor during the season of 1885. Walter Damrosch, the son of the founder of German opera in New York, was the assistant conductor. The company was enlarged, and Lehmann and Fischer were added to its casts. Later on Niemann also became a member of the company. Seidl achieved such excellent results with his forces that the contract was extended for three years, and, under the lead of this authoritative conductor, German opera achieved something like permanency in New York, and in the smaller cities. What Theodore Thomas was in the field of general orchestral music to America, that Anton Seidl became in all that pertained to a comprehension of Wagner. He came to America as an apostle of the new school, and he made clear much that had been obscure and doubtful. False readings, careless performances, slighted rehearsals, bad stage management, all these faults that had sometimes reduced a Wagnerian performance to mere cacophony, he speedily eliminated. Some of the early American Wagnerian performances must have been riddles to every earnest auditor. Mme. Pappenheim once gave a perversion of "Die Walküre" that was almost unrecognizable, while the mystified auditors thought that all the strange results were "the new school." Anton Seidl let in a flood of light upon the matter. His readings were *ex cathedra*, and he was a sincere and enthusiastic conductor. This eminent musician (a friend of Wagner and twice conductor at Bayreuth) was born at Pesth, Hungary, May 7, 1850, and died at New York, March 28, 1898. Had he lived, there might have been a permanent symphonic and operatic orchestra in New York, for his friends were starting a movement to this effect when death ended a great career only too suddenly.

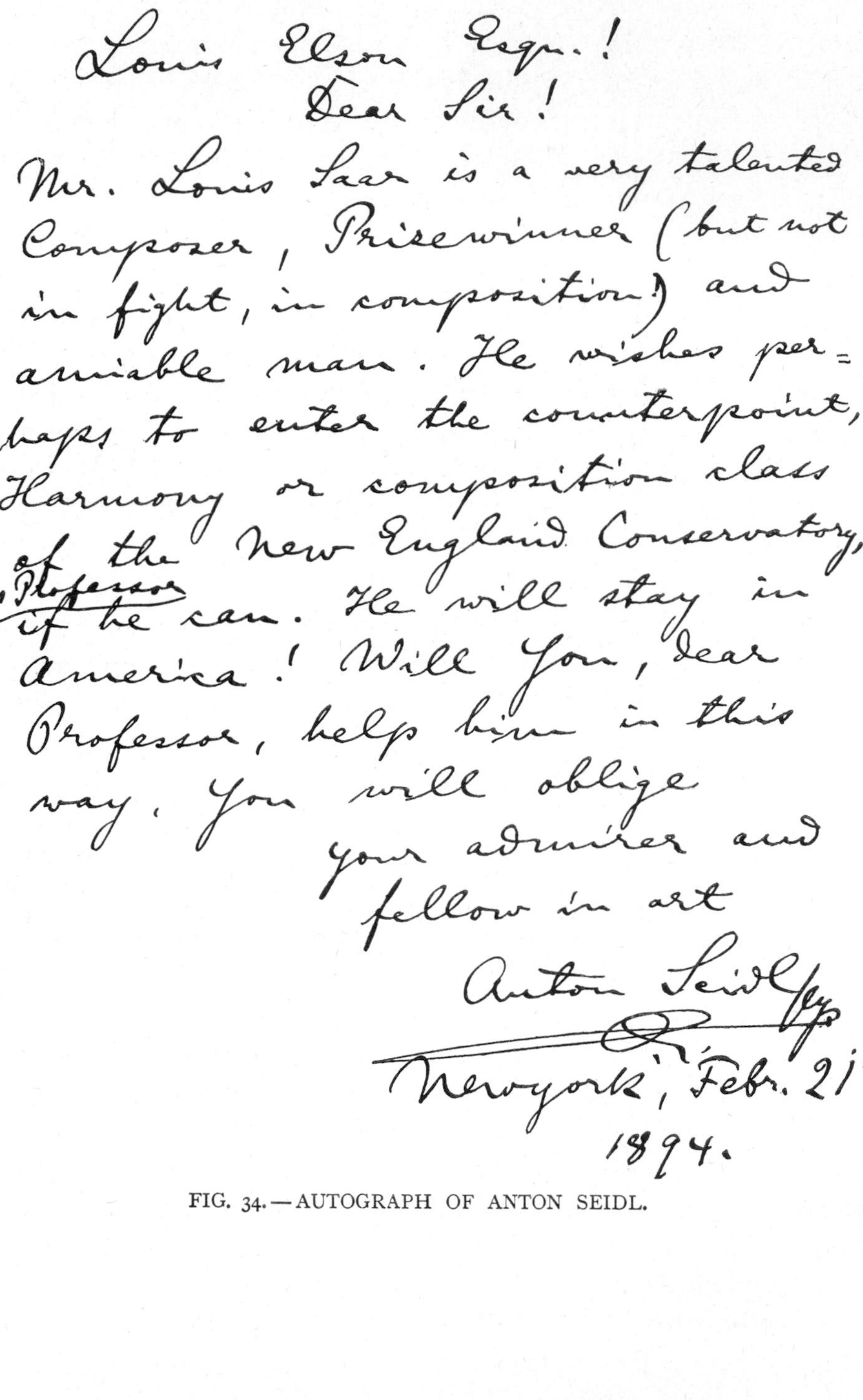

Louis Elson Esqu.!
    Dear Sir!
Mr. Louis Saar is a very talented
Composer, Prisewinner (but not
in fight, in composition) and
amiable man. He wishes per=
haps to enter the counterpoint,
Harmony or composition class
of the New England Conservatory,
as Professor if he can. He will stay in
America! Will You, dear
Professor, help him in this
way. You will oblige
            your admirer and
            fellow in art
                Anton Seidl
Newyork, Febr. 21st
            1894.

FIG. 34.—AUTOGRAPH OF ANTON SEIDL.

In speaking of this culmination of German opera, a swift view may be taken in retrospect. In 1853 the first Wagner orchestral selection ever heard in America, was given by Bergmann, in Boston, — the "Tannhäuser" overture. In December of the same year Bergmann gave Boston "a Wagner night" with his orchestra. Thus the first Wagner performances were due to the Germania Orchestra. In New York it was the Philharmonic Orchestra and the Arion and Liederkranz societies that brought Wagner to the public first. After this Bergmann became the leader of the new school in New York, and was followed by Adolf Neuendorff, Eugenie Pappenheim, Leopold Damrosch, Theodore Thomas, Anton Seidl, Carl Anschütz, Walter Damrosch, Emil Paur, Arthur Toscanini, and Gustav Mahler, who have been the most important propagandists of Wagner in America.

A few words may be fitly spoken of Neuendorff. This conductor was, from 1866, one of the earnest advocates of German opera in New York and the Eastern cities; he even carried the Wagner cult as far as Mexico, where he gave a very successful season of the master's operas. He was born in Hamburg in 1843, and died in New York, December 4, 1897. It is not necessary to dwell upon the Wagnerian festivals which Neuendorff and Thomas gave at different times in New York. Although these men came first, chronologically, it must be emphatically stated that the culmination of Wagnerian opera in America was reached only with Anton Seidl, and his very sudden death was even a greater calamity to the cause than the unexpected passing of his predecessor, Dr. Damrosch.

On February 28, 1886, there was launched a new scheme in opera, founded upon that "Americanism" which has been rather a burden than a benefit to the native musician. The American National Opera Company gave its first performance at the Academy of Music. It was an impracticable affair from the start, a cheap exploitation of the "national" idea (in a country which had as yet no national school), as may be judged by the following excerpt from the prospectus : —

"It has been deemed not only desirable, but it has been felt to be just, that a broadly American spirit should animate the direction of the movement. . . . The plan upon which it is based is so thoroughly national, and its execution so characteristically American, that its most bitter opponents will scarcely decry it as being tainted by foreign influence."

Such an appeal in a country which was at the time drawing all its chief musical sustenance from abroad was worse than useless. It has been one of the handicaps of American music that some of its would-be friends have brought the "know-nothing" steed out of his stable on every possible occasion. Such an effort at protection in art was foredoomed, and the National Opera Company, well-equipped and thorough as it was under Thomas, failed at the end of two seasons, in spite of heavy subscriptions on the part of its misguided backers. Its plan to bring forth companies of American singers and musicians, and to encourage American works, was futile because it was too sweeping and too ambitious. American opera on a less ambitious scale is at present beginning to succeed.

In 1897 a new manager entered the operatic field, — Mr. C. A. Ellis, who had long managed the Boston Symphony Orchestra. He associated himself with Walter Damrosch, and although their labors proved very profitable, Mr. Ellis retired from the management before he met the Waterloo that seems to await all operatic managers in America. The Metropolitan Opera Company, larger and more "starry" than ever, from 1898 was managed by Maurice Grau. The audiences, as well as the expenses, have been enormous in the most recent days. Under Grau's régime Mancinelli has conducted the leading Italian and French operas, and Walter Damrosch and Emil Paur the German ones. The work of Emil Paur in Wagnerian conducting as well as in the introduction of the most modern orchestral compositions, the symphonic poems of Richard Strauss and Hausegger, for example, calls for hearty commendation. Of Walter Damrosch we shall have occasion to speak again in connection with his compositions.

The advent of Mr. H. Conried as manager of the Metropolitan Opera caused a decided lean to the German side. Italian and French operas were often given, but the great successes have been won in the Wagnerian works. Such conductors as Alfred Hertz and Felix Mottl have revived in some degree the enthusiasm that Anton Seidl was wont to evoke. The season of 1903–4 was also made memorable by the first production on the American operatic stage of Wagner's "Parsifal." Boston had heard two performances of this work as a concert, long before this time, but without an adequate orchestra and an authoritative conductor. Heinrich Conried was the first to cause this opera to be performed outside of Bayreuth, and as the interpretation was, if anything, somewhat

better than the present performances at the Wagnerian stronghold, the American representation of "Parsifal," in New York, on Christmas Eve, 1903, may be considered one of the epoch-making events in the history of music in this country, and perhaps even of international importance.

The National Opera Company, or American Opera Company, for it bore both titles, as above stated, came to a sad end. In 1887 Theodore Thomas resigned from its direction, minus six months' salary, and in 1888 the affair was

FIG. 35. — SUZANNE ADAMS AS MARGUERITE.
(Copyright by Aimé Dupont.)

put into bankruptcy and the troupe dispersed. A few years afterwards a more sensible effort to start popular operatic performances in English was made at the Castle Square Theatre, in Boston. A company of resident singers was gathered together, a good repertoire was studied, and such operas as "Lucia," "Martha," "Trovatore," and more difficult ones, were presented, the price of admission being twenty-five cents. The enterprise was decidedly successful, and was followed by a similar attempt on a larger scale.

Mr. Henry W. Savage, a wealthy resident of Boston, soon followed this with a series of performances of operas in English, with several American singers in the cast.

Of the rise and prosperity of so-called comic opera (really a cross between opera bouffe and vaudeville) in the United States, it is unnecessary to speak beyond stating that it has become a permanent fixture in our theatres.   The purer and wittier school of Gilbert and Sullivan, which steered between the Scylla of Offenbach's indelicacy and the Charybdis of Rice's ballet processions, has deservedly had great vogue in America as in England.   The best style of light German opera, as, for example, the works of Lortzing, or of some veins of French opera comique, as the works of Adam, or the lighter operas of Auber, are very seldom given in America, and are practically unknown to the general public.

It has been stated that the Italian opera companies of the highest grade gave seasons in many other American cities besides New York.   It was Mapleson who first ventured to carry a really great opera company as far as California.[1]   Perhaps the most widely known of American travelling companies in operatic work have been the " Ideals," which afterwards merged into the " Bostonians." These troupes, however, seldom went beyond " Fra Diavolo " or " The Bohemian Girl " in the regular operatic repertoire; they generally gave light operas of native origin.

In speaking of opera in English one ought not to forget the services done in this field, in America, as in England, by Parepa-Rosa, nor the constant succession of important works given in a translated form by Emma Abbott.   Thanks to these singers, and to such artists as Clara Louise Kellogg, Miss McCulloch, Adelaide Phillips, and others, there was a time when such works as "Zampa," " Luisa Miller," " The Star of the North," and a host of other standard operas of the foreign repertoire were heard in English in New York and Boston.   Of special operas by American composers of the present, mention will be made in detail in another portion of this volume, as also of most recent enterprises.

---

[1] For a full record of the music of San Francisco. see the *Musical Courier*, of July 4, 1898, National Edition, No. 1.

CHAPTER VI

THE FOLK-MUSIC OF AMERICA

EVER since music began as an art (the date may be approximately set in the thirteenth century) the skilful composers have availed themselves of the songs of the people as a foundation for many of their more elaborate works. Thus Di Lasso and Palestrina used the folk-melody of " L'Homme Armé " for masses, Bach employed a simple and popular love-song for the chief choral of his largest " Passion Music," Beethoven used a couple of Russian themes in his string quartettes. The folk-music of a nation is an important factor in determining its musical rank — after it has passed to the artistic stage and possesses skilful composers.

It must be admitted that in this field America is rather barren. Canada has a folk-song repertoire springing out of the old French life (a romantic and beautiful existence), which transmutes itself readily into music. The more prosaic life of the New England colonists led to no such musical development, and the Southern colonies at first only reflected the manners, and therefore the music, of the mother country. American folk-song in its true sense can only be derived from Indian or plantation life.

It would be quite impossible to detail all the ramifications of Indian music in this place. The researches of John Comfort Fillmore, Theodore Baker, Henry E. Krehbiel, Alice Fletcher, Frank H. Cushing, Frederick R. Burton, and Jesse Walter Fewkes, have preserved much to the world that is not only of great antiquarian interest, but is sometimes melodic and impressive as well. But one must bear in mind that Indian music is not that of a single race, but of many races. Some of the Indian tribes were quite unmusical, others were fairly cultivated in the art; some were not poetic in the slightest degree, others produced poets that deserved

to become known to the world.   Among the tribes in New Mexico
there are relics of ancient music that lead back to a mysterious
civilization that existed on this continent, no one knows how many
ages ago, and the researches of the Peabody Museum in Honduras,
at the buried city of Copan, may yet reveal an antiquity that will
astound archæologists.   Professor Gordon, the Central American
archæologist, recently submitted to the present writer a wind instrument of terra-cotta, found at Copan; it proved to be shaped
exactly like the instruments discovered at Nineveh and in other
parts of ancient Assyria (Fig. 36).

Again, it must be borne in mind that almost all the Indian scales
differ somewhat from our diatonic scale, and that when we reproduce

the melodies in our notation, or upon our
instruments, we generally find a distortion
of the original.   Harmonizations of Indian
tunes, such as Mr. Burton or Mr. Sousa
have given, may be interesting as music,
but are not valuable as contributions to
science.   The author was once present at
a gathering where several Indians sang
their songs to a piano accompaniment.
The deflections from the pitch of the instrument which the singers intentionally produced was very noticeable.   The most
learned and enthusiastic of our investiga-

Fig. 36.—Nineveh Flute.

tors of Indian history and customs, Dr. Fewkes, considers many of
the specimens of Indian music unreliable because of this defect, as
much of the individuality is lost in forcing the Indian melodies
to conform to our scale intervals.

The Ojibways, the Zuñis, the Moquis, and the Omahas have a
fairly large repertoire of songs; the Iroquois, Apaches, and Coman-
ches possess far less and of a more primitive character.   Almost
every one of the Indian songs is given without harmony, being
sung in unison by either male or female voices, seldom both
together.   As with all savage music, gesture and pantomime play
an important part in the songs, which thus become "dances"
(Fig. 37) rather than purely vocal works.   Ghost-dances, war-dances,

snake-dances, and many other semi-religious species of music exist. An extremely strong rhythm is often the chief characteristic of the Indian song, which is seldom varied enough for the purposes of the composer who desires to weave it into the larger forms of music.

Circle dances are to be found among the Indians as among all nations. This is the most ancient form of festival dance, and is believed by many to come down from the time of the ancient sun-worshippers, the circular motion representing the movement of that celestial body. Certain it is that the ancient Hebrews performed a circular dance about the golden calf, and that they copied it from the Egyptian dance about the bull-god Apis. It was known also to the ancient disciples of Zoroaster. Traces of sun-worship are numerous among some of the tribes of American Indians.

A good proof of the antiquity of some of the Indian songs is found in the fact that occasionally words are sung of which the meaning is lost. The same fact may be stated about some of the more advanced songs of the Maoris of New Zealand. In the mystery dances of the Chippewas the statement is frequently chanted: —

> " Thus did our fathers. Is it not so, brothers?
> Thus did they teach us.
> Our fathers taught us this.
> We hold fast to the good customs of our fathers." [1]

The Iroquois, more warlike and less musical than many of the tribes of the South, have left no love-songs or historical ballads (with an exception to be noticed later), and with them the women were not allowed to join in the songs, but were the only performers in one of the dances of this nation (or rather five nations) while the young men sang. The women of the Senecas, however, were allowed to sing a mourning song by themselves. The pantomime was almost continuous in all these dances and compensated for the lack of extended text in some of the songs. Thus the great Iroquois song, "Wolf Runs," has only these two words, but the gestures depicting the lupine course tell a more varied tale.

[1] Quoted by Baker: " Die Musik d. Nord Amerikanischen Wilden," p. 4.

That the Indians have a better ear for musical intervals than they are generally credited with may be judged by the fact that even in the midst of the utmost excitement and abandon they do not get out of time or disturb the unity of the song. There is usually a monotony of figure in almost every one of the Indian songs, and they resemble each other so greatly in most instances (in musical content) that the mine of folk-music in this direction is far more restricted than the large repertoire would seem to indicate. The most advanced of the tribes do not seem to indulge in two-part music, and this absence of harmony is so pronounced that one may even doubt their recognition of a fundamental key-note, although Fillmore and Miss Fletcher have adduced some melodies which are reasonably definite in tonality. In the matter of poetic metre there is great difference between the more or less cultivated tribes. The Southern tribes, which have probably descended from a Mexican ancestry (the Zuñis and the Moquis), have something of rhythmic structure in their poems, of tonality in their music, and in many ways show traces of an ancient development of the sister arts. Among some of these nations we find women participating regularly in the music. On the other hand, some of the nations constituting the Iroquois (the Senecas for example), while possessing rhythmic form in their music, have a less marked tonality and but slight development.

Yet even among the most warlike, and least artistic tribes, there was often a forcible expression that might be called impressive in spite of its roughness and its many repetitions. We have spoken of the Iroquois as possessing no repertoire in the historical or amatory field. There is one exception to this lack of historical music. At the congress of musicians, at the Columbian Exposition in Chicago, Mr. H. E. Krehbiel sang part of a historical recitation of the Iroquois, in which the names of fifty original councillors of the great league are preserved. The league of five nations, which formed the Iroquois, was made up of the Senecas, Mohawks, Cayugas, Oneidas, and Onondagas. Hiawatha, who founded this league, was an Onondaga who subsequently became a Mohawk, and is celebrated in this song.

The song appears to do little else than mention the names of

M. Wright Gill

FIG. 37. — MARCH OF FLUTE PRIESTS.

From "Report of Bureau of Ethnology."

the chiefs and councillors.   The meaning of the verses (as translated
in Horatio Hale's "Iroquois Book of Rites") is as follows: —

> "Hai! Hai!
> Continue now to listen.
> Hai! Hai!
> Thou who wert a ruler,
> Hai! Hai!
> Hiawatha!"

And after three chiefs had thus been mentioned, with their quota
of "Hail!" (or "Hai!"), that section of the song ended with: —

> "That was the roll of you, —
> You who were joined in the work,
> You who completed the work,
> The great League!"

HIAWATHA.

In the songs of some of the Indian tribes coincidences have sometimes occurred that have set investigators upon fanciful and futile
paths of research.   Thus one of the Jesuit priests, hearing the
Indians of Canada sing a refrain that sounded like "Ha-li-loo-hah,"
at once concluded that the word was "Hallelujah," and that he
had discovered the missing tribes of ancient Israel.   Adair, finding
the Cherokees and other related tribes singing "Yo-hee-wah!"
immediately took this as a variant of "Jehovah," and calls the
Indians "the red Hebrews."

As regards the execution of the songs of the Indians, although
there are many grades of vocal culture present among so many
different tribes, it is generally somewhat poorer than would be
found among white singers.   There is, as has been already noticed,
a keen sense of interval and pitch, but the quality of the voices
is not generally attractive.   One of the nearest approaches to a

K

civilized performance, by Indian singers, was heard by the author, at Indian Island, Cape Breton, on St. Ann's Day, a few years ago. This was a Catholic service given by the Micmac Indians. The Gregorian chanting was remarkably true in pitch and displayed that certainty of interval which the Indian possesses in a marked degree, yet for which he has seldom received credit. Mr. William E. Brigham, who has studied some of the music of the Ojibways, finds these Indians appreciative of harmony, although not employing it.

The amount of music which Miss Fletcher and Mr. Fillmore have collected from Omaha and Pawnee sources makes the melodies of these tribes more accessible than those of any other nations, but even after following their long and enthusiastic research, one does not feel quite convinced that the Indian music is a substantial foundation for the native composer to use in classical work. It is not folk-song in the true sense — it is too local and too little understood for that; it is not closely enough allied to our tonal system; it is too often merely figure repetition instead of a presentation of the flowing melodic beauty of folk-music. That some Indian numbers exist that can be called tunes, has been abundantly proven by Fillmore, Fletcher, Farwell, Cadman, and many others, but if one compares these examples with the folk-tunes of Scotland, Russia, Hungary, or Germany, one realizes the poverty of the repertoire.

In the matter of instruments there is also much restriction. Although there exist flageolets, flutes (Fig. 38), Pan's pipes, one-stringed harps, and in a few cases even more developed instruments, yet the drum is the most used of all, and many songs and dances are accompanied by drums (Fig. 39) alone, or by drums and rattles.

The classification of the songs and dances is about as follows: —

1. War-dances, generally wild and furious.

2. Religious dances, which are danced and sung at regular seasons of the year, with many ceremonies, the Indian having a very complicated and highly developed ritual.

3. Mystery dances, sometimes used to heal the sick, to banish evil influences, to bring rain, etc.

4. Historical songs, sometimes merely a roster, as the one given above, sometimes giving a clew to American pre-historic times.

5. Songs of mourning. Sometimes given by women alone (as, for example, among the Senecas), and thus recalling the " mourning-women " spoken of in Jeremiah and other portions of the Scriptures.

6. Love-songs. Chiefly found among the more cultivated tribes. Some of the more warlike nations seem to have had no love-songs.

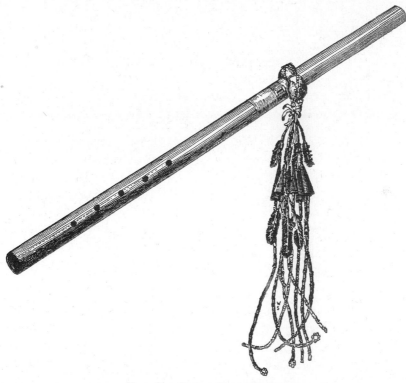

FIG. 38. — OMAHA LARGE FLUTE.
From " Report of Bureau of Ethnology."

7. Convivial or social songs, for many different gatherings. Baker describes some of these as having a semi-religious and often a mysterious character.

Interesting as such a music and poetry must be to the ethnologist, it still falls short of forming a national folk-song, and we are not surprised to find but little use made of it. The most important and beautiful work as yet evolved from Indian sources is Mac-Dowell's " Indian Suite," and this charms far more because of its poetic presentation of phases of Indian life and romance than because of the fact (which scarcely anybody would know unless expressly informed of it) that the figures which are developed in the work are chiefly taken from Indian sources.　Hugo Kaun's beautiful symphonic poems "Minnehaha" and "Hiawatha" also introduce Indian themes.　We present two actual Indian tunes : —

The words are merely "I go" endlessly repeated.

Charles Wakefield Cadman and Arthur Farwell have composed beautiful and popular songs on Indian themes.　Victor Herbert has introduced Indian melody into his opera, "Natoma," and Puccini into his "Girl of the Golden West," yet the foundation of a school of composition on this shifting sand remains as doubtful as ever.

Far more advanced is the folk-song that has grown up around Southern plantation life. Here we find melody, emotion that we can readily understand, and sometimes simple harmony, — in fact all the elements that constitute the power of folk-music in the old world.

The chief instrument of the plantation, the banjo, is also much more advanced than any instrument which we find used by the Indians. It has been charged, however, against the negro music of the South, that it is not American at all, but African. To this one may reply that although the melodies have been brought forth by Africans, or Afro-Americans, the music is distinctly a result of American surroundings. The African in his native land never brought forth anything akin to the songs of the plantation. It was the life of the cotton-field, the cabin, and the river, that gave birth to these expressive musical numbers, and as music is most frequently the child of sorrow, the slave life speaks its melancholy in some of these songs. The ecstatic religious vein, far removed from African music, also is heard in many of the measures.

Many of the songs are easily accessible in different collections, and one need only allude to the tenderness of "Swing Low, Sweet Chariot," or the plaintiveness of "Nobody knows de Trubble I've Seen," as examples of the sorrow and religion combined in this music. Some of the camp-meeting songs are less dignified than these, but their improvisational style, their strong rhythm, their feverish ecstasy, and their strong dramatic action, carry us back to a remote past, being strongly akin to the song of Deborah and Barak, or that of Miriam, in the Scriptures. There is a very close analogy between the slave music in its religious phases and the music of the Bible.[1] Sometimes we find the sound held superior to the sense, by the dusky singers, as when they give the refrain of "Jews, screws, defidum" to one of these camp-meeting songs, utterly unconscious of the original state of the poetry, — "Jews crucified him," — but these are after all only exceptions, the poetry, even when illiterate, being often earnest and genuine.

Here, then, is the true folk-song of the United States, if it possesses any at all. It is unfortunate that a pseudo-plantation school

[1] See Elson's "Curiosities of Music," Chap. II ; "Hebrew Music."

of composition has been built upon this foundation, and pushed so far that it has wearied many.   Unluckily most people imagine this false vein to be derived from the negro music of the South.   " Rag-time " (*i.e.* " ragged time ") is the euphonious epithet applied to this temporary apparition.   The plantation music sometimes employs syncopation, but it certainly does not suffer from such a St. Vitus's dance as is portrayed in the compositions of this modern class. This rubbish must be cleared away before a true use can be made of the plantation music as a folk-song foundation.

There have, however, been some remarkable applications of the negro music in classical forms.   Mr. G. W. Chadwick, in the Scherzo of his second symphony, has made use of this native material, and Antonin Dvořák has built an entire symphony and considerable chamber music upon it.   It has been elaborated as folk-song, with a beautiful simplicity and directness, by Foster, who is as truly the folk-song genius of America as Weber or Silcher have been of Germany.

Stephen Collins Foster (Fig. 40), although born in the North, came to his Southern instincts by inheritance, for his father emi-

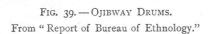

grated to Lawrenceburg (now a district in the city of Pittsburg, Pennsylvania) from Virginia.   In this town the boy was born on a most appropriate date, July 4, 1826, the fiftieth anniversary of American independence, while a band was playing " The Star-spangled Banner " in the wooded grounds of his father's estate.

FIG. 39. — OJIBWAY DRUMS.
From " Report of Bureau of Ethnology."

The father had been a prosperous merchant in Virginia, and was the most prominent citizen of the Pennsylvania town in which he subsequently settled.[1]   His mother was Eliza Clayland Tomlinson, a descendant of one of the oldest families of Maryland, the Claylands, and it was from her that Foster inherited his keen artistic tastes.   There was something of foreign blood also in Foster's veins,

---

[1] The senior Foster actually laid out Lawrenceburg, which he at first intended to call Fosterville, but afterwards named in honor of Captain Lawrence.

for his great-grandfather was an Irishman, a citizen of Londonderry, who emigrated to America early in the eighteenth century. The father was musical in some degree, playing upon the violin, but only in the family circle. The mother was poetic and of most refined and cultured nature.

In 1840 Foster was sent to Athens (Pennsylvania) Academy, and in 1841 to Jefferson College, near his home. He had shown musical taste from childhood, teaching himself the flageolet, and studying the works of such masters as Mozart and Weber. He was of an untrammelled nature, and much of his knowledge was self-acquired. He taught himself French and German, but he seems never to have been brilliant in the schoolroom. At Athens Academy he wrote out his first composition, a work for four flutes, entitled the " Tioga Waltz," and had the pleasure of hearing it performed at a public exercise of the school, the composer playing the first flute himself. In 1842 he published his first song, " Open thy Lattice, Love," in which, contrary to his subsequent custom, the words were not by himself. He made a friend of Mr. Henry Kleber, a musician of Pittsburg, and this artist, without becoming a regular teacher, helped him greatly by advice and by occasional correction of his manuscripts.

Foster had a group of five friends (including his brother), young men, who met at his house twice a week to study singing under his direction, and in 1845–46 he composed many excellent folk-songs for this club, among them " Oh, Susannah " and " Old Uncle Ned," both true types of plantation music. About this time a minstrel troupe came to Pittsburg, and " Oh, Susannah " was submitted to them for approval. The song was performed publicly, and at once won such a success that Foster decided to make this style of composition his vocation. His friends desired him to study composition thoroughly, and his family were willing that he should do so, but he knew how little he had benefited by academic work, and feared that scientific study would only pervert his natural bent in song-creation.

For a little while, at this period, he acted as bookkeeper for his brother at Cincinnati, and was not only pursuing his work in music and languages unaided, but was also teaching himself drawing and painting as well. He attended many negro camp-meetings to

study the style of singing in which he had become deeply interested.   As already intimated he wrote the words to all of his most
successful songs, and his poetry is as natural and spontaneous as
his music, forming one of the great charms of his works.

As examples of Foster's most beautiful folk-songs we may mention " My Old Kentucky Home," " Massa's in de Cold, Cold Ground,"
" Old Uncle Ned," " Nellie. Bly," and above all " The Old Folks at
Home," or " Suwannee River," as it is often called.   He wrote
about 160 songs in all.   " The Old Folks at Home," which may
be called the chief American folk-song, sold very close to one
million copies, and appeared in dozens of different arrangements;
yet the composer received almost nothing for it.   " Beautiful
Dreamer," published in 1864, was Foster's last work.   The charm
of all his popular songs was their directness and pathos.   The same
tender melancholy that one finds in the actual songs of the plantation, such as " Swing Low, Sweet Chariot," or " Nobody knows de
Trubble I've Seen," will be discovered in such a lament as " Massa's
in de Cold, Cold Ground," or " My Old Kentucky Home."   The
utmost simplicity is in all of these songs, the harmonies seldom go
beyond the three chief chords, yet when one tries to imitate this
simplicity it is found to be most difficult to acquire.   Some of the
greatest composers might try for it in vain.

In more elaborate work Foster was not so successful.   Such a
love-song as " Come where my Love lies dreaming " shows fluency
of melody, but by no means compares in rank with the charming
spontaneity which is to be found in the composer's other works.
Ritter, in his " Music in America," while paying a touching tribute
to Foster's memory, falls into the error of stating that Foster's
" Ellen Bayne "[1] (he misprints it " Ellen Boyne ") was the original
melody of " John Brown's Body," and is, unfortunately, followed in
this misstatement by other writers.   " Ellen Bayne," while possessing the same metrical structure as " Glory Hallelujah," is not the
same melody, and is not nearly as good a marching tune as the
latter.   One can find a much closer resemblance between Foster's
" Willie, we have missed you " and the old Scottish " Jock o'
Hazeldean " than between these two songs.

[1] Ritter also omits all mention of Foster's chief song, " The Old Folks at Home."

If the chief American folk-song writer had little musical education, he possessed glorious poetical instincts. He lived unhonored and unrecognized, he died poor, he was one of the gentlest and sweetest of natures; but he was too convivial and too easily led by his companions. His love for his parents was pathetic in its intensity, and his reverence for the memory of his mother, whom he idolized in life, bordered upon mania. His business abilities were about on a par with those of Schubert, and like that

FIG. 40.—STEPHEN C. FOSTER.

composer he would rush his manuscript to the publisher almost before the ink had dried. Many of his later songs were, therefore, "pot-boilers" of the most pronounced type. Yet some publishers paid Foster larger royalties than greater composers have received. Pond & Co., of New York, sent him checks aggregating thousands of dollars, for royalties, during one part of his career.

His later years were, however, most pathetic and painful. Foster married, in 1854, Miss Jennie McDowell, a lady of good family and of fine character. The union was unfortunate; Foster's irregular habits were growing upon him, and he was the last man in the world to build up a home. A separation was bound to ensue, which was, however, not total, for correspondence was kept up, and the wife hastened to New York when Foster died there. A pathetic incident is told of his receiving a picture of his little daughter, who lived with the mother. He opened the envelope containing it, upon the street, and burst out weeping, bitterly deploring the fate that prevented him from living with those he loved, and who loved him.

The New York days were Bohemian enough, in all conscience.

Foster's appearance was not unlike that of a tramp, during much of this time; a shabby coat, a cheap glazed cap, a scar upon his upper lip, one would scarcely imagine this to be the chief folk-song composer on this side of the Atlantic.

He had a great love for poetry, and it is not surprising to learn that Poe was his favorite poet. He could recite pages upon pages of this author from memory, and his declamation evinced a keen appreciation of the subtleties of the works. He had another and very different source of inspiration; he was always incited to composition by a trip in one of the Broadway stages, and would often ride up and down the great thoroughfare in one of these public vehicles, thinking of new melodies as he journeyed. Spite of the amount of money that he received during these years, his was a hand-to-mouth existence, and he and his friend George Cooper, the poet, would often concoct a song in the morning, sell it at noon, and not be a penny the richer by night.

The end came suddenly. He was staying at the American House, one of the most inexpensive of lodging-places, and there one night he fell (while in his room) and cut himself severely. An artery was severed, and he was too faint to summon assistance. By the time he was discovered he had lost so much blood that there was no hope of recovery. In the common ward of a New York hospital this genius died. Unidentified at first, his body was taken to the morgue, but the speedy advent of friends prevented its being buried in the potter's field. The accident occurred January 10, 1864, and Foster's death took place three days later, he being at that time only thirty-seven years old. He was buried at Pittsburg, beside the father and mother whom he had loved so dearly. At his grave a band played "Come where my Love lies dreaming" and "The Old Folks at Home," — a most fitting requiem. His daughter was his only descendant. One cannot deny that Foster could have attained to higher paths in art, and that dissipation obscured his genius somewhat, in later years; and yet one cannot help feeling the deepest sympathy with this wild-brier rose of music, growing all by itself, a product of the soil, not of the hot-house.

The personality of Foster was attractive, but not impressive; he was of slight form and under the middle height ; his manner and the expression of his countenance was shy and diffident; he had soft and most expressive dark eyes (his most characteristic feature) and a high forehead.   Had he been of taller stature, he would have been of a distinctly Southern type.   He was courageous, yet gentle, and kind-hearted in a superlative degree.

In thus raising the curtain upon the unhappy life of Foster, the most typical of all American song-composers, we feel that the reader will perceive that one may not here apply an ordinary standard of judgment; that censure must be mute.   It was said of Burns that "the light that led astray was light from Heaven," and surely this gentle, sensitive, and diffident nature caught something of the celestial gleam   The busy American life was not a pleasant environment for such a poet.   He should have lived the dreamy, lazy life of the Southern plantation, of which he has given us such graphic pictures.   Foster's is the most pathetic story of American music, the tale of a tortured and troubled career, extinguished in misery.

CHAPTER VII

NATIONAL AND PATRIOTIC MUSIC

THE patriotic songs of a nation, those which are generally called "national anthems," are often closely intertwined with history, and most frequently spring up spontaneously, in response to some urgent need. Very seldom is a national song deliberately thought out and created according to a preconceived plan, and still more rarely are the melodies borrowed from some other nation. As exceptions to the above rule one may mention the Austrian national hymn, which was composed by Haydn in deliberate imitation of England's powerful anthem, — "God save the King," — and the use of the melody of the latter anthem as national music by Germany.

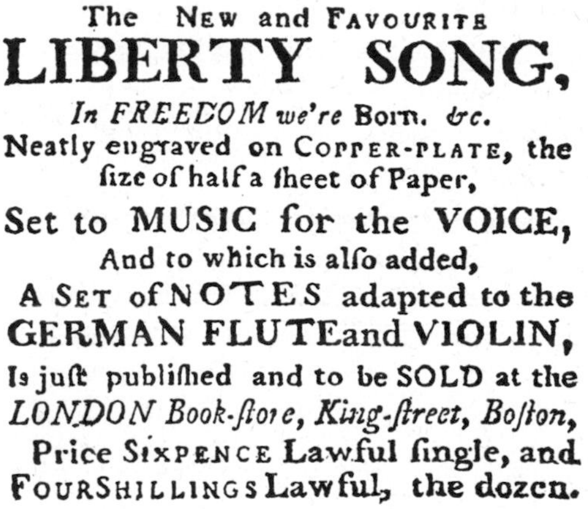

The New and FAVOURITE
LIBERTY SONG,
In FREEDOM we're Born. *&c.*
Neatly engraved on COPPER-PLATE, the
size of half a sheet of Paper,
Set to MUSIC for the VOICE,
And to which is also added,
A SET of NOTES adapted to the
GERMAN FLUTE and VIOLIN,
Is just published and to be SOLD at the
LONDON Book-store, King-street, Boston,
Price SIXPENCE Lawful single, and
FOURSHILLINGS Lawful, the dozen.

FIG. 41. — ADVERTISEMENT OF "LIBERTY SONG."

America borrowed the English tune and many others during the evolution of its patriotic music. Having no good composers during the stirring times of the Revolution or the War of 1812, this country was obliged to appropriate to its own use the tunes of other nations. We shall therefore find, in the course of this chapter, that America possesses very few national tunes of its own, and that our patriotic music is almost wholly an imported article, so far as its melodies are concerned.

The earliest patriotic song in America that we have been able to unearth is a "liberty song" that was advertised in the *Boston Chronicle*, of October 16, 1768 (Fig. 41). The words were by Mrs.

Mercy Warren, wife of General James Warren, of Plymouth, Massachusetts, who began the old American custom of setting patriotic verses to an English melody, the tune in this instance being Boyce's "Hearts of Oak." The words of this ante-Revolutionary production ran as follows: —

"Come join hand in hand, brave Americans all,
And rouse your bold hearts at fair Liberty's call;
No tyrannous arts shall suppress your just claim,
Or stain with dishonor America's name.

Chorus.

"In freedom we're born, and in freedom we'll live;
Our purses are ready;
Steady, friends, steady!
Not as slaves, but as freemen, our money we'll give.

"Our worthy forefathers, let's give them a cheer,
To climates unknown did courageously steer;
Through oceans to deserts for freedom they came,
And dying, bequeathed us their freedom and fame.

Chorus.

"Their generous bosoms all dangers despised,
So highly, so wisely, their birthrights they prized;
We'll keep what they gave, we will piously keep,
Nor frustrate their toils on the land and the deep.

Chorus.

"The tree their own hands had to Liberty reared
They lived to behold growing strong and revered;
With transport they cried, — 'Now our wishes we gain,
For our children shall gather the fruits of our pain.'

Chorus.

"Swarms of placemen and pensioners soon will appear,
Like locusts, deforming the charms of the year;
Suns vainly will rise, showers vainly descend,
If we are to drudge for what others shall spend.

Chorus.

"Then join hand in hand, brave Americans all;
By uniting, we stand; by dividing, we fall;
In so righteous a cause let us hope to succeed,
For Heaven approves of each generous deed.

Chorus.

" All ages shall speak with amaze and applause
   Of the courage we'll show in support of our laws ;
   To die we can bear, — but to serve we disdain ;
   For shame is to freemen more dreadful than pain.

Chorus.

" This bumper I crown for our sovereign's health,
   And this for Britannia's glory and wealth ;
   That wealth and that glory immortal may be,
   If she is but just, and if we are but free.

Chorus.

" In freedom we're born, and in freedom we'll live ;
      Our purses are ready ;
      Steady, friends, steady !
   Not as slaves, but as freemen, our money we'll give."

Of the first edition of this song, as advertised above, we have been unable to find a copy. It was reprinted in an almanac during the ensuing year, but without harmony, no credit being accorded to its composer, and the impression being given that Mrs. Warren had evolved both words and music. This lady wrote many subsequent political pieces, and died at Plymouth in 1814.

In 1770 a new version of the song was written and published in Bickerstaff's almanac, the title now being changed to " The Massachusetts Song of Liberty." The sentiments were now no longer so gracious toward the glory and wealth of Britannia, as the context will show : —

" Come swallow your bumpers, ye Tories, and roar,
   That the sons of fair freedom are hampered once more ;
   But know that no cut-throats our spirits can tame,
   Nor a host of oppressors shall smother the flame.

Chorus.

" In freedom we're born, and, like sons of the brave,
      Will never surrender,
      But swear to defend her ;
   And scorn to survive, if unable to save."

The music was as follows : —

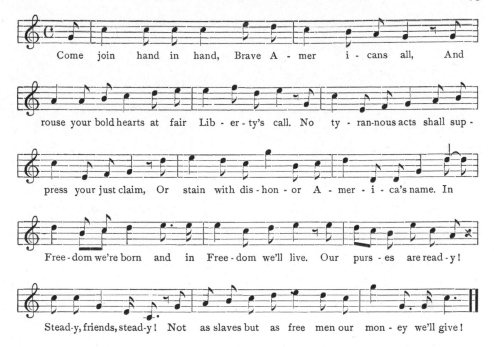

Come join hand in hand, Brave A - mer i - cans all, And rouse your bold hearts at fair Lib - er - ty's call. No ty - ran-nous acts shall sup - press your just claim, Or stain with dis - hon - or A - mer - i - ca's name. In Free - dom we're born and in Free - dom we'll live. Our purs - es are read - y! Stead - y, friends, stead - y! Not as slaves but as free men our mon - ey we'll give!

"Yankee Doodle" (Figs. 42, 44) antedated the above song, but not as an American patriotic work, for it was originally set as a song in derision of the Americans. The origin of the melody of this song is veiled in mystery. For a full account of all that has yet been unearthed regarding the tune, we refer the reader to "The National Music of America,"[1] but we may here state that the origin of the melody has not yet been discovered, although an old Dutch melody (a nursery song) bears a strong resemblance to the first part of the tune, and there is also a German street-song which has similarity to it. It was possibly an old English folk-dance, although this is rather surmised by its general characteristics than by any original yet discovered. The statements that it was sung in derision of Oliver Cromwell, that it is a Hungarian national melody, or that it is a Dutch harvest song, are not true. Equally fictitious is the assertion that the melody was sung to the words of "Lucy Locket lost her Pocket" during the reign of Charles II.

The tune was first brought into prominence by an English surgeon, Dr. Shuckburgh (the name has been misspelled in many ways), who was in Albany with either General Abercrombie or General

---

[1] Elson, "The National Music of America," Boston, 1889.

Allegretto.

i sing U - lys - ses and those chiefs Who

out of near a mil-lion So luck-i-ly their

ba-con sav'd Be-fore the walls of Il-ion.

Yan-kee doo-dle, doo-dle, doo, Black

ne-gro he get fum-bo; And when you come to

our town We'll make you drunk with bum-bo.

FIG. 42. — OLD ENGLISH SETTING OF
"YANKEE DOODLE," 1788.

Amherst, during the French-Canadian War, and either in 1755 or 1756 set words to the melody (giving no clew as to whence he took the tune) in derision of the New England troops which were then moving toward Albany in very motley array. The Americans admired the tune although it was used in sarcasm against them not only by Dr. Shuckburgh, but by the British soldiers in Boston in the first years of the Revolution and the epoch immediately preceding. It became the chief national air of America during the latter part of the Revolution, a melody taken from the enemy.

The most important tune, which was boldly appropriated from English sources very early in our national career, was "God save the King." The origin of this melody has also given rise to much contention; for a full presentation of the facts of the case we refer the reader to Mr. W. H. Cummings's recent book on this topic.[1] The following may be quoted from a review of this book: —

"Dr. Cummings, who has devoted some time to the study of the song, says that it was written by Dr. John Bull, who was born about 1563, was Gresham professor in 1596, and left England about

[1] "God save the King," London, 1893.

1613. It is not improbable that the air is one of those composed by him for the banquet given by the Merchant Tailors' Company to James I, on July 16, 1607, when the composer is said by a contemporary chronicle to have performed upon a 'very rich pair of

organs.' Or the air may have been composed for the Chapel Royal with the Latin words. There seems to be every probability that the tune as Bull composed it has undergone from time to time various changes, such as popular airs are likely to meet with. Who wrote the words is a matter not so easily discovered, and it is not certain that it is capable of exact settlement. According to Dr. Cummings's book, it assuredly was not Ben Jonson, as some persons have argued.

"'The first public performance of the song was not mentioned for nearly a century and a half after

130   THE AMERICAN

SONG L.

AN ODE FOR THE FOURTH OF JULY.

Come all ye fons of fong, Pour the full found along

In joyful ftrains;   Beneath thefe weftern fkies,

FIG. 43 a.—EARLY AMERICAN SETTING OF "GOD SAVE THE KING."

it was written by Bull. This took place at the Drury Lane Theatre on September 30, 1745. A few weeks later a version of the song in the form of a trio by Dr. Arne was sung at Covent Garden, and it was referred to as "An old anthem that was sung at St. James's Chapel for James II, when the Prince of Orange was landed."

L

"'That the tune belongs to England is shown beyond dispute by this writer. The old charge that Bull merely took the tune from Lully is disproved by the fact that Lully was not born until five years after the death of Dr. Bull.

MUSICAL MISCELLANY.   131

See a new empire rife, Burſting with glad ſurprife

Ty - ran-nic chains.

Liberty with keen eye,
Pierc'd the blue vaulted ſky,
Reſolv'd us free;

FIG. 43 *b*. — EARLY AMERICAN SETTING OF "GOD SAVE THE KING."

"'The Dutch version of the hymn printed in 1763 is plainly traced to the English anthem. There were several Jacobite versions of the words, and in this fact is found all the ground for the statement that the tune is of Scotch origin.'"[1]

As early as 1779 the melody was adapted to American use, a set of patriotic verses being written to it and published in the *Pennsylvania Packet* of Philadelphia, in that year. A little later an "Ode for the Fourth of July" was set to the same tune, and became very popular throughout the country. We give a facsimile of this from the *American Musical Miscellany* of 1798 (Figs. 43 *a*, 43 *b*, 43 *c*). Many other poetic settings to the same melody followed, and the tune had become fairly national in character long before it took its present American shape.

[1] Cummings, "God save the King."

A children's celebration took place in Park Street Church, in Boston, July 4, 1832, and for this occasion Rev. Dr. Samuel F. Smith, then a theological student at Andover, wrote the words of "My Country, 'tis of thee," which have since become the favorite, and in fact the only, mode of singing this melody in the United States, on patriotic occasions. Nevertheless, not a few Americans have felt dissatisfied that Dr. Smith's words should be sung to so markedly foreign a melody. The society of the Cincinnati (descendants of officers of the Revolutionary army) offered a gold medal for a new tune that should prove available for the American words. In 1903 this medal was awarded to Arthur Johnstone, of New York, for writing such a musical setting; but, as yet, "America" is sung constantly to the old English tune.

"Hail Columbia" was, from the birth of the poem, accepted as one of the chief national tunes. It had, however, existed as an instrumental work for nine years before it was wedded to poetry. During the last quarter of the eighteenth century, "Washington's March" was the leading instrumental work of the American repertoire, which, by the way, confined itself largely to march music and military subjects. A reproduction of this march from an early edition is shown herewith

132   THE AMERICAN

From her Imperial feat,
Beheld the bleeding ftate,
Approv'd this day's debate
    And firm decree.

Sublime in awful form,
Above the whirling ftorm,
    The Goddefs ftood ;
She faw with pitying eye,
War's tempeft raging high,
Our hero's bravely die,
    In fields of blood.

High on his fhining car,
Mars, the ftern God of war,
    Our ftruggles bleft :
Soon victory wave her hand,
Fair Freedom cheer'd the land,
Led on Columbia's band
    To glorious reft.

Now all ye fons of fong,
Pour the full found along,
    Who fhall control ;
For in this weftern clime,
Freedom fhall rife fublime,
Till ever changing time,
    Shall ceafe to roll.

FIG. 43 c. — EARLY AMERICAN SETTING OF "GOD SAVE THE KING."

(Fig. 44).   When Washington was elected President, a German musician wrote a new work in honor of the inauguration, and called it " The President's March."   It is not clearly ascertained who this musician was, but the claims for the composership are divided between Johannes Roth and a Professor Phylo, with rather more evidence for the former than for the latter.

Johannes Roth was a musician of Philadelphia, where he was familiarly known as " Old Roth."   His composition (if it was his) is said to have been played for the first time, by a band, as Washington crossed the bridge at Trenton, on his way from Philadelphia to New York, to the inauguration ceremonies.   It was soon after played in New York, also, and was instantly taken into popular favor as " The President's March," supplanting the old " Washington's March " for good and all.   But the new march itself would have died out had it not suddenly been wedded to patriotic words.   It was composed in 1789; for nine years it remained in its original state.

In 1798 the country was much excited by political matters. The two parties were sharply divided on the question of assisting France in her difficulties.   The Federalists (who believed in the nation as the supreme power) were desirous of avoiding all possible alliance with France, while the Anti-Federalists (who believed more in state rights than in the Federal union) were very anti-English, and pro-French, dancing the Carmagnole in the streets of New York, and committing various other rabid absurdities.   The latter party, of course, detested John Adams, who was then President. During this excitement, Gilbert Fox, a young actor seeking to sell tickets for a benefit performance, bethought him of a plan whereby he might sell his tickets more rapidly.   He induced his friend, Joseph Hopkinson, to write a set of words that were a glorification of Adams and Federalism, and he then advertised the new song, which was written to the tune of " The President's March," as an attraction of the forthcoming benefit.   In those days a new patriotic song was a most important matter, and its first performance became almost a national affair.   The theatre was crowded.   Mr. Fox was obliged to sing the song over and over, and finally the audience joined in the chorus.   The line, " Behold the chief who now commands," referring, of course, to President Adams, and the exaltation

GENERAL WASHINGTON'S MARCH

Boston Printed and fold by GGraupner at his Mufical cademy Nº6 Franklin Street Franklin place
Piano Fortes For fale to Let. and Tuned in Town and Countr at the fhortest Notice

Pr 12 Ct

YANKEE DOODLE

FIG. 44.—EARLY PRINTS OF "WASHINGTON'S MARCH" AND
"YANKEE DOODLE."

of national unity (which the Anti-Federalists looked at askance) was applauded to the echo. Eventually the political song became a national one. Yet at the time there were plenty of dissenting voices. The "antis," led by Jefferson and Madison, held it to be adverse to France and a covert attack on state rights. Bache's *Aurora* of April 27, 1798, said: —

"The song is the most ridiculous bombast and the vilest adulation to the Anglo-monarchical party."

The careful reader will find considerable exaggerated metaphor in the verses, a prevalent fault of the time. A reproduction of the first edition of this song, while it was still known as a political affair, is given herewith (Figs. 45 *a*, 45 *b*). It will be seen that the harmonization is of the crudest sort. Almost all national songs undergo a polishing process before they become permanent in the repertoire, and "Hail Columbia" has been considerably revised since it began its career as a "Federal song."

"The Star-spangled Banner" is a borrowed work, as far as its tune is concerned, and it was very well known in America under different titles for at least sixteen years before Francis Scott Key set his celebrated words to it. The melody is of English origin, and it was at first a drinking-song. The bold and spirited style of its progressions and the forcible character of its final cadence fitted excellently to the Bacchanalian adjuncts of its earliest performances, but these points make "The Star-spangled Banner" rather an unsingable anthem for great public occasions.

There is some doubt about the year of its origin. In the eighteenth century the Anacreontic Society of London was a wild and jovial association in which the artistic members were often heard in original works of an hilarious character. In short, it was a Bohemian gathering not unlike the Savage Club, of London, in its palmiest days. Between 1770 and 1775, Ralph Tomlinson, Esq., was the president of the Anacreontics. During his presidency he composed the words of a song which he entitled "To Anacreon in Heaven." It was either Dr. Samuel Arnold or John Stafford Smith, Esq. (both members of the society), who furnished the tune. It has been stated that it is an old French tune, but this has not been substantiated. There is certainly no tune resembling it in John Stafford Smith's

" Musica Antiqua," in which he set forth the most remarkable old tunes that he had collected. If, as is probable, Dr. Arnold composed the tune, he did not claim it in its printed editions, for neither author nor composer are named in the old copies of the drinking-song. It appeared as a masonic hymn in Holden's " Selection of Masonic Songs," which is dated " Dublin, A.L. 5802 " (A.D. 1802), but America had appropriated the tune to her own purposes four years before this.

The Massachusetts Charitable Fire Society celebrated its anniversary on June 1, 1798, with a meeting and a banquet in Boston. To this festivity there came Mr. Thomas Paine (he afterwards changed his name to Robert Treat Paine, because of the notoriety of Thomas Paine, the radical and free-thinker) with a new patriotic song which was to be the feature of the occasion. Announcements had been made of this in the press beforehand. The *Columbian Centinel,* on Wednesday, May 30, 1798, printed the following : —

ADAMS AND LIBERTY

On Friday morning will be published from the press of Thomas & Andrews, and sold at all the book-stores, the BOSTON PATRIOTIC SONG called ADAMS AND LIBERTY.

Written by THOMAS PAINE, A.M.

To be sung at the anniversary of the Massachusetts Charitable Fire Society on that day.

And on Saturday, June 2, the following statement appeared in the same newspaper : —

" The Boston Patriotic Song of 'Adams and Liberty,' written by Mr. Paine, was sung and re-echoed amidst the loudest reiterated plaudits. Dr. Fay did great justice to its merits."

This setting was the first patriotic use of the tune of " The Starspangled Banner " in America. It had nine long stanzas (for the patriots feared no prolixity), and it became so universally popular that Mr. Paine received $750 from the publishers for his copyright — an enormous sum for those days. A stanza is herewith given as an example of the style of the song : —

> " Ye sons of Columbia, who bravely have fought
> For those rights which unstained from your sires had descended.
> May you long taste the blessings your valour has bought,
> And your sons reap the soil which your fathers defended.

Sung by M.r FOX ———————— Written by J:HOPKINSON Efq.r

FIG. 45 a. — FIRST EDITION OF "HAIL COLUMBIA."

Brothers joind peace and safety we shall find.

2

Immortal Patriots rife once more
Defend your rights — defend your fhore
  Let no rude foe with impious hand
  Let no rude foe with impious hand
Invade the fhrine where facred lies
Of toil and blood the well earnd prize
   While offering peace fincere and juft
   In heav'n we place a manly truft
   That truth and juftice will prevail
   And every fcheme of bondage fail
     Firm — united &c

3

Sound found the trump of fame
Let Wafhingtons great name
  Ring thro the world with loud applaufe
  Ring thro the world with loud applaufe
Let every clime to Freedom dear
Liften with a joyful ear —
   With equal fkill with godlike pow'r
   He governs in the fearful hour
   Of horrid war or guides with cafe
   The happier times of honeft peace —
     Firm — united &c

4

Behold the Chief who now commands
Once more to ferve his Country ftands
  The rock on which the ftorm will beat
  The rock on which the ftorm will beat
But arm'd in virtue firm and true
His hopes are fix'd on heav'n and you —
   When hope was finking in difmay
   When glooms obfcur'd Columbias day
   His fteady mind from changes free
   Refolved on Death or Liberty —
     Firm — united &c

For the FLUTE or VIOLIN

2d time Chorus

FIG. 45 *b*.—FIRST EDITION OF "HAIL COLUMBIA."

Mid the reign of mild Peace,
May your nation increase
With the glory of Rome and the wisdom of Greece.
And ne'er shall the sons of Columbia be slaves
While the earth bears a plant or the sea rolls its waves."

Nor was this the only setting.   Very soon thereafter a new version of the song appeared in Philadelphia.   As the original had
been in praise of President Adams, this second one paid homage to
his successor, and was entitled " Jefferson and Liberty."   Still later,
when Napoleon had met with defeat and disaster at Moscow,
another set of words was sung in Boston to celebrate the Russian
victories — for there was a strong anti-French feeling there in those
days.   It is very probable that Francis Scott Key (Fig. 46) was as
familiar with these as with the first setting.   It may therefore be
accepted as an established fact (and there is much misinformation
on this matter) that the author of " The Star-spangled Banner " was
thinking of the tune of "Adams and Liberty," the melody of the
old English drinking-song (Figs. 47 a, 47 b), when he penned his
lines.

The circumstances attending the poem were sufficient to arouse a
poet.   Mr. Key had come to the British fleet, in Chesapeake Bay, as
an envoy from President Madison, to request the release of Dr.
Beanes, of Maryland, a non-combatant who had been unjustly arrested.
The British commander, fearing that Key would betray the prepara-
tions for attack which were actively going on throughout the fleet,
detained him until the battle of the next day (the bombardment of
Fort McHenry, below Baltimore) should have been fought.   We
can imagine with what anxiety the American gazed toward the fort
on the morning of the 14th of September, 1814, after the night's
bombardment.   When he saw the stars and stripes floating upon
the fort, he wrote the first stanza of the poem on the back of an
old letter which he had with him.   Released and on his way to
Baltimore, he composed the remaining verses.   Arrived at a hotel
in the city, he made a clean copy in ink and carried it to the office
of the *Baltimore American*, where it was at once published as a
" broadside."   Immediately thereafter it was printed in the paper
itself.   It was labelled from the first, " to be sung to the tune of

'Adams and Liberty,'" and all stories of the tune being subsequently chosen by an actor of Baltimore are misleading. For a more detailed account of the story of "The Star-spangled Banner," the reader may be referred to "The National Music of America."[1]

Outside of "The Star-spangled Banner" the patriotic music of the War of 1812 was chiefly a series of songs in celebration of our various naval victories, "Hull's Victory," narrating the capture of the *Guerrière* by the *Constitution*, the latter commanded by Captain Isaac Hull, being the most important of these.

At the outbreak of the Civil War it was found that none of our national songs had words fitting to so unforeseen an event. Efforts were made, both North and South, to add verses to " The Starspangled Banner" that would suit the emergency. The South at first wished to appropriate both the flag and the song celebrating it. The verses had been written by a native of the South in the first place, and such men as General William C. Wickham and Admiral Semmes hoped for the retention of the banner itself. In the North no less a poet than Oliver Wendell Holmes attempted additions to the verses. The following verse written by him was printed in the *Boston Evening Transcript* in 1861 : —

"When our land is illumined with Liberty's smile,
If a foe from within strike a blow at her glory,
Down, down with the traitor who dares to defile
The flag of her stars and the page of her story !
　　By the millions unchained
　　Who their birthright have gained
　　We will keep her bright blazon forever unstained.
And the Star-spangled Banner in triumph shall wave
While the land of the free is the home of the brave ! "

But none of these attempts succeeded in bringing the old song up to date, and finally an effort was made to evolve a new national anthem. There are, however, as we have stated, very few instances on record of a national anthem being composed or written in accordance with the commercial law of demand and supply.

The South, when it evolved a new flag, created a new song about it, " The Bonnie Blue Flag." The North tried to force a

[1] Elson, " The National Music of America and its Sources," Boston, 1899.

new song into being by offering a prize of $500 for a national hymn. This offer was published May 17, 1861, and a committee of thirteen appointed to examine the musical and poetic results. The responses were numerous if not powerful. Every Northern and Western state, and even England, Italy, and Germany sent contributions. Five wash-baskets were filled with the compositions and poems. Then came three months of hard labor in examination, with the disheartening result that not one of the works was found powerful enough to be classed as a really national song.

FIG. 46. — FRANCIS SCOTT KEY.

Meanwhile a couple of national songs grew up, as such things will, by mere chance, and one other by plagiarism. The latter was "Maryland, my Maryland," which was simply the old German folk-song, "O Tannenbaum," sung by students abroad to the words, "Lauriger Horatius," to which James Ryder Randall set fiery words. The other two songs were "Glory Hallelujah" and "Dixie." "Dixie" has a very simple history. It was written as a song and dance, in 1859, for Dan Bryant's negro minstrel show, and was sung by his troupe at his theatre, 472 Broadway, New York. It was composed by a member of the company, Daniel D. Emmett, an Ohio man (died at Mt. Vernon, Ohio, June 27, 1904, aged 86), and became a war-song entirely by accident. It was a rollicking picture of the plantation, it had something of the dash and insouciance of "Yankee Doodle," and it became the Southern song because the soldiers and the people liked it. It is the only bit of war music that has outlived the Southern confederacy, and bids fair to become national.

If the North gave to the South her chief song, the compliment was returned in the most important song of the war, "Glory Hallelujah" (Fig. 48). This was begun as a hymn-tune in Charleston, South Carolina. The music is claimed by William Steffe, a popular composer of Sunday-school music. The song was used at many a Southern camp-meeting before the war, and was also employed in many of the colored congregations. It even made its way into the Methodist hymnals at the North.

When the war began, the second battalion of Massachusetts Infantry (then known as " The Tigers") was at Fort Warren, in Boston Harbor, with numerous other recruits from various sources. " The Tigers" hoped to go to the front in a body, and offered their service as an organization to the government. This was declined since the regimental formation could not be altered by the government, but the men were advised to enlist individually in the Twelfth Massachusetts Regiment, under Colonel Fletcher Webster. Most of them did this. We therefore find " Glory Hallelujah " closely entwined with the history of the Twelfth Massachusetts Regiment, as the following (gathered by the author from Captain Henry J. Hallgreen and other officers of the regiment) will clearly show. As there are some spurious tales told regarding the song we venture into some detail in the matter.

One day, while the regiment was still at Fort Warren, Captain Hallgreen heard two new recruits from Maine, in the throes of homesickness, most mournfully singing the hymn, " Say, Brothers, will you meet us ? " He was struck by the melody, and taught it to some of " The Tigers." It spread like wild-fire, and at once became a camp-tune. As there was no rhyme or complex construction to the words, the men soon found that they could add their own improvisations to the tune, a fact which made it all the more popular. Meanwhile Gilmore, who frequently came to the fort with his band, caused his men to "vamp" the tune (that is, to improvise harmonies to it), and often accompanied the singing of it. The words grew chiefly about a good-natured Scot, named John Brown, who had enlisted in the regiment, and all the allusions to " John Brown " are merely rough fun made out of the similarity of names, and are not tributes to the celebrated hero of Ossawatomie and Harper's Ferry. They often sang the musical jests standing around their companion, who took all their fun good-naturedly. This John Brown afterwards lost his life trying to swim a river during a retreat of the Union forces.

FIG. 47 *a*.—ENGLISH DRINKING-SONG FROM WHICH "STAR-SPANGLED BANNER" WAS TAKEN.

CHORUS.

And be-sides I'll in--struct you like me to in---twine, The

And be-sides I'll in--struct you like me to in---twine, The

And be-sides I'll in--struct you like me to in---twine, The

And be-sides I'll in--struct you like me to in---twine, The

Myr--tle of Ve-nus with Bac-chus'-s Vine.

Myr--tle of Ve-nus with Bac-chus'-s Vine.

Myr--tle of Ve-nus with Bac-chus'-s Vine.

Myr--tle of Ve-nus with Bac-chus'-s Vine.

2

The news through Olympus immediately flew;
When Old Thunder pretended to give himself Airs
"If these Mortals are suffer'd there scheme to pursue,
"The Devil a .Goddess will stay above Stairs,
　　"Hark, already they cry,
　　"In Transports of joy,
"Away to the Sons of Anacreon we'll fly,
"And there, with good Fellows, we'll learn to intwine
"The Myrtle of Venus with Bacchus's Vine.

3

"The yellow hair'd God and his nine fusty Maids,
"From Helicon's banks will incontinent flee,
"Idalia will boast but of tenantless shades,
"And the bi forked Hill a mere Desart will be.
　　"My Thunder no fear on't,
　　"Shall soon do it's Errand,
"And, dam'me, I'll swinge the Ringleaders, I warrant,
"I'll trim the young Dogs, for thus daring, to twine
"The Myrtle of Venus with Bacchus's Vine.

4

Apollo rose up; and said, "Prythee ne'er quarrel,
"Good King of the Gods, with my Vot'ries below;
"Your Thunder is useles then, shewing his Laurel,
Cry'd, "Sic Evitabile Fulmen, you know.
　　"Then over each head,
　　"My Laurels I'll spread;
"So my Sons from your Crackers no Mischief shall dread
"Whilst snug in there Club Room, they jovially twine
"The Myrtle of Venus with Bacchus's Vine.

5

Nex Momus got up with his risible Phiz,
And swore with Apollo he'd chearfully join
"The full Tide of Harmony still shall be his
"But the Song, and the Catch and the Laugh shall be mine
　　"Then Jove, be not jealous,
　　"Of these honest Fellows,
Cry'd Jove, "We relent, since the Truth you now tell us,
"And swear by Old Styx, that they long shall intwine
"The Myrtle of Venus with Bacchus's Vine.

6

Ye Sons of Anacreon, then, join Hand in Hand;
Preserve Unanimity, Friendship, and Love,
'Tis yours to support what's so happily plann'd;
You've the Sanction of Gods, and the Fiat of Jove.
　　While thus we agree,
　　Our toast let it be,
May our Club flourish happy, uninted, and free,
And long may the Sons of Anacreon intwine
The Myrtle of Venus and Bacchus's Vine.

FIG. 47 b. — ENGLISH DRINKING-SONG FROM WHICH "STAR-SPANGLED
BANNER" WAS TAKEN.

The officers were not all in sympathy with the "John Brown" verses, and endeavored to get the men to substitute the name of "Ellsworth"[1] for "Brown" in the stanzas, but the soldiers would not make the change. Later on Edna Dean Proctor tried to change the words into a praise of the more famous John Brown, but the new poem met with no marked success.

And now came the moment when the camp-song was to become national property. Fletcher Webster's regiment was called to the front. As the men crossed Boston Common on their way to the old Providence depot, they sang their camp-song, one thousand strong, with a band supporting the harmony. Boston went wild over it that day. The next morning, in New York, the regiment was halted on Broadway, and there again they sang their song amid the wildest frenzy of the public. It mattered little that the people could not fully comprehend the words, the tune was one of the "swingiest" of marches, the whole affair was redolent of the camp, and "Glory Hallelujah" was sung by the Twelfth Massachusetts Regiment from city to city, from camp to camp, until it became national.

In December, 1861, a small party of civilians were allowed to visit one of the outposts of the army, on Virginian soil, and chanced to see a skirmish before returning to Washington. After the flurry they heard the men marching to their quarters, singing "John Brown's Body." Rev. James Freeman Clarke urged Mrs. Julia Ward Howe (both being of the party) to try and set grander words to the tune, and "Mine Eyes have seen the Glory of the Coming of the Lord" was the inspired result. But the song is still sung at the camp-fires to its old words, and foreign troops (Kitchener's soldiers in the Soudan and in South Africa) have marched to its inspiring swing, while England, Germany, Italy, and France,[2] all are familiar with the melody which started out in life as a Sunday-school hymn and finally became the most military song of the present time. We give the words and music of the original hymn, "Say, Brothers, will you meet us?":—

---

[1] Colonel E. E. Ellsworth was the first commissioned officer slain in the Civil War.

[2] The author has heard it, sometimes as an instrumental selection, sometimes with foreign words, in all these countries.

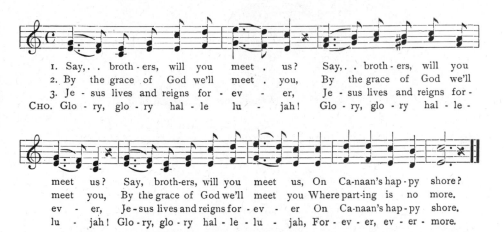

1. Say,.. broth-ers, will you meet . us? Say,.. broth-ers, will you
2. By the grace of God we'll meet . you, By the grace of God we'll
3. Je - sus lives and reigns for - ev - er, Je - sus lives and reigns for -
CHO. Glo - ry, glo - ry hal - le lu - jah! Glo - ry, glo - ry hal - le -

meet us? Say, broth-ers, will you meet us, On Ca-naan's hap-py shore?
meet you, By the grace of God we'll meet you Where part-ing is no more.
ev - er, Je - sus lives and reigns for - ev - er On Ca-naan's hap-py shore.
lu - jah! Glo - ry, glo - ry hal - le - lu - jah, For - ev - er, ev - er - more.

Among the composers who added to the repertoire of famous songs of the Civil War, one must accord a prominent place to George F. Root, who wrote "The Battle-cry of Freedom," which was one of the most successful of the songs of its time. He also produced "Tramp, tramp, tramp, the Boys are Marching" and "Just before the Battle, Mother," both of which were famous in the music of the war. These songs have no especial history attached to them. The composer was born at Sheffield, Massachusetts, August 30, 1820, and died August 6, 1895, leaving a talented musical son (Fred. W. Root) behind him. Dr. Root (he received the title of Mus. Doc. from the University of Chicago) was one of the disciples of the Lowell Mason system, already described, and studied with George J. Webb, and other Boston teachers, besides spending a year in Paris for musical purposes. He was one of the enthusiastic "convention leaders," who followed Lowell Mason in this early method of diffusing music among the masses.

Probably the composer who won the most decided successes with his songs during the Civil War, was Henry Clay Work. He sounded the most characteristic note of all the American composers of the time, and his songs give almost every note in the gamut of expression, from sarcasm to triumph, from gayety to military glory. Yet neither Work nor Root would be called trained composers in these latter days, when the highest and largest forms of music have been attained by our native musicians. But Work was a very earnest man, and no one can doubt the sincerity of his music, or its

John Brown.

ORIGIN, FORT WARREN. Music arranged by C. B. MARSH.

1 John Brown's body lies a mouldering in the grave,
John Brown's body lies a mouldering in the grave,
John Brown's body lies a mouldering in the grave.
His soul's marching on!
CHORUS.
Glory, Hally, Hallelujah! Glory, Hally
Hallelujah! Glory, Hally, Hallelujah!
His soul's marching on!

2 He's gone to be a soldier in the army of the Lord,
He's gone to be a soldier in the army of the Lord,
He's gone to be a soldier in the army of the Lord,
His soul's marching on!
CHORUS.
Glory, Hally, Hallelujah! &c.
His soul's marching on!

3 John Brown's knapsack is strapped upon his back—
John Brown's knapsack is strapped upon his back—
John Brown's knapsack is strapped upon his back—
His soul's marching on!

CHORUS.
Glory, Hally, Hallelujah! &c.
His soul's marching on!

4 His pet lambs will meet him on the way—
His pet lambs will meet him on the way—
His pet lambs will meet him on the way—
They go marching on!
CHORUS.
Glory, Hally, Hallelujah! &c.
They go marching on!

5 They will hang Jeff Davis to a tree!
They will hang Jeff Davis to a tree!
They will hang Jeff Davis to a tree!
As they march along!
CHORUS.
Glory, Hally, Hallelujah! &c.
As they march along!

6 Now, three rousing cheers for the Union!
Now, three rousing cheers for the Union!
Now, three rousing cheers for the Union!
As we are marching on!
CHORUS.
Glory, Hally. Hallelujah! Glory, Hally,
Hallelujah! Glory, Hally. Hallelujah!
Hip, Hip, Hip, Hip, Hurrah!

Published by C S. HALL, 256 MAIN STREET, CHARLESTOWN, MASS.
Entered, according to Act of Congress. in the year 1861, by C. S. HALL, in the Clerk's Office of the District Court of the District of Massachusetts.

FIG. 48.—EARLY EDITION OF "GLORY HALLELUJAH."

originality. He was born in Middletown, Connecticut, October 1, 1832, and died at Hartford, June 8, 1884. He was naturally a strong partisan in politics, for his father had suffered in the cause of abolition. The family removed to Illinois during Work's childhood, and he had the misery of seeing his father imprisoned for his anti-slavery views during this Western sojourn. He seems to have had scarcely any musical education, yet he wrote successful songs even in his boyhood. His songs of "Kingdom Comin'" and "Babylon is Fallen" were his first contributions to war music, and they are as individual as the compositions of that other natural musician, — Stephen C. Foster.

Many other popular songs came from Work's fertile brain, some of them being written in the cause of temperance. But the great success of this earnest writer was "Marching through Georgia," one of the most characteristic, if one of the most partisan, songs of the war. It may be mentioned, as a curious fact, that Stephen C. Foster, the best of the native song-writers of this time, made no marked success in the domain of war music. On the Southern side Mr. H. L. Schreiner and Mr. A. E. Blackmar wrote war-songs of considerable spirit.

We have shown, in the history of "Glory Hallelujah," how a song of peace became metamorphosed into a song of war. In the case of one well-known song this process was reversed, and a hymn of peace was evolved out of a bellicose subject. During the Civil War every musician in the United States seemed to be intent upon composing a new national song. The utter failure of these attempts has already been suggested, yet they went on, unceasingly, during the eventful four years. Among those who strove to compose *the* song that should reverberate through the ages was a modest German living in Boston in very straitened circumstances. Matthias Keller caught the "national-song fever" in the early stages of its epidemic, and promptly produced a lofty, perhaps somewhat grandiloquent, "hymn," entitled "Save our Republic, O Father on High!" This had its momentary vogue, and was then laid aside. When Gilmore planned his second Peace Jubilee (see Chap. IV), he desired to have some special song of peace to commemorate it. He thought of Keller and his moribund hymn. The composer's permission secured, he hastened to Oliver Wendell Holmes with the music and a request that the poetic doctor set new and peaceful words to the tune.   Dr. Holmes consented to assist at this unusual placing of the cart before the horse, and reversed the usual order of things by allowing the music to inspire the poem.   The result was unexpectedly good, and the latest contribution to our national songs was the result.   " Angel of Peace, thou hast wandered too Long " is not of the profoundest music nor of the most thrilling poetry, yet its sentiments admirably fit a nation that is not aggressive or bent on conquest, a nation that brings beneficence to the world at large and that offers welcome to the oppressed and is supposed to oppress none, a nation such as America is — when at her best.

It is very probable that the giant strides made in composition in this country may very soon result in some other national song replacing those above described.   Among the many composers who are now creating a repertoire of important works in America, there must be one who will some day feel impelled to write us a true national anthem.   Possibly the reader of this chapter will come to the belief that the ideal national song in America is not yet written or composed.

PLATE V

EDWARD ALEXANDER MacDOWELL

CHAPTER VIII

AMERICAN TONE-MASTERS

ALTHOUGH it may be a difficult task to grade justly each member of the host of composers which has sprung up in recent times, it is by no means so difficult to select the leaders. Such selection, however, ought not to be based merely upon the size of works created, nor even upon general influence. Seidl and Thomas and Zerrahn exerted a vast influence, yet were not composers; B. J. Lang printed very few compositions, yet his teaching, his leadership of important clubs, his production of many masterpieces which were unattainable to the majority of conductors, make him one of the most prominent of American musical figures. But in the proper classification of "American Tone-masters" these celebrated names must be passed by.

The Nestor of the American composers in the great classical forms was Professor John Knowles Paine (Pl. XII). He was born in Portland, Maine, January 9, 1839, and made his first appearance as an organist and composer in public at eighteen years of age. A pupil of the celebrated Kotzschmar, in Portland, he afterward, in 1858, went to Germany, studying, in Berlin, the organ under Haupt and composition under Wieprecht and Teschner. This continued for three years, during which he appeared many times in German cities as an organ virtuoso. Returning to America in 1861, he became the chief organist of the country, judged by the German standards. It was largely through his influence that the great organ set up in Music Hall in 1860 became appreciated by the public, and he had been a moving spirit in the purchase of this instrument, while he was yet in Germany. In 1862 he began the Harvard College musical course, which will be described later.

In 1867 he directed his first great work, a Mass in D, at the
Sing-Akademie, in Berlin, in the presence of some of the royal
family and a large public. The European press complimented
the young composer heartily upon his attainments, yet seemed to
agree that the composition did not strike into any new path, but
kept to the beaten track. His next work in the large forms received
its first performance in the composer's native land. This was
nothing less than an oratorio — " St. Peter " — which was first publicly given in Portland, Maine, June 3, 1873, and repeated the following year in Boston. It is interesting to note the care which the
composer took in this work. He frequently consulted with a prominent vocal teacher, John O'Neill, regarding the practicality of this
or that solo; he showered forth all his contrapuntal gifts in the
choruses. The orchestral parts were extremely difficult, and the
work as a whole showed much more of ingenuity than of inspiration. The Handel and Haydn Society did its full duty by the
first American composer, by its performance of the work in 1874,
after which it was seldom heard except in excerpts. But it
certainly proved that America had made a great advance in
music, and now possessed at least one leader who could write
respectably in the most difficult musical form of all. It was
Mr. Paine's inaugural as the first thorough composer in the
classical forms in America; it was the first oratorio written on
American soil.

The next epoch-making work was Paine's first symphony, in C
minor, a composition sufficiently classical to be played by Theodore
Thomas's orchestra, in Boston, January, 1876. This work (Op. 23)
was afterwards given many times by the same orchestra. The
second symphony, in A, entitled " Spring," was, however, a much
greater performance. In the earlier works, Paine allowed the rules of
music to master him, becoming somewhat pedantic and *Kapellmeis-
terish;* now he became master of the rules, and his poetry began
to assert itself. The final movement of the " Spring " symphony
(Op. 34) is a glorious outburst of thanksgiving almost comparable
with the finale of that other tribute to spring, the great B flat symphony by Schumann. The symphony was composed in 1880. It
was the composer's favorite work among his orchestral compositions.

When the Centennial Exhibition of the United States took place in Philadelphia, in 1876, there were only two prominent native composers to whom the nation could turn for a lofty opening hymn,— Paine and Dudley Buck.   Paine's "Centennial Hymn" was decidedly more of a success than Wagner's "Centennial March," which was also composed for the opening ceremonies ; a success was also made by Buck, with a choral work.

In 1877 Professor Paine composed a symphonic fantasy based on Shakespeare's "Tempest," which was the first important American composition performed by Gericke at the Boston Symphony Concerts.   Soon after he prepared a musical setting of the "Œdipus Tyrannus" of Sophocles, for a set of Greek performances at Harvard, in 1881.   Here at last we find, and for the first time, an American composition that not only equalled but excelled European settings.   Mendelssohn had set music to Greek plays with success, introducing double choruses, strophe, and antistrophe, and many other skilful contrapuntal devices.   Paine did not follow this lead, nor did he, on the other hand, attempt to reproduce the unison simplicity of an ancient music which, after all, we understand but hazily. He allowed himself to be inspired by the loftiness of the text, and he employed unison, harmony, counterpoint, merely as they evolved themselves from the tragedy, and not with any preconceived attempt at a system.   The performances of the play were powerful in the extreme, and not the least part of them was the dignified music, — the greatest composition which up to that time had been written in this country.

Among subsequent works we may mention "Phœbus, Arise" (1882); Milton's "Nativity," composed in 1883 for the Handel and Haydn triennial in Boston, a work of fine contrapuntal texture and much beauty; "Song of Promise," a cantata composed for the Cincinnati Musical Festival of 1888; "Columbus March and Hymn," composed for the opening of the Columbian Exposition of Chicago, in 1892; and a great number of songs, organ compositions, part-songs, and chamber-music.   Some of these works, especially the "Spring" symphony, have had hearings in European concerts; in fact, Professor Paine was the first American orchestral composer who gained anything of a transatlantic reputation.   To-day there are many who have planted the American musical standard upon European soil.

One of Professor Paine's orchestral works may be mentioned as illustrating the connection between music and painting.   It is called "An Island Fantasy," and may be classed as a symphonic poem.   Composers are very frequently inspired by poems, even in their instrumental works.   In this case the inspiration was a

FIG. 49. — MANUSCRIPT MUSIC BY PROF. JOHN K. PAINE.

couple of paintings (of the Isles of Shoals, in New Hampshire) by an American artist, — J. Appleton Brown.   The work itself suggests both the menace and the beauty of the sea.   Since the composition of this symphonic poem more than one modern musician has taken his themes from painting.   Böcklin, the Swiss artist, has inspired Weingartner to a symphonic poem, by his painting, — "The Elysian Fields," — and Hans Huber has written an entire symphony, each movement of which represents one or more of the paintings of the same artist — a veritable picture gallery in symphonic music! But Professor Paine was, next to Liszt, one of the earliest to translate paintings into instrumental music.

In 1901 he composed the music for Aristophanes' "The Birds," which was performed by the Harvard Classical Club in May, 1901; and his latest and best work is an opera — "Azara" — which has been translated into German and published with German and English text. The libretto is by Professor Paine himself, and is derived from the old Trouvère story, the poetic "Aucassin and Nicolette." Any one who reads this charming mediæval idyl will note the many sylvan touches, the Saracenic scenes, and the bold contrasts. All these present a splendid series of pictures for the composer, and Professor Paine has taken full advantage of them. The action is rather slow for these days of "Toscas" and "Bohêmes," but the artistic effect attained is undeniable.

Professor Paine may be classed as a moderate conservative in music. At one time he was bitterly opposed to the Wagnerian school, and even wrote some magazine articles against it. Time soon mellowed his views of Wagner as it eliminated the pedantic element from his later music. Professor Paine never had the pleasure of hearing his opera in public performance. He died at Cambridge, April 25, 1906, and "Azara" has never reached the stage.

Nothing can better prove the rapid advance of music in America than the fact that when Professor Paine began his career he stood alone, the one classical composer of America; while to-day there are at least three men, Chadwick, MacDowell, and Horatio W. Parker, who might dispute the field with him, and there are a score of others who have won transatlantic reputations. Music has made even more rapid strides than literature among us. Less than a century ago it was contemptuously asked by a British reviewer, "Who reads an American book?" To-day some American writers have surer reputations in England than in their native country. But in music it is much less than half a century since Paine was first heard as a curiosity in Europe, while now, in many conversations with the present writer, such men as Rheinberger, Reinecke, Lamoureux, and Massenet have shown familiarity with the works of the three men mentioned above and with many others of our native composers. The appearance of an American composition on a European programme no longer causes the slightest surprise; and, more than this, England has ordered compositions from our leading musicians for her chief musical festivals. All three of the men named as possible rivals for the chief place among our native composers are young men, or comparatively so, and give promise of more important works to come.

George Whitfield Chadwick (Pl. VIII), the most versatile and chronologically the first of the group, was born in Lowell, Massachusetts, November 13, 1854. He comes of the purest American stock, his great-grandfather having fought in Stark's regiment, at the picket-fence, at the battle of Bunker Hill. Both of his parents were musical; his father taught in an academy and singing-school near Concord, New Hampshire, and his mother sang in the church choir. All of his uncles and aunts were more or less active in the old style of psalmody, which we have described in connection with New England's earlier days. The family moved to Lawrence, Massachusetts, in 1860. The father being occupied by business affairs, the elder brother taught Chadwick piano and harmony, and during his boyhood he sang alto in a church choir in Lawrence. His first connection with organ-playing was at the handle of the bellows, but he was soon promoted from the blowing to the playing of the instrument, and attained some knowledge of the manipulation of the organ before 1869. His first attempts at composition were made while a pupil at the Lawrence High School, and were chiefly songs and dances for the piano. Some of these he preserved and used a quarter of a century later, in his successful comic opera, "Tabasco."

Chadwick's first regular instruction in music began at the New England Conservatory (of which he afterwards became director) in 1872, his chief teachers there being Dudley Buck and George E. Whiting. There seems to have been no "juvenile prodigy" element in Chadwick's life, in spite of his strong love for music. He was a clerk in his father's insurance office for three years, — 1873–76. Yet his musical studies went bravely on, and Eugene Thayer became his organ-instructor to such good purpose that at this time he did such feats as playing several of Bach's greatest organ fugues from memory, besides composing in the small forms and even essaying small orchestral compositions as well as a couple of overtures and two piano trios.

His father opposed his musical tendencies as likely to be quite unremunerative; and this was the most discouraging period of the composer's life. He was compelled to drudge along in a business for which he had not an iota of inclination; no further money was allowed for musical tuition, and there seemed no prospects for the future. At last, taking a bold step, the young man of twenty-two went to a college in the pretty town of Olivet, in Michigan, and there began a professional career. This was brief, for it only lasted a year, but in that time, by teaching organ, piano, and harmony, by conducting a large chorus, and by giving a series of organ concerts, the young Chadwick saved enough money to go to Leipsic in 1877 and begin his first thorough study of composition. His teachers there were Reinecke and Jadassohn, the latter taking a most friendly interest in the young genius who was so bravely battling against odds. The writer has Jadassohn's personal assurance that Chadwick, the young American, was the most brilliant student in his class.

At this time Chadwick wrote much, his "Rip Van Winkle" overture and two string quartettes being publicly performed at the *Prüfung* of 1879. He even made sketches for a symphony. He soon left Leipsic for Munich, where he entered the Royal School of Music, being among the first American pupils of Rheinberger (we shall find many famous Americans there a little later) and studying score-reading and conducting with Abel. Meanwhile the score of the "Rip Van Winkle" overture had been sent to Boston and performed at the Harvard Symphony concerts, where it made a fine impression, showing that one more American was entering the higher fields of music.

In the spring of 1880 Chadwick returned to Boston, and in May of that year he conducted the "Rip Van Winkle" overture at a Handel and Haydn festival. In 1880 he became a teacher at the New England Conservatory of Music, and since that time he has dwelt in Boston. In 1897 he became musical director of the

above-named conservatory, and the broad curriculum of that institution, especially the orchestral, operatic, and chorus work, are
chiefly due to his personal efforts.

Such versatility is difficult to classify in a history of this character. Chadwick might be spoken of under the head of " Organists,"
" Conductors," or " Teachers," and some of the musicians spoken
of under these heads might also be described, fairly, as " Composers."
Mr. Chadwick has succeeded in each of these capacities. As an
organist he has held position at the South Congregational Church,
in Boston, and has had many other prominent posts, yet, in spite of
his early efforts in this direction, he has not made this his chief aim
except as a vehicle for musical composition. As a teacher he has
had remarkable success, and some of his pupils have become leaders
in the American musical advance. Horatio W. Parker, Arthur
Whiting, J. Wallace Goodrich, and Henry K. Hadley were each
and all students under Mr. Chadwick's guidance. His method is
by no means a conservative one. He says: " I believe in a sound
contrapuntal education, *then* as much harmonic breadth as possible.
I believe in form, but not in formality." Such a teacher is broad
enough to perceive the greatness of every school from Bach or
Palestrina to Wagner or Richard Strauss. Chadwick's harmony
book is the result of his own methods of teaching. He always
regrets that he could not have taken lessons from Cesar Franck,
for whom he has a profound esteem.

As a conductor Chadwick was one of the earliest Americans to
make a record, after Professor Paine, and, by coincidence, his
career as a conductor began with Paine's " Œdipus " at the Globe
Theatre in Boston and at Booth's Theatre in New York, in 1881;
before this he had only conducted his own " Rip Van Winkle "
overture, in America. For seven years he was conductor of the
Boston Orchestral Club; from 1889, for ten years, he led the Spring-
field (Massachusetts) music festivals, and here he brought out
Beethoven's Ninth Symphony and many more modern works. He
was conductor of the Worcester Festival for four years, leading,
among other great works, Berlioz's " Damnation of Faust " and the
first performance in English of Franck's " Beatitudes." At one of
these festivals he also brought out his own sacred opera of " Judith."

As a composer Chadwick is to be reckoned as the equal of any one on this side of the Atlantic. His "Rip Van Winkle" overture was recognized at once as rivalling any American composition of its time. In 1880, therefore, there were only two prominent orchestral composers in America, — Chadwick and Paine.

Without attempting a catalogue of Chadwick's compositions, which extend into every field of music, we may examine a few details of those works on which his reputation chiefly rests. He

FIG. 50. — MANUSCRIPT BY GEORGE W. CHADWICK.

has always been the foremost composer of overtures in America. In "Rip Van Winkle," he holds well to classical form, as was to be expected in a score submitted as a graduation work in a German conservatory. His "Thalia" and "Melpomene" overtures are finer works and are true concert overtures, giving the spirit of comedy and of tragedy, without becoming programme music — *i.e.* instrumental music attempting to tell a definite story. To hold to the proper sonata-form without becoming rigid, is one of Chadwick's great gifts; he has reconciled the symmetrical form with modern passion.

Especially is this the case with his concert overture, "Adonais."
It is astonishing how much the American composers have been
attracted by Keats. With Chadwick it was the threnody which
Shelley sang to the memory of Keats that inspired the musical
work. Not that it becomes in any degree programme music, — it
is too subjective for that; but it gives the mood of the poet, the
brooding over loss, the *Weltschmerz*, that is in the poem. The
thought of Shelley, that one learns in suffering what one teaches
in song, is carried out. Noble music is too often the offspring of
sorrow, and in this overture we have

"the Pard-like spirit, beautiful and swift,"

harried and pursued by relentless fate until

"Life, like a dome of many-colored glass,
Stains the white radiance of eternity."

There is Hellenic dignity in this work and in the "Melpomene"
overture that is like the portrayal of an Orestes pursued by the
Furies, a Euripidean picture of human helplessness.

It speaks well for Chadwick that, while able to portray the
tragic, he has also a bright sense of the humorous. In his second
symphony these two contrasted phases lie side by side; the
second movement is full of jollity, while the third presents dignity,
loftiness, double counterpoint, and science in combination. In
this work there is continuity of thematic material in the last two
movements, and in a return of the opening thought at the close
of it all.

Chadwick has composed three symphonies. He himself considers that his real "pace" was begun with the second, in B flat.
In this work one may also find the first real effort of an American
composer to utilize the only folk-song which our country possesses,
— the music of the South, the themes of the plantation. This
occurs in the Scherzo, the second movement, spoken of above.
And it may be remembered that this work was composed long
before Dvořák came to America and began the same quest.
The third symphony, in F, though less characteristic, shows much

facility in scoring.   Thus much for the orchestral works, which have been performed in the Boston Symphony concerts alone more than twenty times.

In chamber-music Chadwick has achieved the best that America can show to-day.   His piano quintette, in E flat, is a work of highest rank, and his latest string quartette is not only noble in development, but beautiful in melody.   In all of his large works he deserves laudation for avoiding the demon of cacophony which has run rampant in some of the modern music.   Many of the recent American composers seem to have adopted all the faults of Wagner and assimilated none of his great merits.

Naturally such a composer shines forth well in the vocal forms. If any proof were necessary that Chadwick combines tune with his classicism, it would be furnished by the fact that he has written a comic opera — " Tabasco " — that won a decided popular success, one of its tunes (the march) having been whistled all over the country. But a higher application of the vocal gifts can be found in the composer's " Phœnix Expirans " and the " Lily Nymph," two cantatas much used by choral societies.

The most ambitious work of all is Chadwick's " Judith," which is a sacred opera, and was intended for performance upon the stage, but has thus far been given as an oratorio, upon the concert platform. In this work the composer shows his most modern tendencies, even using the *leit-motif*, but with far more conservatism than is found in the Wagner operas.   The composer calls the work "a lyric drama," but it is a good guide-post on the path that is being taken by the twentieth-century oratorio.   Splendid contrasts occur between the religious loftiness of the old Hebrews (chiefly broad chorales or contrapuntal choruses) and the brutal sensuality of the Assyrians, expressed in dances or in bombastic marches.   A combination of these two elements, in the second part, gives a most skilful display of the composer's ability; and the simultaneous presentation of the sighs of the prisoners and the laughter of their conquerors is supported with some of the most graphic orchestration imaginable. There is one well-developed fugue in the work, and other fugal and canonic passages.   The love-scenes are somewhat too long, and will probably demand pruning if the work is to be given upon the stage.

The end of the second act, with the cry of " All's Well," given by the receding sentinel, is a masterful touch.

Chadwick's songs are not equal (possibly he has written too many of them), and yet some of them are among the best of American lyrics. His " Allah" (a noble conception), " Bedouin Love-song," " The Lily," the " Two Folk-songs," and many others might be cited as comparable with the best German *Lieder.* The piano compositions are not important, but there are some skilful works for organ, especially some studies of canon, that deserve mention. Chadwick received the honorary degree of M.A. from Yale University in 1897. See supplementary chapter for later works.

Horatio William Parker (Pl. VI), or Horatio Parker (for he has dropped the middle name), was born at Auburndale, a suburb of Boston, September 15, 1863. His family was originally an English one, and his ancestors came to America in 1635. His father, Charles E. Parker, was a distinguished architect, and many prominent edifices throughout New England are monuments to his skill. Parker's musical talents were undoubtedly inherited from his mother, who was for a time the organist of Grace Church, in Newton, Massachusetts, and is a lady of considerable literary attainments. The libretto of the composer's " Hora Novissima" was translated from the Latin by her, and the librettos of " The Holy Child" and " St. Christopher" have come from her pen. As a child the young Horatio disliked music; he enjoyed literature, and gave evidence of excellent gifts of memory by repeating poems when he was but five years old, but all of his mother's efforts could not awaken any musical enthusiasm in the boy.

At the age of fourteen, however, a sudden change seemed to come over the lad in the matter of musical appreciation. His mother says: " In October, 1877, Horatio suddenly began to take great interest in music, to ask all sorts of questions about it, and to spend literally whole days at the piano, beginning at daylight, and stopping only when his father sent him to bed, perhaps at 11 P.M. From this time onwards he had but one object. Sports and recreation were left out of his life, and the necessary education was with great difficulty imparted in the intervals of music study." [1]

[1] Quoted from the London *Musical Times,* September 1, 1902.

His mother gave him his first piano lessons. He began to compose at this time, without, however, being trained in the science. He was not daunted by lack of knowledge, but is said to have set fifty of Kate Greenaway's poems to music in two days, with good melody and sufficient accompaniment. His mother also taught him the organ, and at sixteen he became organist at St. Paul's Church in Dedham (Massachusetts), and later at St. John's Church, Roxbury (Boston). He began his studies in harmony with Stephen A. Emery, the gentle musician who did such constant pedagogic service at the New England Conservatory of Music. He also studied piano with John Orth. Finally he began studying composition with Mr. Chadwick, who laid a thorough foundation, and then sent the lad of eighteen to his own old teacher, Rheinberger (Fig. 51), in Munich. Parker studied three years with the famous contrapuntist, and Rheinberger seemed to regard him as a favorite pupil. His organ technique, thanks to his mother, was sufficiently good for Rheinberger to intrust him with the solo part in his

FIG. 51. — JOSEF RHEINBERGER.

organ concerto (in F) at a public performance in Munich. At this time, too, several of Parker's own compositions were performed by the orchestra of the Royal Music School, of which Rheinberger was the inspector, and these received very favorable notices from the Munich press.

Returning to the United States, in 1885, the young man of twenty-two at once found occupation. He became director of music at St. Paul's and St. Mary's schools, at Garden City, Long Island, near New York, and soon was appointed organist at St. Andrew's Church, in Harlem (New York) where he directed a boy choir. He left this to become organist and director of the Church of the Holy Trinity, New York, and then became one of the faculty of Mrs. Thurber's "National" Conservatory, being for some years

N

teacher of counterpoint in that institution.   In May, 1893, he was appointed organist and musical director of Trinity Church, in Boston. The next year, 1894, he accepted the professorship of music at Yale University.   The chair of music was founded at Yale, in 1893, through the donation of Robbins Battell, an alumnus of the university.   Mr. Parker was its second occupant, and has held the position from 1894 to the present time.   He has received the honorary degree of M.A. from his university.

As regards the music course at Yale, it is largely upon the lines of the curriculum of Harvard University; but, as New Haven has not the orchestral facilities of Boston, Professor Parker has extended his work somewhat to meet this deficiency.   He teaches harmony, counterpoint, and composition, as Professor Paine does at Harvard, and also gives lectures on the history of music; but besides this he teaches a class in orchestral scoring, and conducts orchestral concerts every year.   The university supports the orchestra as a proper adjunct to its music course, and, to make the connection still closer, one concert each season is devoted to the performance of orchestral compositions by Yale students.   These concerts are not mere college functions; the public is permitted to attend, but, in order to make the occasions as educational as possible, Professor Parker prefaces the orchestral work with a short lecture, analyzing the compositions and playing the different themes and figures upon the piano.   As was the case in Harvard, the accommodations of the music department were soon outgrown.   At present a large concert hall has been erected (it is called Woolsey Hall), and there is soon to be a building devoted exclusively to musical studies, a memorial to Albert A. Sprague, a graduate of 1859.

Parker's compositions extend into every kind of musical work from symphonies and oratorios to piano pieces and songs.   He is less impassioned than MacDowell, less poetically melodic and dramatic than Chadwick, but he has created dignified contrapuntal works which not only hold high rank in America, but have compelled the highest respect abroad.   We append a list of Parker's works as an example of the versatility of the American composer (for similar lists might be shown to the credit of all the five men whom we have classed as the tone-masters of America).

OP.

1. The Shepherd Boy. Male chorus.
2. Five part-songs.
3. Psalm 23. Female chorus, organ, and harp.
4. Concert overture in E flat.
5. Regulus. Overture in A.
6. Ballad of a Knight and his Daughter.
7. Symphony in C minor.
8. King Trojan. Ballad for chorus and orchestra.
9. Five pieces for pianoforte.
10. Three love-songs for a tenor voice.
11. String quartette in F (MS.).
12. Venetian overture in B flat (MS.).
13. Scherzo in G minor. Orchestra (MS.).
14. Blow, thou Winter Wind. Male chorus.
15. Idylle (Goethe). Cantata.
16. Ballad of the Normans. Chorus (MS.).
17. Four organ pieces. (Set 1.)
18. Morning and evening service in E.
19. Four pieces for pianoforte.
20. Four organ pieces. (Set 2.)
21. The Kobolds. Chorus and orchestra.
22. Three sacred songs.
23. Six lyrics for pianoforte.
24. Six songs.
25. Two love-songs.
26. Harold Harfager. Chorus and orchestra.
27. Two choruses for female voices.
28. Four organ pieces. (Set 3.)
29. Overture to Count Robert of Paris (MS.).

OP.

30. Hora Novissima. Cantata.
31. The Dream King and his Love. Cantata. Prize composition.
32. Five organ pieces.
33. Six choruses for male voices.
34. Three songs.
35. Suite for violin, pianoforte, and violoncello (MS.).
36. Four organ pieces.
37. The Holy Child. Christmas cantata.
38. Quintette for strings in D minor (MS.).
39. Four choruses for male voices.
40. Cáhal Mór of the Wine-red Hand. Baritone solo and orchestra (MS.).
41. Suite for violin and pianoforte (MS.).
42. Ode for Commencement.
43. The Legend of St. Christopher.
44.
45. Adstant Angelorum Chori (*a capella*). Prize composition.
46. A Northern Ballad, for orchestra (MS.).
47. Six old English songs.
48. Choruses for male voices.
49. Three pieces for pianoforte.
50. A Wanderer's Psalm. Cantus Peregrinus.
51.
52. Three songs.
53. A Greek ode, for chorus and orchestra, for the celebration of Yale Bicentennial, 1901.
54. A star song, for solo, quartette, chorus, and orchestra.
55. Organ concerto — organ and full orchestra.

(For most important later works, see supplementary chapter.)

"Hora Novissima," a setting of the old poem of Bernard de Morlaix, is one of the most important works that America has yet produced. It was fitting that, in such a subject, the composer should reproduce some of the intricacy and asceticism of the old school of pure counterpoint, and that he should sometimes introduce the unaccompanied vein (*a capella*) of the ancient composers. The work was completed in 1893, and was first performed by the New York Church Choral Society, in the Church of the Holy Trinity, in New York. The fugal writing in the work is of the most praiseworthy character, and such numbers as " Pars Mea " and " Urbs Syon Unica " show that Mr. Parker drinks deeply at the Palestrinian spring. " Hora Novissima " has been performed repeatedly by the Handel and Haydn Society, and once at the Worcester (England) Festival, where it was conducted by the composer. This last-named performance took place in 1899, and is memorable as being the first English musical festival at which the work of an American composer was presented. Such a success was won that Parker was commissioned to compose a work for the Hereford Festival of 1900, for which he furnished "A Wanderer's Psalm." Since then England has most cordially received " The Legend of St. Christopher," — one of the most fluent and attractive on the above list. The pure style of "Jam sol recedit" of this cantata, or oratorio, is an exhibition of Parker at his very best. The fugue — " Quoniam tu solus " — shows him at his contrapuntal height. It has one peculiar vocal defect (like Handel's " Unto us a Child is Born "), which is that its short phrases too often end on *s*, which, in a chorus, causes an incredible amount of hissing. Better, however, that the hissing should come from the singers than from the audience, and the fugue, *per se*, is an excellent specimen of the best American work in this school. It has a subject somewhat like that of Bach's fugue in D major (" Well-tempered Clavichord," Book II, No. 5), finely developed both in a direct and an inverted manner, and there is very ingenious stretto treatment.

It is in such touches as these in " St. Christopher " that Parker is greatest; he is less so when he deals with such a fiery subject as a picture of the infernal regions and the cohorts of Satan. Although he pictures hell as full of syncopations and diminished seventh chords, and the chromatic progressions lead to a tonal jungle where none but expert singers can find the path, Satan (accompanied by castagnettes and glockenspiel, instead of piccolo) is not quite as convincing as the pious hermit with his serene and rather Gothic sacred music.

FIG. 52. — THE ALLEN A. BROWN ROOM, BOSTON PUBLIC LIBRARY.
The largest musical collection in America.

The organ concerto, named last upon the above list, is an interesting work, but not as practical as it might be. Organ concertos are rare, but the Frenchmen, Widor, St. Saëns, and Guilmant, have managed to unite orchestra and organ without making a *mésalliance*. Mr. Parker follows the Rheinberger solidity rather than the Gallic grace in this work. He banishes the woodwind as being too near the organ color, and causes the harp and the solo violin to become the foils to his chief instrument. The second movement shows much ingenuity, particularly in the introduction of some bizarre kettledrum effects, and the finale is again the display of the skilful contrapuntist.

Much of Mr. Parker's work is music for musicians; his rather ascetic, somewhat undramatic, style can scarcely appeal strongly to the masses, — which is a failing that leans to virtue's side. At his best he is a really great composer (least so, perhaps, in songs or piano pieces), but the copiousness of his writing hardly does justice to the loftier numbers of his repertoire. He has received a most remarkable compliment for an American musician, the honorary degree of Mus. Doc. from Cambridge University, England.

Earnest, dramatic, passionate, and romantic, Edward Alexander MacDowell (Pl. V) was most powerful in just the field where Parker is least strong. The training of MacDowell served to nourish just those qualities which were to a certain degree innate, with the most fortunate results. He was born in New York, December 18, 1861, and his best and chief teacher was the tropical and fiery Teresa Carreño. To her he dedicated his Second Piano Concerto. But many other teachers contributed to equip this most dashing of American composers. He went to Paris in 1876, and enrolled himself in the conservatory there, studying theory with Savard, and piano under Marmontel. In 1879 he went to Wiesbaden, where he studied with Ehlert for a time. Then to Frankfort, where Karl Heymann taught him piano and, best of all, Joachim Raff guided him in composition. This was the chief influence in the career of MacDowell, for Raff taught him routine work as no other could have done, and it was too late for the elegant vein of Raff to import effeminacy into the virile style of his pupil.

Possibly because the two were opposites in their natures they became friends, and, through the influence of Raff, MacDowell became a prominent piano teacher in the conservatory at Darmstadt, when he was but twenty years of age. Liszt soon recognized the genius of the young American, and obtained a hearing for his first piano suite before the leading society of Germany. There followed three years of concert touring, and then, in 1884, MacDowell settled down to teaching in Wiesbaden. In 1888 he came to Boston, where he taught and composed, giving concerts occasionally, with great success. Princeton University soon conferred upon him the degree of Mus. Doc. and, in 1896, MacDowell was called to the chair of music in Columbia University, New York. Here he followed in the path which Paine had originated at Harvard and which Parker was treading at Yale. He resigned this professorship, however, in 1904, and was succeeded by a Dane — Cornelius Rübner.

MacDowell is more radical than many of his contemporaries, but he was so well endowed with vigorous ideas that this becomes decidedly more of a virtue than a fault. Naturally the continental countries of Europe appreciate his works more keenly than the English, the latter having been educated in a rather precise school of musical conservatism which is only at present beginning to thaw out. On May 14, 1903, he made his appearance before the London Philharmonic Society, by invitation, playing his Second Concerto. This work, dedicated to Teresa Carreño, was played by her at the Crystal Palace popular concerts, three years before the composer performed it in London.[1] Before this England had become fairly familiar with some of MacDowell's songs, and with his beautiful " Indian Suite." The concerto, which we value as one of the best of the composer's works (yet do not rank with the First Concerto), won a popular triumph under Dr. F. H. Cowen's direction, but it set the critics by the ears at once. To cause heated discussion is generally the proof of individuality in music, and the English re-viewers could not grasp the boldness of MacDowell as they had comprehended the counterpoint of Parker. Some found traces of Brahms in the concerto! They might better have discovered indica-tions of MacDowell's Scottish ancestry in it. Others found touches of " Parsifal"; others discovered Tschaikowsky. The utter lack of unanimity of judgment showed that the reviewers were face to face with a modern whom they could not fully comprehend.

Yet MacDowell was not iconoclastic. He had been trained too thoroughly by Raff to become formless, but he applied the old forms with a new spirit; he modernized, and was far removed from pedantry. The reviewers of London were unanimous in praise of his piano playing, and he certainly stood in the front rank of American artists in this field. As a teacher, too, he has been an inspiration to many students, and this part of his work has been of great importance to the development of piano playing in America.

But it is as one of the tone-masters of America that MacDowell stands forth most prominent in our musical history, — one of those American composers who first won recognition for American music of classical form in Europe. It is no doubt too early to give a full judgment of the value of MacDowell's work. Some excellent reviewers have gone, perhaps, to extreme lengths in their praise

[1] MacDowell's First Concerto has been heard in Amsterdam, Dresden, and a number of other European cities ; in fact, all of his large works have been heard in Europe.

of his compositions. Henry T. Finck, in his "Songs and Song-writers," places MacDowell with the very greatest of the world in his *Lieder*. One may, however, dissent from this opinion because, even when the musical thought expressed is noble, the songs are often instrumental rather than vocal in their spirit. Rupert Hughes, in his "Contemporary American Composers," states: —

"An almost unanimous vote would grant him rank as the

FIG. 53. — THE NEW ENGLAND CONSERVATORY OF MUSIC.

greatest of American composers, while not a few ballots would indicate him as the best of living music writers."

The French have a saying, "*Il n'est plus lourd fardeau qu'un grand nom acquis trop tôt!*" One must not forget Chadwick's Second Symphony and his fine overtures, Paine's "Œdipus" and "Azara," and Parker's "Hora Novissima," in passing judgment on the value of MacDowell's works. Yet one can grow enthusiastic easily enough over the juiciness, the romance, the originality of this great composer. He was, thank Heaven, not a cacophonist. In the midst of all his freedom of development and his most fiery moods he did not turn to musical ugliness as a necessary adjunct of modern composition; he did not strain for uncouth progressions, nor purchase his originality at the expense of sanity.

To us his "Indian Suite" is one of the best examples of his art. He has built this orchestral work on actual Indian themes, but we .do not value this proceeding, since the figures used are utterly unfamiliar to almost every auditor, and do not, of themselves, suggest anything national; the composer could evolve a hundred original figures, equally effective, if he wished to do so. But the development and the treatment of these figures is another story. We find here a poetic presentation of phases of Indian life that is equal to anything ever evolved from this subject; and, as this life exists (or has existed) nowhere but in America, this work becomes our own in a double sense. The composition presents a wide scope of emotion, from the exquisite tenderness of a "love-song" to the fierce exposition of the panoply of war, with galloping of horses and cries of warriors. One can also pay tribute to MacDowell's scoring, although he does not try to attain modern extremes here either; he achieves the fitness that characterizes Tschaikowsky rather than the extreme difficulties and complexities which too often mar the modern orchestral web. The expressive tone-coloring of the dirge and the powerful use of the woodwind in the third movement of the suite may be referred to in illustrating our meaning. The welding together of the piano with the orchestral forces, in the two concertos, is further evidence of the ability of the composer in this direction.

One sometimes finds evidence of MacDowell's Scottish forefathers in his songs, and he has won, perhaps, his best results in setting poems by Burns. Mr. Finck thus speaks of some of the vocal works:[1] —

"Were I asked to name the two greatest living song-writers, I should say Edvard Grieg and Edward MacDowell. There is a certain affinity between these two composers, traceable, no doubt, to their Scotch ancestry. Grieg and Wagner are the only composers whose influence can be distinctly traced here and there in MacDowell's songs, but it is no more than a harmonic atmosphere which he

[1] "Songs and Song-writers," p. 238.

breathes in common with them when he gets into certain emotional spheres. His ideas are always his own, and there are plenty of them. . . . MacDowell is undoubtedly a genius."

In piano composition MacDowell was first among his contemporaries. Not only has he composed some very graceful works in the smaller forms, but he has also written sonatas which have indicated what the twentieth-century composers must do with the old form if they wish to perpetuate it.

It will thus be seen that MacDowell succeeded in three different directions, — orchestral composition, piano works, and songs. Yet the future only can reveal what place this most individual of American composers is to occupy permanently. That it is to be a high one there can be no manner of doubt; that much has been demonstrated already. As against the very contradictory English criticisms above spoken of, it may be stated that Massenet, in Paris, spoke of MacDowell's concerto with great enthusiasm. He has fairly won all the important European critics and musicians to his music. An anecdote connected with his First Concerto may serve to show how a great pianist and brother-composer appreciated him. Eugen d'Albert, the noted pianist, had taken Mac-Dowell to one of Liszt's afternoon receptions in Weimar, at which the modest young American musician began, as the French say, to " efface himself," according to his wont. But d'Albert had other things in view than MacDowell's self-effacement. He was begged to perform to the assembled company, and, seating himself at the pianoforte, announced that he would play something entirely new, that existed as yet only in manuscript. He then proceeded to play the first movement of MacDowell's First Pianoforte Concerto, which was received with enthusiastic acclamations, everybody present naturally thinking the composition must be his own. Liszt was especially delighted. When the expressions of admiration had in a measure subsided, d'Albert quietly pointed to MacDowell as the real composer of the novelty.

There is one point (a minor one) on which one may disagree with MacDowell: he wrote almost all of his expression and tempo-marks *in English*. It is no affectation that causes most musicians (Wagner, Schumann, and Berlioz excepted) to use Italian terms.

Music has become almost a universal language; its written form (notation) is more wide-spread than any other. We must not localize such a universal tongue by writing its signs in the vernacular. By priority of usage Italian should be the language attached to music. Beethoven himself gave up the German language, after trying it one year in this connection, and returned to the use of Italian for expression and tempo-marks. A MacDowell piano work, for example, could be understood in every European country; but his mark — "Slow and with much feeling" — would mean nothing to a dozen nations which would have comprehended "*Lento e con molto espressione!*" In his "Indian Suite" this is obviated by the use of German, English, and French (with Italian also used for expression marks), but his shorter works are not thus supplied.

Inspiration drawn from the poets is not lacking in MacDowell's work. Indeed, at one time he thought of taking up poetry instead of music. "Lancelot and Elaine" is an orchestral outcome of Tennyson's poem. "Hamlet" and "Ophelia" are two orchestral poems direct from Shakespeare.

The end of this great composer was most pathetic. His work had been constant and conscientious, but it was too severe for his mind, and symptoms of mental aberration gradually appeared. His was the fate of Schumann, of Smetana, and of Hugo Wolf. But his disease did not lead to violence. He became as a simple child, and he died in New York, Jan. 23, 1908. At Peterborough, New Hampshire, where he often worked, his compositions are given annually as a memorial service.

In selecting five names as the chief composers of this country, we must acknowledge the verdict but a temporary one, for there are other composers who have rivalled their work in this or that separate performance; and there are important symphonies, operas, and chamber-music to be mentioned later in connection with other men and women. Our reasons for the selection are many. These five were the first to write worthy compositions in the classical forms in America. They were the first to achieve a transatlantic reputation. They were the first to win successes in all the different fields of musical creation, as, with the exception of Chopin, all the great masters of music have done.   And these five names (up to the present time) have appeared far more frequently upon the programmes of our symphonic concerts than any others.   Four of the five have also been important factors in public musical education, Paine being the head of musical training at Harvard, Chadwick at the New England Conservatory of Music (Fig. 53), Parker at Yale, and MacDowell at Columbia.   The fifth man, Mr. Arthur Foote, has employed his excellent abilities as a teacher only in a private capacity thus far.

Arthur Foote (Fig. 54) was born at Salem, Massachusetts, March 5, 1853.   He first studied composition with Stephen A. Emery, in Boston.   Entering Harvard, he took the classical course and graduated with the class of 1874, but remained to study music in Paine's department (before the professorial chair was established), and obtained the degree of A.M. for his work here, in 1875. After this he studied organ with B. J. Lang, who has educated many of the leading American musicians, as will be seen later.   Foote became organist of the First Unitarian Church in Boston, in 1878, and has held that post ever since.   He teaches piano and composition in Boston.

FIG. 54. — ARTHUR FOOTE.

Foote has little of that dramatic force which one finds in the works of Chadwick and MacDowell; he charms rather by grace and ease and by his easy leading of voices in contrapuntal passages.   Naturally therefore, in such a work as " The Wreck of the Hesperus," he falls short of one's ideal.   On the contrary, in his suite for orchestra in D minor (Op. 36) he equals any composer of this form — even Franz Lachner, its modern progenitor. This suite must not be confounded with his suite for string orchestra, in D major (Op. 21).   The last named, although graceful, symmetrical, and well-constructed, is not to be compared with the greater suite, which is for full — very full — orchestra. In the D minor suite, piccolo, English horn, trombones, tuba, triangle, and harp appear, over and above the regular forces, and the large orchestra is handled with an ease and beauty that is very attractive. The work has been given more than once by the Boston Symphony Orchestra, and ought to take high rank in the standard repertoire of native orchestral compositions.

The dramatic cantatas are less inspired. In the "Wreck of the Hesperus," for example, the chorus repeat the unimportant words, "The Hesperus," in contrapuntal manner until the dramatic effect is entirely lost. In another similarly vigorous topic, the "Skeleton in Armor," we find the same fault, a display of counterpoint where terse directness is required. The sentiments of the viking (at once suggesting a baritone or tenor robusto solo) are given to chorus and quartette. There is not an iota of difference between the triumphant "Skoal to the Northland! Skoal!" and the prosaic "Thus the Tale Ended!" The "Corsair's Crew" are too suave and well bred for actual sea-rovers, and the hero himself is a contrapuntal and gentlemanly viking. The other excellent contrapuntist, Horatio Parker, met with similar musical shipwreck upon the Arctic seas in his orchestral "Northern Song."

Foote's string quartette (Op. 4) and his piano quintette (Op. 36) have both been performed with great success by the Kneisel Quartette and other string organizations. The latter has a folk-song element that is especially effective. His "Francesca di Rimini," held by some to be his greatest work, is not as convincing to us as the above-mentioned suite; it is too reserved for the anguished tale which Tschaikowsky and Liszt have told so well. His overture, "In the Mountains," is a fine work, and his pianoforte trio in C minor has won success both in America and in England, this and other of his works having been played at the Monday popular concerts in London. He has also won decided success with his songs, and his "Irish Folk-Song" is a gem in its way, and deserves its great popularity. Foote's piano quartette in C is held by some musicians to be the best example of his chamber music; it is a scholarly rather than an impassioned work.

Among Foote's larger works of especial power we may mention a sonata for violin and piano (Op. 20, G minor) which has been played successfully in England, a serenade for string orchestra (Op. 25), and a remarkably skilful motet for mixed chorus, "Vita nostra plena Bellis," which has been sung by our chief choral societies. All together Mr. Foote is a conservative and classical composer who never has written anything trivial or unworthy.

Foote's orchestral suites have a dignity and an easy leading of the voices, that place them in the front rank of American compositions. He has also orchestrated some of his piano works, notably four tone-pictures derived from "Omar Khayyam." These show a romantic style which differs from his earlier music and show that the composer is still advancing in his work.

PLATE VI

HORATIO PARKER

CHAPTER IX

THE ORCHESTRAL COMPOSERS OF AMERICA

In classifying the many well-known names which follow, there has been an endeavor to give prominence to the chief feature of the work of each composer. Thus, for examples, although Dudley Buck won his laurels in organ composition, and has written an orchestral overture, yet his fame rests chiefly upon his cantatas, and he will be spoken of in the chapter devoted to such forms; Walter Damrosch has composed in almost every branch of music, yet his most prominent compositions have been operatic ones, and we shall speak of his other works in connection with that school of creation. Almost all of the American composers of rank have done more or less orchestral work, but the men now to be passed in review have achieved their chief laurels in this field.

Henry K. Hadley (Fig. 55) was born in Somerville, Massachusetts, in 1871, and is one of the strongest of the American composers who are attempting the large forms. His father was a prominent musician in Somerville and was certainly one of the most efficient of instructors in the public school music of that city. The younger Hadley, after some instruction from his father, studied harmony with Stephen A. Emery, of Boston, counterpoint and composition with George W. Chadwick, and violin with Charles N. Allen. Under Mr. Chadwick's guidance he advanced far enough to complete an orchestral overture and a string quartette, before he was twenty-one years of age. At twenty-three he went to Vienna and studied further with Mandyczewski, and here he wrote several orchestral works, including an excellent suite — his third work in this form. In 1896 he was again in America, at Garden City, Long Island. Soon after this he was operatic conductor in Germany, then orchestral conductor at Seattle, and after this (1911–14) became symphonic conductor at San Francisco.

He now entered into the symphonic field, writing two symphonies which are virile and powerful in a high degree. The stamp of Seidl's approval certainly means a great deal, and that conductor produced a Hadley symphony a year before his death. His Third Suite also had the honor of performance by the American Symphony Orchestra, under Franko. A festival march, a heroic overture, a cantata, and a number of songs indicate that the young composer is at present very active. One may pay the sincerest tribute to Hadley's music in its freedom from morbidness and excessive dissonances. He has advanced amazingly in recent years. His symphonic poems " Salome " and " The Culprit Fay " are most worthy compositions. A symphony " The Four Seasons " is becoming rapidly famous. His " Youth and Life " symphony is very effective. His symphony " North, East, South, and West " is full of strong contrasts. All together, Henry K. Hadley is the most promising of the younger American composers.

The name of Van der Stucken scarcely indicates an American, and the wearer of it is of Belgian descent (German on his mother's side), yet Frank van der Stucken (Fig. 102) was born in Fredericksburg, Gillespie County, Texas, October 15, 1858. In spite of the fact that much of his life was spent abroad, he has worked in this country to such good purpose that he certainly ought to be classed with Americans, according to his birthright. The father was a captain of Texas cavalry, in the Confederate army during the Civil War, who went to Europe after the defeat of the Southern cause. In Antwerp the son studied under Peter Benoit, and he lived in Europe from 1866 until 1884. The thoroughness of his compositions may be judged by some of the honors that were paid him during his European career. He became *Kapellmeister* of the Stadt Theatre of Breslau; in Antwerp his music was sung in the churches and a ballet performed in the theatre; Grieg wrote enthusiastically of his songs; Liszt, in 1883, was his sponsor when he gave a concert of his own compositions in Weimar, and in 1891 he was invited to give a similar concert in Antwerp.

It was in 1884 that Van der Stucken became conductor of the Arion Male Chorus of New York. In 1892 he took this society on a tour through Europe, showing the foreign critics something of the standard of vocal execution among organizations in this country. He conducted novelty concerts and other symphonic concerts in New York, 1885–88, and was the first orchestral conductor to give a concert entirely made up of "American compositions"—not the most judicious thing in the world to do, with all the repertoire of the world from which to choose. What was far better than this, he frequently placed American compositions on his regular programmes, when our composers stood the test of comparison with the masters of the old world. Nevertheless it must stand to his credit that he gave a concert of American compositions at the Paris Exposition of 1889, and several other exclusively American concerts in different cities.

From 1891 to 1894 he did good work for the German male choruses in America, establishing festivals and training large masses of singers. In 1895 he became conductor of the Cincinnati Symphony Orchestra, and in 1897 dean of the Cincinnati College of Music, retiring from the latter post in 1903. Therefore it is not only as composer that Van der Stucken deserves notice, but as conductor, teacher, and propagandist as well.

FIG. 55.— HENRY K. HADLEY.

As orchestral writer Van der Stucken is decidedly modern. He deals with an orchestra of the largest proportions, and some of his scores (the revision of the symphonic prologue, " William Ratcliffe," for example) are as complex and as highly colored as even the Richard Strauss phantasmagoria. His great work, a symphonic prologue entitled " Pax Triumphans," has been performed in Hanover and Brunswick with great success. On American soil there is only one composer who can equal the skill with which he draws highly spiced effects from the ultra-modern orchestra, — Charles M. Loeffler, — of whom hereafter.

Van der Stucken's breadth of treatment is well shown in his " William Ratcliffe," a symphonic prologue, which represents the

o

composer in his most modern guise.   Heine's tragedy, on which this
is founded, is lugubrious enough to require a Tschaikowsky in its
darker moods.   In the play McGregor kills Edward Ratcliffe, Fair
Betty dies of grief, Ratcliffe kills two suitors for the hand of Maria,
and winds up the cheerful proceedings by killing McGregor, Maria,
and himself.   Two ghosts also appear at intervals to add to the
blitheness of the plot.   Here is the orchestra employed by the composer: piccolo, two flutes, two oboes, two English horns, two clarinets, a bass clarinet, two bassoons, a double bassoon, four horns, two
cornets, two trumpets, three trombones, a bass tuba, a pair of kettledrums, triangle, a snare-drum, cymbals, a bass drum, gong, two bells,
two harps, a pianoforte, and the usual forces of stringed instruments.
Add to this that the composer blends cornets and trumpets, *à la*
Berlioz, that he employs a bass-drum trill, *à la* Verdi (and Berlioz
does this also), that there are guiding motives as definite and as
freely used as in Wagner, that "fff" occurs many times and "ffff"
once, and the reader will readily comprehend that it is with a modern we are here dealing.

Van der Stucken has not attempted Scottish local color in this
work, and here he has been wise.   Only one to the manner born
can achieve the Scottish lilt; perhaps MacDowell, of all American
composers, does it best, because of his Scottish ancestry.   Even
the German composers, Beethoven, Schumann, Bruch, and Franz,
have failed to catch the Scottish style, and the lesser men have
stumbled over it, although Mendelssohn proved that a foreigner
could succeed in attaining it.

Van der Stucken gives a dignified picture of tragedy rather than
a local sketch; ghosts are ghosts the world over, and speak no
especial dialect.   Although the work is continuous, he has at least
outlined the character of the four-movement symphony, each division, however, being very freely treated.   It is programme music
(instrumental music telling a definite story) from first to last, and
has its printed synopsis.   Love idyl, destroyed happiness, catastrophe, lament, William's sorrows, the ghosts, another catastrophe,
retrospects, and general lamentations, — these are a few of the emo-
tions depicted in this sombre tale.   Not every one will sympathize
either with the subject or the ultra-modern treatment, but all will

unite in tribute to the composer's orchestral skill and to the grandeur of his climaxes.

We have spoken of Van der Stucken as the pupil of Benoit; but he had some guidance from Reinecke, Grieg, and Langer. It was not from these, however, that he gained his brilliancy of scoring and his employment of guiding motives; it was probably from Liszt, whose works he studied and with whom he was thrown in contact for a short period. Before this time he is somewhat more conservative, and, to our thinking, more beautiful. His music to Shakespeare's "Tempest," for example, which he wrote in Breslau before the Liszt-Grieg epoch, is a fine work of which any composer might be proud.

In his songs (Fig. 56) Van der Stucken is also very modern, working up great climaxes with much skill, yet in defiance of all conservative rules. He was for long the dominating musical influence of Cincinnati, and he restored to the city some of the prestige which it lost when Thomas went to Chicago. He was the chief composer in the West, before he departed for Europe.

But Chicago has also had its orchestral composer, and again we find a thorough New Englander achieving high rank in composition. Frederic Grant Gleason (Fig. 57) was born in Middletown, Connecticut, December 18, 1848, and his first studies were made with Dudley Buck, in Hartford, Connecticut, to which city his parents moved when Gleason was five years old. In 1869 he went to Germany to study in the higher branches of music. He studied in Berlin (not at the *Hoch-Schule*, as is sometimes stated) with Oscar Raif, C. F. Weitzmann, Albert Loeschhorn, and August Haupt, being a private pupil of these celebrities. He also studied at the Leipsic Conservatory under Moscheles, Plaidy, Richter, and Lobe. Returning to America, Gleason became organist of different churches in Connecticut until, in 1877, he was appointed teacher of piano, composition, and orchestration at the Hershey School in Chicago. From that time on he was a prominent pioneer in the cause of good music in the West.

With Mr. Gleason we again find an example of the versatility of the American in music. He became famous as a composer, but he also did yeoman service as a musical critic, being musical editor

of the *Chicago Tribune* from 1884 to 1889.   He exerted great influence as a teacher from 1877, when he was in the Hershey School,
and he was the director of a Chicago conservatory until nearly the
day of his death.   He was a member of the New York Manuscript
Society, almost from its organization; he was first president of the
Chicago Manuscript Society (these are societies for the encouragement of the American composer), and at the time of his death was
again its president, having been elected by a unanimous vote.   Mr.
Gleason died in Chicago, December 6, 1903.

The compositions of Gleason are many of them in the largest

FIG. 56. — MANUSCRIPT BY VAN DER STUCKEN.

forms: a grand opera, " Otho Visconti," of which the overture has
been performed in Leipsic; another grand opera, " Montezuma ";
a cantata, " The Culprit Fay "; two symphonic poems, " Edris " and
" The Song of Life "; important organ works, including a sonata
for the instrument, and many other choral and instrumental works.
He is also the author of the text of his two operas.   In addition,
he composed a symphonic cantata for the opening of the Auditorium
in Chicago.

The quality of his work can best be judged by the fact that
Theodore Thomas, who is not given to flattering the American
composer, has directed many of Gleason's compositions.   Thus, at

the World's Fair at Chicago, the prelude to " Otho Visconti " was given by the Thomas Orchestra; the procession of the " Holy Grail," a richly scored work, and the symphonic poem " Edris " have also been performed by the same organization in its Chicago concerts. " The Song of Life," rather a tragic composition which dwells upon the dark side of life, bears the motto (from Swinburne): —

> " They have the night, who had, like us, the day ;
> We, whom the day binds, shall have night as they ;
> We, from the fetters of the light unbound,
> Healed of our wound of living, shall sleep sound."

This work was given by Thomas, November 30, 1900, in Chicago.

Mr. Gleason was decidedly a modern; he used the *leit-motif* in his operas and in his cantatas, was fond of the most extensive orchestral effects, and cared more for breadth than for mere melody. He was not very strict in his part-writing, and broke harmonic laws without always getting a powerful result, but he was often noble in his orchestration and poetic, rather than dramatic, in his operatic work.

There was another American orchestral composer in Chicago, who may be mentioned as an important contemporary. Henry Schoenefeld was born in Milwaukee, October 4, 1857. His father was a musician and taught the boy until his seventeenth year, when he went to Leipsic and became the pupil of Reinecke, Papperitz, and others. He won a composition prize there, for a choral and orchestral work, which was brought out at the *Gewandhaus*, the young Schoenefeld directing. Subsequently a year was spent with Lassen at Weimar. In 1879 he came back to America and settled in Chicago, where he became the conductor of a large male chorus (the Germania), and a teacher. He left Chicago in 1904 and became a resident of Berlin, where several of his works were produced; after which he settled in Los Angeles.

The chief claim of Schoenefeld is his clear and unaffected style and his hearty Americanism. He has from the first tried to bring definite American melody into classical music, and to accomplish this he has used exactly the means that Dvořák suggested, a development of plantation music, but, like Chadwick, he did this before Dvořák made the discovery. Schoenefeld's suite (Op. 15) has a movement that is as distinctly plantation as the banjo itself. This use of local color was increased after the Bohemian composer had set our concert audiences hunting negro melodies, and in an overture entitled "The Sunny South," Schoenefeld became very frankly American.

Dvořák was strongly attracted toward this young composer, and complimented him highly when his "Rural Symphony" won the prize of $500 offered by the National Conservatory, of which Dvořák was then director. Nor was this the only prize that Schoenefeld captured. In 1899 he won Marteau's award for the best American sonata for violin and piano, with some of the first musicians of France serving on the jury. In this work again our American took his cue from the banjo and sent a new music to Europe. Notwithstanding the foreign performances of Schoenefeld's works, and the prizes won, some of the orchestral numbers have not yet been printed. There is, unfortunately, no public demand for large works among us that can impel a publisher to take the risk of adding to the scanty printed repertoire of American orchestral music.

Turning again to the East we find a colony of young American composers in New York, and some of them dauntlessly writing orchestral works. Henry Holden Huss is one of the leaders of this band, and one of those Americans whose compositions have an international repute. He was born June 21, 1862, in Newark, New Jersey. His father, an esteemed musician, directed his early studies. Otis B. Boise was his teacher of harmony, counterpoint, and composition. In 1883 Huss went to Munich where at the Royal Music School he was a fellow-student with Horatio Parker and Arthur Whiting, under Rheinberger. He has inherited some of that composer's love of form, and he does not break away from the highway of music and scratch through the brambles of dissonance. Several of his compositions were performed publicly in Munich during his stay at the school, and, at his graduation, he played the solo part in his rhapsody in C major, for piano and orchestra. This work at once achieved success, and immediately after Huss's return to America it was brought out by the Boston Symphony Orchestra. With this same orchestra he played his "Piano Concerto," in 1894, under Mr. Emil Paur. The work was played again at these concerts by Adele Aus der Ohe (to whom it is dedicated), in 1903, and has been performed in many other cities with great success. It is well within the lines of form, although the cadenza of the first movement does not come at the end, but in the centre, and the development is very skilful.

Mr. Huss has written an "Ave Maria" for female chorus, soli, string orchestra, organ, and harp, which has been performed under the direction of Thomas, Lang, and other famous leaders. A trio in D minor (violin, violoncello, and piano) has been given at many classical concerts, including those of the Kneisel quartette. His "Andante and Polonaise" for violin and orchestra has been heard at the Trocadero, in Paris, and Raoul Pugno has performed several of Mr. Huss's piano compositions abroad. He has composed a fine Recessional, for mixed chorus, organ, and orchestra, and many songs and piano works. He is sometimes too extended in developing figures, but he is always in good form, melodic even in his *Durchführung*, and he works up his climaxes well. It is probable that with greater simplicity, with less ingenuity of figure treatment, this composer would be yet more attractive, for his melodic gifts are sometimes hidden by his learning.

Another of the New York set of composers is Harry Rowe Shelley, who was born at New Haven, Connecticut, June 8, 1858. He studied at Yale University, under Professor Gustav J. Stoeckel, and was organist of the Center Church, in New Haven, when only fourteen years of age. Subsequently, he was for a long time in New York, under Dudley Buck, Max Vogrich, and Dvořák. He also studied some in Paris and London, but the larger part of his musical education was achieved on American soil. At twenty he was organist of the First Church, in New Haven, and three years later he became musical director of Dr. Storrs's Church in Brooklyn. He has since then been organist at the Fifth Avenue Baptist Church.

Shelley has written two symphonies, the first, in E flat, having been performed in New York in 1897, a violin concerto which has also been heard in various concerts, a cantata, and an opera. He has essayed about all the forms. His fantasia for piano and orchestra is one of his most successful works. His life has, however, been passed more in the atmosphere of church music than in the concert room. He is very graceful in the smaller forms, and his organ music deserves special mention.

Another New York composer who is a quaint combination of classicist and radical, who seeks to reconcile extreme popularity and classical form, is Silas Gamaliel Pratt. He was born in Addison, Vermont, August 4, 1846. His youth was devoted to commercial pursuits, but he employed all of his spare moments in musical study. His boyhood and youth were spent as a clerk with different musical firms in Chicago. His musical career practically began at twenty-two, when he gave a series of piano recitals, in Chicago, and, immediately thereafter, went abroad for further musical study. In 1868 he was in Berlin, studying piano with Bendel and Kullak, and com-

FIG. 57. — FREDERIC GRANT GLEASON.

position with Wuerst and Kiehl. Like Schumann, he studied too assiduously at the piano and achieved the same result, — a lame wrist, which, as was the case with the great German, sent him into composition. Some of his works were performed in Germany before he returned to his native heath. But Chicago, just after the great fire, was by no means the place for a musician to thrive, and Mr. Pratt was forced back into the selling of music, and obliged to leave the making of it to a more favorable time. In 1875 he was again in Berlin, studying score-reading with Heinrich Dorn. On his return home he stopped in London, and was able to direct two of his compositions in the Alexandra Palace, in London. After his return he began work on his opera, "Zenobia."

There never was a better example of the irrepressible Yankee in music than Mr. Pratt at this time. A hundred schemes seemed to form in his mind simultaneously. Large musical events and great musical compositions, many of them intensely patriotic and even of the " spread-eagle " order, were planned.   Had Mr. Pratt not had the advantage of a good European musical training, he might have been a second Gilmore, but, fortunately, his classical studies kept his aggressive Americanism somewhat in check, and his work grew better and better.   When the bombast is eliminated from some of his "patriotic" works, there is a residue of good technique and worthy music, and in the less magniloquent works Mr. Pratt is often very effective.   He has achieved something in all of the large musical forms.   A partial list of his compositions presents operas, " Zenobia " and " Lucille "; cantatas, " The Last Inca " and " The Triumph of Columbus," although the latter may be called a patriotic opera; three symphonies, one of which is entitled " The Prodigal Son "; a grand centennial overture; an orchestral work on Paul Revere's ride; " The Battle of Manila "; an anniversary overture on the centennial of American Independence; a brilliant march called " Homage to Chicago "; several shorter pieces for the orchestra which have been successful; and over fifty pieces for the piano, most of which are practical and pleasing.   Mr. Pratt's restless energy has caused him to direct several of these works in London, Amsterdam, Berlin.   He is at present director of an important School of Music in Pittsburg.   Had this composer been less ambitious, he would have achieved more; yet he has won his triumphs, and stands as an example of American energy and pluck.

And now we come to the opposite type, the quiet musician who composes without any effort to astonish the world, a faithful slave to the tyrant Frau Musica, asking no reward but the privilege of laying his offerings upon her altar.   Too few musical readers, in the earliest years of the twentieth century, have heard of Louis Adolphe Coerne (Fig. 58).   This is an oversight that later years must rectify. He has written a host of works in almost every musical form, and is a poetic as well as a prolific writer.   He was born in Newark, New Jersey (the city which also claims Henry Holden Huss as its citizen), February 27, 1870, and therefore is among the younger of the American composers in the large musical forms.   Like Pratt, he has also written a " Zenobia," a grand opera, which serves to suggest that the story of the Queen of Palmyra has considerable attraction for the American operatic composer.

The father of Coerne was an American citizen, though of Dutch and Swedish ancestry. His mother was an American woman and a descendant of English settlers. He spent his early childhood in Germany and France, and at the age of six he began the study of the violin. Returning to America, he entered the Boston Latin School, where for six years he had a thorough training in the classics. Upon graduating, he was admitted to Harvard University, where, together with other subjects, he studied harmony and composition under J. K. Paine. Simultaneously he continued his violin studies under Franz Kneisel, then of the Boston Symphony Orchestra. While at college, Coerne wrote as musical critic for the *Cambridge Tribune.*

In 1890 he went to Munich, where he studied organ and composition under Rheinberger at the Royal Academy of Music. Upon graduating with honors in 1893, he directed his symphonic poem " Hiawatha," a work which he afterwards directed in 1894 with the Boston Symphony Orchestra in Cambridge, Massachusetts. In Munich he also played his organ concerto, which he later played at the Columbian Exposition and again at Buffalo. Before returning to this country he made several protracted tours through Italy, France, and England. He presently received an official invitation to visit the Exposition at Chicago as solo organist, and after his arrival there the Bureau of Music made request for the composition of a festival overture, to be played at the closing exercises of the Exposition. In the fall he went back to Boston, his former home, and accepted, first, the position of organist and choir-master of a boy choir in Roxbury, and afterward a position at the Shepard Memorial Church in Cambridge. During the winter he was actively employed in publishing earlier works and in teaching.

In 1894 Coerne was called to Buffalo, New York, as director of the Buffalo Liedertafel and Buffalo Vocal Society, and subsequently took the position of director and organist of the Church of the Messiah there. During these years he composed his first opera, entitled " A Woman of Marblehead." He went to Columbus, Ohio, in 1897, to fill the position of organist and choir-master of Trinity Church, and subsequently assumed the directorship of the Arion Club and the Columbus *Maennerchor.* From 1899 to 1902 he lived abroad, devoting himself to composing, publishing, and teaching. An order to finish an uncompleted mass of his former master, Rheinberger, was given him, and he also composed his second opera, "Zenobia." This latter work has been accepted for performance at the Berlin Royal Opera House.

At the close of the year 1902, Coerne returned to Boston. He was called to take charge of the department of music at Harvard University for the Summer School of 1903, then became musical professor at Smith College, afterwards at Olivet, and after that at the Wisconsin University.

Like most of the American composers of the present, Coerne has been in search of American subjects for his muse. His first opera, "A Woman of Marblehead," deals somewhat with the Floyd (or Flood) Ireson episode. We may add, parenthetically, that it is a pity that poor Floyd Ireson should be held up to scorn by the good poet Whittier, and the librettist, who follows his lead, as a hard-hearted man. It has been abundantly shown that he was innocent of the crime for which the women of Marblehead punished him. The opera is a worthy work, has some broad climaxes in its first act, and a sufficiency of melody throughout. The second opera, "Zenobia," from its acceptance abroad, would seem to be a work of some importance.

Mr. Coerne has done his best orchestral work in "Hiawatha," something not so highly colored as the great cantata of Coleridge Taylor (the only negro composer of classical music), nor yet so directly derived from the aboriginal music as MacDowell's "Indian Suite," but clear and well-developed music nevertheless. Sometimes Coerne yields too much to his skill in elaboration, but he is by no means to be classed with the dissonance-mongers, nor has he the consecutive-fifth habit, which too often covers a paucity of ideas. He is sane, healthy, a little too diffuse at times, but always musicianly and earnest.

Every branch of music is represented in the list of this young composer's writings — concert overtures, symphonic poems, operas, a string quartette, organ compositions, canons, songs, piano pieces. Most of them have been published in Europe — German publishers having accepted many of them. The organ works are of excellent worth, thanks to the evident contrapuntal ability of the composer. Mr. Coerne has also written a valuable book on " The Evolution of Modern Orchestration " (Macmillan, 1908) which is a careful commentary upon a most important topic, with many musical examples.

Another name that has now found its place among the leaders of our music is that of Frederick S. Converse. This composer was born at Newton, Massachusetts (a fashionable suburb of Boston), January 5, 1871, and is therefore still at the early part of his career. He was educated in the schools of Newton, and studied piano under

FIG. 58. — LOUIS ADOLPHE COERNE.

local teachers. He went to Harvard College in 1889 and, of course, came under the influence of its musical director. He graduated in 1893 with the highest honors in music and, at that time, a violin sonata, his Op. 1, was publicly performed. It is not every composer who begins his career with a large classical composition.

A few months of commercial career convinced the young Converse that he was unsuited to business, and he then decided to make music his profession. He thereupon studied pianoforte for two years with Carl Baermann (whom we shall speak of again) and composition at the same time with Chadwick. After this he went to that Mecca of so many American composers, the Royal School of Music, at Munich, from which he graduated in 1898, with honors in composition. His symphony in D minor (Op. 7) was first produced at this time. The following winter the Boston Symphony Orchestra performed the first movement of this work. After graduation Mr. Converse came back to America, and is now resident in Boston, where he was for two years a teacher in the New England Conservatory of Music.

He has written several large orchestral works and much chambermusic. Among the works that have been performed in America are two symphonic poems, inspired by Keats, one entitled the " Festival of Pan " and the other "Endymion's Narrative," which the composer calls " Romances for Orchestra," — a term quite as applicable as

"Poëmes Symphoniques." He has also written a concert overture, "Euphrosyne," a string quartette, a sonata for violin and piano, a suite for piano, and a ballad for baritone voice and orchestra, "La Belle Dame sans Merci," — all of which have been performed or published.

Of the works mentioned above we prefer "Endymion's Narrative," which is a most worthy addition to the orchestral repertoire of the present. There is no straining for effect in this romance, no endeavor to invent new and impossible progressions, yet it is thoroughly modern withal, and deals with the largest orchestral score without attempting unnecessary tumult. Nor does Converse disdain melody when it is requisite, and there is a march theme in the work which is the happy medium between classical and popular music. Best of all, the work is in the dreamy, sylvan style of Keats, and is a noble translation of the spirit of the poem "Endymion" into the tonal form. It is a good illustration of the saying that music begins where language ends. The "Festival of Pan" was inspired by the same poem, but is less romantic, less melodic, and more skilful. One can scarcely imagine Keats inspiring a fugato, such as occurs in a portion of this work. Neither of the two compositions are to be regarded as "programme music," for the composer does not schedule his meanings, but leaves the auditor free to read his Keats and make his own application. More recently Mr. Converse has written operas of some importance. The "Pipe of Desire" is in one act and of idyllic character. "The Sacrifice" is an American subject, very dramatic and in three acts. His orchestral tone-poem "Ormazd" is a masterpiece.

There is another Converse who has also written in the largest orchestral forms. This is Charles Crozat Converse, who was born in Warren, Massachusetts, October 7, 1832. This earlier composer drifted from music into law, and his larger works are mostly in manuscript. We confess a lack of familiarity with them, yet the list is formidable enough. There are two symphonies, ten orchestral suites and overtures, three symphonic poems, an oratorio, six string quartettes, and a very popular hymn, "What a Friend we have in Jesus," which we know and do not find very musical. Theodore Thomas, Walter Damrosch, and Anton Seidl have produced some of his works.   Mr. Converse was a student at Leipsic Conservatory, and several of his compositions have been published in Europe.

Yet another modern American symphonist may swell the list. Howard Brockway was born in Brooklyn, November 22, 1870.   In his youth he studied with Kortheuer, in New York.   At twenty he went to Berlin, and studied piano with Barth and composition with the American teacher there, O. B. Boise — his own father-in-law.   The latter trained his fellow-countryman and relative so well that by twenty-four he had written a symphony, a symphonic ballad, a violin sonata, a romanza for violin and orchestra, and many other works.   Many of his compositions were published abroad, and he conducted a concert of his own works at the Sing Akademie in Berlin, where he received much praise.

Brockway's "Sylvan Suite" for orchestra was performed under Gericke at the Boston Symphony concerts.   This suite is very cleverly written, is quite genial and agreeable throughout, yet introduces some counterpoint in a tricksy fugue given to the Will o' the Wisps, which shows that these fairies are more classical than has been supposed.   There are semi-popular touches in the "Dance of the Sylphs," a neat waltz, and a march theme in the fourth movement, while the finale, "At Daybreak," is a strong climax to a pleasant sylvan suavity.   A graceful composer is Brockway, who will no doubt grow broader.   He is at present engaged as instructor at the Peabody Institute, in Baltimore, where O. B. Boise was at one time professor of composition.

In speaking of the West in connection with musical progress, we have up to this point confined ourselves to two cities, Chicago and Cincinnati; and these two cities have certainly been the most important in the orchestral advance, in music festivals, in operatic performances.   Yet a few orchestral writers have appeared outside of them.   Cleveland, the home of several good composers, has one orchestral writer, Beck, who, under more encouraging circumstances, might have become, may yet become, a great influence in the art that is growing stronger each day in communities which but a short time since were entirely commercial.

Johann H. Beck was born in Cleveland, Ohio, September 12, 1856.   He studied violin, first in Cleveland, afterwards in the

Leipsic Conservatory. Returning to Cleveland from Germany, he at once devoted himself to the large forms of composition. It is needless to say that there was little encouragement for this in his native city at that time. Nevertheless Beck kept bravely on, writing overtures, a cantata, chamber-music, and a few songs. His teachers in Germany (in composition) had been Reinecke and Jadassohn, and of course they taught him expression without subverting the rules of form and harmonic progression. Beck's large works are, unfortunately, not accessible, being in manuscript. Yet they have been played both in America and in Europe. We can only judge of them by the little that has been heard at concerts of the Music Teachers' National Association, but it would seem as though Beck with his manuscripts, in Cleveland, and practically unknown in the Eastern cities with large orchestras, is like a giant in a closet. But he is no longer a solitary classicist in Cleveland. Wilson G. Smith, James H. Rogers, and others have brought that city into line with the modern school of composition and made it in some degree a musical centre.

St. Louis, large metropolis as it is, has lagged behind somewhat in the musical field. Even its great International Exhibition (of 1904) produced little in the field of music (save organ recitals) that compared with the new compositions, the symphonic concerts, the musical congress, that marked the Columbian Exhibition at Chicago, in 1893. Yet St. Louis, too, has its symphonic orchestra, and also an important native composer.

Ernest Richard Kroeger (Fig. 59) was born in St. Louis, August 10, 1862. His father was a native of Schleswig-Holstein, his mother was of English birth. The young Kroeger was at first obliged to enter a business career, and from fifteen to twenty-three the only musical study that he had was gained in the moments left free from commercial pursuits. At twenty-three, however, he decided to make music his profession. All his studies have been pursued in America, and chiefly in the West, wherefore he may stand as a typically Western composer. He has aimed high in his writings. His list of compositions includes a symphony, a symphonic overture on " Sardanapalus " which has been performed by Seidl in New York, and another overture entitled " Hiawatha," in which he used actual Indian themes. This work was given at Omaha by the Thomas Orchestra. The American theme has rather drawn him. Not only his "Hiawatha" shows this, but in "Ten American Sketches" (Op. 53), he portrays Negro, Indian, mountain, and prairie life, and sounds a characteristic note founded upon the idea of the folk-tone. Victor Herbert's Pittsburg Orchestra produced his "Thanatopsis" overture. Like F. S. Converse, he has been inspired by Keats's poetry, and has written an overture entitled "Endymion." He has composed in many veins of chamber-music, and some of his works in this field have been published by the German firm of Breitkopf & Härtel. His "Masque of Dead Florentines" is a most poetic vocal suite.

FIG. 59. — E. R. KROEGER.

A whole host of piano and vocal compositions by Mr. Kroeger have been published, and among these are anthems, quartettes, choruses, and the like. He has written organ compositions of substantial worth, and his contrapuntal skill may be judged by his prelude and fugue for piano, a skilful and serious work. Mr. Kroeger's labors in music have been many (for the musician in America must needs be versatile). He has been organist, choirmaster, conductor, founder, and leader of clubs, head of a college of music, and has been most prominent in teaching and developing music in his native city. He has received his reward (for cities are not always ungrateful). He was appointed chief of the Bureau of Music of the St. Louis Exhibition, of 1904, and the many important organ recitals, given there by artists from every part of the United States, were due to his efforts.

It is doubtful if Pittsburg would accept the title of a "Western" city; but the term may be applied to dissociate it from New York and Boston, the Eastern musical centres, and New Orleans, the Southern musical city. Pittsburg has, thanks chiefly to Andrew

Carnegie, become a musical centre in recent years, and in organ playing, as we shall see in a later chapter, it has had advantages beyond many an Eastern city.   It had its own symphony concerts, and it has its little group of composers.   Of these one stands forth as a representative American composer.

Adolph Martin Foerster was born in Pittsburg, February 2, 1854.   He inherited his musical gifts from his mother, who was his first teacher.   For a time he had no intention of following music save as an accomplishment, but, after three years spent in commercial pursuits, he came to the conclusion that in music only could he achieve success.   The serious study of the art began with him in 1872, and for three years from that time he was in Leipsic a pupil of Richter and Papperitz in composition, Grill and Schimon in voice, and Wenzel and Coccius in piano.   On his return to America he became a teacher at the Fort Wayne (Indiana) Conservatory, but after a year in this post he returned to Pittsburg, where he has since remained.   Here he at once pushed to the front in musical matters.   He was very soon made conductor of the Symphonic Society, and in 1883 he directed the Musical Union and the Choral Society.   The influence of Robert Franz, in Halle, Germany, upon this American composer, has not been a slight one. Foerster's six songs (Op. 6), are dedicated to the German master, who was his close friend.

Many of the orchestral works of Foerster remain in manuscript, although most of them have been performed.   " Thusnelda," by Foerster, a characteristic orchestral piece founded upon a poem by Schaefer, has, however, attained the dignity of print.   His " Dedication March " was composed for the opening of Carnegie Hall, in Pittsburg (1895), and has some most effective and ingenious touches. It presents, for example, a development of the notes " A–C," — " Andrew Carnegie," — and it brings in a touch of " The Old Folks at Home," by Foster; thus paying tribute to the founder of the Hall and the first composer of Pittsburg, in a very fitting manner. The work has been heard in its orchestral form at the St. Louis Exposition (1904), in Cleveland, and in other American cities.   A " Faust " overture (in spite of Wagner), a march-fantasia, a festival march (performed by Seidl), and some others, yet await their pub-

P

lisher.   In songs and in piano compositions Foerster has been very successful.   He is sufficiently melodic and romantic, without becoming mawkish, and he is clear in what he wishes to say.

Perhaps nothing can show the growth of music in America more vividly than the fact that one can find great artists and good composers even in the cities most remote from what we have called "musical centres."   San Francisco and Los Angeles possess orchestras and conservatories, and in far Colorado there has been not only a good conservatory, but a composer, an orchestral composer of native birth, Goldmark, who is likely to be heard from frequently in the near future.

Rubin Goldmark is a nephew of the great composer of the same name, in Vienna.   He was born in New York, in 1872, and received his education in the public schools there, and in the College of the City of New York.   He took his first musical studies in New York, with Alfred Livonius, with whom he afterwards went to Vienna.   Arrived in the Austrian capital at seventeen, he began earnest study with Door, in piano, and Fuchs, in composition.   On his return to New York he studied both branches further with Joseffy and Dvořák.   His health sent him to Colorado Springs, where he established a college of music, and where he resided until 1903, when he again returned to New York.

At nineteen Goldmark composed a theme and variations, for orchestra, which was performed by Seidl, in New York, with much success.   At twenty there came a piano trio, which caused Dvořák to say, " There are now two Goldmarks ! "   A " Hiawatha " overture and a symphonic poem — " Samson and Delilah " — both very dramatic works, have been played by the Boston Symphony Orchestra ; a violin sonata, a host of songs, and a liberal list of other .compositions form the contributions of this young composer to our art.   What has been heard and seen of these works proves the young Goldmark to be a remarkably scientific musician, graceful in his thoughts, and fine in his orchestral coloring.

Another composer from the middle West is Carl V. Lachmund, who was born in Booneville, Missouri, in 1854, and went abroad at a very early age to study music.   At thirteen he was at Cologne, under Heller and Seiss ; a little later at Berlin with the two Scharwenkas and Moszkowski; finally with Liszt at Weimar, where he stayed for some years. Lachmund was active in the opera at Cologne, and became known to the German concert-rooms through a trio for harp, violin, and violoncello, and also a concert prelude that was quite popular. Since his return to America his "Japanese Overture" has received performance by Thomas and Seidl, and he became prominent in New York, but finally settled in Portland, Oregon, where he has founded a female string orchestra.

This chapter may be fittingly brought to a close with one of the more important names, that of a composer who, by some, is considered one of the very few Americans to be called a master. Arthur B. Whiting (Fig. 60) has written in almost all the musical forms, both great and small, and has won success in many of them. His works have been played by all of the great orchestras of America, and many of them have had interpretations abroad. And in this connection a clear statement may be made. The single performance of a large work does not always prove much. So many wires are pulled, there is so much playing of musical politics, that works of an inferior order sometimes appear upon a programme of the highest class. Some conductors, and notably Thomas, Gericke, Paur, and Seidl, have sought to stem this tide, and their indorsement means much. The works of some native composers, however, are in actual demand and are played over and over again. The concertos of MacDowell, the overtures of Chadwick, the suite in D minor by Foote, and numbers by Paine, Horatio Parker (chiefly vocal), and Arthur Whiting, are played purely because they are worthy compositions, just the same as a work by Brahms, or R. Strauss, or Grieg.

Arthur Battelle Whiting (who is a nephew of the organist and composer G. E. Whiting) was born in Cambridge, Massachusetts, June 20, 1861, and is a member of a remarkably musical family. His father was a musician of some prominence, and the young Whiting was given instruction of the best character from the very beginning. William H. Sherwood was his teacher in piano, J. C. D. Parker in harmony, and George W. Chadwick taught him the higher grades of composition. Then came the trip to Munich, where he formed one of the excellent band of Americans which Rheinberger instructed, and of which Chadwick was one of the earliest members.

On his return to America he settled in Boston, marrying into one of the oldest New England families. Within the last few years, however, he has made New York his home. He is not a composer who gives forth a large list of compositions, for he works slowly and seems to prize finish as much as inspiration. Almost all of his early works were instrumental or orchestral. But he has nevertheless won a striking success in a vocal setting of Oliver Herford's cycle of poems entitled "Floriana," in which he has displayed a charming delicacy and a thorough comprehension of the needs of the vocalist. It is in the dainty and graceful moods that we find this composer at his best, and we find him lacking when vigor and fiery dramatic expression are required. Yet he has been

FIG. 60.—ARTHUR WHITING.

fairly successful in setting some of Kipling's "Barrack-room Ballads," which certainly are not over-delicate. Yet it is not to be doubted that "Floriana" is, up to the present time, his most successful and artistic work in the vocal field.

Naturally, as Mr. Whiting is a clever pianist and a prominent teacher of the instrument, most of his works tend in that direction. Yet some of his piano works are combined with orchestra in such an advanced manner that it gives the composer the right to appear in this chapter. He has written a piano concerto, in D minor (Op. 6), which has been heard in American symphony concerts as long ago as 1888. The orchestration of this work is quite advanced, and there are bold modulations in it that are beyond the suavity of some of Mr. Whiting's later works. Even before the composition of this concerto the composer had brought forth classical pieces. A piano trio, performed in Munich, we have never heard, but a concert overture, performed by the Boston Symphony Orchestra, in 1886, made a very favorable impression, although not of the power of the Chadwick overtures, which had preceded it. In 1891 a suite, in G minor, for string orchestra and horn quartette (Op. 8) made its appearance. The combination of musical forces was an unusual one, yet it was very successful. In this suite Mr. Whiting showed that he was a master of sonata form, and his grace and elegance were well exhibited. About the same time the Kneisel quartette concerts presented a violin sonata by the young composer, the performers being Mr. Kneisel and Mr. Whiting.

But the most ambitious of Mr. Whiting's works is the fantasia for piano and orchestra, in B flat minor (Op. 11). In this the composer not only has more of virile power than in his other large compositions, but he even manages to innovate in musical form, giving a pastorale, nominally as a second movement, but really as the contrasted second portion of the first movement, for it is followed by a condensed return of the first movement before the finale begins. This is a form which we do not recall ever having met before, yet it is symmetrical and decidedly useful in classical treatment, shortening the composition, yet not depriving it of any of its effective contrasts. As might have been expected from a pianist, the chief instrument is made rather prominent, having long stretches of absolute solo; but this can be readily condoned in so free a form as a fantasia.

All together, then, Mr. Whiting, beginning in too suave and Chesterfieldian a manner, has grown constantly, and is now one of the prominent composers in the larger forms. His compositions become more and more powerful with each successive number, and his piano works are among the most useful in the entire American repertoire.

PLATE VII

ANTON SEIDL

(Copyright by Aimé Dupont, New York)

CHAPTER X

OTHER ORCHESTRAL COMPOSERS OF AMERICA

AFTER narrating the advent of American compositions in Europe it now becomes necessary to speak of some Americans who have expatriated themselves — those who studying abroad, at the end of their musical course, tempted by the musical atmosphere of foreign climes, and possibly believing that success in the higher branches of the profession was difficult at home, settled in Europe almost permanently. This list is happily a short one.

The first of these is Otis Bardwell Boise, who taught music in Berlin for many years. Boise was born in Oberlin, Ohio (a very active musical town), August 13, 1844. He was educated at the public schools in Cleveland, Ohio, and was an organist at fourteen years of age. In 1861 he studied in Leipsic, under Hauptmann, Richter, Moscheles, and others; and in 1864 there came still further study in Berlin, under Kullak. Then he returned (temporarily) to his native land, and from 1865 to 1870 engaged in teaching, and playing the organ, in Cleveland. From 1870 to 1876 Boise was in New York, as a teacher of composition in the New York Conservatory and organist in the Fifth Avenue Presbyterian Church. He was in Europe again in 1877, composing and studying; and now he won the friendship of Liszt, who helped him in his work and undoubtedly aided him in his recognition abroad. Another attempt in New York followed, from 1878 to 1881, and then came seven years of business affairs instead of music. Finally, in 1888, there began the period of his expatriation, and from that time (until very recently) Boise remained in Berlin. There has been a good reflection of his work in America, for Howard Brockway (his son-in-law) studied with him in Berlin, and Huss was his pupil before he left America. Boise has written symphonies, overtures, concertos, and other large works, but these are better known abroad than in his native land. He has also written an educational work entitled "Harmony made Practical," which is decidedly modern in its tendencies. In 1902 he returned to America, taught in Baltimore, and died there, December 2, 1912.

Arthur Bird, the second of the American group in Europe, was born in Cambridge, Massachusetts, July 23, 1856. He went abroad before he was twenty-one, and studied in Berlin for two years under Haupt, Loeschhorn, and Rohde. Returning to America he settled for four years in Halifax (Nova Scotia) as organist and teacher, and founded there the first male chorus in Nova Scotia. In 1881 he went back to Berlin for more extended study, under Heinrich Urban, at Kullak's school. The attention of Liszt was drawn to his work, and the summer of 1885 was spent with that master at Weimar, as also part of the following year. A concert given in Berlin in 1886 served to introduce some of his own works to Germany, and so successfully that his path became easy in that musical centre.

Another visit was made to America in 1886, but eventually (about the same time that Boise settled abroad) Bird became a regular teacher and composer of Berlin. He has composed in almost all forms and is an excellent contrapuntist, yet uses his skill in this direction as a means rather than as an end, seldom making a display of his knowledge. His works include a symphony, in A, three orchestral suites, some excellent piano compositions (including two fugues), a ballet, and an opera comique entitled "Daphne."

A third American composer abroad is Templeton Strong. He is the son of the late G. T. Strong, once president of the New York Philharmonic Society. Just as Arthur B. Whiting, Henry K. Hadley, and Horatio W. Parker have dropped part of their names (there are hosts of instances of this in musical biography, outside of William Richard Wagner), so George Templeton Strong has curtailed his name to Templeton Strong. Born in New York in 1855, of a distinguished and wealthy family, his musical education was fostered from the very beginning, and after some study in his native city he was sent to Leipsic, where, in the great conservatory, he studied composition and piano for some years. In 1891 he came to America to take a position in the New England Conservatory as teacher of harmony and counterpoint.   He became very popular with all who came in contact with him, pupils and faculty alike, but was soon obliged to return to Europe on account of his health, which suffered from the rigorous New England climate.   He at present makes his home in Vevay, Switzerland, composing amidst the most picturesque surroundings.

Strong has written much orchestral and cantata music.   He possesses a grace in delicate romance that is altogether charming, and in his control of the modern orchestra he is the equal of any of the American composers.   He has written two symphonies, of which one, "Sintram," has been given in the United States, Anton Seidl performing it in Brooklyn, in 1892.   This work may be taken as Strong's *magnum opus*.   It is too prolix, but it has much power and is brilliantly scored.   More artistic and poetic to our thinking is " The Haunted Mill," a work for chorus, baritone solo, and orchestra, which is as successful a work as anything of its kind in the repertoire, being full of true inspiration from beginning to end.   A symphonic poem, " Undine," has not yet been heard in America. Strong's piano works are full of poetry, and his cantatas (mostly with German text) are all worthy of translation and performance in America.

If we have loaned to Germany three good American composers, that country has returned the compliment tenfold, by sending us a host of creative musicians who, having taken up their residence among us, have become part and parcel of the advance movement which is now so strongly marked in musical matters on this side of the Atlantic.   In such a list as that which is to follow, we shall not include sporadic visitors, who have been sojourning here from the time of Jullien to that of Richard Strauss, but only those who have definitely Americanized themselves and have given their permanent efforts to compositions of an American character.

Among these one man stands preëminent for mastery of the most modern orchestra, for originality of thought, as well as for remarkable devices in combinations of instrumentation.   This modern Berlioz is Charles Martin Loeffler (Fig. 61).   He was born in Mühlhausen, Alsatia, in January, 1861.   A few of his early works were published as by Loeffler-Tornov, the latter being part of his family name, which, however, has been omitted from later works. In his fourteenth year he decided to make music his profession. He then studied violin with Leonard in Paris, with Massart, in the same city, and with Joachim, in Berlin, becoming a violinist of the highest rank. He studied composition with Friedrich Kiel, in Berlin, and orchestration with Guiraud, in Paris. Loeffler himself doubts, however, whether he ought to be called a pupil of Kiel, as his studies with him were interrupted and very brief. His chief studies of orchestration were made from the orchestra itself, or with men who (he says) are quite unknown to fame. His work with the Pasdeloup Orchestra, in Paris, and with other European orchestras, gave him a practical training that has been of the greatest value to him.

More than half of Loeffler's life has been passed in America, three years in New York and the later years in Boston.[1] In the latter city he has been one of the most prominent violinists of the Boston Symphony Orchestra and a teacher of the highest rank. At present he has dissociated himself from the orchestra in order to have more time for composition. Few of Loeffler's works have been published, although about all of them have been performed either in Boston or New York. Most of the published scores have appeared in Paris, and include a few songs and a berceuse for violin and piano. Recently he has produced four remarkable songs with French text (the poetry by Gustave Kahn), which have been published in New York. They prove that even without the glow of orchestral color, this composer can present impressive music.

In the main, however, Loeffler's work has been largely orchestral. His chamber-music is very effective and practical, as might be expected from so thorough a violinist. In some of it he has developed Russian themes very brilliantly. His tendency toward Russian and French subjects has been marked, as also a decided morbidness that is a characteristic of the ultra-modern school. There is a distinctly Russian flavor in Loeffler's violin concerto, as also (and here it is more attractively employed) in his string sextette.

Such a subject as Maeterlinck's " Death of Tintagiles " would

[1] The portrait of Loeffler which is reproduced herewith is a famous painting by John S. Sargent, presented to Mrs. John L. Gardner of Boston, and is at present in her Italian palace.

FIG. 61. — C. M. LOEFFLER.

After the painting by John S. Sargent.

(Copyright by Thomas E. Marr.)

naturally appeal strongly to the *morbidezza* which we have spoken of as prominent in this composer's work.   It is made into a large symphonic poem, and the composer's individuality in scoring is shown by his resuscitating the obsolescent viol d' amore, and employing two of them to picture the pathetic hero and his sister, a thoroughly adequate tone-color which speaks the orchestral mind. The present writer may perhaps be pardoned for introducing here an extract from a review of the work written by him after the first hearing.   It will serve to point out Loeffler's merits and defects.

"Now followed a very talented, but very radical, composition, by C. M. Loeffler, entitled ' La Mort de Tintagiles.'   Mr. Loeffler has already proved that he is thoroughly imbued with ultra-modern pessimism.   He has given us a *carnaval des morts*, and has revelled in the verjuice of Verlaine, and now he plunges into the still deeper gloom of Maeterlinck.   It is but the tendency of most modern art; music is no longer to be beautiful, but is to become a hopeless wailing, a thrice-intensified *Weltschmerz*.   One may acknowledge that shadows are needed to give the best effect to lights in painting, that evil must contrast against good in literature, that dissonance must enhance consonance in music; but to present shadows only, to portray only crime and misery, to sound only dissonances and unrest, is bad art.   In the Maeterlinck cult the religion is hysteria, the temple a morgue.

" Maeterlinck is so steeped, soaked, and sodden in horrors that, to a healthy mind, some of his tricks become comical.   His castles and palaces are always in bad repair, built in a malarial district, with bad drainage, and perfumed with blood.   Heavy iron doors, dark passages filled with horror, mysterious presences, melancholy children abound.   Everybody goes about in the deepest gloom and terror ; the characters never speak but always stammer their gruesome tales to each other ; there is murder in the air, there is death at the end of every play.   Shakespeare's (if it be Shakespeare's) ' Titus Andronicus ' is sunshine compared to these tragedies ; and what would one have said of Shakespeare had he brought forth one ' Titus Andronicus' after the other ?   And now we are to have this pernicious art, with its only ambition that of the fat boy in ' Pickwick,' — ' I wants to make your flesh creep ! ' — exerting its funereal influence

in music.   Mr. Loeffler does not beat about the bush; he plunges
bodily into the brambles of the modern path.   He begins with a dissonance that makes the first chord of the finale of Beethoven's Ninth
Symphony seem sweet by comparison, and, once launched, there are
no stopping-places, no cadences of repose — all is restless, agonized,
sorrowing.

"It was in good taste, however, to use a couple of viols d'amore
to represent the two children, Tintagiles and Ygraine, although their
wretchedness was pushed to such great length that it became
monotonous at last.   The two viols d'amore were not the only
instrumental novelty of the wonderful score, for a pedal clarinet,
the deepest of the single reed instruments, was heard in America, in
this work, for the first time.   And there were still more striking
novelties in the application of older instruments; from harps to
cymbals the composer showed himself a master of orchestral combinations.   Setting all the lugubrious ideas aside, Mr. Loeffler has
suddenly shown himself as ranking among the most famous masters
of the modern orchestra.

"The odd effects produced upon the cymbals (not unlike Wagner's rattling in the Venus-scene in 'Tannhäuser'), the impressive
tolling of midnight upon the harps (Berlioz and St. Saëns may stand
sponsors for this), the bold use of bass drum and of percussion generally, the muted horns, the 'ponticello' work of the strings, the
short trumpet-blasts, the mournful organ-point against the viols
d'amore, these, and a host of other striking touches might be mentioned to prove what a master of scoring we have in Mr. Loeffler."

Mr. Loeffler has recently rescored this work and has eliminated
one of the viols d' amore, giving the single obbligato instrument
more prominence.   In its new form the work shows even more masterful control of the modern orchestra.   If the extremely sombre and
radical school be accepted, it may be cordially admitted that Loeffler
is a master of it, a rival to any of its modern exponents.

Other orchestral works by Loeffler show the same qualities.   A
divertimento for violin and orchestra presents a charming eclogue,
with just the tender pastoral feeling that ought to dominate such a
movement.   The finale, however, rushes into the extreme of frenzy
with a *carnaval des morts* in which all the *diablerie* in which the

composer revels is introduced. In the eclogue the violins are omitted from the orchestra, a point which gives especial prominence to the solo instrument. Other ingenious touches of orchestration occur, even muted trumpets (a very rare effect in orchestration) being employed.

All Loeffler's morbidity bursts forth in his symphonic poem "La Villanelle du Diable," founded upon an eccentric poem by Rollinat. It is not a Miltonian Lucifer that here appears, but a very restless gentleman with the rickets. Led by the poet, Mr. Loeffler has created a *Till-Eulenspiegel* kind of a devil, and sent him prancing through a most complicated score. Muted horns give forth their baleful tones, piccolos shriek, the "Ça Ira" and the "Carmagnole," and the blood-stained tunes of the Reign of Terror blend in fierce confusion in this picture of Satan.

FIG. 62. — LOUIS MAAS.

In exquisite contrast to such orgies is a symphonic poem founded on "La Bonne Chanson," one of the finest works of Verlaine. His "Pagan Poem" for orchestra, founded on Virgil's 8th eclogue, is also a masterpiece. The climax, at the return of the lover, is very masterly; and this Loeffler has turned into music in a noble manner. Loeffler has shown himself to be a great tone colorist — the best in America.

A great musician, Louis Maas (Fig. 62), took up his residence in America in 1880, and, but for his early death, would have become a leader in the musical advance. He was born in Wiesbaden, Germany, June 21, 1852. Pupil and subsequently teacher at the conservatory in Leipsic, he came to Boston, one of the most learned musicians of the Boston coterie at that time. He conducted the Philharmonic Orchestra; sought out American sub-

jects in music, and finally wrote a symphony (inspired by his Western tours) entitled " On the Prairies." He wrote much orchestral
and classical music, was a pianist of foremost rank, a very successful
teacher, and stood very high in his work at the New England
Conservatory of Music. A most prosperous career seemed opening
to him in America, but it was cut short by his death in Boston,
September 18, 1889.

Richard Burmeister is another of the foreigners who has identified himself with American musical progress. He was born in
Hamburg, December 7, 1860. He was a teacher in the Hamburg
Conservatory and also a pupil of Liszt, in the general sense in
which this term is applied. That is, Liszt advised him, heard
him play, admitted him to the coterie at Weimar, and guided
his performance and his compositions in a large degree. He
was also with Liszt in Buda-Pesth and in Rome — an exceptional
privilege. He has written a piano concerto, has rescored the
Chopin F minor concerto, and has added an orchestral part to
Liszt's own " Concerto Pathetique." In 1885 he came to America,
and for twelve years was the head of the piano department of the
Peabody Institute in Baltimore. After that he settled in New York,
where he became head of the Scharwenka Conservatory and whence
he made concert tours all over this country and Europe. His
present residence is Europe, where he has many American pupils.

Asgar Hamerik (born in Copenhagen, April 8, 1843) was
director of the same Peabody Institute Conservatory, from 1871.
He has composed an enormous list of large works, including five
symphonies; but none of these are especially American, so far as
they are generally known. He has written much sacred music,
and many of his compositions are Danish in their trend and
inspiration.

Otto Singer was more thoroughly Americanized than Hamerik.
Born at Sora, in Saxony, July 26, 1833, he studied in Dresden, in the
Leipsic Conservatory, and with Liszt (the usual reservation is to be
made here), and was a teacher in the two cities named above. He
came to America in 1867, and taught here for more than a quarter
of a century. Such foreigners have had a more important rôle in
American musical history than some of our native-born composers,

and it is quite in line with the purpose of this volume to trace their influence. At first Singer was a teacher in New York — until 1873. In that year he was called to Cincinnati to be assistant conductor of the first May Festival in that city. After this musical occasion he accepted the post of teacher of piano and composition in the College of Music in Cincinnati, and remained there for almost the rest of his life. In 1893 he returned to New York, where he died, January 3, 1894. Much of the best chorus singing in Cincinnati is due to Otto Singer. For years he trained the choruses for the May festivals. In 1876 he wrote an American cantata for one of these festivals, " The Landing of the Pilgrim Fathers," which had much success. Besides this he has composed symphonies, a symphonic fantasia, concertos, and many other works. His " Symphonic Fantasia " was performed by Gericke with the Boston Symphony Orchestra and with good success. Singer stood on the neutral ground between the conservative and the radical. Even his " Symphonic Fantasia " followed the outline of the symphonic shape, giving the effect of four distinct but continuous movements.

Another of the band of foreign composers in America is Gustav Strube, who, after playing in the Gewandhaus Orchestra in Leipsic, and being one of the faculty of the Mannheim Conservatory, came to America in 1889, joined the Boston Symphony Orchestra, and composed some masterly overtures and symphonies. He afterwards left Boston and became a teacher in the Peabody Institute, Baltimore.

Such composers as Eichberg, Singer, and Loeffler, who have lived among us for a generation or longer, who have taught hundreds of American pupils, who have written works on American subjects or have had all their works brought out first in America, — these men, although of foreign birth, are part of the warp and woof of the American musical fabric, and their honors belong to this country as Handel's glory belongs to England, the country of his adoption.

In no city is the beneficent character of foreign influence on American music so well illustrated as in Milwaukee. This city has been, even more than Cincinnati, the home of the *Maennerchor*, great " Saengerfeste " often being held there, and the fiftieth anniversary of the *Musikverein*, originally the Musical Society (celebrated

Q

in May, 1900) showed a remarkable record of many worthy musical achievements. The programmes of this society have included chorus works with orchestra, entire operas and extracts from operas and oratorios, symphonies, overtures, etc. Among the directors have been such men as Balatka, Mickler, Luening, Catenhusen, and Christoph Bach, and among the presidents Mr. Henry M. Mendel and Dr. Louis Frank. Mr. Mendel, born in Breslau, Silesia, October 15, 1839, is (like Mr. Higginson, of Boston) a prosperous business man who delights to advance the cause of music; and his successful career as a merchant has not hindered him from becoming an excellent violinist. He has been a most prominent factor in Milwaukee's musical advance for the last half century.

The American side of choral music in Milwaukee has been chiefly in the hands of the Arion Musical Club, an organization with both male and female chorus. Its chief conductors have been Mr. William L. Tomlins, Frederic Archer, Arthur Weld (who has done much orchestral work in Milwaukee), and Daniel Protheroe, and it has given large musical masterpieces and important musical festivals.

There were composers in Milwaukee even from the early days. Of Schoenefeld we have already spoken; Balatka wrote large cantatas and choruses with orchestra; but Hugo Kaun was the greatest of the resident composers of the city. He was born in Berlin, March 21, 1863. He came to Milwaukee in 1887 and remained there as conductor and teacher, leading a *Maennerchor* which he founded, until 1901, when he returned to Berlin.

Kaun is possibly the best of the German-American band of composers. He has produced symphonies, symphonic poems, operas, chamber music, etc. He has created American works also, among which are two noble symphonic poems (as great as anything yet evolved on any American theme) named " Hiawatha " and " Minnehaha," and there is a third, on a similar topic, in manuscript. Kaun's compositions have won much favor in Germany and have been played by almost all American orchestras.

There is a sorrowful tale of the wasted efforts of a German composer connected with Milwaukee's musical history. Edward von Sobolewski was born October 1, 1808, in Königsberg, of an ancient noble family of Poland. He studied music with the great von Weber and was Kapellmeister and prominent director in several German cities. He wrote operas which were performed in Königsberg, in Bremen, and even in Berlin. In 1859 he came to America. He at once interested himself in American music and wrote an opera on Indian subjects, entitled " Mohega, the Flower of the Forest." He had come before his time! He was a Wagnerian, a pioneer of the neo-Germanic school, and the rich seed was thrown upon a sterile soil. The first performance drew a large audience; at the second the house was empty. Poor von Sobolewski, who in Germany had won the praises of Schumann and Liszt, fought against sneers and jealousies of much lesser men for a time, but at last broke down; he died, a disappointed and embittered man, upon a little farm near St. Louis, May 18, 1872. It might be well for some enterprising manager to look up the score of this early opera (it was in the possession of Henry M. Mendel, Esq., of Milwaukee) and render a tardy justice to the memory of Edward von Sobolewski by performing it.

It is perhaps fitting that this chapter should close with a figure essentially American, and one which is entirely familiar to most of our readers. It is not the figure of a great orchestral conductor, it is not a composer of the classical forms, yet the man whose name is to follow has had more performances of his work in France, Germany, and England than all the names thus far cited put together. One may recall the fable of the bat among the birds and the mice. The birds declined to associate with it because it was too much like a mouse; the mice declined its companionship because it too closely resembled a bird. Some such dilemma confronts one in the classification of John Philip Sousa (Fig. 63). In Germany they hold his music so typically representative of America that they play his marches on international occasions, as, for example, the festivities connected with the Wagner monument in Berlin. In America his tunes are familiar to all classes, and many a musician who knows that Sousa does not belong among the great masters might be obliged to confess greater familiarity with the melodies of the former than with some of the themes of the latter.

Sousa was born in Washington, November 6, 1856. His mother was German, his father a political refugee from Spain, who became a trombone player. Sousa's youth was decidedly variegated. His musical teachers were John Esputa and George Felix Benkert. At eight he was fiddler in a dancing-school, at sixteen he led an orchestra in a variety theatre, at eighteen he was musical director of a travelling theatrical troupe, and had composed music for their play. A little later he blacked his face and appeared with a negro minstrel company; at nineteen he had moved a little higher, and was a member of the orchestra with which Offenbach toured the United States. Then he became director of a " Pinafore " opera company; and finally, in 1880, at twenty-four years of age, was appointed leader of the United States Marine Band. August 1, 1892, he resigned the leadership, and formed his own band, which has since become celebrated in its peculiar field.

FIG. 63. — JOHN P. SOUSA.
(Copyright by E. Chickering, Boston.)

Although Sousa has written operas of the lighter kind, waltzes, and songs, his chief claim to fame lies in his marches. It is said that over twenty thousand bands in the United States alone play, or play at, his marches, while in England and Germany, at present, one cannot escape hearing the well-remembered rhythm of the " Washington Post " or the " Liberty Bell " march. The prices received for these two marches varied somewhat. The composer sold the first for $35, the second has thus far netted him $35,000. The latter is far more than any sum received for any composition mentioned elsewhere in this volume.

PLATE VIII

GEORGE W. CHADWICK

CHAPTER XI

OPERATIC, CANTATA, AND VOCAL COMPOSERS

In this chapter may be examined the works of those composers who, whatever other compositions they may have written, have won their chief successes in the vocal field. In the domain of sacred music, America has a writer of much importance in the person of James Cutler Dunn Parker (Fig. 64). Not only are his works of intrinsic worth, but Parker was the earliest of all the native composers to study music thoroughly in Germany. As his era of teaching activity antedates that of John K. Paine, one may call him the father of the American school of musical pedagogues.

He was born in Boston, June 2, 1828, and graduated from Harvard in 1848. At that time it was deemed impossible for any American of social prominence and ample means to take up music as a profession. In consequence, Parker studied law for three years. At the end of that time, however, he made up his mind that he would not develop into a great legal luminary, and that there was a career before him in the realm of tones. Three years of study in Leipsic followed, under such teachers as Hauptmann, Richter, and Rietz, and especially with Moscheles, who took much interest in the young American student in the days when few Americans studied music in Germany. Returning to America in 1854, Mr. Parker entered upon a musical career that continued until 1912, when he retired from active work in music. He became the organist at Trinity Church, was the organist also of the Handel and Haydn Society, and entered the New England Conservatory as piano and harmony teacher. In this last capacity Mr. Parker's influence has been extensive. The pupils that he has graduated during his long era of activity would form a good-sized regiment. Among those who studied under him may be mentioned John A. Preston, Fred. H. Lewis, Alfred D. Turner, Henry M. Dunham (Fig. 65), Allen W. Swan, J. H. Howe, Charles H. Morse, — the list of celebrities might be extended much farther. He was for some time examiner at the New England Conservatory, in Boston.

Although Parker's teaching in Boston began as early as 1854, it was not until 1877 that he brought out a large composition. In that year the Handel and Haydn Society gave his " Redemption Hymn," a cantata that has held its place in the standard repertoire ever since. Nine years later he wrote a secular cantata, " The Blind King." " St. John " was the next important work, and finally there came a small oratorio, " The Life of Man." Mr. J. C. D. Parker does not attempt the intricate style of Horatio Parker (not a relative), but combines graceful melody with sufficient counterpoint to lend dignity to his work — the *juste milieu* between the classical and the popular. The last-named work was produced by the Handel and Haydn Society, April 14, 1895. " The Life of Man " may be called Parker's best work. Although quite melodic, fugal work is not wanting in its numbers, the first chorus being a well-developed fugue with a fine stretto as climax. Subsequently fugal expositions and excellent canonic writing occur. In the portrayal of the Resurrection the composer has won a powerful effect by soprano solo against chorus, as Rossini did in his famous " Inflammatus." There is also some masterly canonic writing in the portrayal of the seven churches of Asia, in which seven voices enter in beautiful imitation. A tendency to oversweet-ness, a desire to be melodic and singable at all hazards, is the only weak spot in this composer's work.

Just as one feels that J. C. D. Parker should be classed among the great teachers, as well as among the composers of America, so Dudley Buck (Fig. 66) impresses one as a celebrity among organists and a famous instructor. Yet it is by his compositions, and chiefly by his cantatas, that he is known to American readers. He was born in Hartford, Connecticut, March 10, 1839, the son of a prominent merchant of that city. He had no musical instruction whatever until his sixteenth year; but when he began, he took up the study with so much ardor that his father was obliged to change his plans regarding his commercial career, and, determining to give the young man all possible equipment in his chosen profession, sent him to Leipsic in 1858. There he studied under Plaidy, Richter, Hauptmann, and Rietz. When the last-named professor went to Dresden, Buck followed him there to continue his work and now added organ study with Friedrich Schneider. A year in Paris followed this, and in 1862 he was a well-trained young musician, engaged as organist at the Park Church, in Hartford. Subsequently Buck became organist at St. James's Church in Chicago, where he had all his early compositions burned in the great fire. In 1872 he came to Boston, where he was organist at St. Paul's, and in 1874 he went to New York, where he became Thomas's assistant conductor and the musical director at St. Ann's. Still later, in 1877, he was appointed organist at Holy Trinity, in Brooklyn, which position he retained until 1902, when he became organist at the Brooklyn Tabernacle. He died at Orange, New Jersey, October 6, 1909.

Naturally some of Buck's most important works are organ compositions, and his two sonatas, his "Triumphal March," and his pedal studies are known to most musicians in America, and are sure to remain in the standard repertoire. As an organist he wielded much influence through his concert tours, which extended all over America at a time when it was very important to guide the taste of the multitude. His first "Motette Collection" also came at a time when a better influence was required in the vocal music of the church in America. Buck has been surpassed in this field and in some points of composition by our modern native tone-masters, but he has been a very healthful influence in music in America at just the right time, and it may be borne in mind that if he had been too radical in his forward steps he would have been beyond his public; he would have had no influence at all.

We have said that Buck's most ambitious work was done in the cantata forms. As long ago as 1876 this composer gave a choral contribution to the Centennial Exhibition in Philadelphia, which was sung by one thousand voices under Theodore Thomas's direction. Even before this he had published (in 1874) the "Legend of

Don Munio," a very successful secular cantata. "The Voyage of Columbus," for male voices, deserves mention, and "The Light of Asia" (founded upon Sir Edwin Arnold's poem) is the most elaborate of all Buck's cantatas. All of these works are popular and all are melodious.

Among the most effective of his compositions for the church are the series of four short cantatas, "The Coming of the King," "The Story of the Cross," "Christ the Victor," and "The Triumph of David." The first three are historically and thematically connected;

FIG. 64. — J. C. D. PARKER.

in them the composer has consecutively depicted the main events relating to the prophecy, the birth, the death, the resurrection, and the ascension of Christ, presenting somewhat dramatically, within a suitable time-limit, and with moderate musical difficulty, the chief episodes of the Christian year. "The Triumph of David" treats of a happening distinct and separate from the other three. And in the same class with the cantatas also belongs the "Midnight Service for New Year's Eve." In the field of male-voice music Mr. Buck has achieved fame.

Many of his compositions, notably "Twilight," "The Nun of Nidaros," "King Olaf's Christmas," "Chorus of Spirits and Hours" from Shelley's "Prometheus," "On the Sea," and "Paul Revere's Ride," besides a long list of male quartettes, were written for the Apollo Club (of which he has been for many years director). His songs and ballads number upward of thirty, and among them are such well-known numbers as "Sunset," "The Silent World is Sleeping," "Crossing the Bar," "The Tempest," "The Bedouin Love-song," "The Village Blacksmith," "The Creole Lover's Song." Many of these songs are too saccharine for the purest taste. Frequently Mr. Buck is his own librettist. In "Don Munio," "Columbus" (English and German), "The Festival

Hymn," and "On the Sea," the words are original with the composer.

Buck's setting of the Forty-sixth Psalm, for soli, chorus, and orchestra, first produced by the Handel and Haydn Society of Boston in 1873, requires mention, as also the symphonic overture to Scott's "Marmion" (1880), a work which Thomas first produced with the Philharmonic Society of Brooklyn. His works have won quite as much success in England as in America, his "Light of Asia" having been given in London with such artists as Nordica, Lloyd, and Santley in the cast. As a teacher he has had such pupils as Harry Rowe Shelley, C. B. Hawley, John Hyatt Brewer, Frederic Grant Gleason, and W. H. Neidlinger.

Some reviewers consider Buck too suave and too popular to rank with the best American composers. "Because thou art virtuous shall there be no more cakes and ale!" Must we be eternally condemned to the dramatic dissonances of Loeffler and Van der Stucken because there is a modern school which countenances them? In literature one may enjoy Browning and yet not discard Tennyson; a taste for Wordsworth is not considered incompatible with a delight in Swinburne. Let us have some of this toleration in music too, and enjoy the suave as well as the heroic.

In the domain of opera America has as yet done but little. There are hosts of light operas which, combined with a lavish display of the charms of the chorus girls, have won box-office success in the large cities. Of these musical history need take no note. In the more earnest field, which yields the composer no reward except the faint hope that posterity may appreciate him, there have been, as yet, no startling successes. Chadwick has made the experiment of a sacred opera, "Judith," Paine completed his romantic "Azara," and Coerne has written two operas already spoken of. It fell to the lot of a composer of foreign birth, however, to find a subject well suited to the people of the United States. Walter Damrosch found inspiration in the noble novel of Hawthorne, "The Scarlet Letter."

Walter Damrosch, already spoken of in connection with orchestral and operatic leadership, was born in Breslau, Silesia, January 30, 1862 (Fig. 22). His father was the celebrated Dr. Leopold Damrosch. The son studied music first with his father and afterwards in Dresden with Draeseke.   Although born abroad, he has so thoroughly identified himself with music in America, particularly with the Wagner propaganda here, that it is difficult to think of him other than as an American composer.   Coming to New York in his early childhood, conducting German opera at the Metropolitan Opera House, leading symphony orchestras and the Oratorio Society, marrying the daughter of so prominent an American as James G. Blaine, Damrosch has been steeped in American life for so many years that it was natural to find it seeking expression in his music.

"The Scarlet Letter" was his first great work.   It committed the error of treating a plot thoroughly American in a manner decidedly German.   The libretto was made by George Parsons Lathrop, the son-in-law of Hawthorne.   Few liberties were taken with the powerful novel.   Little Pearl, however, was very curtly done to death before the rise of the curtain, the Rev. John Wilson finishing her story in these lines —

> " A child to thee was born,
>   Bringing disgrace and scorn.
>   Heaven's wise decree
>   Hath taken thy daughter away,
>   Wafted on wings of Death " —

which makes short work of one of Hawthorne's charming characters.   More important than this, Hester finally dies upon the pillory, with Dimmesdale, because ever since " Romeo and Juliet " it has been impossible to kill one lover and save the other; they must go together like a brace of ducks.   For all that, however, one may rebel at the idea of finishing off so grand a character as Hester Prynne by suicide, in the conventional manner of operatic heroines.

As regards the music of this most important operatic work of its time in America, one cannot grow very enthusiastic.   Damrosch has been steeped in the Wagner cauldron, but not to the depth of Achilles, and there is a good deal beyond the heel which remains vulnerable.   The Wagnerian idea in " The Scarlet Letter " is carried out by *leit-motiven* (but not very many of these), by its continuous flow of music (a very few exceptions were made to this), by heavy and dramatic scoring, and by the use of dramatic recitative (*melos*) rather than direct melody.   All this is well enough, but

Wagner revelled in sharp musical delineation of character, and of this Damrosch scarcely exhibited a trace. A little psalm-singing is introduced, — rather too contrapuntally, — and is a proper touch; but to have a band of Puritans marching about, in Massachusetts, circa 1650, singing "'Tis Time we go a-Maying," is stretching probability somewhat. Only Morton's roisterers at Merrymount would have done anything like that.

Nevertheless this madrigal, the forest music, and the prayer of Hester are the finest bits of the opera, and deserve to live even

though the opera dies a natural death. The contrapuntal chorus of the finale of the opera is most un-Puritan in character, although displaying much skill. The whole opera is soaring, too soaring, and the orchestra is heavy enough to suit the gods in Walhalla rather than a simple pair of Puritans.

A further proof of Walter Damrosch's Americanism was given when he devoutly wrote a "Manila Te Deum," giving thanks for the beginning of our national worries in the Philippine Islands. Later on Mr. Damrosch set to music a less

FIG. 65. — H. M. DUNHAM.

national topic and one whose intensity attracted him. He has made an opera out of four acts of Rostand's "Cyrano de Bergerac," the text being by that well-known writer, W. J. Henderson. He has also become conductor of the New York Symphony Society, which his father founded, of which more in the supplement.

It is a long step from such a work as "The Scarlet Letter" to the light operas of America. A great number have been written of which a few stand forth as worthy. One of the best composers in the less ambitious school is Edgar Stillman Kelley. His largest work is called "Puritania." Kelley was born in Sparta, Wisconsin, April 14, 1857. He is of old American stock, both his paternal and maternal ancestors having settled in this country before 1650.

His collegiate education was interrupted by ill health. An accidental hearing of Blind Tom, a half-witted negro pianist, turned his attention seriously to music, though he inherited some musical gifts from his mother (Mary C. Bingham-Kelley), who was his earliest teacher. He went abroad and studied in Stuttgart, graduating from the conservatory there in 1880. He had become something of an organist before that, thanks to Clarence Eddy with whom he studied in Chicago; but his chief knowledge of composition came from Max Seifriz, Royal Court Conductor at Stuttgart.

On his return from Germany Kelley settled in San Francisco, where he exerted a strong and beneficent influence upon California musical life. He was the first well-equipped musical critic in the far West. His first important work here was a setting of dramatic music to Shakespeare's " Macbeth." Strange, bold, and modern it was, but scarcely of a popular cast. Yet backed financially by John Parrott, and played by McKee Rankin, the tragedy with its incidental music ran successfully for three weeks in San Francisco. Local pride may have helped this somewhat, for the same music has never gained a foothold in the East. But this was only the beginning. C. M. S. McLellan offered him a libretto to set to music, and the result was his opera of " Puritania," first produced in Boston in the summer of 1892.

One may speak of " Puritania " as a light pendant to " The Scarlet Letter," for it also deals with Puritan life, but in a playful vein. The music may be heartily praised as being as good as anything achieved by an American in comic opera up to its time, but the libretto has an indelible fault; it deals with witch-hunters and the Salem witchcraft craze. A thinking auditor will always regret seeing so awful a subject used as a comic libretto. The tears of one century can never furnish the laughter of another. To one who reads history, the martyrdom of Giles Corey and Rebecca Nourse would forbid ever jesting about Salem witch-finders.

Kelley may be called the most graceful of our musical humorists, and his comical symphony, " Gulliver in Lilliput," his Chinese suite, " Aladdin," which has been played in Germany very successfully, and his Chinese song, " Lady picking Mulberries," indicate a class of work of which he may be recognized as the originator.

He makes most ingenious use of the Chinese five-toned scale (our own diatonic scale with the fourth and seventh notes left out), and Oriental critics have admitted the genuineness of his treatment of topics relating to the celestial kingdom.

But, although Kelley must be characterized first and foremost by his delicate fun in music (a musical Bret Harte perhaps), his serious works are also musicianly. This versatile composer has advanced rapidly in the large orchestral forms, and his recent " New England " symphony is a work which will take its place in the standard repertoire of great American symphonies. His incidental music to " Ben Hur " is also to be commended for a true presentation of Arabic music and the old Greek modes. Mr. Kelley has recently done excellent service to music by his lectures in university extension, and he is at present instructor in composition in the Oxford, Ohio, College.

Much more popular, although also much more conventional in his music, is Reginald de Koven, who has composed several light operas and a host of songs. His works are not those which create a new school or make musical history, yet his melodic charm, his fluency, his tact and grace, may not be doubted. He was born in Middletown, Connecticut, April 3, 1859, of a distinguished family, his father being an eminent divine. He had exceptional advantages in his education, — his final literary and classical studies being made at St. John's College, Oxford, England, where he took his degree in 1879. Before this he had studied music in Stuttgart, afterwards he went to Frankfort, Vienna, Florence, and Paris, for further study. Vanuccini, Genée, and Delibes may be mentioned as among his teachers. On his return to America success soon came to him, and has continued with him ever since. Such operas as " Robin Hood," " Don Quixote," " The Begum," and such tremendously popular songs as " Oh, Promise me," show that this composer is at least in close touch with his public. " Robin Hood " has been sung many thousand times in the last twenty-five years, and it is said that a full million of copies of " Oh, Promise me " have been sold ! De Koven has composed a dozen light operas. All of them are graceful and fluent, and in none of them can one find anything cheap or meretricious. To win such a marked success in a manner which does not depreciate art or public taste is worth its meed of praise, even if his works bear a strong family resemblance to each other, and are not epoch-making.

We have stated that a quarter-century of active work in America's musical affairs may be considered sufficient naturalization for any composer of foreign birth. Victor Herbert has now completed over that period in America. He is of a famous Irish family, his grandfather being Samuel Lover, the celebrated novelist and poet, and was born in Dublin, February 1, 1859. He was sent to Germany, at seven years of age, to be educated in music. He became a famous violoncellist, and while a mere youth was the principal player of this instrument in the Court Orchestra at Stuttgart. He came to the United States as solo violoncellist with the Metropolitan Opera Company in 1886. Since that time he has been connected with the Thomas, Seidl, and other orchestras, sometimes as violoncellist, sometimes as conductor. In 1894 he became bandmaster of the Twenty-second Regiment Band. From 1898 Herbert was the conductor of the Pittsburg Symphony Orchestra, succeeding Archer in that position, and resigning it in 1903.

Although Herbert's American reputation rests chiefly upon his light operas, he has done nobler work. He has written a short oratorio, "The Captive," for the Worcester Festival Association, two excellent concertos for violoncello and orchestra,[1] and other orchestral works.

Mr. Herbert's recent works have been in the school of Grand Opera, and his successful "Natoma" goes far towards establishing that desideratum, a really native grand opera. The subject is American, and even actual Indian themes are introduced. It is possible that "Natoma" may be more permanent in the repertoire than the operas (see supplementary chapter), which have won great prizes and which at present seem to overshadow it. It was produced in New York and made its way to other cities. Mr. Herbert has also composed a serious one-act opera, entitled "Madeleine," a fine musical setting of the French play "Je dine chez ma Mère."

It should be mentioned here that a young American musician, Mr. Homer Moore, of St. Louis, is at present writing nothing less than

---

[1] Herbert's Second Concerto for violoncello is probably his finest work, and is one of the best existing works of this school.

an American trilogy; three operas founded upon American themes. He says of them: —

"In these works I am trying to so use our national history, traditions, legends, manners, customs, superstitions, and beliefs as to bring out thoroughly their dramatic significance, and to reveal, not so much history and historic characters, as social atmosphere and the forces that prevailed at the time and characterized the minds and opinions of those who did things and were the foundation upon which our national structure, temperament, etc., have been built."

The three operas are to be entitled "The New World," "The Pilgrims," and "The Puritans." Of these the present writer has been able to examine a portion of one opera only, but in that both the plot (Mr. Moore's own libretto) and its treatment promised something fairly worth while. The scheme is, however, somewhat too Wagnerian. Guiding motives are copiously employed and definite melody is not prominent enough.

FIG. 66. — DUDLEY BUCK.

It is doubtful if in a country where single operas by native composers (unless they are "comic") are looked at askance, a native trilogy will have any chance of success. Yet we mention Moore's work as an example of the amount of striving in every part of our country, east and west, to bring forth something "American" in music — and something gigantic!

Another operatic composer, who, like Herbert, won his title of American by years of work in this country, is Bruno Oscar Klein, who was born in Osnabruck, Hanover, June 6, 1858. He settled here in 1878, although occasionally he would make concert tours in Germany, as organist, pianist, and composer. His teaching was done chiefly in New York, where he was connected with several schools, including the National Conservatory of Mrs. Thurber. His single grand opera is not of especial import to American history, being founded on Scott's novel and entitled "Kenilworth." It was performed in Hamburg (in 1895), but has never had an American performance. Klein's shorter compositions are of a high order of merit. He died in New York, June 22, 1911.

Returning to the cantata field and to the strictly American composer, we find an excellent example of sturdy musicianship in a city which has only recently begun to take its place in the ranks of musical centres, — Philadelphia. William Wallace Gilchrist was born in Jersey City, January 8, 1846. Both his parents were musical, and Gilchrist heard good music from his earliest childhood. His musical education was gained entirely in America, chiefly at the University of Pennsylvania, under Dr. Hugh A. Clarke. He was gifted with a good baritone voice and sang in public for some years. His setting of the Forty-sixth Psalm won the $1000 prize offered by the Cincinnati Festival Association. In addition to this, he has won prizes from the Abt Male Chorus of Philadelphia, and the Mendelssohn Glee Club of New York.

Gilchrist's teacher, Professor Clarke, is a devout formalist in music, and it must be said that his pupil follows in his footsteps with obedience. One constantly sees in Gilchrist's compositions a strong composer fettered by contrapuntal rule and by an evident desire not to stray from the highroad of art. There is never anything astonishing, but rather a constant display of skill and ease in the leading of voices. Whenever counterpoint can be used it is present, and always correct, ingenious, and commendable; but one sometimes longs for an outburst of ferocity, for a touch of Loeffler's dissonance and freedom. In songs Mr. Gilchrist has achieved some genuine successes, especially in the gentler moods. He has written some excellent Episcopal music, for in this his dignity and his contrapuntal interweavings are perfectly in place. He is also one of our orchestral composers, and has written a symphony, an orchestral suite, and much chamber-music. All together, he is a thorough musician, a well-equipped composer, with melodic, contrapuntal, and rather formal tastes. In his school he is the equal of any of our composers, and he is, as already intimated, an unquestionable home product.

We now come to an American composer (and not a Catholic) whose chief work is neither a cantata nor an opera, but a mass. Benjamin Cutter is the composer who has won this unique distinction.   He was born in Woburn, Massachusetts, September 6, 1857, his father being a physician of high repute with an inclination toward music.   He studied violin with Julius Eichberg, in Boston, and harmony with Emery, in the New England Conservatory.   Then came further study in Stuttgart, Germany, Seifriz being his teacher of composition.   Mr. Cutter became a good violinist, and was for a time a member of the Boston Symphony Orchestra.   His musical life was passed wholly in Boston, Massachusetts, where he long taught harmony and analysis in the New England Conservatory.   As a teacher his work averaged very high, and he graduated hundreds of pupils.   But his mass in D entitles him to rank with those who have added something permanent to the American repertoire.   It is lofty and majestic in thought and sufficiently free to be classed with the modern school.   Cutter's setting of " Sir Patrick Spens," for chorus and orchestra, is of sufficient dimensions to be called a cantata.   His chamber-music is voluminous.   In his later years his pedagogical work pushed aside the muse.   He has written some standard works, notably a text-book on harmonic analysis and a series of exercises in harmony.   He died in Boston, May 10, 1910.

And finally we may speak of one of the younger American composers of cantata, who, contrary to the usual custom, studied abroad, not in Germany, but in France.   Homer Albert Norris was born in Wayne, Kennebec County, Maine, in 1860.   After a course of musical study at the New England Conservatory in Boston, he went to Paris, where he studied under Dubois, Guilmant, and others for four years.   Norris, on returning from Paris, settled as a teacher in Boston, where he published a work on practical harmony based on the French method.   He has written some romantic songs, but his chief works are two cantatas.   The first, " Nain," would scarcely entitle him to rank with our chief cantata composers, but the second, while it cannot be classed as a masterwork, is at least an effort to contribute something original to the American stock.

Norris has turned to Walt Whitman for his inspiration in this latter composition, and surely a more American poet would be hard to find.   " The Flight of the Eagle " is the name of the cantata.   It is bold, not to say blood-curdling, in some of its progressions, but then Whitman is as unconventional as shirt-sleeves.   Much play is

R

made with a series of diatonic major seconds rising in a continuous scale.   This device is used enough to call it a guiding motive.   It is not certain that eagles fly in this manner, but the originality of the device cannot be denied.   Of Norris's songs " Protestations," with its well-developed violin obbligato, is perhaps the best, although some of his later songs show so much grace and originality that one is inclined to believe that this composer belongs rather among the song-composers than among the creators of those larger works which require sustained effort.   To write songs cleverly, to do good work in the smaller forms, is not to be despised, as all will acknowledge if they study the song-albums of Schumann, Schubert, or Robert Franz.

PLATE IX

KING'S CHAPEL, BOSTON

CHAPTER XII

AMERICAN SONG-COMPOSERS

IN 1892, just before his death, Robert Franz, one of the greatest of song-composers, said to the present writer regarding the smaller vocal forms in music : —

" In this country they looked quite condescendingly upon these small forms, taking the silly notion that these forms arise only incidentally in music. Yet the song-form is really one of the chief foundations of our art; I know that you share this conviction with me."

In another letter (dated March 23, 1889) he says : —

" Until now they have looked upon this form with a shrug of the shoulders, and yet there rests upon it one of the chief factors of music. As regards myself, I have never regretted for a single moment that I have devoted myself exclusively to this branch of music, and with my predecessors have lifted it into its proper position of honor" (Fig. 67).

These words serve as a fitting introduction to those American composers who have won their chief reputation in the domain of songs. What the orchestral and cantata composers have done in this direction we have already seen; but there have been some composers who, attaining only mediocrity in the orchestral field, have reached almost to genius in the production of smaller sketches. Such a composer was Ethelbert Nevin (Fig. 68). His cantata entitled " The Quest" is anything but satisfactory, and yet this same composer has brought forth songs that are as dainty, as inspired, as any that have been composed in this country.

Ethelbert Woodbridge Nevin was born at Edgeworth, Pennsylvania, near Pittsburg, November 25, 1862. His father was a literary man and editor of a newspaper in the last-named city. He inherited his musical tendencies from his mother, who is said to have owned the first grand piano that ever was seen in that section of the country. The boy showed an inclination toward music even in his infancy. His father took him abroad in 1877, and he had the benefit

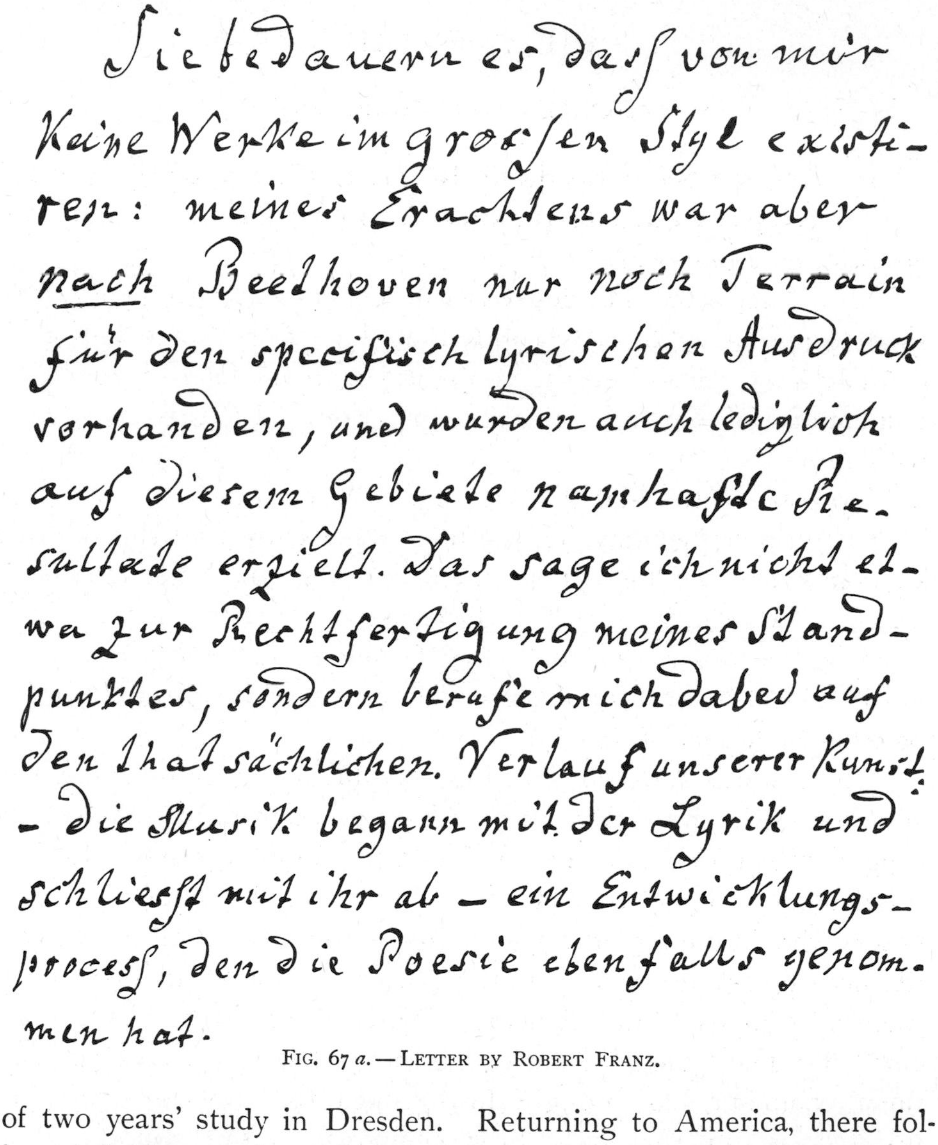

Sie bedauern es, dass von mir keine Werke im grossen Styl existiren: meines Erachtens war aber nach Beethoven nur noch Terrain für den specifisch lyrischen Ausdruck vorhanden, und wurden auch lediglich auf diesem Gebiete namhafte Resultate erzielt. Das sage ich nicht etwa zur Rechtfertigung meines Standpunktes, sondern berufe mich dabei auf den thatsächlichen Verlauf unserer Kunst — die Musik begann mit der Lyrik und schliesst mit ihr ab — ein Entwicklungsprocess, den die Poesie ebenfalls genommen hat.

FIG. 67 a.—LETTER BY ROBERT FRANZ.

of two years' study in Dresden. Returning to America, there followed further study under B. J. Lang and Stephen A. Emery, in Boston. After that there were some years of music-teaching on his own account, in Pittsburg, until enough money was saved up to take a thorough musical course in Berlin. Three years, 1884–86, were

spent in the German capital, during which Nevin studied with
Bülow, Bial, and Klindworth. To the last-named pedagogue he
ascribed nearly all of his musical abilities. He constantly spoke of
Klindworth as a great inspiration to all who came near him. Klind-

Indem ich Ihnen nochmals für
die Theilnahme, welche Sie zu Gunsten
der von mir eingeschlagenen Richtung
bekundeten, Dank sage, bin ich

Ihr
ergebenster

Rob. Franz.

Halle d. 23? März
89.

FIG. 67 *b.* — LETTER BY ROBERT FRANZ.

worth's aim was not only to make good musicians, but cultured men,
and he held that one result could not be reached without the other.
Bülow seems also to have appreciated the talent possessed by Nevin,
and the American student was admitted into that master's "artist's
class."

In 1887 Nevin returned to America again, this time settling in Boston. But his was a restless career, and a few years afterward he went to Paris, achieving good success there as a teacher. A year later he reappeared in Berlin, working so hard that his health broke down, and he was ordered to Algiers. After that came concert tours, piano recitals, in this country. His attack of nervous prostration caused the postponement of some of these concerts, but in 1894 he was able to appear again. Those who heard him play at these concerts realized that while he had not a technique comparable to the Rosenthals, D'Alberts, or Paderewskis of piano work, he had a most poetic conception, free from mawkishness, and was a delightful interpreter. In these concerts both his piano works and his songs made the best possible impression. It is not necessary to give a list of Nevin's songs.[1] His "Rosary" is the most famous American song ever written; it won a fortune for the composer and his heirs. His "Narcissus" for piano was almost as popular. His piano works have all the poetry of Schumann; his songs are like the *Lieder* of the best German writers. He was a master of his *genre*.

His roving life went on; Florence, Venice, then Paris again, and finally America once more, followed in quick succession. Some work in New Haven seemed to promise a permanent position in America when suddenly there came — death! The constant study, the fever of composition, the ceaseless travel, had done their work, and in 1901 Nevin's short career ended. One can pay tribute to him as being one of the most poetic of American composers; and to him might be applied the epitaph which Grillparzer wrote for Schubert: —

> " Fate buried here a rich possession,
> But yet greater promise ! "

The lesson of Nevin's work might profitably be taken to heart. If only there were less of striving to create symphonies that no one wishes to play or hear, of operas that show straining and labor in every part, and more of genuine unforced music in the smaller forms! The chief trouble with most of the American composers is an ambition that o'erleaps itself. In justice to the memory of Nevin

---

[1] A good analytical list may be found in Rupert Hughes's "Contemporary American Composers."

it ought to be added that he felt that his efforts in the larger forms were misplaced. Even the cantata mentioned at the beginning of this sketch was not published or performed during the composer's life. It is a posthumous work.

Close to Nevin, perhaps his equal in some ways, is Clayton Johns (Fig. 69), whose smaller works are known not only through America, but are popular in Germany and England as well. He was born in Newcastle, Delaware, November 24, 1857, and as a boy he taught himself to play the piano, with the usual weak result. Study at the Newcastle schools and at Rugby Academy in Wilmington, were preliminary to an intended entrance into Princeton University. The boy wished to study music, the father (James McCallmont Johns) wished him to study law. A compromise was effected by which both plans were given up and architecture substituted, and the young man entered an architect's office in Philadelphia, where he spent three years. He then came to Boston to enter the Institute of Technology, in pursuance of this profession, but the musical influence of Boston awakened all his dormant passion for that art. Architecture has been described as "frozen music," and with Johns it had already begun to thaw.

This was in 1879, and being now of age and free to choose, the young man went to William H. Sherwood for piano lessons, and to William F. Apthorp for instruction in harmony. Two months' experience with the new pupil led both these teachers to recommend his devoting himself entirely to music, and (continuing with Sherwood in piano study) he went to Harvard where he took the musical course under John K. Paine. In 1882 Johns went to Berlin, where he studied piano under Grabow, Raif, and Rummel, and composition under Kiel. He returned to Boston in the autumn of 1884, and has resided there ever since.

At present Mr. Johns busies himself with teaching, composing, and occasionally with a concert tour here and there. He has given recitals of his compositions in Boston, Philadelphia, Washington, and many other cities. Although he has written a few choruses and some works for string orchestra, it is not by these that he will be judged. It is true that the Boston Symphony Orchestra once performed two movements for string orchestra (a berceuse and a scherzo with trio) by Johns, but these made no very decided impression. The berceuse had the usual saccharine touches with muted violins, but at least it had direct melody and not too much of complex development. The scherzo with trio was in the accepted song-form, dainty and delicate enough, and a carillon-like returning passage was ingenious. Coming, as it did, after Liszt's discordant " Mephistopheles " movement (" Faust " symphony), the work was welcome, but taken by itself it is only a magnified song-form.

Mr. Johns's piano works are practical, melodic, and interesting, but his songs overtop them, and with few exceptions are graceful, elegant, and unforced. He has written over a hundred of these, in English, French, and German. He does not voice intense passion, but is something of an American Mendelssohn in this field. He knows how to choose his subjects well, and in setting Dobson, Herford, or Arlo Bates he has reached perfection. It is to be hoped that he will some day try his hand at Herford's " Floriana," for, in spite of Arthur Whiting's excellent treatment of the theme, one feels that it was made for Clayton Johns. Of course he has set Heine's " Du bist wie eine Blume " — who has not? This poem has been far more frequently set to music than any other. There are nearly four hundred settings known, and more are constantly arriving. But Johns's setting has a *raison d'être*, for it is very refined and fitting to the poem.

It may be mentioned also that Johns's compositions are known in England, where some of his part-songs and a chorus for female voices and a string orchestra have been sung and played with much success. The reprints of his songs also find a good market in Germany. All together, he, like Ethelbert Nevin, has won success by not attempting more than he could easily and artistically accomplish. At times he reminds one of Robert Franz, who is also delicate rather than intense. The accompaniments of Johns's songs are especially praiseworthy, for he does not become trivial in this part of the song, nor, on the other hand, does he ever write piano compositions with vocal attachment, as Jensen and even Richard Strauss have sometimes done.

Since we have spoken of the great song-composer Franz, in

FIG. 68.—ETHELBERT W. NEVIN.

this chapter, we may speak of a man who exerted much influence in the days when Boston's classical taste was forming, and who was the strongest representative of Robert Franz in this country. Otto Dresel was a foreigner, for he was born in Andernach, in 1826; but he lived in America nearly forty years, dying at Beverly, Massachusetts, July 26, 1890. He not only taught in Boston, but he upheld the standard of classical music in America, at a time when Dwight, Thayer, and a small band of pioneers were striving to lead New England away from its eternal psalmody. Dresel wrote a book of *Lieder* that, although little known, was one of the most sterling things in vocal work that had, up to its time, been produced in America. He edited Bach's "Well-tempered Clavichord," made a great piano accompaniment to Handel's "Messiah," and was one of the moving forces in the musical growth that began in America a little over a half-century ago.

FIG. 69. — CLAYTON JOHNS.

Although, strictly speaking, George L. Osgood should be classed with the prominent teachers of America, yet his song compositions are sufficiently important to be treated of here, particularly as that portion of his work has not been recognized by those who have heretofore written of American compositions. Osgood is one of the finest melodists that America has ever possessed, and the accompaniments of his songs and the harmonies of his part-songs, are among the most fluent and singable in our repertory. His part-song, "In Picardie," his "Wake not, but hear me, Love," may be cited as examples of the sweetness which does not cloy, and which is not akin to musical vulgarity. Few composers have so tastefully united the popular and the classical as this excellent musician.

George Laurie Osgood was born in Chelsea, Massachusetts,

April 3, 1844 — a lineal descendant of John Osgood, the Puritan, who landed at Salem in 1632. He was graduated from Harvard in 1866. In college he was conductor of the Glee Club and of the orchestra, with inclinations and faculties from the start indicating a musical career. In 1867 he went to Berlin for the study of composition under Haupt, and vocal expression under Sieber. In Halle he formed an intimate friendship with Robert Franz. He went to Italy in 1869, and for three years studied the art of singing with Lamperti, in Milan. In 1871 he repaired to Germany, and gave a series of concerts in Vienna, Leipsic, Dresden, Berlin, and other cities. Returning to America, he soon made an engagement with Theodore Thomas, and traveled through the country in connection with the Thomas orchestra. Finally he settled in Boston, where he soon became celebrated as a teacher, composer, and conductor. In 1875 he assumed the directorship of the Boylston Club, a promising choral organization then in its third year, and soon refined its singing, aroused its enthusiasm, and gave to Boston one of the most noteworthy clubs in its musical history. Under Mr. Osgood's direction the perfection of its performances became known throughout America. Among his many works are a "Guide in the Art of Singing," a volume of two hundred pages, already passed through eight editions, and numerous choral works for concert and church. He now dwells in England.

Boston has been peculiarly rich in song-composers, among whom Frederic Field Bullard (Fig. 70) was not the least. He was born in Boston, September 21, 1864, and was at first destined for the science of chemistry, studying in this branch at the Massachusetts Institute of Technology when twenty-three years of age. But finally he turned to music as his life-work, and, at twenty-four years of age, he began a four-years' course in composition and organ playing, at the Munich Royal School, under Rheinberger. This German teacher (Fig. 51) almost deserves a chapter to himself in an American history of music, for, since 1878–79, when Charles D. Carter, of Pittsburg, and George W. Chadwick studied with him (they were, we think, the first of the American band), an endless procession, including H. W. Parker, Arthur Whiting, Henry H. Huss, F. F. Bullard, Wallace Goodrich, and others, has passed through

Munich and come back to the United States perfected in composition through his influence. The recent death of Rheinberger will be felt as a distinct loss, since his influence upon American composition has exceeded that of any other European teacher.

To return to Bullard: his public reputation rests chiefly upon his songs and part-songs. He holds well to the laws of form and harmony, which is a marvel in these days when so many composers feel that every emotion must break at least six rules of harmony. But Bullard does not become weak through harmony; indeed, his strongest charm is his virility and straightforwardness. His drinking-songs suggest wine rather than lemonade, and when he deals with warlike themes he has a viking vigor that has often been felt at the Apollo concerts in Boston.

FIG. 70. — FREDERIC FIELD BULLARD.

Bullard also worked in some of the larger forms. He wrote a series of Christmas and Easter cantatas (published by Schirmer, New York), and edited several collections of songs, particularly a college song-book for his own Alma Mater, the Institute of Technology. Bullard died in Boston, June 24, 1904. He left numerous compositions in manuscript. Judging by the vigor of his " Stein Song" this man would have had much to give to the world. It is not too much to say that he was the most promising of American composers. Here, if at all, was an American Bizet.

Frank Lynes is another of the Boston group of song-composers. He was born in Cambridge, Massachusetts, May 16, 1858, and studied at first at the New England Conservatory. Subsequently there was some study of organ and piano with Mr. B. J. Lang, and harmony with Professor John K. Paine. Then came the Leipsic Conservatory with Reinecke, Richter, and Jadassohn as teachers. Lynes followed the highway of music, not seeking any new and dangerous paths, but his songs, piano works, and choruses are well constructed and very singable. He was a charming worker in the small forms. Mr. Lynes died at Bristol, New Hampshire, June 24, 1913. He left a large number of creditable compositions, none of them in the large forms. One of his songs may be objected to upon æsthetic principles. As the words have been set by other American composers in a similar manner, the impeachment here may be considered as against a school rather than an individual. The poem is by Kingsley : —

> " When all the world is young, lad,
>   And all the trees are green,
>   And every goose a swan, lad,
>   And every lass a queen, —
>   Then hey for boot and horse, lad,
>   And round the world away !
>   Young blood must have its course, lad,
>   And every dog his day.
>
> " When all the world is old, lad,
>   And all the trees are brown,
>   And all the sport is stale, lad,
>   And all the wheels run down, —
>   Creep home, and take your place there,
>   The spent and maimed among ;
>   God grant you find one face there
>   You loved when all was young ! "

If ever major and minor were represented in poetry, it is in these two stanzas. To set them both to the same music is little short of a crime. Yet just this matter of the proper illustration, the interpretation of the verse by the tone, is what song-writers both in America and England have failed to study sufficiently. Balfe set " The Sands o' Dee," four contrasted word-pictures, to the same music ;

Hullah set "The Three Fishers" (security, anxiety, and disaster) to the same melody; and American composers have given Tennyson's "Ask me no More,"—which pictures first stanza, indifference; second stanza, sympathy; third stanza, the utter yielding of love—to *one tune* thrice repeated. Germany is beyond us in musical interpretation. England and America must needs study Wagner's theories regarding the wedding of poetry and music.

Before leaving the Boston colony of composers we must again speak of a man of foreign birth, whose influence has been far more extensive in his adopted than in his native country. Augusto Rotoli (Fig. 71) was born in Rome, January 7, 1847. His Italian reputation was high enough before he came to America, for he was a choir-boy at St. Peter's, founded a great choral society and directed it, was vocal teacher to the Princess Margherita, and was maestro of the Cappella Reale del Sudario. For all this his twenty years of American work represent the maturer portion of his life, and certainly show the more far-reaching influence. He has composed a Roman festival mass and a host of songs in the passionate Italian school. In 1885 he was one of the faculty of the New England Conserva-

FIG. 71. — AUGUSTO ROTOLI.

tory of Music, and he continued in that position until his death, which took place in Boston, November 26, 1904. He had many very famous vocal pupils.

Jules Jordan, living in Providence (Rhode Island), and leading the Arion Club there, has considerable reputation as a composer of songs. He was born in Willimantic (Connecticut), November 10, 1850, and has been the chief vocal conductor of Providence for nearly a quarter of a century. He is a pupil of George L. Osgood, Sbriglia, and Shakespeare. An opera, a large cantata, and some orchestral works stand to his credit, but his songs and his vocal conductorship form his chief services in the cause of American music.

A list of others who have built up the song-form in America, both in its instrumental and vocal application, would include William Harold Neidlinger (born in Brooklyn, July 20, 1863), a pupil of Dudley Buck; Homer Newton Bartlett (born in Olive, New York, December 28, 1845), whose work embraces many sterling compositions; Harvey W. Loomis (born in Brooklyn, February 5, 1865), who won Dvořák's hearty commendation when that master was teaching in New York, and who has written many large works, but whose best expression is found in his songs; James H. Rogers (born in Fair Haven, Connecticut, in 1857), who studied in Berlin and Paris, and whose songs and short piano pieces are of much excellence; George W. Marston (born in Sandwich, Massachusetts, in 1840), whose songs deserve more attention than has been paid to them; Alfred G. Robyn (born in St. Louis, April 29, 1860), who has composed in the large forms, but whose best works are his poetic and artistic songs; William Victor Harris (born in New York, April 27, 1869), whose songs again are better than his cantata and operatic works. All of these men are still living except Marston, who died in 1901, and as most of them are not old, much may yet be expected from them. Of this band two have worked in the West, Robyn in St. Louis, and Rogers in Cleveland, but Robyn is now in Brooklyn.

Even in the far West one begins to find earnest composers who are no longer isolated from the musical world. San Francisco, for example, has at present its own orchestral concerts, directed by Alfred Hertz, and musical conservatories of good rank. Most of its musical leaders are, however, of foreign birth. Its chief organist is an Englishman, but his service of nearly a score of years in this country causes his work to be of greater import to America than to England. Humphrey John Stewart was born in London, but came to this country in 1886. Since that time he has been almost constantly in San Francisco, engaged as the organist of leading churches. For one year, 1901–02, he was organist of Trinity Church, Boston. At present he is at St. Dominic's in San Francisco. He was solo organist of the Buffalo Exposition of 1901, and has received the honorary degree of Mus. Doc. In spite of his prominence as performer, Dr. Stewart is of chief importance to the far West as a

composer.   He has written three operas, which have been performed, and has composed an oratorio.   Many organ recitals have
been given by him.   Yet his songs, part-songs, and his church
music (vocal) are, to our thinking, the important factors in his work.
California has many musicians within its borders, but, as yet, very
few worthy composers.   Mr. Stewart is also a factor in the Western
musical advance by his able criticisms.   He is the leading musical
reviewer of the Pacific coast.

PLATE X

BENJAMIN JOHNSON LANG

CHAPTER XIII

ORGANISTS, CHOIR AND CHORUS LEADERS

IT may be accepted as an axiom that, while vocalists are frequently not thorough musicians, organists are the most versatile, the best musically trained of all. Among the leading organists of America, we find many of the men who have made the brief musical history of the country. John K. Paine was an organ virtuoso, as well as a composer; Chadwick, Parker, Dudley Buck, and a host of those whose names have already been passed in review, were organists. In this chapter, therefore, while speaking of celebrated musicians who have won their fame upon the organ or by organ composition, it should be remembered that in almost every case they have won equal fame by chorus direction, by piano playing, or by other achievements in the musical field.

No better example of this can be cited than Benjamin J. Lang. He was a most prominent organist of Boston for years, and was the organist of the Handel and Haydn Society for more than a generation; but he has also been one of the foremost piano teachers of the country, has been conductor of some of the chief musical clubs of America, and has introduced many of the most important musical works of the world into this country. In short, he was so thoroughly interwoven with musical progress of every kind, in the United States, that there is scarcely any classification of musicians in which his name would not fitly find place; yet, as his work in Boston began as an organist, and as he has published none of his compositions, we may speak of him among those composers whose favorite instrument is the organ.

Benjamin Johnson Lang (Pl. X) is one of the most typically American figures that we can find in our musical history. He was a man of enterprise beyond any European comprehension — a man who was a perfect organizer.   He was born in Salem, Massachusetts, December 28, 1837.   He studied music at first with his father, who was a good organist and piano teacher.   After this the lad took lessons in Boston, to such good purpose that he became a church organist and choir leader at fifteen.   There was some study abroad from 1855 to 1858, and Satter, Jaell, and Liszt himself aided in forming the piano playing of the young musician.   Studies in composition were not neglected.   On his return to America, Lang became organist of the South Congregational Church, and held that position for twenty years.   His service in the same capacity at the Old South and at King's Chapel also extended over many years.   He was one of the movers in the matter of bringing the first really great organ to America, and his work with the Handel and Haydn Society was only second in importance to that of Zerrahn in the evolution of that organization.   Still more important than this has been his career as conductor and interpreter of great works.   It is not an exaggeration to state that no one man achieved more for the educational advance of Boston in music than B. J. Lang.   As a pianist he had won some laurels, although he scarcely could rank with the great virtuosi of the instrument. Nevertheless, his certainty in ensemble work was something to grow enthusiastic over, and in chamber-music or in playing an accompaniment none of our native musicians could excel him.

Lang's conducting was generally stronger on the vocal than upon the instrumental side.   He could not play on an orchestra as Gericke, Paur, Nikisch, or Thomas have done, but he equalled almost any of these men in conducting or in training a chorus. Fortunately, his chief work led him into that path.   The Apollo Club, a male chorus, was formed in 1868.   From that time, until 1901, Lang was its director, and he made it for a time the best club of its class in America.   In 1874 the Cecilia Club was founded, a mixed chorus, and from its foundation until the year 1907 Lang was its sole conductor.   Of his year of conductorship of the Handel and Haydn Society, we need say little, for he took the society when it was at a low ebb and torn with dissensions; but as conductor of the Apollo and the Cecilia clubs it is simply impossible to overrate his labors.   Just as Liszt in Weimar did missionary work in teaching, in presenting great works which might otherwise remain unknown, in bringing great artists before the public, so, in a less promising field (and therefore in a less degree), did Mr. Lang work for Boston, and through Boston for the entire East, in developing art.   No work was too great or too difficult for him to undertake its rehearsal with the forces under his control.   Berlioz's " Damnation de Faust," and his Requiem, Bach's B minor mass, Brahms's Requiem, Wagner's " Parsifal,"—the list might be greatly extended beyond this,—were all introduced to our concert audiences by this great worker.

As a composer we cannot speak of this remarkable musician, for although he had written much, he never printed anything, and very seldom allowed any of his work to be heard.   The present writer has, long since, had a few auditions of some of the smaller compositions of Mr. Lang, and they were fluent, graceful, and musicianly.   But it is evident that this veteran conductor did not wish to be considered as a composer.   Both he and Mr. Thomas have, in letters, declined the composer's title, yet their work for music in America has gone far beyond the creation of a symphony or an opera, for they have taught the public how to appreciate the best music, and have made it familiar with the modern masterpieces.

Mr. Lang's influence as a teacher was also far-reaching.   He gathered around him a circle of distinguished pupils who have become in a degree disciples.   Among these one may mention Arthur Foote, Ethelbert Nevin, William F. Apthorp, his own daughter, Margaret R. Lang, and a host of others.   It was very fitting that Yale University, in 1903, should have given an honorary degree of M.A. to Mr. Lang.   His was a talent of high order, working in a sensible and practical manner.   One may recognize limitations while acknowledging all the great results achieved.   He was most active in all the various branches of music we have outlined above, almost to the day of his death, which occurred in Boston on April 3, 1909.   The time will come when America will recognize him as among the very foremost of those who created a musical taste among us; and when one views the many directions in which this beneficent influence has been exerted, one feels tempted to call Mr. Lang a musical " Admirable Crichton."

In a chapter devoted to organists it may not be amiss to speak of the advent of the first great organ in this country. We have already, in speaking of Pilgrims and Puritans, shown the slowness with which the organ was accepted in New England. There were churches in Boston, in 1810, that still held the organ as a godless instrument. To this same city, however, there came, in 1863, the first thorough concert organ of this country (Fig. 72). The organ was built by E. F. Walcker & Son, of Ludwigsburg, in Germany. The Music Hall corporation, chiefly through the efforts of Dr. George B. Upham, at first appropriated $10,000 toward the organ which (as they stated in their prospectus) would stand in Boston "for centuries of years." When the instrument finally came, after some delay because of the troubles of the Civil War, it cost about $70,000. The first to play upon it, when it was erected in Music Hall, were B. J. Lang, John H. Wilcox, John K. Paine, Eugene Thayer, Dr. S. P. Tuckerman, and G. W. Morgan. This was probably the most famous gathering of organists that had ever assembled in America. It occurred November 2, 1863.

The history of the great instrument may be very briefly recited. Some of its stops were beautiful beyond compare; its mechanism was less excellent. It spoke rather slowly, and the organist had to keep well ahead of the conductor's beat when accompanying. When the Boston Symphony concerts began to crowd Music Hall, it was found that the organ took up too much room, and it was sold, in 1884, to Hon. William Grover, who presented it to the New England Conservatory of Music, hoping that that institution could build a hall for it. Before it was taken down Frederick Archer gave a concert that proved the instrument to be still a marvellous one. It became, however, a white elephant; the conservatory found it impracticable to build a hall as vast as such an instrument would require, and finally the great organ that was to stand for "centuries" was sold, thirty-four years after it had been set up, for the sum of $1500, as old metal and lumber! Since that time, however, America has built many great organs (Fig. 73) (there is no longer the necessity of going abroad for them), and Cincinnati, New York, Chicago, and other cities now boast of instruments that, if they do not equal every stop of the first-named instrument in tone-quality, greatly surpass it in mechanism.

FIG. 72. — MUSIC HALL ORGAN, BOSTON.

The chief names in the older generation of concert organists in America, the men who were pioneers in the modern musical movement, are John H. Wilcox, George W. Morgan, and Samuel P. Tuckerman.   Dr. Tuckerman was born in Boston, in 1819, and studied here with Carl Zeuner.   He became organist of St. Paul's Church, and afterwards went to England, where he carried on extensive studies.   On his return to America he gave many recitals and lectures, and wrote much good church music.   George W. Morgan was born in England (1822), and had an excellent musical training before he came to America.   His influence was exerted in New York after 1853.   John Henry Wilcox was a Southerner, having been born in Savannah, Georgia, in 1827.   His work was chiefly done in Boston, where he gave many popular concerts.   Wilcox was fond of sugar-coating the classical pill, and his programmes would scarcely stand severe criticism, but he was full of good taste in registration, and he generally managed to smuggle in a little of Bach among his more "catchy" pieces.   Eugene Thayer, born in Mendon, Massachusetts, in 1838, became another of the early virtuosi upon the organ in this country.   He was a good composer of sacred music, and one of his cantatas gained for him the degree of Mus. Doc. from Oxford University.

To come to the men of the present, some of our best composers of sacred music are to be found among the organists.   One of the most practical writers for the instrument that this country has yet produced is George Elbridge Whiting (Fig. 74).   Mr. Whiting was born in Holliston, Massachusetts, September 14, 1842.   He played the organ publicly when thirteen years of age, and at sixteen he succeeded Dudley Buck as organist of the North Congregational Church at Hartford.   He studied with George W. Morgan in New York, but soon went to England, where he became one of the most talented pupils of the renowned Best, of Liverpool, frequently taking the place of that master.   On his return to America Whiting became organist at St. Joseph's, in Albany, where the celebrated Albani (then Emma la Jeunesse) was the soprano of his choir.   After this he moved to Boston (where he had been organist for a short time before), becoming leader at King's Chapel and concert organist at Music Hall.   Another trip abroad followed, this time to Berlin, where Whiting studied harmony with Haupt, and orchestration with Radecke.   On his return to America he became teacher of the organ at the New England Conservatory, holding that position (with the exception of three years spent as a teacher at the Cincinnati College of Music) until 1898.   He was also for many years the organist and musical director of the Church of the Immaculate Conception, in

FIG. 73. — ORGAN IN JORDAN HALL, BOSTON.

Boston.   As a teacher, he has educated many of the leading young organists of America.

But it is as a composer that Mr. Whiting takes rank above the organists thus far mentioned.   He is the best organ composer of America.   His organ sonata and his pieces and studies for the organ, are well fitted to become a model in the organ music of the world.   He has also written much vocal church music which not only is in good form and singable, but gives all necessary dramatic effect without breaking rules.   He is a master of the Gregorian tones, — tones far too little used and understood by modern writers; and he has written four masses, a great Te Deum, and some worthy cantatas, of which "The Tale of the Viking," "Henry of Navarre," and the "March of the Monks of Bangor" are the best. His orchestral works include a symphony, an overture, a piano concerto.   He has also recently completed an Italian opera in one act, entitled "Lenore."   Mr. Whiting has a charming gift of melody and is far removed from the ultra-modern noise-makers.   Regarded as an organ virtuoso, as a teacher and as a composer (and particularly as an organ composer), George E. Whiting must be accorded a prominent place among the workers in the field of American music.

Probably the most talented pupil of Mr. Whiting is Henry M. Dunham, who has himself become a prominent virtuoso and composer for the instrument.   Henry Morton Dunham (Fig. 65) was born in Brockton, Massachusetts, July 27, 1853.   He comes of a musical family, many of his relatives being professional musicians of rank.   His chief studies were at the New England Conservatory of Music, under Mr. Whiting, and his contrapuntal training came in large degree from John K. Paine.   A short trip abroad followed his student life and, on his return to this country, he was appointed a member of the faculty of the New England Conservatory and is still teacher of the organ in that institution.   Mr. Dunham has been an organist in many of the leading churches of New England, his work at the Ruggles Street Church in Boston being very prominent in Boston's choral music.   As a composer for the organ he has accomplished not a little.   His compositions include an Organ School, two organ sonatas, fantasia and fugue in D minor, a festival march, theme, and variations for piano and organ, and some thirty other works for the latter instrument.

One can trace out musical descent as one would follow any other genealogy.   Speaking after the Biblical manner, one might say that Best begat Whiting, Whiting begat Dunham, and Dunham begat Goodrich; for Wallace Goodrich, one of the most promising of all the younger organists and conductors, studied the organ with Dunham and composition with Chadwick.   Wallace Goodrich (Fig. 75) was born in Newton, Massachusetts, May 27, 1871.   At nine years old he began studying piano; at fourteen he was giving organ recitals and had a public position as organist in a Newton church. He went to Europe when twenty-three years of age (1894) and followed that great American procession already spoken of, to Munich, where he became a pupil (of course) of Rheinberger, and also of Ludwig Abel.   He won a silver medal at this school by his com-

FIG. 74. — GEORGE E. WHITING.

position and organ playing.   In the fall of 1895 he went to Paris, where he studied with Widor.

It may be said in passing, that Charles M. Widor is an organist and composer whose greatness has not as yet been fully recognized. More powerful and solid than the suave and facile Guilmant, the style of the organist of St. Sulpice does not win so speedy an appreciation as that of his competitor and contemporary, but Widor is building to last, nevertheless.   It was of immense benefit for Goodrich to study in Paris, for to the solidity of German attainments he now added Gallic grace; and the Frenchmen broke the fetters in which the Germans play Bach, for the young organist.   Study of operatic conducting followed in Germany and close acquaintance with plain song and ancient church music in Italy; so that when, in 1897, Goodrich came back to this country and began teaching in the New England Conservatory, he was one of the most broadly educated musicians imaginable.

Goodrich has not composed or published much as yet.   A Latin hymn, an overture for orchestra, an " Ave Maria " for chorus and orchestra, an operetta, and a requiem (in English) are still in manuscript.   He has, however, written valuable essays upon organ playing and is exerting a wide influence by his teaching.   He has done some very important work in conducting different societies, and was conductor of the Boston Opera Company for some time.   He is now Dean of the New England Conservatory of Music, in Boston.

As an organ soloist Mr. Goodrich has appeared in the symphony concerts of different cities, and is one of the surest ensemble
players that we possess.   He has also been the organist of Trinity
Church, Boston.   The work of this man extends in so many directions (we must not forget to add that he has lectured on church
music), that we can confidently predict that if the mantle of Mr. Lang
is ever to descend to any one, it will fall upon the shoulders of
Mr. Goodrich.

Everett E. Truette is another of Mr. Dunham's pupils.   He has
given some four hundred organ recitals throughout the United
States, and yet perhaps the best work he has done for organ playing
has been his writings upon that theme.   These have been many
and interesting.

Probably one of the chief figures in connection with the music
of the Anglican church was Samuel Brenton Whitney.   This veteran of high-class church music was born in Woodstock, Vermont,
June 4, 1842.   Although he studied at first with local teachers, and
afterward with Charles Wels, of New York, yet his chief musical
education came from John K. Paine, whose substitute in organ work
he frequently became.   Soon after this period of study Mr. Whitney
was appointed organist and choir-master at the Church of the
Advent, where he soon introduced the beautiful English Cathedral
service in all its musical glory.   For more than thirty years Mr.
Whitney held this post.   At the twenty-fifth anniversary of his
entrance into it, several of his old choir-boys, now grown to famous
men, sang in the service, and Dr. H. H. A. Beach and the celebrated
tenor, Charles R. Adams, were in that chorus.

Naturally the boy choir is an important factor in such a church.
Mr. Whitney stood as the chief conductor in this field in America.
His boy choir has been the musical model of many other churches.
Phillips Brooks longed for such a choir and hoped to have the
director as well, but Mr. Whitney held to his old post, and the
famous clergyman was too high-minded to make any efforts (beyond
his expressed wish) to draw him away from the Church of the
Advent.

Mr. Whitney established another valuable English custom in
New England; he brought about parish choir festivals, and

directed many of them, and at the New England Conservatory of Music he established what was probably the first "Church Music Class" in America.   As a performer he was one of the best organists of the country, yet he seldom displayed his abilities in this field outside of his church.   His Bach playing was remarkably dignified, and without that rigidity with which German organists too often invest it.

The compositions of this modest musician are of high quality. A piano trio by him has been heard in many American concerts in many American cities.   A processional by Mr. Whitney has become as famous in London as in America, and has been republished abroad.   It has been rearranged for piano, for orchestra, and there is even an edition, in raised notation, for the use of the blind.   A canon in G has become nearly as popular.   His hymn, "The Son of God goes forth to War," has become world-famous, being even translated into Portuguese.   The church services (Anglican) that Mr. Whitney has composed are numerous.   This great worker in the music of the Anglican Church died in Vermont (the state in which he was born) in 1914.

FIG. 75.—J. WALLACE GOODRICH.

It may be claimed that New York had such church music before Boston, and quite as good; but the fact is that the chief Episcopal composers in New York have been Englishmen.   The most prominent American in this field belongs to New England.   Yet there is one man whose career in New York may parallel that of Mr. Whitney in Boston, although his musicianship was not upon the same level.   Mr. George W. Warren, born in Albany, August 17, 1828, was almost entirely self-taught in music, although he had a broad education in other directions at Racine University. He was for ten years the organist and director of Holy Trinity Church, in Brooklyn, and for thirty years the organist and director at St. Thomas's Church in New York. On his twenty-fifth anniversary of service a great commemorative festival was held, as for Mr. Whitney in Boston. He has left some effective church music and a son, Richard Henry Warren, who is musical director at the Church of the Ascension, and is also a sterling composer.

But a greater Warren once labored in New York — a man who may stand with the church organists of any country and not be relegated to an inferior position. And this man, although born in Canada, belongs to the United States, for his father was a Rhode Island organ-builder, who had moved to Montreal to carry on his manufacture in that city. In Montreal, therefore, on February 18, 1841, Samuel Prowse Warren was born (Fig. 76). His childhood was spent amid the surroundings of organ manufacture, and he was familiar with the instrument even before he began its study. While a mere lad, he became the organist at the American Church in Montreal. After finishing his general studies at college, in 1861, he started for Berlin to complete his musical education. In his case it was Haupt for the organ, Wieprecht in instrumentation, and G. Schumann as piano teacher. In 1864 he came back to Montreal, but soon went to New York, where he dwelt thereafter. All Souls' Church, Trinity Church, and Grace Church have had him at different times as a leader. He was one of the great concert organists of America, and has given many recitals. In New York alone he has played hundreds of times in public. Mr. Warren has added to our store of church music, yet by no means in the degree of Whiting or Whitney. He died in New York in 1915.

In Edward Morris Bowman we again find an organist whose work in music is not to be bounded by his instrument. Mr. Bowman's influence has been exerted as a teacher and most prominently as an organizer of associations to protect the American composer. He was born in Barnard, Vermont, July 18, 1848. After considerable desultory training in music he came under the influence of Dr. William Mason (whose work we shall describe in the succeeding chapter), and finally went to Berlin, where Bendel, Haupt, and Weitzmann were his instructors. Afterwards Guilmant, Batiste, and Macfarren in Paris and London, helped his musical studies still further. Mr. Bowman, as the originator and first president of the American College of Musicians, and as a very active president of the Music Teachers' National Association, did very much for the native composer. As the head of the musical department of Vassar College from 1891 to 1895, he worked faithfully in the cause of college education in music, and as a director he has also done permanent service to American music. He organized the famous " Temple Choir " of Brooklyn, and conducted that and many other societies. His death took place in Brooklyn, August 27, 1913.

FIG. 76. — SAMUEL P. WARREN.

Two other eminent American organists are musical descendants of Samuel P. Warren, and both have claims to be recorded in a historical account of America's music. Gerrit Smith, born in Hagerstown, Maryland, December 11, 1859, in addition to his important work as church and concert organist, held a conspicuous position as a composer; William C. Carl, born in Bloomfield, New Jersey, March 2, 1865, is to be ranked as one of the founders of the American Guild of Organists, and a very active concert organist, whose recitals have extended throughout this country. He is also a church organist in New York and a conductor of vocal societies in that city. In addition to their organ study with Warren, Smith studied with Haupt, in Berlin, and Carl with Guilmant, in Paris. In connection with organ playing it may be mentioned that Haupt and Guilmant have had as direct an influence upon American organ work as Rheinberger upon American composition.

Haupt has taught more than one hundred and fifty American organists, among them being Thayer, Whiting, Warren, Bowman, Morgan, Eddy, Paine, and Arthur Bird.

Before leaving the New York colony we must mention Louis Arthur Russell (another Warren pupil), who has written much good music and musical literature; Charles H. Morse, who, although more constantly engaged in college work, and no longer resident in New York, has done prominent work in Plymouth Church, and has been an indefatigable worker in organizing societies for the benefit of American musicians; John Hyatt Brewer, who has been very active along the same lines, conducting societies, organizing associations, and composing worthy music; and, finally, Raymond Huntington Woodman, who has the exceptional honor of having been a pupil of Cesar Franck, the French Schumann. Woodman, who was born in Brooklyn, January 18, 1861, has added many compositions to the American stock, and has been a teacher of the organ in New York for many years past.

Charles H. Morse's influence, apart from his service in Plymouth Church, has been extended over many parts of the country. He was born in Bradford, Massachusetts, January 5, 1853, and his musical studies were pursued in America, chiefly under John K. Paine, J. C. D. Parker, George E. Whiting, and Carl Baermann. For a time he was a teacher at the New England Conservatory, then director of the musical department of Wellesley College, and then director and founder of the Northwestern Conservatory at Minneapolis. After that came his work at Plymouth Church, and much organizing of musical associations in New York state and New England. In 1901 he was made musical director of Dartmouth College, which position he held for many years.

The West has also begun to advance rapidly in organ music. In San Francisco we find Dr. H. J. Stewart (already spoken of as a composer), and in Chicago a larger number of prominent organists headed by Harrison M. Wild, a good concert organist and a sterling conductor. Every large city of the West now boasts its coterie of educated organists. Probably, however, no city of its size, in America, has been so well provided with organ music of a high class as Pittsburg. Thanks to Mr. Andrew Carnegie, a large hall

T

and an excellent organ have been provided, and regular organ concerts are given to the public every Sunday afternoon. One can scarcely imagine a better employment of part of the Sabbath than listening to the excellent programmes that have been given in Pittsburg. Frederick Archer (1838–1901), the eminent English organ virtuoso, was the organizer of these educational concerts, and until the year of his death he gave programme after programme of excellent music to audiences which filled every part of the great hall. Never, in America, has there been such an impetus given to public taste in organ music; the Pittsburg concerts (which still continue) have been one of the most important factors in the history of organ music in the United States.

On the occasion of great public festivals in America, the organ has almost always played a prominent part. At the World's Fair in Chicago, in 1893, for example, there were sixty-two organ recitals given by the following artists: —

Clarence Eddy, twenty-one recitals; Guilmant, of Paris, four; R. Huntington Woodman, four; Samuel A. Baldwin (Dudley Buck's successor at Holy Trinity, New York), William C. Carl, Walter E. Hall, William Middleschulte, Frank Taft, George E. Whiting, and Harrison M. Wild, three each; J. Fred. Wolle, whose direction of Bach music in Bethlehem, Pennsylvania, has already been chronicled, gave two recitals; G. Andrews, Louis A. Coerne, N. J. Corey, C. A. Howland, B. J. Lang, Otto Pfefferkorn, W. Radcliffe, W. S. Sterling, Henry G. Thunder, a talented Irishman, pupil of Thalberg, who died in New York in 1891, and A. S. Vogt, one recital each.

During 1897 and 1898 the Twentieth Century Club of Boston, impelled by the lack of public appreciation of organ recitals characteristic of that city, gave a series of free concerts in various churches in Boston. The following were the performers: —

Edgar A. Barrell, two; P. B. Brown, two; G. A. Burdett, five; G. W. Chadwick, two; E. Cutter, Jr., two; Ernest Douglas, one; Henry M. Dunham, two; Arthur Foote, one; Wallace Goodrich, four; Philip Hale, one; Warren A. Locke (the organist of Appleton Chapel, Harvard), two; Hamilton C. MacDougall, three; Charles H. Morse, one; Homer A. Norris, one; John O'Shea, one; Horatio

W. Parker, two; Charles P. Scott, two; Charles A. Safford, one; Walter R. Spalding (assistant professor of music at Harvard), three; William Stanfield, one; Allen W. Swan, two; Everett E. Truette, five; Benjamin L. Whelpley, three; and S. Brenton Whitney, two. The effort was a praiseworthy one, although it did not accomplish as much as the array of organ virtuosi deserved.

Regarded from the standpoint of virtuosity, there is one American organist, Mr. Eddy, who has won a remarkable reputation both in America and France, the latter country being the land of great brilliancy in organ playing. Clarence Eddy (Fig. 77) was born June 23, 1851, in Greenfield, Massachusetts, and began his musical education at the age of eleven. In 1867 he studied under Dudley Buck, at Hartford, Connecticut, and from 1868 to 1871 was organist of Bethany Church, Montpelier, Vermont. Then he went to Berlin, and studied under August Haupt and Albert Loeschhorn. This was followed by a concert tour through Germany, Austria, Switzerland, and Holland, during which he played at the

FIG. 77. — CLARENCE EDDY.

Vienna Exposition of 1873. Returning to America in 1874, he became organist of the First Congregational Church in Chicago, and after two years went to the First Presbyterian Church, where he was organist and choir-master for seventeen years. In 1876 he became general director of the Hershey School of Musical Art in Chicago, and gave there his famous series of one hundred organ recitals without a repetition of any composition.

Besides the Vienna Exposition, Mr. Eddy has played at the Centennial Exposition, Philadelphia, in 1876; the International

Exposition, Paris, in 1889; the World's Fair, Chicago, in 1893 (twenty-one recitals); the Pan-American Exposition, Buffalo, in 1901, and has given recitals in all the chief American and European cities. During the season of 1900–01, from October 16 to May 1, he made a tour of the United States and Canada, and played over one hundred recitals.

Mr. Eddy has lived much in Paris during recent years, and has won many European tributes for American organ works, which he has often brought to foreign notice. Regarding his own perform- ance, Haupt, in Germany, Guilmant, in France, and Sgambati, in Italy, have ranked him with the greatest virtuosi on the instrument.

As a composer Mr. Eddy is not regarded as the equal of Whiting or Whitney among our organists, yet he has published a worthy series of fugues, canons, and other organ works. He has been more of a specialist than the two composers just named, and it is gratifying to find an American in music so eminently successful in his speciality.

FIG. 78. — DR. WILLIAM MASON.

CHAPTER XIV

THE AMERICAN COMPOSERS FOR PIANOFORTE

Among the composers who have made piano composition their chief work, we find many who are also celebrated as teachers of the instrument, and who have influenced the course of music in America as much by their pupils as by their musical productions. There is probably no country in the world where piano playing is so wide-spread as in the United States. Almost every home, even among the humble, possesses its instrument and some amount of piano music. Although this latter is not always of the quality that one might desire, the universal gift or habit of playing the piano, or playing at piano music, in America, is undeniable.

Even the mechanical attachments to the piano, the musical automata, have contributed to further piano music, and most of these appliances are of American origin. Add to this that America is to-day making more and better pianos than any other country, and we can readily see that piano composition must be, for good or for evil, one of the most important factors of our music. The amount of piano teaching that is carried on in the United States is something stupendous, and the leaders in this field have a most important task in forming a national taste in music, and in checking certain pernicious influences that have grown up only too rapidly.

Dr. William Mason (Fig. 78) of New York ought to be given precedence in treating of this topic, for he is the pioneer among our native piano composers and teachers. He was born in Boston, January 24, 1829, the third son of Dr. Lowell Mason, that important figure in American musical history, whose work we have already recorded. Naturally his father was his first teacher. Mason made his first public appearance as a pianist in Boston. As long ago as March 7, 1846, he played at an orchestral concert of the Boston

Academy of Music, in days when Beethoven was a novelty in that city, and Music, heavenly maid, was decidedly young. Mason's life, like that of Moscheles, is a chain leading from the old to the new. In his youth he saw the beginnings of secular music in a country which had been steeped in psalmody and sacred concerts; but he lived to see America give orchestral concerts equal to those of Europe. He witnessed a race of native composers in the classical forms grow up; and his own work has formed an important part in the fabric which he thus watched in the weaving.

In 1849 Mason went to Europe to complete his musical studies. Leipsic, thanks to Mendelssohn (who had passed away but two years before), was then a musical centre, and this pilgrim from the new world was taken as a pupil by such men as Moscheles, Hauptmann, and Richter. Then there came study at Prague with Dreyschock, and finally the five years of apprenticeship were rounded out with nearly two years of Liszt.

It was very different with the American student abroad, in the middle of the nineteenth century, from what it is to-day. There was no great band of cisatlantic enthusiasts to be found in the conservatories at that time; J. C. D. Parker, the superficial Richardson (who subsequently wrote a poorly arranged piano method and sold over a million copies of it), and Mason were three of the earliest of the American Jasons. And it was different with Liszt, also, in 1853, from what it became in his later years. There was no cosmopolitan crowd of worshippers at the Weimar shrine, but in its place a small, highly appreciative artistic coterie. The young Mason became the companion and friend, as well as the pupil, of the great pianist.

During the European sojourn Mason played in public, twice in London, and several times in Weimar, even at the court of the Grand Duke. This was probably the first time that American musical talent had attracted attention in Germany. In 1854 his American career began. It was to be a long and an extremely important one. New York at once had a classical impetus given it by a series of excellent chamber concerts, which were instituted by Mason, with the assistance of a string quartette composed of Theodore Thomas, Carl Bergmann, J. Mosenthal, and George Matzka

(Fig. 27). For about thirteen years these classical chamber concerts were continued, and America first became acquainted with Brahms and many of Schumann's noble inspirations through this medium. There was also a long concert tour through the different states made by Mason, but he did not care much for this arduous and distracting work. In 1872 Yale University conferred the degree of Mus. Doc. upon Mason, — a well-deserved tribute.

How sincere and intense the love of this American musician for his chosen art has been, may be best understood by that little band of auditors who have been privileged to hear him give daily recitals during his summer vacations at the Isles of Shoals, at the home of Celia Thaxter, the eminent poetess. His geniality and unstrained manner speak in his compositions. These are almost wholly pianoforte works, although a few part-songs and an early serenade for violoncello also exist. There are about fifty works for his favorite instrument, and (with Mr. W. S. B. Mathews) Dr. Mason arranged a piano method that has become famous. In this latter he advocates an especial touch, a drawing of the finger (further used in his later instruction books and essays) in certain passages, which has become known as the "Mason touch."

Many of Dr. Mason's compositions have been republished in Germany. His "Silver Spring," "Reverie Poetique," "Improvisation" (Op. 51, composed when Dr. Mason was over seventy-one), and "Danse Rustique" are among his best works. None of his compositions attempts the large classical forms. There is no sonata or concerto to his credit; but in the domain of pleasing and instructive drawing-room music he has had great success. Many technical points are introduced in his piano pieces in such a deft manner that the pill of study is sugar-coated. It is, however, rather as teacher, as introducer of classical music in America, as educator of the public, that Dr. Mason's memory is to be honored. He has had some famous pupils, including William H. Sherwood, E. M. Bowman, and others. He died in New York, July 14, 1908.

Another American composer, born in the same year with Dr. Mason, seems far more remote from the present epoch, and his foreign descent, his constant European tours, and his French predilections, all combine to make us think of him as cosmopolitan rather than distinctly American.   Louis Moreau Gottschalk (Fig. 79) was born in New Orleans, May 8, 1829, his father being an Englishman, his mother a Creole.   He was emphatically an infant prodigy, for he showed his musical taste at the early age of four, and played the organ on one occasion, in church, at six!   Piano, organ, and violin constituted his early musical studies.   At thirteen he was sent to Paris to complete his musical education.   He became a great favorite in the French metropolis, being idolized by impressible female auditors after the fashion that Liszt had been and Pade-

rewski was to be.   Chopin heard him play at a concert at the Salle Erard, in 1845, and predicted that he would become the king of pianists.   He gave a series of concerts with Hector Berlioz, and that celebrated composer said of him that he had sovereign power, that he was a consummate pianist. Tours were made all over the world and honors were won everywhere.   In Spain a celebrated bull-fighter presented him with his sword and the Infanta made a cake for him with her own royal hands; in almost every European country he received orders and decorations from royalty.

FIG. 79. — LOUIS M. GOTTSCHALK.

Occasionally Gottschalk would stoop to meretricious effects, and more than once he arranged a work for a whole battalion of pianos together.   Yet, over and beyond this, he was a poet of his instrument.   His own compositions show this.   One can find few works more expressive than the couple of sketches entitled " Ossian," which were among his early works.   His tropical dances are full of fervor and passion, and his reveries are filled with the languor of the South. Among his works are two operas, which never were performed, a couple of symphonies, marches for the orchestra, and a dozen

songs, but his influence as a composer rests with his piano compositions. None of these was in the largest forms; he was satisfied to
win his triumphs in salon composition, which was well, since a poetic
drawing-room *morceau* is worth a dozen uninspired sonata forms.

Gottschalk was the first American to achieve European fame by
performance or composition, for he was playing publicly in Paris
while Mason was yet occupied with Boston concerts. But Gottschalk was far less distinctively American than Mason, and his work
by no means exerted such direct influence upon American musical
development. He gave, to be sure, many concerts in the United
States, — it is said as many as eighty concerts in a single season
in New York, — appearing more than a thousand times in this
country; but he came as an exotic and was a foreigner in the land
in which he was born. He was French by taste, language, and
maternal descent, and his compositions are in no sense American,
but lean heavily to the Spanish or French school. He was a great
artist, born, by chance, in New Orleans, but in art belonging to
other climes. It was a wild, Bohemian life, the typical career of
the world artist, that Gottschalk led, yet with all its excitement, the
constant tours, and the green-room atmosphere, the earnest side of
the composer's nature would often assert itself; and, amid much that
is temporary and some that is unworthy, many of Gottschalk's compositions are characteristic and powerful enough to hold their own
in the standard repertory of to-day.

The excited and irregular life of Gottschalk could not last very
long. He was an exhausted man at forty. In 1869, he was giving
a musical festival at Rio Janeiro, Brazil. On November 26, of that
year, as he was seated at the piano (it is said that he was playing his
latest composition, " Morte "), he fell senseless. He had been stricken
with yellow fever during the year, and was in an enfeebled condition
that precluded recovery. He was taken to the suburb of Tijuca,
about three miles away, in the hope that in its higher altitude he
might recover; but he died there, December 18, 1869. It is morti-
fying to state (yet strictly true) that Gottschalk was far more appreciated abroad than in his native land, America.

Leaving these two dissimilar exponents of piano music in America, we come to the native composers who are at present adding to

the library of American music.   As we have seen the orchestral and operatic composers occasionally composing for the piano, so we shall find our piano composers (those who have won their chief triumphs in this field) sometimes winning successes in song or operatic composition as well.   One of the most versatile of those American composers who have won success in various styles of musical work is Wilson George Smith, who, with Mr. Beck and Mr. Rogers, aids in giving musical importance to Cleveland, Ohio.

Mr. Smith was born in Elyria, Ohio, August 19, 1855.   He was a pupil of Otto Singer, at Cincinnati, and was so promising in his work that the veteran teacher urged him to go to Germany to complete his musical education.   Therefore, in 1880, he set to work in Berlin, under Kiel, Scharwenka, Moszkowski, Raff, and others.   In 1882 he came back to Cleveland, and has remained there ever since as a teacher of piano, voice, and composition, and a concert pianist.

He has composed a large number of works, among which are about half a hundred songs, but his chief reputation rests upon his piano works.   Some of these, entitled " Homages," are in the style of European masters.   A " Homage to Schumann " runs along the line of the novelettes of that composer; a " Homage to Grieg," toward whom Smith seems specially attracted, consists of five piano works in the Norwegian vein, and these brought warm commendation from the Northern master.   He has written other piano works in the Norwegian and Swedish style, for which he has an evident *penchant*.   In two other piano homages Smith has laid wreaths upon the altar of Schubert and Chopin.   His more individual compositions are not vast but always fluent, attractive, and graceful.   He is not an iconoclast by any means (although not afraid of fifths upon occasion), but a very agreeable traveller along the musical highway.   His transcriptions of works by Grieg and Raff, for two pianos, are very broad and effective.   His pedagogic works are commendable.   Every teacher finds Smith's octave studies and the studies for especial finger development useful and practical.   His chromatic studies and his set of studies in transposition have won approval from Grieg, Godowsky, Xaver Scharwenka, Mason, and other authorities.

Less prominent as a composer, but exerting a great influence as a teacher and performer, was William Hall Sherwood (Fig. 80), whose sphere of action, at first in Boston, then in Chicago, has been remarkably wide.   He was American by birth, by descent, and by his aggressive labors for the native composer.   He was born in Lyons, New York, January 31, 1854.   His father, a good musician, was his first teacher; Dr. William Mason was another of his instructors, and took great interest in him.   A very thorough European training followed, during which Sherwood studied with Kullak, Weitzmann, Deppe, Richter, Doppler, Scotson Clark, and Liszt.

FIG. 80. — WILLIAM H. SHERWOOD.

He gave a series of successful con- certs in Germany, and then, in 1876, returned to his native land, where he at once started upon a large and brilliant concert tour.   After this he settled in Boston, and began teaching.   Sherwood soon went to Chicago, where he started a conservatory.   After 1889 his chief work was done in the West, where his teaching (with that of Emil Liebling and W. S. B. Mathews) soon made Chicago a centre for piano music.   Yet his work in Boston also left its mark, as witness such pupils as Arthur Whiting, Clayton Johns, and many others. His published works (all for the piano) contain a couple of suites, a scherzo, and some other compositions.   Perhaps the "Scherzo Caprice" (Op. 9), although one of his early works, is his best.   He died in Chicago, January 7, 1911.

But it is as a performer and teacher that Sherwood won his spurs.   His concert tours have extended everywhere, north, south- east, and west.   Canada and Mexico have heard him, as well as the United States.   Every great symphonic orchestra in the country has had his services in concerts at one time or another.   All together, it is not too much to say that the first American piano virtuoso of the beginning of the century was William H. Sherwood.

More prolific than the composers we have mentioned is a Boston pianist and teacher, Charles Dennée, who was born in Oswego, New York, September 1, 1863. He studied music chiefly in Boston, taking his harmony lessons of Stephen A. Emery, and his piano of Alfred D. Turner. It was Turner's guidance and friendship that made Dennée a musician. He has written some successful light operas of the vaudeville type, a large number of songs, and a still greater number of piano works in the small forms. A piano method is also to be placed to his credit. He has toured the United States as a concert pianist. Frank Addison Porter (born at Dixmont, Maine, September 3, 1859) is a pupil of the same teachers, and has also composed some useful pedagogical works, as well as songs and piano *morceaux*.

To such a list of piano composers Albert Ross Parsons also belongs, although of a somewhat more ambitious school. Parsons was born at Sandusky, Ohio, September 16, 1847. He studied at first with F. L. Ritter, the famous litterateur and conductor, and afterwards with Reinecke, Papperitz, and Richter, in Leipsic, with Taussig, Kullak, and Weitzmann, in Berlin. Parsons's translations of important foreign musical works, his careful editing of classical reprints, and his own compositions entitle him to very honorable mention.

New York once had an American virtuoso, who attempted other flights, in John Nelson Pattison. He composed a " Niagara," a symphony for the orchestra and military band. There are many of his piano works in print, and he added much to the more agreeable class of drawing-room music. In Philadelphia, Michael Hurley Cross (born there April 13, 1833, died there September 26, 1897) and Charles H. Jarvis (born there December 20, 1837, and died there February 25, 1895) were standard-bearers in the best school of piano work.

Of the youngest workers in the field it might be dangerous to predict the full result as yet. Boston has two of these in its musical ranks. Harry N. Redman is writing not only many songs, piano pieces, and studies, but also violin sonatas and larger concerted works. Redman is distinctly modern in his vein, and has studied deeply in the works of the neo-Russians Tschaikowsky, Balakireff, and others. Alvah Glover Salmon has drunk at the same fountain, and has even gone to St. Petersburg and Moscow for musical study. He has composed much brilliant and difficult piano music and has appeared in public, both as a pianist and lecturer. His chief teacher in America was John D. Buckingham, of Boston.

In speaking of piano composition we must again turn to foreign influences that have had their effect upon American musical education. In no direction have these influences been more marked than in the development of our piano playing and its repertoire. Attracted to a country where the piano fever was assuming the proportions of an epidemic, some of the best artists and teachers from abroad settled here, and became virtually leaders in the onward movement of that kind of music. The mere accident of birth must be ignored in such a case. Such men as Joseffy, Baermann, Hoffmann, Mills, who have spent the riper years of their lives among us, and have trained many of the best of the present generation of our pianists, are certainly not to be ignored in any work that speaks of the development of music in America. The native band of advanced pianists and piano composers, was, as we have seen, a very small one, twenty years ago. The European leaven came, and it stayed in the loaf. Such a man, for example, as Carl Baermann, who was born in Munich, has had far more to do with American music than Gottschalk, who was born in New Orleans.

Carl Baermann (Fig. 81) belonged to one of those families where music seems to run in the blood and is transmitted from generation to generation. His grandfather, Heinrich Joseph Baermann, was one of the most brilliant clarinettists of the world, and was a close friend of Weber and Mendelssohn, both of whom wrote compositions for him. It may be recalled that both of these masters were the earliest in the true usage of the clarinet, and who can say how much they were influenced in their scores by personal contact with the famous clarinettist, Baermann! A granduncle was a celebrated bassoon player, and the father, Carl Baermann, Sr., was also celebrated for his clarinet work. Both Heinrich and Carl Baermann, Sr., wrote many works for their instrument. Both were held in high esteem at the court of Bavaria, and the father has left a clarinet method which is still one of the most famous in existence.

From such ancestry came Carl Baermann, the pianist. In

Munich, among other teachers, he had as instructor the thorough and conservative Franz Lachner.   Subsequently he was one of the pupils of Liszt, not merely in name, but in fact, for he possessed the most laudatory letters from that master, and was literally one of his favorites.   Soon after his studies were completed Baermann became well known for his concert performances, and was appointed piano teacher at the Royal Music School of Munich, that academy where so many American composers have studied; and here many Americans came under the influence of the excellent musician.   Soon after this, King Ludwig of Bavaria gave to him the title of Royal Professor.

FIG. 81.—CARL BAERMANN.

In 1881, Professor Baermann received a furlough of two years, in order that he might visit America. The visit resulted in a permanent residence in this country, and for fully thirty-two years this teacher and pianist became a leader in classical piano music in the United States. He gave many recitals and appeared at the large symphony concerts under all the celebrated conductors; but his influence as teacher has been the most important of all.   His pupils represent almost every state in the republic, and many of them have become famous in their own right.

Professor Baermann has not published a large list of piano compositions, but his few works are of a high order.   A series of twelve studies (André, at Offenbach) may be spoken of as belonging to the finest piano literature of the present.   They do not pale, as so many similar compositions do, even before the studies of Chopin. A piano suite, of high order, is in manuscript, as are several other compositions.   We know of but one orchestral work by Professor Baermann, and that has not yet been heard in America.   This is a festival march, which was performed recently in Munich on the occasion of the celebration of the centennial of the Bavarian State

Museum.   The work won the highest praise, even the Prince Regent growing enthusiastic over it.   In Professor Baermann's later years his pupils, friends, and admirers formed a "Baermann Society," which was to perpetuate his conservative and valuable work.   This society dissolved after his death, which occurred in Newton, Massachusetts, January 17, 1913.   Nevertheless it is to be hoped that some organized effort will be made to publish the many piano works which this modest composer has left in manuscript.

In speaking of foreign teachers of piano in Boston a prominent place should be given to Ernst Perabo, who, although born abroad (in Wiesbaden, in 1845), came to this country when but seven years old.   He returned to Leipsic for his musical education, which was especially thorough, but was again in Boston in 1865, a young man of twenty.   Since that time his life has been almost wholly spent in Boston in teaching.   As one of his pupils was Mrs. Beach (who also studied with Carl Baermann), one can see the direct result of his teaching.   Mr. Perabo's compositions are few and brief, although he has made some remarkable transcriptions of great difficulty.   He is not as frequently heard in public as could be wished for.   He is a superb Beethoven player.

In Rafael Joseffy (Fig. 82) America won to herself a remarkable genius of the piano.   Born in Miskolcz, in Hungary, July 3, 1853, his childish efforts at the piano were so noteworthy, that he was early sent as a pupil to Moscheles, and from him to the greater Tausig.   A marked success attended his debut in Vienna, and a series of concert tours around the world followed.   He came to America in 1879, and at once made a sensation by his great virtuosity.   It is to Joseffy's honor that he rose to something higher than this in later years.   He lost nothing of his brilliancy but gained decidedly in musicianship in his riper manhood.   For over five years he disappeared from the concert platform, studying most zealously during that time; then a new Joseffy came back, — an earnest and powerful musician who strove for the best in art, not for immediate success.   He gave all his best work to America.   As a teacher (in the National Conservatory of New York), Joseffy has done much for piano playing with us.   His pedagogic works and his editing of Chopin (his last work) are valuable legacies.   He suffered from

U

nervous maladies during his last years, which somewhat impaired his teaching. He died in 1915, universally honored.

Much more prominent as a composer, and the most thoroughly Americanized of our foreign contingent, was Richard Hoffman. He was born in Manchester, England, May 24, 1831, and was taught by Rubinstein, Thalberg, Moscheles, and Liszt. He came to America as a mere lad of sixteen, — at a time when such pianists as he were most rare, — and, as he became a resident of New York, his influence was very great with the few musical societies existent there in 1847. He made musical tours through America, first with Burke, the violinist, then with Jenny Lind. He often played duets (on two pianos) with Gottschalk, who had a great predilection for concerted music of this character, when a good orchestra was not obtainable. He played duets also with Von Bülow, when that pianist came to America.

FIG. 82. — RAFAEL JOSEFFY.

For more than fifty years, Richard Hoffman remained a notable figure in American music, as concert performer, as teacher, and as composer. Nor does his work fall wholly in the earlier times of New York's musical activity. Even in the last days of Seidl, this pianist appeared in a concerto directed by the great conductor.

As a composer Mr. Hoffman has a list of compositions which extends to more than 125 works. Songs and some excellent Episcopal church numbers are among these, but his most successful

pieces are for the piano.   Most of these are of the higher order
of drawing-room music, and such works as " Le Crepuscule," "Im-
promptu" (Op. 6), and " Venice" were much better than the average
American piano composition at the time they were published.   In
short, in Richard Hoffman we have had a musician who has been
actively intertwined in the growth of our art in New York from
Jenny Lind concerts to " Parsifal" performances, even if he had
not the influence of a William Mason.   Hoffman died August 17,
1909.

Scarcely less of an American record in length of time, and more
brilliant in the matter of public work, is that of Sebastian Bach
Mills, another Englishman who certainly belongs to American
musical history if nearly forty years of active service in the cause
can constitute a claim.   Mills was born in Cirencester, England,
March 1, 1838.   His name may indicate that his father was a musician.   Cipriani Potter and Sterndale Bennett were his early teachers,
and he played before Queen Victoria when he was seven years old.
After that came a Leipsic Conservatory education and public performances even in Germany, at the celebrated Gewandhaus concerts.
Finally, a debut in New York, in 1859, was so successful that Mills
settled in that city permanently.   A few tours of Germany were
made in later years, but most of Mills's concert appearances were in
America.   He appeared in New York every season from 1859 to
1877.   By his teaching, his composing, and his concert playing,
Mills greatly assisted the cause of good music in that city.   He
died in Wiesbaden, Germany, December 21, 1898.   His compositions, so far as we know them, were all for the piano, and were none
of them in large or classical forms, but all graceful and attractive
works.

Mr. Perry is an American artist who stands in a class by himself
—a concert pianist who is totally blind, yet tours the country from
one end to the other.   Edward Baxter Perry was born in Haverhill,
Massachusetts, February 14, 1855.   He was not born blind, but lost
his sight in childhood.   Some of his training was given at the
Perkins Institution for the Blind, at South Boston.   A European
education in piano playing began with Kullak in Berlin and was
continued under Pruckner in Stuttgart.   Then came assistance and

tuition from Liszt and from Clara Schumann.   During his stay in
Germany he gave a recital before the Emperor.   On his return to
America, he began teaching in Boston, but the large number of
engagements for recitals and lectures forced him away from musical
pedagogics.   He has given more recitals than any other American,
and, as already stated, enjoys a unique position in American musical art.

Hundreds of other musicians who, by teaching or composition, or
public performances, have added something to American piano music,
might be passed in review, but to do so would turn musical history
into a musical directory.   Yet some of these have also done yeoman
service.   Hanchett has lectured and taught in New York and elsewhere through the country; Boekelman has done good work at Miss
Porter's famous school at Farmington, and has invented a color
scheme of analysis of Bach's fugues and inventions that is enormously valuable to all musicians; Constantin von Sternberg, the
celebrated Russian, has helped musical education both in Atlanta,
Georgia, and in Philadelphia; W. C. Seeboeck and August Hylle-
sted have done in the West what Sternberg has achieved South
and East.   Frederick Brandeis gave the larger part of his life to
composition, organ playing, and teaching in New York, bringing
forth large and classical works in many branches of music.   All
of these pianists, and many others, have helped to make us the
most piano-playing nation of the world.

PLATE XI

MRS. H. H. A. BEACH

CHAPTER XV

AMERICAN WOMEN IN MUSIC

CAN a woman become a great composer? Will there ever be a female Beethoven or a Mozart? In Europe most authorities have decided the question quickly and in the negative. Carl Reinecke, long the director of the Leipsic Conservatory, once gave his views on this subject to the present writer. He believed that there was a point where woman stopped in music. His experience was, that, up to a well-advanced point in the interpretation of the ideas of others, the female student often outstripped the male; but in the highest realms of musical performance, where individuality needed to be blended with the text of the composer, there was a timidity that militated against progress. In the purely creative field he found scarcely any progress comparable to that of the intelligent and poetic male student. Svendsen, in Norway, and Gade, in the Conservatory of Copenhagen, long ago expressed almost identical views to us.

But, in Europe, prejudice alone might well hold back many a woman from entering the field. Fanny Mendelssohn composed several of the songs without words, and some of the vocal songs, which went under her brother's name; but that brother firmly repressed any thought of her entering the field upon her own account. Once, when Queen Victoria, at the English court, told him how much she enjoyed singing his song " Italy," he was obliged to reply that this particular song was the composition of his sister Fanny! Rubinstein warningly said to the sister-in-law of Chaminade: " I hear your relative publishes compositions of her own. She ought not to do that!"

Nevertheless, this is a woman's epoch; Rosa Bonheur has succeeded in painting, George Eliot in literature, Madame Curie discovers radium and sets a new pace in science, and in music, too, a

Chaminade, a Clara Schumann, an Augusta Holmés, have broken down many barriers. We venture to believe that it has been insufficient musical education and male prejudice that have prevented female composers from competing with their male brethren in art. In the United States, where this prejudice has not existed, the female composer was in the field contemporaneously with our Chadwicks, Parkers, and MacDowells; and America can boast at least one female composer who can compare favorably with any woman who has yet entered creative musical art.

Mrs. H. H. A. Beach (Pl. XI) was born (Amy Marcy Cheney) in the town of Henniker, Merrimac County, New Hampshire, on September 5, 1867. She is of American parentage, a descendant of the earliest colonial settlers. From the same ancestry came William Larned Marcy, who was successively governor of New York, United States senator, Secretary of War, and Secretary of State; Randolph Barnes Marcy, the explorer of the Red River; Charlotte Cushman, the eminent tragedienne; and Major-General Dearborn of Revolutionary fame. Mrs. Beach's musical inheritance appears to have been a natural sequence of the devotion to music of her mother, and her maternal ancestry; while her strong taste for the scholastic and mathematical side of her art seems like a reflex of her father's mental qualities. His family had never shown any active interest in music, but had devoted attention to political, collegiate, and other educational affairs.

Gifted with absolute pitch and an accurate memory, the child constantly surprised her family and their friends with startling feats from the time when she was a year old. It is said that at that period she had unmistakably memorized forty separate tunes which were always accurately sung by her. At times she would insist upon their being sung to her, until her mother was exhausted. One of her favorite anthems was, "The moon shines full at His command and all the stars obey." Of the songs sung to her, she always remembered the way in which they were first rendered, and never permitted any variation from the original version. All substitutions and cadenzas were met with the stern reproof, "Sing it clean." When two years old she was taken to a photographer for a sitting, and when all was ready for the picture she suddenly surprised her

FIG. 101.—MUSIC HALL AND COLLEGE OF MUSIC, CINCINNATI.

audience by singing at the top of her voice, "See, the Conquering Hero Comes." The photographer, who had been practising (as one of the chorus of the first Peace Jubilee) the celebrated chorus of Handel, exclaimed: "Why, that baby is really singing it! That is more wonderful than anything we shall see at the jubilee." The picture was a success.

No other punishment was ever needed than a little minor music for the little hands that occasionally were mischievous, for this would make her disconsolate at once. Violin music gave her great pleasure, and she would sit quietly for hours listening to it with keenest enjoyment. She also exhibited phenomenal literary appreciation and memory at a very early age, but the musical side of her nature rather outran the literary.

At this time the child was accustomed to show preference for certain pieces of music that her mother played, by designating it as the blue, pink, or purple music. Little attention was at first paid to this manifestation of musical feeling, because it was supposed to be connected with the color of the outside paper, with which musical publications were covered. Afterwards it was clearly demonstrated that the music played was not satisfactory to the child, because it did not correspond with a scheme of color that she had *in her mind*, and had no correspondence with colored wrappers. When carefully questioned, it was found that she associated colors with certain keys. For instance: —

Key of C . . . . White	Key of A major . . . . . Green
Key of F sharp minor ⎱ . . . Black	Key of A flat major . . . . Blue
Key of G sharp minor ⎰	Key of D flat major . . . . Violet
Key of E major . . . . . Yellow	Key of E flat major . . . . Pink
Key of G major . . . . . Red	

This association of keys and colors continues with Mrs. Beach to the present time; but we must add that, while many composers share this association of tone and color, their color-schemes are by no means unanimous.

When four years old this precocious child was allowed, after much begging and to her great joy, to stand on a hassock at the piano and play an improvised secondo to a primo played by her aunt. From that time she had daily access to the piano, and played correctly in their original keys, and with full harmony. hymn-tunes that she had heard in church and Sunday-school, improvised melodies and accompaniments to children's poems, and played without fault chorales of "St. Paul," operatic duets, Beethoven's "Spirit Waltz," and many of the Strauss waltzes. She also

FIG. 83. — MISS MARGARET RUTHVEN LANG.

composed a few piano pieces which she named "Golden Robin Waltz," "Marlboro Waltz," "Mama's Waltz," "Snowflake Waltz." The latter was composed while on a three months' visit in the country where there was no piano. She played it with great spirit and precision the first time she touched the piano after reaching home. She had no difficulty in making transpositions at her pleasure. Even before she had taken *any* theoretical instruction, her writing was found to be musically correct. It seems as if she must have always understood the relations of intervals, for, before she studied harmony, a glance at the page of music she was playing, enabled her to use four-part harmony and in the correct key. At that time she did not know the names of the notes or keys, but when she was six years old nothing would satisfy her but lessons. These were begun by her mother giving her regular instruction three times a week for the following two years. In that time among the large variety of pieces she studied and played were: —

> Heller's Études, Op. 47.
> Czerny's Études de Velocité (Book No. 1).
> Handel's "Harmonious Blacksmith."
> Mozart's Andante and Variations in G major.
> Mendelssohn's "Songs," arranged by Dresel.
> Chopin's Valse, Op. 18, and others in order.

Beethoven's Sonatas, Op. 49, Nos. 1 and 2, Op. 2, No. 1 ; Op. 14, No. 2 ; with all the slow movements and minuets of the sonatas as far as Op. 49.

These were played with accuracy and much feeling.   Best of all, the child loved Beethoven's music, which she would play until compelled by force to leave the piano.   Her greatest sorrow now was that her hand could not reach a full chord, and was occasionally obliged to omit the lower notes that she easily read, but could not touch.

When seven years old she made a limited number of public appearances, playing works by Beethoven, Chopin, and others, and introducing a waltz of her own composition.   At this time the writings of Bach attracted her warm interest, which later developed into the greatest enthusiasm, especially for fugal compositions.   At eight years of age, her parents settled in Boston, and here, while her school studies occupied a large share of her time, the course in pianoforte instruction so well begun by her mother was continued by Mr. Ernst Perabo, and later by Professor Junius W. Hill and Professor Carl Baermann.   At the same time she was insensibly educating her judgment and feeling for orchestral music by carefully studying the scores of standard works at the many concerts and rehearsals she was able to attend.   Her feeling for the clarinet was, and is, deeper than for all other orchestral instruments. Her reverence and love for its timbre has an interesting connection with the fact that her maternal grandfather was a good performer and great admirer of the instrument.

While studying with Professor Hill in the winter of 1881–82, the young lady's instruction included a course in harmony.   This course was afterwards supplemented by systematic studies in counterpoint, fugue, musical form, and instrumentation pursued *alone* for several years.   She made translations of the treatises by Berlioz and Gevaert to aid her in the last-named study.   As an exercise in the study of fugue she was accustomed to committing Bach fugues to memory, and then writing out their voices on separate staves.   Her interest in choral works was very strong, and she was a close student of the diversified productions of our many choral societies.

The present writer recalls a test of the fourteen-year-old prodigy, made with Teresa Liebe, the violinist, wherein the young miss not only played fugues from Bach's " Well-tempered Clavichord," but transposed them into any required key.   Her memory, her expression in playing, her enthusiasm, her exhibitions of the sense of absolute pitch, were wonderful.   Her teachers considered her, at that time, the greatest musical prodigy of America.

Her subsequent marriage to one of Boston's most eminent physicians, Dr. H. H. A. Beach, in December, 1885, eliminated the element of struggle from her art career.   There was no German aftermath of study, and Mrs. Beach is a composer whose entire education has been completed in America.   She was withdrawn, too, from the professional career — her subsequent appearances as a pianist being almost invariably to aid some charity.   Whether this was an unmixed advantage we may not judge.   When one considers the more luxurious road of ease that was opened, it is sufficient to be thankful that Mrs. Beach did not become in any degree sybaritical, but went bravely on, encouraged by her cultured husband, in the work of composition.   All of her best works followed her marriage.

Her first public appearance in Boston as a pianist was on October 24, 1883, she being then sixteen and still Miss Amy Cheney.   On that occasion she played Moscheles's G minor concerto (Op. 60) with orchestra, and as a solo Chopin's rondo in E flat.   During the ensuing winter she gave several recitals.   At the age of seventeen she played Chopin's F minor concerto with the Boston Symphony Orchestra under Mr. Gericke, and the Mendelssohn D minor concerto with Mr. Theodore Thomas's Orchestra.   Since then she has appeared at concerts and given recitals in Boston, New York, Philadelphia, Chicago, Brooklyn, and various other places almost every season, the programmes of some of her concerts and recitals being made up wholly of her own works.   With the Boston Symphony Orchestra she has played concertos by Beethoven, Mozart, Chopin, St. Saëns, and herself.

Her first large work was a grand mass in E flat major, brought out by the Handel and Haydn Society in February, 1892, under the direction of Carl Zerrahn.   On the same evening Mrs. Beach

FIG. 84. — MRS. JULIA RIVÉ-KING.

afterwards appeared and played with the society and orchestra the piano part of Beethoven's Choral Fantasy. Upon her appearance she received an ovation. Following the mass, she composed a scena and aria for contralto and orchestra, taking for her text the "Eilende Wolken" from Schiller's "Mary Stuart." It was sung for the first time in the same year as the mass, by Mrs. Carl Alves at a concert of the New York Symphony Society, under the direction of Mr. Walter Damrosch, and was the first work written by a woman produced at these concerts. The scene is that of Mary's first release from prison, just before her meeting with Elizabeth. Behind her is the dungeon, about and above her the free open air, the beautiful foliage and the "wandering clouds," to which she intrusts messages of love to her native land. Through the music, to give the scene more local coloring, is heard an old familiar Scotch air.

In the following year Mrs. Beach was invited by the Executive Board to write a composition for the dedication of the Woman's Building of the Columbian Exposition at Chicago. As the occasion celebrated in the nineteenth century the enterprise in discovery of the fifteenth, Mrs. Beach felt that her share of the music should in some way represent the union of the two centuries. She therefore selected themes characteristic of Gregorian writing, augmented, harmonized, and orchestrated in the modern style, and produced the Festival Jubilate, for chorus and orchestra, in exactly six weeks. It was successfully performed under the direction of Mr. Theodore Thomas and again later in New York City. During the Columbian Exposition Mrs. Beach played with Miss Maud Powell her romance for piano and violin, for the first time in public, at one of the concerts of the musical congress.

Soon after this Mrs. Beach began the Gaelic symphony — so called from the use of a number of genuine Gaelic themes. It was finished in the spring of 1896 and first performed by the Boston Symphony Orchestra under the direction of Mr. Emil Paur in October. Later performances were given in New York, Brooklyn, Buffalo, Kansas City, San Francisco, and Chicago, the latter under Mr. Theodore Thomas. A sonata in A minor for piano and violin was written in the six weeks following the completion of the symphony.　Mrs. Beach played the work with Mr. Franz Kneisel at one of his quartette concerts in the following January (1897).　The same artists played it again in Boston, New York, and in Cambridge at one of thé university concerts.　Mrs. Beach has performed it on numerous occasions with other violinists.　It was given in Berlin by Carreño and Halir, in Paris by Pugno and Ysaye, and in London by Henry Bird and Sigmund Beel.

Regarding these two works, one can say that they are the most important ever written in America by a woman.　Yet one would have preferred a less epic form than a symphony for the composer's best expression.　Better a fluent suite than a labored symphony. Yet it would be unjust to say that this Gaelic symphony is dull. It is not nearly so Scottish, however, as the symphony in A minor by Mendelssohn; and the title must of necessity provoke a comparison.　The first movement betrays a lack of ease, although the mastery of the form (at least, of the sonata movement) is pleasingly evident.　As in Mendelssohn's " Scotch " symphony, there is much use made of the clarinets in this work, even the unusual bass clarinet being very boldly employed in the lento movement. The scherzo is an orchestral gem, and the slow movement, which here comes third, is also beautiful, although perhaps carried out at too great length.

The violin sonata is best in its first and last movements, the largo (the third movement) being less spontaneous.　Mrs. Beach in her classical productions holds loyally to the sonata form, and is never vague or meaningless in her development-work.　Good counterpoint and thematic treatment are present in both the symphony and the sonata.　She seeks the largest forms by choice.　The violin sonata has an extra movement in its largo, and the piano concerto, in C sharp minor, has also an interpolation.　In this concerto, played by Mrs. Beach with the Boston Symphony Orchestra for the first time April 7, 1900, the scherzo is altogether charming, and the finale is powerful enough to make any critic, who does not believe that woman can create music, become rather doubtful about his position. Strangely enough, in a piano concerto written by a pianist, the orchestra dominates matters throughout almost the whole work. The finale presents some excellent figure development.

FIG. 85. — MME. HELEN HOPEKIRK–WILSON.

It must not be imagined that this composer has only aimed at symphony, mass, concerto, and sonata; she has gone beyond the fiftieth opus number, and some of these *opera* are made up of several numbers each. There are many piano compositions in the small forms, from easy pieces for children to transcriptions of Richard Strauss, and a furiously difficult (yet properly developed) cadenza to the first movement of Beethoven's C minor piano concerto. In her songs Mrs. Beach shows a tendency to complexity, — the ingenuity that is born of skill in figure development. But in her simplest moods she is very charming. The "Western Wind," "The Blackbird," and "The Year's at the Spring" are good examples of direct and unaffected musical utterance.

To those who believe that women who achieve greatness in ·any art or science must be masculine in mind and manner, unsexed phenomena, we may say that Mrs. Beach is most womanly in all her ways. Art does not recognize sex, and, if we have spoken of Mrs. Beach at some length and apart from her brother composers, it has been done to point a moral, which is, that it will be time to express unbelief in woman's musical powers only after equal chances have been given to both sexes and all trace of prejudice has disappeared.

Boston presents the name of still another woman among its host of composers. Miss Margaret Ruthven Lang comes by her talent quite legitimately, for she is the daughter of Benjamin J. Lang, the musician, who has won all his great successes in conducting and teaching and has published nothing. His daughter is rapidly restoring an average and publishing much. Miss Lang (Fig. 83) was born in Boston, November 27, 1867. There was paternal influence shown in her musical tastes; but it may be added that something may have been inherited from the maternal side as well, for Mrs. B. J. Lang is of musical predilections and an excellent amateur singer. Miss Lang began her attempts at composition before she was twelve years old. It was at this juvenile period that she wrote one movement of a piano quintette. She studied violin in Boston under Louis Schmidt, but in 1886 went to Munich, studied with Drechsler and Abel in violin and Victor Gluth in composition. Nor were her studies neglected on her return, for she became a pupil of George W. Chadwick

x

in orchestration, E. A. MacDowell in composition, and worked also with other teachers in Boston.

Miss Lang has aimed at the large forms; if not at symphony or concerto, at least at classical overtures for orchestra, of which she has written three, and also an orchestral ballade and songs with orchestra. Yet we like her work best when it seeks the smaller forms. Some of her songs have a keen poetic instinct and originality as well as grace. Her "Irish Mother's Lullaby," "Lament," and "Ghosts" are instances of masterly efforts in the vocal direction. Her overture, "Witichis," was performed in Chicago by Theodore Thomas and again under Max Bendix. This work we have not heard yet in the East. Her "Dramatic Overture" (Op. 12) has been given by the Boston Symphony Orchestra under Nikisch. It has some strong contrasts, especially between the chief theme and the subordinate. The first is grim and mediæval, the second tender and human. To place these two in juxtaposition in itself gives something of dramatic power, and the development of both is singularly unconventional.

The concert aria for soprano and orchestra, entitled "Armida," is made from a version that deals rather too freely with Tasso. The setting is by no means as dramatic as its poetic subject, and the composer seems to have missed the majestic power of the great death-scene. But in less intense work, and in the smaller forms especially, Miss Lang has won a leading position among song-writers.

From the host of women composers in America who have not gone beyond dilettantism in their numerous works, a few may be singled out as having achieved real success in the smaller forms of vocal or piano music. Miss Helen Hood is the first of these. Born in Chelsea (a suburb of Boston), June 28, 1863, she pursued her piano studies under Benjamin J. Lang, and subsequently under Moszkowski in Berlin. Her teacher of composition was George W. Chadwick. Miss Hood has occasionally composed in the larger forms, and a piano trio, a Te Deum, and a string quartette are to be placed to her credit; but her fame rests chiefly on her very graceful songs and piano sketches. Her trio for piano, violoncello, and violin is the first that was composed by an American woman, and her sets of violin and piano pieces deserve record. She received a diploma and medal from the Columbian Exposition for her meritorious work in composition.

In a smaller field again, but especially successful in it, is an American lady who was born in St. Louis. Mrs. Jessie L. Gaynor has written piano works and vocal quartettes, but her *metier* is the production of songs for children. In this juvenile vein she has no equal among American women. She was a pupil of A. J. Goodrich and Frederic Grant Gleason, and she also studied with the eminent composer, Dr. Louis Maas. Some of her songs are more developed than one would expect to find in juvenile compositions, and may readily be used by children of a larger growth. They are all poetic, so far as we have seen them, and unite words and music closely.

Some other American women-composers should be mentioned here. Mrs. Edith Noyes Porter has written orchestral works and chamber-music, and has published some graceful songs and instrumental works. She is a pupil of Chadwick and others, and has had the assistance of Emil Paur, who has spoken of her work as very promising. She is of an old American family, and her mother, Jeannette Noyes (Mrs. George B. Rice), was a prominent alto singer. Miss Mabel Daniels also comes of a musical family, her father, George F. Daniels, being president of the Handel and Haydn Society. Miss Daniels has written a pretty operetta and many shorter compositions. She went to Germany in 1903 to finish her studies, and has made great advance recently.

Among foreign women-composers who have settled in the United States, Mrs. Clara Kathleen Rogers ("Clara Doria") holds high rank. She is English by birth, and comes of very musical lineage. She has had the best of training in Germany and Italy in harmony, counterpoint, piano, and voice. She is, therefore, one of those rare people (of whom Sembrich is an excellent type) who are musicians as well as vocalists. Her compositions comprise a string quartette, a violin sonata, a violoncello sonata, a large number of songs, and a few piano works. She has made her home in Boston for the last quarter of a century.

Helen Hopekirk (Wilson) is a Scottish artist who has also resided in Boston for a long time. She is a brilliant concert pianist who has, however, not rested upon her platform fame alone. She has composed many orchestral works, among them a *concert-stück*, which was performed in Edinburgh under Henschel, in 1894, and a large number of powerful songs and advanced piano *morceaux*.

One of Mrs. Hopekirk's most valuable works is a volume of Scottish folk-songs. Almost every editor in this school of music has

FIG. 86. — MME. CAMILLA URSO.

tampered in some degree with the old Gaelic tonality; but this composer has kept both the spirit and letter of the ancient scales intact. It may be recorded, therefore, that one of the most important contributions to the most varied and expressive repertory of foreign folk-music, was made in America, by this talented composer.

There is also a purely American pianist who must be mentioned here as a composer. Mrs. Julia Rive-King (Fig. 84) was born in Cincinnati, October 31, 1859. She studied in America with William Mason and S. B. Mills, finishing in Europe under Reinecke and Liszt, and has played in many concerts with Seidl and Thomas. She has composed several brilliant works for piano, and made some concert transcriptions of Liszt's and Scarlatti's works.

The United States has produced or adopted artists in every field of musical execution. It may not be the purpose of a history of American music to speak of them in detail, for, while they have undoubtedly aided the development of musical taste in our country, they can hardly be regarded as leading factors in the development of American music. They are interpreters rather than creators of music. Yet a list of the chief of these is appended.

In piano playing, America has one of the greatest artists of the present in Mrs. Fannie Bloomfield-Zeisler, who, although born in Austria (July 16, 1866), has dwelt in Chicago almost continuously since she was two years old, making her extensive American and European tours from that centre. She has composed little, however.

In violin playing the American women have been numerous and notable, as, for example, Arma Senkrah-Harkness (New York, 1864), whose career was so sadly terminated a short time ago; Nettie Carpenter (New York, 1865); Maud Powell (Aurora, Illinois, 1868); Leonora Jackson (Boston, 1879) (Fig. 85); and Geraldine Morgan, daughter of the New York organist. Possibly the large list of American lady violinists is due in some degree to a lady who was not an American. Camilla Urso (Fig. 86) was born in Nantes, France, in 1842. But she came to America when only ten years of age, and a concert tour as long ago as 1852 made a strong impression on the violin playing of America. Other American tours caused many of our young musicians, particularly of the female sex, to take up the instrument, and it is not too much to ascribe much of the success of our female violinists to the inspiration derived from Camilla Urso. She died in New York, January 20, 1902.

The name of the great American vocalists, of both sexes, is legion. One can begin the list in the early days of American musical performances, with the great basso, Myron W. Whitney (Ashby, Massachusetts, 1836), and continue with Clara Louise Kellogg (Sumterville, South Carolina, 1842); Charles R. Adams

(Charlestown, Massachusetts, 1845?); Annie Louise Cary, noblest of contraltos (Wayne, Maine, 1846); Emma Abbott (Peoria, Illinois, 1850); Emma Thursby (Brooklyn, 1857); Marie van Zandt (New York, 1861); David Bispham (Fig. 30) (Philadelphia, 1857); the most triumphant of American *prime donne*, Lillian Norton — Nordica (Fig. 31) — (Farmington, Maine, 1856); Emma Wixom — Nevada — (Nevada City, 1860); Ella Russell (Cleveland, 1862); Emma Eames (Fig. 32), who, although born in Shanghai, China (1867), is to be ranked as an American, being of American parentage; Sybil Sanderson (Sacramento, California, 1865); Suzanne Adams (Fig. 35); Louise Homer (Fig. 33). The list could be extended much farther, but as it stands it will show that the preponderance of America's vocal contribution to the world is in great sopranos.

Ambroise Thomas once said to us, "Your country seems to be the natural home of the soprano!" No scientist has yet investigated the cause of national characteristics of voice. It may be climate, or food, or heredity, that causes north Spain to bring forth tenors; Switzerland, male falsetto singers ("jodlers"); England, contraltos; Russia, basses; and America, sopranos. But the fact remains, that as regards great musical executants and interpreters America has given more prominent operatic sopranos to the world than it has of pianists, organists, or violinists. Yet in these fields, too, we have not been without worthy and world-famous representatives.

CHAPTER XVI

MUSICAL CRITICISM AND AUTHORSHIP

WE have already outlined the beginnings of musical criticism in America. The earliest musical journals were of a very mild description, combining music and *belles-lettres* in a rather incongruous manner, and worshipping at the shrines of Handel and Haydn, with a very limited knowledge of even these two masters. The reviews were almost entirely rhapsodical. An example of what "criticism" meant in 1820 may be given in the following citations (we include their misprints and grammatical errors), not better or worse than dozens of other essays of the same epoch: —

"MR. OSTINELLI'S CONCERT

" The exertions of this truly scientific and accomplished musician, were never more conspicuously exhibited, than on Thursday evening, at Boylston Hall. The selections for performance, were chaste and well arranged, the applause resounding from every part of the Hall, was reiterated in thundering peals. We have not room, at this late hour, to particularize the several masterly scintillations of genius, fancy, and taste, and can only add,

> "'He wak'd the soul by tender strokes of art,
> He showed his genius, and he's won a heart.'"

"MISS DAVIS'S CONCERT

" The sudden and unexpected departure of this young lady from our City, and particularly from her numerous pupils, is a source of considerable regret, the more so from the evident and rapid improvement they have acquired, during the very short term of her stay. At the instigation of her most immediate acquaintances, Miss Davis was induced to give a Concert of vocal music, on which occasion the

Government of the Handel and Haydn Society generously tendered the use of Boylston Hall, and Doct. G. K. Jackson, with several amateurs volunteered their services.

"It is a circumstance of notoriety, we notice that the Gentleman of St. Paul's Church Choir (who alone volunteered their services on this occasion) have manifested a sensible regret, at the sudden departure of this interesting and truly classic vocalist, who has so essentially contributed her aid and assistance as first Soprano, in the performance of Handel's Music in a style of superiority, to which we are in a degree unaccustomed, to hear in this country. Nor can we omit to add our reluctance, in the acknowledgement, that a public loss will be incurred by her absence.

"Miss Davis made a very happy selection of Songs, which were received by an admiring audience, who were fully persuaded, that,

"'Her last notes were the sweetest.'"

At this time the daily press had nothing that could, even by the wildest stretch of the imagination, be called musical criticism. If a great concert was given in Boston or New York, a brief mention of it was sometimes made two or three days after the event, often merely chronicling the fact that the hall was crowded, or stating that the affair was "very successful." The first attempt at anything like critical reviews of music and musical performances was made by Dwight's *Journal of Music* (established in 1852), which became a powerful factor in moulding musical opinion, although it had but a limited circulation.

John Sullivan Dwight (Fig. 87), the founder of this periodical, may therefore be justly called the father of American musical criticism. He was born in Boston, May 13, 1813, and graduated at Harvard College in 1832. He studied in the Cambridge Theological School, and then entered the ministry, continuing in that field for six years. He wrote some excellent essays and reviews for literary magazines while in the ministry, but seems always to have had a predilection for music. As he had a refined (although very conservative) taste, his work, intrinsically valuable, was doubly and trebly so at a time when there were no well-equipped guides for public opinion in this art. It is amusing to note that sometimes his musical essays were held as somewhat more valuable than the works they chronicled. The eminent Theodore Parker once exclaimed, after reading one of Mr. Dwight's eloquent reviews, " Fancy making all that out of a musical work!" In the beginning Dwight worked with great zeal to acquaint the public with the beauties of Handel, Bach, Mozart, Beethoven, and the accepted classics in music. In his later years he fought against monster musical festivals, and was bitterly opposed to the more radical works of such men as Berlioz and Wagner.

FIG. 87. — JOHN S. DWIGHT.

In these days of Richard Strauss and Vincent d'Indy, we have gone far beyond what Dwight would have called musical blasphemy. The rapid advance in music may be illustrated by the statement that Dwight was regarded in his early years of journalism as too radical, yet long before the end of his days his views were held to be entirely too conservative!

Dwight had the advantage of associating with the brightest American men of letters and science, the broadest thinkers of his day. In 1842 he joined the Brook Farm Association, a gathering of the chief idealists of the time. It would be aside from our purpose herein to speak of this association, but one obtains the clew to some of this early critic's enthusiasm in studying his friends. He had a long and successful career, and Boston honored him in his declining years in many ways. He was for a long time presiding officer of the Harvard Musical Association; Otto Dresel and Hugo Leonhard, and a host of other advanced musicians of that day, became his close friends and advisers; finally a great benefit concert was given him by the leading musicians of the city. But the tide had swept past him, when, for a short time, he reëntered criticism and became musical reviewer of the Boston *Transcript*. Many skilled reviewers had gone beyond him, and his poetic views and conservative standard no longer attracted much attention.   He died, full of years, September 5, 1893.   His journal had gone out of existence a dozen years before.

Dwight was the pioneer of our musical critics.   His paper, during the first fifteen years of its existence, is the history of music in America.   Its contributors were in themselves a band of notable reviewers.   A. W. Thayer, the famous American biographer of Beethoven, was one of these, Otto Dresel was another, and Leonhard, Mathews, and many other celebrities often contributed to its columns.

In the musical literature of America, the name of Alexander Wheelock Thayer must certainly be accorded a foremost place; yet, by a strange irony of fate, his best work is scarcely known at all to American readers.   Thayer was born at South Natick, Massachusetts, October 22, 1817.   He graduated from Harvard University in 1843, and was then appointed assistant librarian at the college.   During six years of service in the library Thayer became imbued with a fixed purpose, which was nothing less than to devote his life to writing a biography of Beethoven.   It was a bold undertaking for a young American and a man none too well off in this world's goods, but he set about his task with grim determination.   He went abroad for two years (1849–51) and collected much material in Germany, supporting himself by newspaper correspondence.   In 1852 he was in New York as one of the editorial staff of the *Tribune*, but this was only a temporary makeshift, for, two years afterward (1854), he was back in Germany arranging for his monumental work.   He was again in Boston in 1856 and found friends who entered into his project with enthusiasm.   Among those who assisted him toward achieving results one may mention especially Lowell Mason.   Mrs. Mehitable Adams also gave material aid, and 1859 found Thayer hard at work at his chosen task. The first volume appeared, in German, in 1866.   Thayer had determined to give the original edition of the life of the great German composer to his own countrymen, and in their vernacular.   Therefore the manuscript, written in English, was translated into German by Dr. Herman Deiters, himself a musical biographer of note.

By this time, fortunately, Thayer's circumstances had altered somewhat for the better.   In 1862 he had been attached to the

American embassy in Vienna, with every opportunity for prosecuting his researches. Three years later President Lincoln (but a short time before his assassination) appointed Thayer United States consul at Trieste, a post which he held until his death. Thayer preceded the first volume of his biography with a thematic and chronological list of Beethoven's works, the most thorough list of the kind in existence. The second and third volumes of the biography appeared in 1872 and 1878, and several contributions to Beethoveniana had been published by the indefatigable researcher in the meantime.

English publishing houses offered Mr. Thayer tempting sums for the privilege of translating the volumes of this biography, but, although the consul was quite poor, he could never be induced to accept these offers. His plan was, after the work had been completed in German, to give forth a complete revision of it in English. This was, however, not to be; for, exhausted with his unceasing efforts, his health gave way and he died at Trieste, July 15, 1897, before the fourth and final volume of the German version was finished. Thayer's great work has suffered the fate of many other vast literary enterprises, such as Ambros's great "History of Music" ("Geschichte der Musik"), and Fetis's "Histoire Générale," and remains an unapproachable but unfinished edifice. Nevertheless it is with pride that the bibliographer records that the chief life of the great musician — possibly the greatest musical biography ever written, when one takes minuteness, size, general interest, and reliability into account — was achieved by an American author.

But in other fields of musical biography Americans have also won laurels. The American works upon the Wagner topic have found for themselves a place beside the German essays upon the same theme. Finck, Kobbé, and Krehbiel have written remarkable books on this subject.

Henry Theophilus Finck (Fig. 88) was born September 22, 1854, in Bethel, Missouri, not far from Mark Twain's birthplace, and was brought up in Oregon. In 1872 he entered Harvard College with the intention of becoming a physician; but he found the study of philosophy, under Professors Bowen and Palmer, so attractive that he changed his mind and decided to become a professor of psychology.   In 1876 he graduated with high honors in philosophy, and two years later Harvard gave him the Harris fellowship, which enabled him to continue his studies in psychology and sociology at the universities of Germany for three years.   At Harvard he had taken Professor John K. Paine's courses in music, and while in Europe he frequently wrote on musical and other topics for New York periodicals.   This led to his receiving an invitation to join the editorial staff of the *Nation* and also of the *Evening Post*, at the time when Carl Schurz, Lawrence Godkin, and Horace White ruled their destinies.

Mr. Finck began his biography of Wagner soon after the first musical festival at Bayreuth, in 1876.   He made the acquaintance of the great composer there and at once began gathering material for his biographical work.   The completion of the two volumes occupied many years, and it was not until 1893 that the first edition of " Wagner and his Works " appeared.   Since that time it has gone through many editions, and while it is written from the standpoint of a most pronounced admirer, it is one of the most influential books in the field of Wagner literature.

Other musical works of Mr. Finck's are a volume of essays on Chopin and other composers, " Paderewski and his Art," and "Songs and Song-writers."   The most timely work of Mr. Finck is also his most important.   It is a complete American edition of the four operas of the Nibelungen Ring (Cincinnati, 1903).   The work was probably the largest that had issued from the American press as a musical score, and the labor of editing, translating, and correcting it must have been stupendous.   It is a great contribution to the Wagner cause in America, bringing the gigantic work within reach of the music student.   In all of his books Mr. Finck takes very decided ground, and he is a bold iconoclast in many musical matters, attacking the old forms and fighting valiantly for the newer school.   He is, unfortunately, not in sympathy with the sonata and symphony writers.   He has been an ardent champion of Liszt and Grieg, and an opponent of Brahms.   His writings on other than musical topics are also most poetic and interesting.   Although aside from our topic, one cannot refrain from mentioning his " Lotos-time in Japan " and " Romantic Love and Personal Beauty " as

FIG. 88.—HENRY T. FINCK.

books of excellent caliber.   But it is in the field of musical biography and criticism that Mr. Finck has become a power, and his strong likes and dislikes make him one of the most militant warriors in the cause of progress.

The second of the Wagnerian writers above named, Gustav Kobbé, was born in New York, March 4, 1857.   His father, the late William A. Kobbé, was for many years in the consular service, being a native of the Duchy of Nassau.   His mother was Sarah Lord Sistare, a New England woman of Spanish descent, her first ancestor in this country having been a Spanish sea-captain, who, early in the eighteenth century, was wrecked off New London and afterward settled there.   Kobbé studied pianoforte and composition (1867–72) with Adolf Hagen in Wiesbaden; later with Joseph Mosenthal in New York.   He graduated from Columbia College in 1877, and from Columbia Law School in 1879.   He is the author of "Wagner's Life and Works," with the leading motives in notation (two volumes), which has passed through several editions, especially that part relating to the "Ring of the Nibelung," which has been printed separately.   "Opera Singers," "Signora," "A Child of the Opera House," "My Rosary and other Poems," "Miriam, a Story of the Lightship," are among his works, and he is one of the best-known American magazine writers on musical and dramatic matters as well as on miscellaneous subjects.

Kobbé's "Wagner's Life and Works" is valuable to the student for its analytical character, the succinctness and clearness of its statements, and for the care with which the author avoids polemics in his presentation of his subject.   Although a great admirer of the composer, Mr. Kobbé writes with a judicial poise that makes him almost neutral in the midst of conflict.   No man has better avoided the *furor biographicus*.   His work on musical topics for some of the leading encyclopædias has been remarkably exact and painstaking.

Mr. Henry Edward Krehbiel, the third of the above-mentioned writers (Fig. 89), has for many years been the musical reviewer of the New York *Tribune* and has won an enviable position among American musical essayists by his works.   He was born in Ann Arbor, Michigan, March 10, 1854.   He was for a time a journalist in Cincinnati, his studies in music beginning after he had attained an excellent reputation as a general writer. He studied law for a time in the West, but became musical critic of the Cincinnati *Gazette* in 1874 and held that position for nearly six years. He afterwards became musical critic of the *Tribune* as above stated, and also editor of the New York *Musical Review*, his New York career beginning in 1880. His contribution to the Wagnerian literature has been a volume entitled "Studies in the Wagnerian Drama." Besides this work he has written many musical year-books, records of the Philharmonic Society, an important book for the laity entitled "How to Listen to Music," an interesting historical work entitled "Music and Manners in the Classical Period," and has translated and edited innumerable other works. Mr. Krehbiel is soon to complete Thayer's "Beethoven," which will undoubtedly be his *magnum opus*. In 1900 he was a member of the International Jury of Awards in Paris (at the Exposition Universelle), and as a result of his services received the decoration of Chevalier of the Legion of Honor. The collaborator and associate critic of Mr. Krehbiel — Mr. Richard Aldrich — is also to be mentioned as an earnest writer. He is at present the musical reviewer of the *New York Times* and has written many essays on musical topics.

It will readily be seen that the chief musical authors of America have been the principal musical critics as well.

The influence of William H. Fry (already spoken of) was less widespread than that of John S. Dwight, since New York was not as active in musical matters (save in Italian opera) as Boston, in the middle of the nineteenth century. Yet Mr. Fry's enthusiasm for Italian music did much for America in the days when musical appreciation was in process of formation. Since that time New York has evolved a number of able reviewers in addition to the three Wagnerian authors already cited. One of the most trenchant and vigorous of these is James Gibbons Huneker, whose work in the columns of the *New York Sun* has been valuable in a high degree. Mr. Huneker is very modern in taste, and his writing is perhaps the best example of pungency in musical criticism that we have in America. Musical comment with us has generally followed the sprightly style of the French *feuilleton*. This is not to be regretted, and has the warrant of such able reviewers as Hector Berlioz and Edward Hanslick, two of the leading critics of the world. The heavy vein of reviewing that obtained in England until recent times has never taken root in America. In accordance with the literary tendency of the average American critic, Mr. Huneker has been active in authorship. His "Mezzotints in Modern Music"

and his "Melomaniacs" are somewhat bizarre, and at times morbid, but his life of Chopin is an excellent work. It is less detailed than the life by Niecks, but far in advance of that by Karasowski, and his Life of Liszt is decidedly the best at present existing on this topic.

Most of the American critics are practical musicians and Mr. Huneker is not an exception to this rule. He was born in Philadelphia, January 31, 1860, and studied music there with Michael Cross, subsequently

FIG. 89.—HENRY E. KREHBIEL.

continuing his work in Paris. He has been teacher of piano in the New York National Conservatory of Music for many years. He is a dramatic critic of prominence as well.

Another musical critic of New York whose name stands high among the writers of musical literature is William James Henderson (Fig. 90), who was born at Newark, New Jersey, December 4, 1855, and graduated from Princeton College in 1876. His books on music have been chiefly educational in character, but are very bright and

Y

readable as well as reliable. He possesses a style of writing that makes him one of the most popular of art critics. He is able to speak upon musical topics without becoming either technical or dull; and he has the happy faculty of leading his readers into the realms of higher musical appreciation without making them too self-conscious during the process. His terseness and his dry humor are great factors in achieving this result, and his "Story of Music" can be comprehended and appreciated by all of that legion who "don't understand music." Even in such abstruse topics as his explanation of the orchestra he has managed to convey his message to the public in an easily grasped series of descriptions. "The Story of Music," "What is Good Music," "How Music Developed," and "The Orchestra and Orchestral Music" are some of his best-known publications. He has been connected with both the New York *Times* and the New York *Sun;* and aside from music, he has written books on navigation, yachting, and other themes.

All of the writers we have mentioned have written magazine articles, essays, programme annotations, and have given lectures as well. The American musical reviewer is a decidedly active and manifold influence in American musical matters. One prominent New York critic, however, has not entered the field of book-making, — Mr. August Spanuth, who has gone to Germany and become the editor of the famous Leipsic *Signale.*

In Boston, during the latter days of Mr. Dwight's régime, there suddenly sprang up a number of able musical writers. It is good evidence of the rapidity of musical growth, that during the palmy days of Dwight's *Journal of Music*, every newspaper in Boston allowed its musical reviews to be written by any reporter, while at present almost every newspaper of the city has its expert to guide musical opinion. Albert Lavignac, of the Paris Conservatoire, has wisely written in his work on "Musical Education":—

"A critic is not a reporter; he is an initiator and guide, an educator and a professor; his pupil is the public."

Such guides were soon forthcoming in Boston as they had been in New York. One of the earliest, after Dwight and Thayer, was Benjamin Edward Woolf, an Englishman, born in London, February

16, 1836. He came from a family of operatic conductors and studied music practically with his father's theatrical orchestra. He conducted theatre orchestras in many American cities, and finally at the Boston Museum. He brought forth many compositions of his own, and his influence in light opera and in drama was fully as important as his contributions to musical criticism. He wrote " Pounce & Co." and " Westward Ho," two works in the "comic opera" vein which does not represent the best taste in American music; but it is only just to add that these were better than their school. He wrote the libretto for Eichberg's " Doctor of Alcantara," a work of excellent character, and he composed madrigals, overtures, string quartettes, and even symphonies, although the last named were not publicly performed and are yet in manuscript. All together, then, Mr. Woolf was easily the most thorough musician who had, up to 1870, entered American musical journalism. He began in that year on the Boston *Globe*, but soon attached himself to the staff of the *Saturday Evening Gazette*, a weekly paper of some social influence. In his later years he was musical critic of the Boston *Herald*.

From Mr. Woolf's English and rather conservative training it was but natural that he should be out of sympathy with the radical modern school. He was at one time one of the fiercest opponents of the Wagnerian music, and his bitter sarcasm and invective made him feared by many who held different opinions. He was often sublimely savage in his reviews. But, in spite of these limitations, his great musical ability made him an influence to be reckoned with. He died in Boston in 1901.

Almost contemporaneous with Mr. Woolf was William Foster Apthorp, who was thoroughly trained for a musical career, but composed little or nothing. Mr. Apthorp was born in Boston, October 24, 1848, and graduated from Harvard in 1869. He studied music with Professor John K. Paine and Mr. B. J. Lang, and was for some time teacher of theory in the New England Conservatory of Music in Boston. He began his career as a musical critic on the *Atlantic Monthly* in 1872, after which he occupied the same position on the *Sunday Courier*, the Boston *Traveller*, and finally (1881) he became musical and dramatic editor of the Boston *Transcript*. The latter position he held until 1903, in which year he departed for Europe, where he died in 1912.   Mr. Apthorp's volumes are "Musicians and Music Lovers," "The Opera, Past and Present," and several translations, chiefly from the French.   He has done excellent work as the compiler of the analytical programme books of the Boston Symphony Orchestral concerts, and as critical editor of the "Cyclopædia of Music and Musicians."   His influence was chiefly exerted after he became the critic of the *Transcript*.

It was much later than the time of Messrs. Woolf and Apthorp that Mr. Philip Hale began his career in Boston.   He was born in Norwich, Vermont, March 5, 1854, and graduated from Yale in 1876. He was early occupied both with music and with literature, for he had played the organ in the Unitarian Church at Northampton, Massachusetts, before entering college, and in Yale he edited one of the college papers. His chief studies, however, were in the law, and he was admitted to the New York bar in 1880.   His musical education went on with considerable vigor all through this formative period, and subsequently he went abroad, studying with Rheinberger,

FIG. 90. — WILLIAM J. HENDERSON.

Guilmant, and other French and German teachers.   He came to Boston in 1889 as organist at Dr. De Normandie's (Unitarian) church in Roxbury.   He soon became the critic successively and successfully of the *Home Journal* of Boston, the Boston *Post*, and the Boston *Journal*, finally joining the Boston *Herald*.   He has been the editor of the *Musical Record* and the *Musical World*, and has written articles in many musical magazines, notably in the *Musical Courier*, of which periodical he was for a long time the Boston correspondent.   His musical writings have always been bright, witty, and readable.   His chief work in book form has been the editing, in collaboration with the present writer, of a set of three volumes on "Famous Composers" (new series), which deal largely with the most modern developments in music. Mr. Hale has also done splendid work in writing the analytical programmes of the Boston Symphony Orchestra. His work in this direction has been a model for all writers. He stands unrivalled in this field.

[Louis C. Elson, the author of this " History of American Music," also belongs with those who have worked for the advancement of American music. He was born in Boston, April 17, 1848. August Hamann was his teacher of piano. In voice he received instruction from August Kreissmann, the friend of Franz and one of the best singers of *Lieder* of his time. Composition was afterward taken up with Carl Gloggner-Castelli, of Leipsic. In 1880 Mr. Elson entered the New England Conservatory as teacher of voice and lecturer. The department of musical theory was assigned to him, and, after the death of Stephen A. Emery, he became the head of this department in the institution. His lectureship was devoted to explanations of the orchestra and its instruments and to a course upon the history of music. His journalistic work began on the *Vox Humana*, a paper devoted chiefly to organ music. In 1880 this was merged in the *Musical Herald*, of which Mr. Elson became editor. At about the same time he was appointed musical editor of the Boston *Courier*, and when abroad was an occasional correspondent of the New York *Tribune*, the New York *Evening Post*, the Boston *Transcript*, and other papers. In 1888 he became musical editor of the Boston *Advertiser*, a position which he still holds.

Mr. Elson has directed large choruses in Trinity Church, Boston, in the New England Conservatory, and in a musical festival which took place in Boston in 1886, in which music was given representing composers from mediæval times down to the present epoch. In composition he has written much in the small forms. His books are " The Curiosities of Music "; a " History of German Song," which was partially translated in the German press; " The Realm of Music," a series of essays; " The Theory of Music," a technical work; "Great Composers"; "Our National Music and its Sources"; "Famous Composers and their Works," new series; " European Reminiscences," a book of travel; " Shakespeare in Music "; " Mistakes and Disputed Points in Music"; " Elson's Music Dictionary"; "Modern Music and Musicians " (10 vols.); " Elson's Pocket Dictionary." As lecturer on music he has been twice called to the Lowell Institute Course (the most prominent in America), and has lectured repeatedly at Cornell, Brown, Vassar, University of Pennsylvania, the Brooklyn Institute, the Drexel Institute, and has given 250 lectures for the city of Boston, teaching appreciation of music to the masses. — EDITOR.]

In speaking of the growth of musical literature in the Eastern states, the name of Howard Malcom Ticknor must also be mentioned. A Harvard graduate, assistant editor of the *Atlantic Monthly* in the days when Lowell brought that magazine to its highest standard, United States consul in Italy for many years, and instructor in Harvard and Brown universities, Mr. Ticknor brought to musical journalism a refinement and suavity which it had noticeably lacked after the influence of Dwight had spent itself. Mr. Ticknor's writings were chiefly in the Boston *Advertiser*, the Boston *Globe*, the Boston *Herald*, and the Boston *Journal;* he wrote no musical works or books.

In the Eastern states a supplementary factor in the general advance in orchestral taste has been the writing of analytical programme books. These musical essays have been found in evidence at almost every great concert. Mr. George H. Wilson was the pioneer in this work in Boston, and Messrs. Apthorp and Hale, in Boston, Mr. Philip H. Goepp, in Philadelphia, Messrs. Krehbiel and Spanuth, in New York, and others, have done great educational service in this direction. Mr. Goepp has, in addition, written a work entitled "Symphonies and their Meaning" (in three volumes), which is worthy of honorable mention among American musical books. Mr. Goepp was born in New York, June 23, 1864, and studied in Germany. He graduated from Harvard in 1884, and received a degree from the University of Pennsylvania in 1888. He has been a composer as well as an author, yet his chief influence upon American art has been exerted from the literary side.

Philadelphia has been less active in the field of criticism than New York, Chicago, or Boston, yet two names may be mentioned as prominent in her musico-literary annals. Mr. Willard J. Baltzell has written many excellent educational essays and has made an astonishing success with a semi-pedagogical musical journal, — the *Musician*. Mr. Baltzell, like many American musical writers, has composed much music, even in the larger forms with orchestral accompaniment. Mr. James Francis Cooke has done excellent work in conducting a very great musical periodical — *The Étude* — and has also written a History of Music, and various important pedagogical works.

Among the brightest of the present writers on musical and other topics, yet not permanently attached to any of the great dailies, is Rupert Hughes. He is a Westerner, having been born in Lancaster, Missouri, January 31, 1872. He has been somewhat of a rolling stone, yet his gatherings have been many and valuable. Educated in the public schools at Keokuk, Iowa, he afterward graduated from the Western Reserve University. He then became assistant editor of the *Criterion*, in New York, after which a large publishing house sent him to London to do research work. He has written fiction, verse, essays, and criticisms for such leading magazines as *Scribner's*, the *Cosmopolitan*, and the *Century*, but his claim to record here lies in his bright musical reviews in the *Criterion*, his musical sketches in *Godey's*, his popular " Musical Guide," his " Love Affairs of the Great Composers," and his " Contemporary American Composers," which, with the exception of Mathews's " Hundred Years of Music in America," was the first book upon this topic. Mr. Hughes is an indefatigable student of facts, yet one of the liveliest and wittiest of American musical authors. He has won success in novel and play writing.

In the Western states musical literature has been a plant of rather slow growth. Even now it is the exception, rather than the rule, to find an intelligent analytical description of musical events in the columns of the press in Western cities. Chicago has made the most progress in this important matter, and has had at least four writers who are comparable to the best of the Eastern musical critics. Mr. George P. Upton (Fig. 91) holds such rank, not because of his being a composer or a profound musician, but because he was a pathfinder in the West, and, like Dwight in Boston, upheld a standard of good taste and culture in music at a time when such an influence was peculiarly valuable. He was born in Boston, October 25, 1834, and graduated from Brown University in 1854. He became a journalist in Chicago in 1855, and was on the staff of the

Chicago *Journal* for six years. At the end of that period he joined the forces of the Chicago *Tribune* and has been actively engaged there ever since. He wrote the first musical criticisms ever published in the western metropolis, possibly the first of any importance that were ever written in any part of the West.

To illustrate the state of Chicago's music before Mr. Upton's advent, we quote from the Chicago *Tribune*, which thus sums up the musical progress of that city from its earliest stages: —

" Music antedates the drama in this city, for the first concert was given in 1835, in the First Presbyterian Church, the first church built in Chicago. No programme of the concert has been preserved, and all of the singers are gone. Prior to 1835 the only music in the city was that of the Indian's tom-toms, old Beaubien's fiddle, and the Congregational Church singing in a frame tenement, which was used in common by Presbyterians, Baptists, and Methodists, the Rev. Messrs. Porter, Whitehead, and Freeman being the ministers, and Sergeant Burtis, of the fort, leading the singing.

" Music was not well grounded in Chicago until 1850. In that year Mr. Dyrenfurth presented an orchestra composed almost exclusively of German revolutionists whom he had employed upon his farm, but who proved to be better musicians than farm laborers. This was the first orchestra Chicago ever heard. In that same year Chicago heard its first opera at Rice's Theatre, or a part of its first opera, for the season was only half an hour in length. The opera was 'Sonnambula,' and at the close of the first act the audience was dismissed because the theatre was on fire. There were two or three spasmodic efforts to establish opera, but it was not until 1859 that Maurice Strakosch succeeded. The next three years may be called the concert years of Chicago. Anna Bishop in 1851, Teresa Parodi, Catherine Hayes, and Anna Thillon in 1852, and Adelina Patti in 1853, were the concert pioneers."

One would wish to add to the above condensed account a word about the work of Hans Balatka in Chicago's early days. Born in Moravia, March 5, 1827, he came to America in 1849. He founded the Milwaukee *Musikverein* in 1851. Chicago had founded a Philharmonic Society in 1852, and in 1860 Balatka became its first eminent conductor. In developing chorus music in the West,

particularly in Chicago and Milwaukee, Balatka was a pioneer
of importance. He lived to see Chicago advance far beyond
the primitive beginnings described above, for he died there April
17, 1899.

At this time Mr. George P. Upton was most active in diffusing not only a musical taste in Chicago, but also in inspiring musical practice. He was the first president of the Apollo Musical
Club of Chicago, founded as a male chorus directly after the great
fire of 1872, and now a flourishing mixed
chorus. It may suggest the recent growth
of music in the West when it is stated
that Mr. Upton, still living, heard the first
orchestra that ever played, and the first
opera and first oratorio ever given in
Chicago. When this fact is remembered,
it may show more vividly the herculean
task of one man, Theodore Thomas, who,
almost alone, has built a firm foundation
for the best music in that city, and has
led Chicago to a foremost rank among
our western centres.

FIG. 91. — GEORGE P. UPTON.

Mr. Upton did his work for good
music at a time when the poorest was in vogue, and he has lived
to see, not a complete triumph as yet, but incredible advances.
He has written some small but useful volumes of musical essays
under the following titles: "Woman in Music" (written in 1880,
before America's band of women composers had come into being),
"The Standard Oratorios," "The Standard Operas," "The Standard Symphonies," and "The Standard Cantatas." He has translated Nohl's lives of Haydn, Wagner, and Liszt, has published a
volume on the light operas, and has added a host of more purely
literary essays and criticisms.

Another prominent figure in Western musical writing was William
Smythe Babcock Mathews (Fig. 92), who was born in Loudon, New
Hampshire, May 8, 1837. Mr. Mathews studied music at first in his
native town, but afterward came to Boston for better educational
facilities. He was soon appointed adjunct professor in the Wes-

leyan Female College at Macon, Georgia, and was one of the regular contributors to Dwight's *Journal of Music* under the pseudonym of "Der Freischütz." His most active work in music began after he settled in Chicago, in 1867. Here his influence extended in many directions. He was the organist in one of the leading churches, a pianist and a teacher of high repute, and a writer of both reviews and books of training and knowledge. His writing, although very facile and most rapidly done, was reliable, instructive, and interesting. His musical criticisms were among the best that the West has ever had. They have appeared in the Chicago *Herald*, *Record*, and *Tribune*. Besides this he established a magazine of excellent character, entitled *Music*, of which he was not only editor but the most valuable contributor. Mr. Mathews's musical books have been of the most practical character. He wrote numerous books of instructive character and was one of the most successful of teachers. He died at Denver, April 1, 1912.

It will be seen that America is well supplied with pedagogical musical books. It has more of this kind of literature than any other nation except Germany. Musical readers form a very large class in our country, and some of the American musical journals reach a circulation unknown elsewhere. Mr. Mathews has appealed to vast multitudes through this musical press. He was constantly writing essays and articles in such musical journals as the *Étude* and the *Musician*, in addition to the work in his own magazine. He has probably been as great an influence in the moulding of musical taste in the West as Mr. Dwight has been in the East, and he has always been much the better musician.

One must add the name of Emil Liebling to the list of formers of American taste by means of essays and musical articles. His name would lead Western musical literature but for the fact that his influence has been chiefly exerted in the class room. He was also one of the prominent teachers in the country, and his application to this work prevented him from being as active in the literary field as his contemporaries. Yet his articles on musical topics were always the well-considered work of a thorough musician, and he had an enviable vein of humor and piquancy as well. He was an Austrian, having been born in Pless, Silesia, April 12, 1851. He became active in

Chicago in 1872, when he first came to the Western metropolis, and he died in that city, January 20, 1914, deeply mourned. The fourth on the list of Chicago critics was Frederic Grant Gleason, whose chief work has been done in composition, and who has been spoken of elsewhere in this volume.

Cincinnati has never been as well-equipped with musical writers as Chicago, and its musical criticisms have been too largely reportorial until recent days. It has, however, possessed one notable exception to this in the person of John Smith Van Cleve, who was born in Maysville, Kentucky, October 30, 1851. Although Mr. Van Cleve is totally blind (having been so from his ninth year), this handicap has not prevented him from being very active in almost every department of practical music authorship and lectureship. His chief musical studies were made in Boston. For a time he was undecided between music and theology. His work in Cincinnati began in 1879, and he soon became musical critic of the Cincinnati *Commercial* under Murat Halstead. He was subsequently employed upon the *News Journal* of the same city, and did much work in Cincinnati in teaching. His strong literary tendencies made him not only a good writer, but an excellent lecturer on musical topics.

The lecture seems to be a peculiarly American institution. While in Europe it is possible, occasionally, to hear a good series of lectures on musical history in some college or conservatory, America has a constant running fire of public lectures and lecturers on musical topics. Possibly this form of teaching owes its vogue, if not its inception, to the great number of women's clubs which are found in the United States. One phase of the emancipation of woman has been the establishment of lecture courses and the reading of "papers," and a goodly proportion of these papers or lectures is devoted to music.

Mr. Van Cleve left Cincinnati in 1897 and removed to Chicago, where he was as active as in the former city. But, in Cincinnati he was the chief musical writer; in Chicago he was but one among several.[1] He now resides in New York, and is still heard, both as lecturer and writer, in that city.

[1] Mr. Van Cleve is also a composer and a poet, and a volume of his poems and another one of his lectures are among his works.

Cleveland, although not exactly a musical centre thirty-five years ago, had a musical journal even then, and its editor was a writer who left his mark on the musical culture of that city. Karl Merz was born at Bensheim, Germany, September 10, 1836. He came to America in 1854, and taught music in Lancaster, Pennsylvania, in Oxford, Ohio, and in Wooster, Ohio. In 1873 he was appointed editor of the *Musical World* of Cleveland. His essays have been collected in a volume entitled "Music and Culture," and show a well-balanced mind and indicate a thoughtful analyst. He died in Wooster, Ohio, January 30, 1890.

In California one finds musical critics and authors forming that public taste which culminates in classical concerts and sometimes even in native composers. In Los Angeles there resides a musical reviewer who has also added to American musical books. Mr. W. Francis Gates (born in Zanesville, Ohio, March 18, 1865) has written and compiled several volumes of musical essays, and has also been very active in musical journalism. In San Francisco, from 1893 to 1895, there was an excellent critic upon *The Examiner*, Edgar S. Kelley, of whom we have spoken in a preceding chapter.

Many other writers may be named who have added to American musical bibliography without having been critics or musical reviewers. Among these is Edward Dickinson, A.M., professor of musical history at the Oberlin (Ohio) Conservatory of Music, whose "History of Music in the Western Church" is a most scholarly contribution to the sacred side of musical study, and is probably the chief work on this topic that America has yet produced. Theodore Baker, Ph.D., of New York, was the first musician to thoroughly sift the Indian music of North America, and his work (published in Germany) on this topic has been quoted freely in this volume. He has also compiled a biographical dictionary of musicians, which is the chief work on this subject in America. Arthur Elson, of Boston, has added a history of opera, a guide to the orchestra, and a volume on women composers, and "The Book of Musical Knowledge" to the list. John Comfort Fillmore, already quoted in connection with Indian music, has published a practical history of pianoforte music and some lessons on general musical history.

FIG. 92.— W. S. B. MATHEWS.

Women have appeared not too frequently among our musical authors, the most popular book by a woman writer on music in this country being Amy Fay's "Music Study in Germany," which has been translated into various tongues and republished in Europe. It is a record of the fetich-worship accorded by the feminine students to Liszt, not an important historical matter, but so naïvely and charmingly told that it holds the attention from first to last. Making due allowances for the character of the topic, we do not know of any woman among the musical authors who has won a more popular success than Miss Fay. She has also written a pedagogic work, an exposition of the Deppe method of piano playing. Miss Helen M. Sparmann has written an essay entitled "An Attempt at an Analysis of Music,"—a very commendable, though short, pamphlet, and Mrs. Helen D. Tretbar has given forth some useful analytical works and many musical translations.

One of the most promising of the American writers on music, E. Irenæus Stevenson, was drawn away from his subject by other pursuits. He made an excellent reputation as an essayist on musical topics, by articles in the New York *Independent* and in *Harper's Weekly*, and had written some musical novels, and also a collection of musical sketches, when, in 1899, he received an addition to his fortune and his name (becoming Mr. Prime-Stevenson), and went to Vienna to live. His gain was a loss to American musical literature, for he was an intelligent writer upon the modern phases of art, and an influence much needed at the present time.

Any sketch of American musical authors would be very faulty if it did not mention the learning and wide influence of Dr. Frederic Louis Ritter. As will be seen directly, Dr. Ritter's influence was exerted in many other fields besides musical authorship. He was born in Strassburg, June 22, 1834, and studied both in France and in Germany. He came to this country in 1856 and settled in Cincinnati. That city owes a great debt to him; for what Mr. George P. Upton was to Chicago in its musical childhood, that Dr. Ritter became to Cincinnati in the early days. The latter city, to be sure, was an older one than Chicago, and had the advantage of a German element in its population which founded the *Maennerchor*, the embodiment of all that is genial in music, even in the earliest

days of the settlement; but Dr. Ritter built a classical edifice upon
this foundation, and the Cecilia Society, — choral, — and the Philharmonic, — orchestral, — were the result of his labors.   He did
not, however, stay long enough in the city to develop what he so
ably inaugurated.   In 1861 he settled in New York, where he continued in the same line of public musical service.   The Sacred
Harmonic Society made him its conductor, while, as leader of the
Arion, he had control of one of the best German male choruses in
the world.   Both in Cincinnati and in New York he introduced
a large number of new and important works to the American
public, and his name may be mentioned in the same breath with
those of Theodore Thomas and Dr. Leopold Damrosch for the
far-reaching pioneer work which he accomplished.   He arranged
and conducted the first really great musical festival held in New
York, in 1867, and at about the same time was appointed professor of music at Vassar College, a position which he held almost
up to his death, which took place in Antwerp, July 22, 1891.   The
University of New York, in 1874, conferred upon him the degree
of Mus. Doc.

It is difficult to form a just estimate of a man who achieves
so much, and in so many different directions, as did Dr. Ritter.
In musical conductorship he had superiors, and, although his pedagogic influence at Vassar was of the best, other teachers in similar fields deserve equal recognition; but in the domain of musical
literature he was as important a figure as any in America, after
Dwight and Thayer.   He was constantly writing musical essays,
not only in the American journals, but in France and in Germany, and was instrumental in causing Europe to become familiar
with the musical strivings of this country, which before his time
had been deemed semi-barbaric.   His most important work was a
history of music, which was for a long time the best brief book[1]
on this subject in the English language.   He also wrote a volume
on music in England, which is still regarded as an authority abroad.
Another volume on music in America had less of success, for

---

[1] Or rather two volumes, for at first it was in this shape.   It is now published as a
student's history of music, in a single volume.   It is in English very much what Brendel's
" Geschichte der Musik " is in German.

Dr. Ritter approached his subject with little sympathy. William Billings, the first native composer, shocked this classicist with his false progressions; our national music did not appeal to him deeply, and of the American composers he had not a word to say. The work is mainly devoted to opera and to orchestral societies in New York, but is most thorough in these fields.

Dr. Ritter was a profound musician, and composed many works even in the symphonic forms. These were, however, the compositions of a German in America, rather than of a native composer or of a man influenced by American surroundings. Massenet, the French composer, once spoke enthusiastically to the present writer regarding the inspiration that ought to come to the American composer. "Were I in America," said he, "I should be exalted by the glories of your scenery, your Niagara, your prairies; I should be inspired by the Western and Southern life; I should be intoxicated by the beauty of your American women; national surroundings must always inspire national music!" Dr. Ritter, however much he labored for us, worked from without, not from within; he was among us, but not of us. He could not realize what a group of good American composers was growing up around him. In spite of these limitations his will always be a respected name in our musical annals.

The work of Richard Grant White (born in New York, May 23, 1822, and died there April 8, 1885), in musical criticism, is something of a contrast to that of the writers we have thus far mentioned. Ritter, Finck, Huneker, Mathews, and many of the others, were musicians who had entered the literary field; White, like John S. Dwight, was an essayist who had added music to his literary topics. But White had none of the gentleness and suavity of the elder writer; he was keen and bitter in controversy, pronounced in opinions, relentless in polemics. He wrote some of his diatribes with vitriol. His writhing victims made an epigram out of his name,— turning "Richard Grant White" into "Richard Can't Write,"— but he could write far better than he could judge. His was not the judicial mind that saw both sides of any question; with him there was but a single view upon any topic, musical or otherwise,— his own.

z

White's versatility is suggested by the fact that he was a great Shakespearian commentator, a brilliant journalist, one of the leading magazine writers, a learned philologist, a musical critic, and chief clerk in the New York Custom House! Such versatility is dangerous, for it prevents a man from becoming a leader in any one field. Had White given greater attention to the study of music and of its literature, it is probable that he would have been the chief author in this field. As it is, he may be considered the chief literary light that entered musical criticism in America. That his reviewing moulded any national taste, or influenced our musical progress in any permanent manner, cannot be truthfully said.

PLATE XII

JOHN K. PAINE

CHAPTER XVII

THE MUSICAL EDUCATION OF THE PRESENT

WHILE America does not possess, and does not require, an endowed school of music under government protection, such as the *Conservatoire* at Paris or some of the conservatories in Italy, Belgium, or Germany, yet, through the philanthropy and the love of art of private individuals, large schools have been founded that have nobly carried on the movement inaugurated in the Boston Academy of Music and by Lowell Mason over sixty years ago. There is possibly no country on the globe where the rudiments of music are so widely diffused among the masses as in America. Every city gives its public school children some knowledge of part-singing and at least the ability to read notation; conservatories in each large city offer not only well-equipped courses in every branch of music, but free scholarships to pupils of pronounced talent. It must be borne in mind that in this chapter it is not our purpose to give a list of great conservatories. Almost every city has one, New York nearly half a dozen. We speak only of those which are *historically* prominent.

Before the conservatories began, before even the Boston Musical Academy was dreamed of, there was a thorough education in music dispensed at the Moravian and other religious settlements in Pennsylvania. In Bethlehem and at Ephrata, even in the eighteenth century, there was constant study, and Philadelphia was at times glad to borrow musicians from the Moravians for its early festivals. The Moravian and Ephratan music undoubtedly had an effect even beyond the Alleghanies, and it is not impossible that it also influenced the first New England composers; but this Pennsylvania-German school can in itself scarcely be classed as American music. For a record of recent discoveries in this field the reader is referred to Dr. Julius F. Sachse's "Music of the Ephrata Cloister" (Lancaster, 1903).   The Moravians undoubtedly had the first regular music schools of this country.

In speaking of the musical conservatories of America a few may be mentioned as typical.   The largest, the New England Conservatory of Boston, has a curriculum most nearly approaching that of the great European schools, and this broad course has been largely due to the efforts of Mr. George W. Chadwick, its present

director.   But the founding of this conservatory was due to Dr. Eben Tourjée (Fig. 93), a man who, without being a great musician himself, wielded a great influence on musical education in America. Dr. Tourjée (the degree of Mus. Doc. came from Wesleyan University) was born in Warwick, Rhode Island, June 1, 1834, and died in Boston in 1890.   Largely self-taught in music, his first connection with the art was upon the commercial side, for at seventeen he was clerk in a music store at Fall River, Massachusetts; subsequently he became organist and choir director at Newport, Rhode Island.   During the existence of the East Greenwich Musical Institute he visited Europe and studied the conservatory system there.   At this time he also took lessons from Haupt, in Berlin, and from other prominent teachers. On his return to America he established a conservatory in Providence, Rhode Island.   As early as 1859 he obtained a charter for a musical institute in connection with the academy at East Greenwich, Rhode Island.   The Boston Academy of Music, already described, had been too idealistic and had attempted far too much; Dr. Tourjée was the first to establish the class system of musical training upon a practical basis in America.   In 1867 he founded the New England Conservatory of Music.   He was a superb organizer, and soon saw that America needed some modifications of the European system, especially in the matter of careful protection of female students coming from a distance to a strange city.

FIG. 93. — DR. EBEN TOURJÉE.

He incorporated the New England Conservatory in 1870, and the institution had its quarters in Music Hall Building for about a dozen years. After this, in following out the idea suggested above, he secured the great St. James Hotel Building in Boston, and altered it to suit his needs, making it both a conservatory and a home for students from distant cities. Many persons helped the institution, among whom may be mentioned the Hon. Rufus Frost, long its president, the Hon. Richard H. Dana, also a president and the organizer of a fund for its perpetuation, and Jacob Sleeper, who gave a hall for its recitals and concerts. There were many pecuniary difficulties attending the school in its enlarged quarters, but Dr. Tourjée bravely fought on and steered successfully through troubled waters, until his health began to fail. An attack of nervous prostration incapacitated him, and for a year before his death his keen intellect was clouded.

Mr. Carl Faelten, who had been one of the most prominent piano teachers of the institution, now took the helm, but after a few years resigned in favor of George W. Chadwick, who found that the time had come for yet further innovations. He began his régime by separating in some degree the home and the conservatory. A new building (Fig. 53) was erected, probably the most perfect for its purpose of any in America, which is used exclusively for teaching; new dormitories were established, apart from the conservatory itself, yet under its direction and supervision; and two halls were built for lectures and concerts.

The new conservatory found more powerful protectors than ever before, Mr. Charles P. Gardiner becoming its president. Mr. Eben D. Jordan, now president of the institution, was one of the chief of its benefactors. The great organ of the institution is his gift, and the large hall of the conservatory, one of the finest music halls in Boston, is named in his honor. The curriculum of the conservatory is at present probably the most severe of any musical school in this country. Its faculty contains many distinguished names, which have been spoken of in their various fields of work, yet a few of the teachers of the past may be here mentioned.

Mr. Carl Faelten was born in Thuringia, December 21, 1846. He derived the greater part of his musical proficiency from Raff, with whom he was intimately associated in the Frankfort Conservatory. His earlier studies, however, had been under Montag and Schoch, in Weimar and Frankfort. His work was interrupted by the Franco-Prussian War, when military law compelled a term of service, but through the influence of some officers who accidentally became acquainted with his musical abilities, he was spared severe tasks and largely employed in clerical duties. When his term of service had ended, he again began his musical studies, and carried them on so successfully that he was soon able to make several concert appearances in Germany. He was one of the piano

FIG. 94.—STEPHEN A. EMERY.

teachers in Raff's Conservatory, and from 1882 he was active as a teacher in the Peabody Institute in Baltimore. In 1885 he became one of the faculty of the New England Conservatory. He left that institution in 1897 to found a large piano school of his own, which still flourishes in Boston.

Mr. Stephen A. Emery (Fig. 94) was one of the most popular of the harmony teachers in the Conservatory. He was born in Paris, Maine, October 4, 1841, his father being a distinguished lawyer and judge of that state. After preliminary musical study in Portland, Mr. Emery went to Leipsic, where he studied with Richter, Hauptmann, and others. He was a teacher of harmony at the New England Conservatory from its very beginning, 1867, until his death, which took place in Boston, April 15, 1891. Mr. Emery's compositions, almost all of them in the smaller forms, although full of grace and delicacy, are not of great importance in the development of American music, but in his long-continued pedagogic service he did much for the advancement of the art, and hundreds of his pupils are now working successfully in the musical field. Many of the important composers spoken of in this volume derived their early inspiration from the teaching of Stephen Albert Emery.

Another teacher at the Conservatory, whose influence was exerted almost entirely within its walls, was Alfred Dudley Turner, who was born in St. Albans, Maine, August 24, 1854, and studied with Mr. J. C. D. Parker, and also with Mme. Madeleine Schiller. Such musicians as Frank A. Porter and Charles F. Dennée attest the earnestness of Mr. Turner's work. Like Mr. Emery, he wrote chiefly in the smaller forms, and left no very important works even in these. His octave studies, however, are among the most valued contributions made by Americans to musical pedagogy. He died May 7, 1888, when only thirty-three years of age.

The names of Emery and Turner, their unostentatious work, their pedagogic success, may serve to point a moral. European teachers of greater celebrity did not always achieve as much practical result in America as these two men. It was simply the comprehension of the American student, the knowledge of how to reach his heart, how to spur on his ambition, that made their work remarkable. The really successful teacher must have, besides the technique of his art, a full comprehension of the character of his pupils; and this gives an obvious advantage to the American teacher in America.

There were other important teachers in the Conservatory. Mr. Lyman W. Wheeler and his brother Harry Wheeler were prominent in the vocal work, Mr. John O'Neill graduated Lillian Norton (Mme. Nordica) and other prominent pupils, Mr. Otto Bendix taught piano there before going to San Francisco and establishing another conservatory, Carlyle Petersilea, recently deceased, was of the piano group, George E. Whiting was for a long time the chief organ teacher, Carl Zerrahn was its teacher of conducting. Martin Roeder came from Italy to join the forces, as did also Signor Augusto Rotoli, and a musical brotherhood, "The Sinfonia," was founded in the conservatory by Ossian E. Mills, and now has branches in many cities of the United States.

A few additional words regarding Dr. Tourjée may be pertinent before leaving the conservatory which he founded. He was a most active lieutenant in the two peace jubilees given by Gilmore in Boston, and practically constructed the immense choruses of these festivals. He was a strong worker in the cause of music in the public schools, and he was the originator of the " Praise Service " in American religious life.   He was also a diplomat to the finger-tips and had a manner of getting almost everybody to work out his wishes, to educe the maximum of work with the minimum of friction ; in short, he was the man for his place and time, just as Billings had been for the rudimentary stage of American music and Lowell Mason for its advancing stages.

During the early days of the New England Conservatory, while it had no rival in its general curriculum, it had a keen competitor in the domain of violin music.   The Boston Conservatory of Music had been founded by Julius Eichberg, and was, for a long time, the chief violin school of America.   With the death of Mr. Eichberg, however, much of its glory departed, although the good work of its subsequent director, Herman Chelius, in the piano department, is to be chronicled.   The influence of Mr. Julius Eichberg (Fig. 95) upon the violin music of America is incontestable.   He was born in Düsseldorf, June 23, 1824, studied with Rietz, and in his childhood played before Mendelssohn, who put on record his high opinion of the performance of the juvenile prodigy.   Additional study with Fétis and De Beriot and acquaintance with Schumann made the youth of this violinist a memorable one.

Eichberg came to New York, in search of health, in 1857, but soon settled in Boston, where he began his career in 1859.   His first work in that city was as conductor of the little orchestra at the Boston Museum.   There he contributed somewhat to the American repertoire, for he wrote a charming opera, " The Doctor of Alcantara," which was the best light opera that had up to that time been written in this country.   He subsequently composed other operas, all graceful and singable, but none of them of the excellence of the first-named work, which was produced in 1862 (Fig. 96).   In spite of its charm " The Doctor of Alcantara " has become obsolete ; nor can it be fairly called an American work, since the libretto was by B. E. Woolf, the English musical critic (resident in Boston), and the music was, of course, by a German.   Yet Mr. Eichberg became enthusiastically American, as may be seen by his national hymn, " To Thee, Oh Country ! " of which the words were written by his daughter, a lady of much literary ability.   He wrote some chamber-music and became for a time supervisor of music in the public schools of Boston. He died in Boston, January 13, 1898.

The West also has had its musical enthusiasts who were ready to play the part of Mæcenas in endowing educational institutions for the development of the art. George Ward Nichols and Reuben Springer were the chief founders of the Cincinnati College of Music (Fig. 101), the leading musical institution of the West for many years. The first meeting of the stockholders of this college was held on the 16th of August, 1878, and Theodore Thomas was invited to become director of the new enterprise. Mr. Springer gave endowment upon endowment, and the erection of the present large buildings of the college was made possible chiefly through his munificence. Mr. Nichols, as the first president, saw the college outgrow building after building until its present large equipment was achieved. After the de-

FIG. 95.—JULIUS EICHBERG.

ease of Colonel Nichols, Mr. Peter Rudolph Neff became president.

Mr. Thomas, great as is his musicianship, and vast as have been his musical services, was not the most effective musical director possible. There is probably no position in music which demands so much of diplomacy as the directorship of a number of prominent musicians who are not definitely graded, as in an orchestra. Mr. Thomas had his high artistic ideal, and "compromise" was a word which did not exist in his vocabulary. The result was a series of complications for which no one person was responsible, and in two years Mr. Thomas left the post and returned to New York. The college went on under other direction; Mr. Van der Stucken (Fig. 102) (of whom we have already spoken) was its musical director until 1903, when he resigned the post.   It has done great work for Cincinnati and for the entire West.   It has been active in the musical festivals of the city, it has patronized opera and assisted the operatic advance, and it has gathered together a band of excellent musicians who have been like the leaven in the meal through-

, FIG. 96. — MANUSCRIPT BY JULIUS EICHBERG.

out the musical West.   Among its faculty have been such men as Otto Singer, Arnold J. Gantvoort, Albino Gorno, E. W. Glover, John A. Broekhoven, John S. Van Cleve, Dr. Elsenheimer, and many others.   Bushrod Washington Foley was one of the most important of its vocal teachers and is at present at the head of a conservatory of his own in the same city.

There are other conservatories of later origin than the three already spoken of that have had success.   These are such institutions as the Chicago Musical College, which Dr. Florence Ziegfeld brought into existence and guided to prosperity, the Cincinnati Conservatory, which owes its success to Miss Clara Baur, the Oberlin (Ohio) Conservatory, the Peabody Conservatory of Baltimore, the Chicago Conservatory of Music in which Mr. William H. Sherwood was very active, the Philadelphia Academy of Music founded by Richard Zeckwer.   These later institutions are, however, less important from the historical standpoint, even when reaching an equally high artistic standard.   Yet one conservatory deserves especial mention because of a peculiar influence which it exerted upon composition in America.   The National Conservatory of New York, founded by Mrs. Jeanette Thurber, not only brought together a large number of prominent workers in music, such as Joseffy, Finck, and others, but, in 1892, it was under the artistic direction of Antonin Dvořák, the great Bohemian composer, who at once became active in the field of American composition.   Although we have spoken separately of those composers from abroad who have paid visits to America, Dvořák's influence was so direct and pedagogic that we may speak of it in connection with conservatory work.

Antonin Dvořák (Fig. 97) was born at Nehalozeves, in Bohemia, September 8, 1841.   He was thoroughly steeped in the folk-music of his native country, for his principal teacher was Smetana, the chief worker in the cause of the renascence of Bohemian national music.   On Dvořák's coming to New York, he began with composition classes in the National Conservatory at once, and many prominent young musicians became his pupils.   He desired, however, to evolve something distinctly American on his own account, and at once sought to discover what American folk-song was like.   He must have been somewhat disappointed at first, for he found only the Indian music (unfamiliar to almost every American) and the plantation music of the South, the product of an alien race.   Yet, as the latter portrayed phases of American existence and was recognized and understood by almost all the people (a prime necessity of folk-song), he proceeded to employ this material in classical composition.   Music for a string quartette, a sextette, and a symphony were the results of the search for native material.

The symphony, "From the New World," has given rise to considerable contention. Some maintain that it is no more American than were Dvořák's painful attempts in the native language. One may disagree with such a dictum; the symphonic language is not itself a local dialect, but it may properly be founded upon local themes. It is not a Bohemian masquerading as a plantation darky that we find in this work, but an idealization of the typical music of the South, developed, as this epic form demands, yet entirely recognizable. The chamber-music on American figures is still more frankly plantation-like in its vein. But the American symphony (in E minor, Op. 95) will always remain Dvořák's chief achievement in this country. The whole proceeding was a demonstration, on the part of a great composer, that the roots of the music of a nation are to be found in its folk-songs; should there be no such inspiration to draw from, the result will be more generally eclectic and less typical. For that reason it is still a mooted point as to whether a distinctively American school can ever arise, even amid a host of talented native composers.

Although Dvořák was the first to call the attention of Europe to the possibilities of our plantation music, he was not the discoverer of this foundation of classical music. If any musician will examine the scherzo of Mr. G. W. Chadwick's second symphony, they will find that an American composer recognized the adaptability of this material before Dvořák came to these shores.

Dvořák's connection with the National Conservatory continued three years; in 1895 he returned to Prague, where he again directed a conservatory; he died May 1, 1904. Among his pupils while in New York we may mention Harvey Worthington Loomis, William Arms Fisher, Harry Rowe Shelley, Henry Schoenefeld, and Rubin Goldmark.

The conservatories described, and many later ones, are bringing into existence a host of trained musicians in America. The public schools are bringing forth an entire race that shall have some practical acquaintance with music. Yet the result has not, thus far, been equal to the efforts put forth. Perhaps the main reason for this is that the public school courses in music have all started with the assumption that the pupil was to be a singer, whereas a very slight proportion of the graduates are ever active in music after leaving school. If only a small part of the vast sums that are expended by municipalities in America in teaching public school students how to read notes and to sing were to be devoted to instructing them in the general comprehension of music, its architecture, its different instruments, the development of figures which plays so important a part in sonata, sym-phony, and fugue, the different scales used by the nations of the earth, the meaning of the folk-songs of various countries, in short, if classes in *musical culture* were to be established, a much greater general result might be brought about.[1]

FIG. 97. — ANTONIN DVOŘÁK.

Yet, if the premise be granted that it is only desirable to teach singing to the pupil, the public school system of America has accomplished wonders. Luther Whiting Mason (born in Turner, Maine, April 3, 1828, died at Buckfield, Maine, July 14, 1896), a man largely self-taught in mu-sic, reformed the beginnings of music-teaching in the primary schools of America and established a practical course far more carefully graded than anything which had preceded it. His influence spread even as far as Japan, where public school music was for a long time known as " Mason music."

The chief aim of the new system was to enlist the services of all the public school teachers in the musical training instead of allowing it to remain guided by the sporadic efforts of the musical supervisor. The work of Mr. John W. Tufts in this direction deserves hearty recognition; for, while Mason, H. E. Holt, and others in the movement were not of the highest musicianship (however practical their teaching-system might be), John W. Tufts, whose name is not

[1] An article by the present writer on this subject is in the *Atlantic Monthly*, August, 1903.

mentioned in any of the musical dictionaries and encyclopædias, was a finely educated composer, a good contrapuntist, and a thorough musician.   He was able to write all necessary examples and exercises for a most carefully graded course, and placed the training-system of the public school upon a much firmer foundation than it had ever had before.[1]   He died a few years ago.

Many experiments were tried, both east and west.   Chicago for a time employed the tonic sol-fa system, a simplified method of notation which has opened the doors of choral singing to thousands who have not had time or opportunity to master the regular system of notation, yet has numbered very few composers among its followers.   We have it upon the authority of Samuel W. Cole, a man who himself has been most active in spreading good music among the people, that in a well-organized system of schools more than 90 per cent of the pupils sing correctly.   It has been discovered, in this universal application of vocal methods, that heredity plays a less important part than environment, in the production of singers.   It has also been discovered that the child's voice is somewhat higher in natural compass than is generally imagined, such notes as F and G above the staff being by no means a tax upon the juvenile throat.

Among the workers in this field of public school music, in addition to those already mentioned, are: —

William Lawrence Tomlins, who was born in London, February 4, 1844.   He came to New York in 1870, but after five years went to Chicago.   His work in that city was very successful, especially in the training of children's voices.   He has followed out the Mason system by training school-teachers in music for some years past.   Samuel Winkley Cole, above alluded to, who was born in Meriden, New Hampshire, December 24, 1848.   His work in the schools has been so successful that he once produced the entire oratorio of the "Messiah" with the pupils of a high school, probably the first time that this was accomplished with such non-professional forces.   His labors in connection with people's chorus training have already been spoken of.   Dr. Frank Damrosch (Fig. 98) is the son

---

[1] Mr. Tufts modestly writes (from Camden, Maine, August 4, 1903), "It seems to me that what I may have done in music is a matter of small importance to the world."

of Dr. Leopold Damrosch. His work in the public schools began in Denver, Colorado, nearly twenty years ago. Coming to New York he was for a time connected with opera, but soon (1892) organized the people's choruses with which his name is identified. In 1897 he became supervisor of music in the public schools of New York, and is also, at present, conductor of many different choral societies. His influence has been very widespread. Yale University conferred a Doctor's degree upon him, June, 1904. He is director of a great music school, the Institute of Musical Art, New York.

Hosea E. Holt, Leonard Marshall, Sterrie A. Weaver, and many others are laboring in this peculiarly American field with good results. Much has been accomplished; a better musical taste has been instilled in the growing public; yet it is to be hoped that the time will come when public school training in music will mean something deeper, broader, and more comprehensive than merely participation in singing or the reading of notation in single parts.

The musical education in colleges and universities in America has undergone startling changes since the time when Harvard allowed the Pierian Sodality and its offspring, the Harvard Musical Association, to devote its time to other than the sacred music which colleges of old considered the only branch of the art worth practising. At present many of the large colleges and some of the small ones have added a musical department and a chair of music to their regular curriculum. But even in this field there is as yet no class which, leaving the domain of technical construction or performance, devotes its attention wholly to studying the *appreciation* of music. One of the earliest establishments of a chair of music at an American college was accomplished at the University of Pennsylvania, Philadelphia, where, in 1875, Hugh Archibald Clarke was elected Professor of the Science of Music — a position which he still fills. Professor Clarke was born near Toronto, Canada, August 15, 1839. He studied with his father, James Paton Clarke (a Mus. Doc. of Oxford), and played the organ in church at twelve years of age. In Philadelphia he was organist at the Second Presbyterian Church for twenty-two years. He has written much, and among his compositions may be mentioned a setting of Aristophanes's "Acharnians," for which he received the degree of Mus. Doc., a setting of "Iphigenia in Tauris," an oratorio, "Jerusalem," much chamber-music and many smaller compositions. He is an excellent contrapuntist.

It was in the same year (1875) that Harvard established a professorship of music. The establishments were so nearly simultaneous that it may be a disputed point as to which came first. Harvard is, however, generally credited with the earlier beginning, and Professor John K. Paine is usually described as the first possessor of a musical professorship in America. When Professor Paine was appointed to his chair with a musical course in the curriculum, he had been a teacher of music in Harvard for nearly fourteen years, and the department was certainly the first really important one in any American college.

FIG. 98. — FRANK DAMROSCH.
(Copyright by Rockwood.)

The establishment of the chair at Harvard was undoubtedly the incentive which led other colleges to follow in this path, and its origin and beginnings are interesting to trace. In 1862 John K. Paine, who was then organist and musical director at the university, offered to give a series of lectures on the musical forms, without any compensation whatever. There was considerable opposition on the part of the board of direction to this innovation, and when permission was at last granted, the course did not count at all toward a degree. Few attended the lectures, and the outlook was so disheartening that the plan was abandoned. When President Eliot entered upon his duties, however, a new attempt was made, and in 1870 the lectures were resumed. During this year a course in harmony was also established and attracted so large a number of students that two years later counterpoint was added to it. All this work was tentative, however, and helped neither toward the student's degree nor the teacher's affluence, for Professor Paine received no salary. But the effect of the work began to spread, and in 1873 Mr. Paine was appointed assistant professor, and now the course was officially recognized. In 1875 came the full professorship and complete recognition of music as a part of the regular curriculum, it being one of the elective courses.

This Harvard course does not teach piano playing, singing, or any technical musical work whatever. Music 1 (as the first course is called) gives harmony lessons to the freshmen; Music 2 adds counterpoint during the sophomore year. There is a course in vocal counterpoint which analyzes the old masterpieces and allows some composition on the part of its students; there is a course on musical history and æsthetics; there are advanced courses in canon and fugue, sonata and chamber-music composition; and finally there is a course in orchestral composition. A helper in elementary work was found, in 1896, in Walter R. Spalding, who, in 1902, was made assistant professor. Since Paine's death he has been full professor. New buildings are soon to be erected especially for the musical department, including lecture rooms, a concert hall, and the like.

Other colleges have founded their work largely upon the lines described above. The University of Michigan, an institution with a large number of enrolled students, was one of the earliest to follow the example of Harvard and of the University of Pennsylvania. Yet it was not until 1888 that Albert Augustus Stanley was called there as professor of music. Mr. Stanley was born in Manville, Rhode Island, May 25, 1851, and studied music in Leipsic both privately and in the conservatory. He has been most active in the organization of musical enterprises in America; has been twice president of the Music Teachers' National Association, as well as its secretary and treasurer; is one of the founders of the American College of Musicians and honorary vice-president of the Manuscript Society,

an organization for the performance of American compositions.   Mr.
Stanley is a composer as well as a teacher, and the list of his works
includes a symphony entitled " The Awakening of the Soul," which
has not yet been heard in the East, a symphonic poem, " Altis," a
commemoration ode, and a cantata.   He is also an organist of pronounced ability and has often appeared publicly as a performer on
this instrument.

Other colleges have not been very far behind in their recogni-

FIG. 99. — PHILADELPHIA ACADEMY OF MUSIC. AN OPERA HOUSE.

tion of the study of music as part of a thorough education.   Yale
University called Horatio W. Parker to its chair of music in 1894.
Columbia University established a similar chair, with Edward A.
MacDowell as its professor, in 1896.   Dr. Cornelius Rübner succeeded
MacDowell in 1904, and is at present (1915) the director there.   The
colleges for women have, of course, made more of the study of music
and have had professorships of the science from their very beginnings.
In the past Smith College owed everything to Dr. B. C. Blodgett's
conservative and thorough instruction ; he was for many years the

guide of its excellent musical course. Vassar is under the leadership of George C. Gow, a sterling musician and composer. Wellesley has had Charles H. Morse, afterward organist of Plymouth Church, Brooklyn, and Junius W. Hill, one of the most accomplished of musicians, and has now the enthusiastic and thorough Hamilton Crawford MacDougall as its head in this department. Some of these names are absent from the musical encyclopædias, yet their work is as far-reaching and as important as any in the history of American music.

In the pretty little town of Farmington, in Connecticut, Miss Porter established years ago an academy of great thoroughness, and in this school Karl Klauser was musical director as early as 1856. From this retired spot he edited some of the best editions of classical music published in America in the third quarter of the nineteenth century. After him there followed, in the same post, the brilliant Dutchman, Bernardus Boekelman, whose editions, in colored notation, of Bach's fugues and inventions have an international reputation.

Even in the more popular courses of education, known under the name of "University Extension," music has received its full meed of attention. Mr. Thomas Whitney Surette has given many lectures upon the art to large classes. Mr. Surette also deserves mention as a composer, for he has written an operetta, "Priscilla," which has had much popularity, and also many shorter works. He has also done service in the musico-literary field, although not regularly attached to any newspaper, his essays appearing in various magazines. He was a pupil of Professor John K. Paine at Harvard and has also studied with Arthur Foote.

Another example of a composer-lecturer is found in Professor Leo Rich Lewis, who now holds the musical chair at Tufts College. He was born February 11, 1865, in South Woodstock, Vermont, but came to Boston at a very early age. He also is a product of Harvard teaching, graduating from that college in 1889 with highest musical honors. He received the diploma of the Munich Conservatory in 1892, with honorable mention for his compositions, and was installed in the chair of music at Tufts College in 1895. His work has been that of pedagogue, composer, and writer. He has published operettas, a cantata, — "The Consolation of Music," — a sonata for violin and piano, and also a charming restoration of Henry Lawes's old music to Milton's masque of " Comus."

The versatility of America's musical workers will be readily perceived.   Few musicians have kept to one branch of the art alone, few have been entirely specialists.   This may have detracted from the superlative of excellence in a single department, but it has cer-

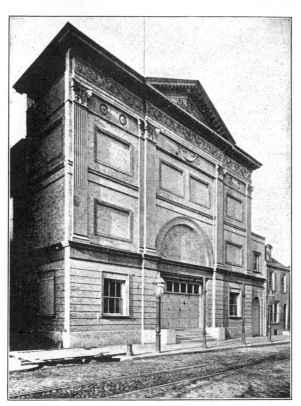

FIG. 100. — MUSICAL FUND HALL, PHILADELPHIA.

tainly made the rapid advance more stable and reliable. We have not yet spoken of technical books on the science of music which have been created in America, and these works show most clearly the educational worth of what has been accomplished.   Some of them are to be compared with the works of Richter, Jadassohn, and Cherubini, of European fame.   George W. Chadwick, Benjamin Cutter, Percy Goetschius, Professor Clarke, John A. Broekhoven, A. J. Goodrich, Thomas Tapper, and J. H. Cornell have all written text-books that speak eloquently for the thoroughness of American musical study, the mere fact of there being a market for such literature proving much.   Although all of them are composers, some of them have made their most marked successes with their text-books, and of these we may speak at once.

Mr. A. J. Goodrich was born in Chilo, Ohio, May 8, 1847, and comes of Scottish ancestry, although his father was American.   His father taught him the rudiments of music, but Mr. Goodrich, like

J. C. Lobe, the great German theorist, was largely self-taught. There is an advantage in self-instruction; it makes one decidedly original and independent, as witness Wagner, Schumann, and many other masters of composition. Although Mr. Goodrich, in his youth, composed much, and in large forms too, in his riper years he has devoted himself entirely to the authorship of technical books with which he has won remarkable success. His chief work, up to the present time, is " Analytical Harmony." He has another work in press on melodic counterpoint, which promises to modernize teaching in this branch. His " Music as a Language" shows great industry and research.

Percy Goetschius is one of the most learned contrapuntists in America. He was born in Paterson, New Jersey, August 30, 1853, studied in the Stuttgart Conservatory, and afterwards became a professor in the same institution. While at Stuttgart he was also very active as a journalist, writing many concert reviews for the German press. Returning to America in 1890, he became a teacher in Syracuse University, New York, and he afterwards taught composition and gave lectures in the New England Conservatory of Music. He is at present professor of counterpoint in the great National Institute of Musical Art in New York City. His principal work is " The Material used in Musical Composition," which has been printed on both sides of the Atlantic. He has also written some valuable books on musical forms. Like almost all the American writers on harmony and counterpoint, both Goodrich and Goetschius have broken away from the old method of constantly building from a bass part and have given more prominence to melodic construction as the prime factor of a musical work. The modern Germans have been disposed to follow in the same path, but Richter's rather too tyrannical rule was overthrown on this side of the ocean. John Henry Cornell, born in New York, May, 1828, and died there March 1, 1894, was an excellent and conservative composer and another writer of educational books. His principal work was the " Theory and Practice of Musical Form."

Mr. Thomas Tapper may be considered the chief of those who have written for juvenile musical students in America, although he

has produced excellent works for adults as well. He was born at
Canton, Massachusetts, January 28, 1864. He has been a very successful journalist, and writes constantly for the musical magazines.
By such works as " Chats with Music Students," " Music Talks with
Children," " The Child's Music World," he has led young students
to a study of musical history, and has made the subject remarkably attractive without yielding to the temptation to substitute
pretty tales for truth. It has been one of the temptations of
musical literature, thanks to the Elise Polkos of Germany and the
Haweises of England, to rush into sentimentality on the slightest
provocation. It is at least to the credit of America that the
sentimentalists have never been in the foreground — not even in
the juvenile branch of musical literature.

CHAPTER XVIII

QUALITIES AND DEFECTS OF AMERICAN MUSIC

THE mother of American music was New England psalmody — a stern and narrow-minded parent, but certainly characteristic of her age. From this psalmody came the earliest singing-schools, then the conventions, finally the music festivals that, however pronounced their faults have been, have spread some degree of musical appreciation throughout the country.

Opera has been an exotic save in two cities, New York and New Orleans, the former having been the musical centre of the country in operatic matters from the very beginning. Opera in English has had many sporadic representations, but only with the advent of the Castle Square Company in Boston at the very end of the nineteenth century did it achieve something like a permanent basis; the company, finally under the management of Henry W. Savage, became for a time national rather than local.

Boston has been chronologically the first in the field of oratorio and orchestra, and may still be considered the centre of these schools of music in America. But the city is provincial in the matter of grand opera, and has but little public taste in organ music. In piano recital and chamber concerts New York and Boston are about equal. These two cities have also the largest number of influential music societies, but almost every city in the Union is at present provided with these in some degree.

Again, almost all American cities at present try to support something classical in orchestral music, while New York, Boston, Baltimore, Philadelphia, Cincinnati, and Chicago have had excellent programmes given for many years past by their own musicians. Indianapolis, Minneapolis, St. Louis, San Francisco, and many other cities are giving their own symphonic concerts and supporting them reasonably well. Each of the larger cities has at least one good musical conservatory, and many have two or three. In these conservatories one finds some of the best European teachers and a curriculum that should give excellent results in vocal and instrumental work. There is this limitation, however, to be noted; the vocal work is almost always solo, and the instrumental study is almost entirely piano. It is to the credit of two or three conservatories that they lead their vocal instruction up to full operatic performances, and that their instrumental aims are not bounded by the piano, but include orchestral and general *ensemble* work. Such conservatory training is likely to lead to true musicianship.

The musical courses in the universities and colleges of America are beyond anything that is done in similar institutions abroad; it is a question whether they are not *too* extensive for schools not exclusively musical. It is desirable, however, that every college in America should have a department devoted to teaching the æsthetics of music in connection with the other fine arts. As for the public schools, they give more attention to music than similar institutions in any other country in the world. It is a pity that, hitherto, the entire effort seems to have been in the direction of concerted singing; for here, also, a study of musical form, theory, and *general appreciation* of music would be in place, since not one pupil in a hundred continues actively engaged with music after graduation.

In the matter of musical instruments America again compares favorably with European countries. The best pianos of the world are made in this country, and the Gemünder violins (made at Astoria, Long Island) are as perfect as any violins of modern make. In cabinet organs, or harmoniums, the American instruments have competed successfully both in price and quality with the European, and in the mechanism of church organs the American leads, although there is a better voicing of stops in some foreign manufactures than one finds with us.

We have no libraries of music comparable to those which enrich Oxford, Cambridge, or the British Museum, the Bibliothèque Nationale or the *Conservatoire* of Paris; but here, too, a great beginning

FIG. 102. — FRANK VAN DER STUCKEN.

has been made, and the Boston Public Library, the Newberry Library of Chicago, the Drexel Institute of Philadelphia, and many other public institutions, have musical libraries that are easy of access and useful for reference. The Allen Brown room of the Public Library of Boston (Fig. 52) is perhaps the national model in this field.

The chief fault of our musical system may be found in the excess of piano playing. Almost every home possesses a piano and some one to play it. If this latter necessity is absent, recourse is had to the piano playing machines (attachable to the keyboard) in which America has distinguished itself as the manufacturer. But of real *music* at home such as one finds in Germany, in Bohemia, in Hungary, in all deeply musical countries, — *ensemble* music, violin, voice, flute, piano, and other delightful combinations, — one finds, as yet, too little. There is too much of display, or of money-getting, in America's musical strivings; we turn out a hundred executants to one composer.

And the composers, as well as the rest of Americans in music, are too often wholesalers. They desire bigness at any cost; they try too early to bring forth symphony, opera, or oratorio; and they seek rather to make their orchestras large than to have them excellent. The eminent German critic, Dr. F. Hiller, once expressed himself to us with some critical reserve: —

"I fear that you are sometimes too gigantic — in musical festivals, for example. It is a natural fault in a young nation that likes to do vast things."

It is no longer ago than the time of the great Columbian Exhibition that some of the Chicago papers were boasting that Thomas would have the biggest orchestra, on that occasion, that ever was led in America — not recognizing the fact that Thomas at the head of one hundred excellent musicians could produce better results than if he were given a thousand or ten thousand of any kind whatever.

Another demon broods over American music, — *Haste!* The good old motto about making haste slowly has only recently been learned by our young musicians. They have desired to rush through their musical studies in a way that would be the despair of an old world professor. It is to the credit of some teachers and some conservatories that they have pulled resolutely upon the check-rein. The evil influence has by no means been overcome yet, and a slower, longer, more thorough course of musical study is still a crying need in many communities in the United States.

In this volume we have endeavored to give a plain statement of what has been accomplished in music in America. Much more has been done than the world at large has been aware of. Much remains, however, to be accomplished, for there are defects as well as excellences in our music and in our musical education. No one can foresee what the future may bring forth, and yet, judging by a retrospect of fifty years of America's musical endeavor, that future may be considered full of promise.

SUPPLEMENTARY CHAPTER TO 1915

LATER MUSICAL DEVELOPMENTS

MUSICAL history is being made very rapidly in America. Not only are there an enormous number of important enterprises launched, in the orchestral and operatic field, in many different cities, but the great number of musical conservatories, and the musical depart- ments of numerous American colleges, are constantly adding to the list of prominent composers. To record all of these events and celebrities would be a task similar to writing a small directory. It is our purpose, however, in this chapter, to mention some of the chief events of the past ten years.

The chief efforts have been made in the domains of symphonic music and in opera. New York, as usual, has been the chief city in the latter branch of Art. The Metropolitan Opera Company has been enlarged and, even if no new Anton Seidl has arisen, there have been important advances made. The saying that "Opposition is the life of Trade" may in some degree be applied to Art also. It was the opposition of Oscar Hammerstein which has made the recent New York operatic seasons more brilliant than ever before. That gentleman founded a Manhattan Opera Company which brought out many new works in the most brilliant manner, with such artists as Mary Garden, Tetrazzini, Trentini, Renaud, Gilibert, etc., and he brought to America a great operatic conductor in the person of Cleofonte Campanini, who continued in America long after Hammerstein had given up opera.

The Metropolitan Company, spurred on by this invasion of their domain, brought equally great artists in Bonci, Caruso, Scotti, the American prima donna Geraldine Farrar, many other great singers, and a conductor who is probably the greatest that ever came out of Italy, — Arturo Toscanini. Gustav Mahler was also brought from Vienna to lead the German operas.

Gustav Mahler's career in New York was a troublous one.   He came over in 1909 and was not only conductor at the Metropolitan opera, but of the Philharmonic concerts.   His bold innovations and independence of interpretation were not understood and he was bitterly criticised by some.   He left New York a bitterly disappointed and worn-out man.   He died in Vienna in 1911.

Toscanini's career has been the opposite of this.   He has been recognized as one of the greatest of conductors from the very beginning.   Yet he, too, had some friction with his forces recently and has temporarily left America.

The rivalry of the Metropolitan and Manhattan opera troupes was most expensive to both of the companies, and it ended by the Metropolitan company buying out Mr. Hammerstein, and it has since remained sole exponent of Grand Opera in New York, under the management of Signor Gatti-Casazza.   But the rivalry left a very good legacy behind.   The two troupes made frequent tours to other cities, and after the taste for high class opera had once been implanted, these other cities began to agitate for opera companies of their own.   Chicago and Philadelphia united their forces, and the habit of interchanging singers between different cities made a species of operatic trust which was beneficent in its results.   Andreas Dippel, who had been one of the managers of the Metropolitan company, in 1910 became manager of the Chicago Opera Company, and the eminent Cleofonte Campanini was soon induced to transfer his activities to that field.   The Chicago company still exists.

Boston also felt the operatic fever, and by the generosity of a merchant-prince, Eben D. Jordan, an Opera House was erected, one of the best equipped in America, and November 8, 1909, the new edifice was opened with "La Gioconda."   Henry Russell was manager, and there were many good conductors, although none so eminent as those of New York or Chicago.   Finally Felix Weingartner was brought to Boston for a short season.   In 1913 this opera company ended its brief career, yet it had given many new works in that period, and in its stage settings, chorus, and ballet, was the equal of any of the other great opera companies.

Some efforts have been made to found a permanent company to give operas in English, the most ambitious of these being the Aborn

Dʳ Karl Muck.

Company in New York, but none of these attempts have as yet succeeded in becoming permanent.

The Metropolitan Company, however, threw its influence into the scale and fostered the project of Grand Opera in English. The result has been that some of the best American composers have brought forth operatic works in the vernacular. Victor Herbert's "Natoma" may be spoken of as the most pleasing of these, an opera upon an American topic and introducing actual Indian melodies also. But a prize of $10,000 which was offered by the wealthy opera company was won by Horatio Parker, in 1911, with an opera entitled "Mona." The subject of this work is druidical, and it deals with early Britain and the Roman occupation. It is a symphonic opera, with very little in it that is truly vocal or strikingly popular. But the libretto, by Brian Hooker, shows that it is possible to achieve a really poetic opera book in English.

The same pair in 1915 won another $10,000 prize with a less ascetic opera, a work in three acts, entitled "Fairyland," which was given by the National Federation of Music Clubs, and was performed in Los Angeles. This attempts to be more popular than "Mona," but the librettist has not been so successful in building a logical work as in "Mona." Parker's oratorio of "Morven," composed for the Händel and Haydn Society's centennial in Boston, is not a successful work.

A new combination was made, in 1915, by Manager Max Rabinoff, who united an excellent operatic troupe with the Pavlova ballet, giving modern ballets as well as operas and reviving Auber's "Masaniello," in various cities.

The orchestral advances have been briefly chronicled in this volume by additions which have been made to Chapter III. But a few especial works may here receive mention. George W. Chadwick has composed a remarkable tone-poem in modern vein, entitled "Aphrodite," which was inspired by an antique bust in the Boston Art Museum, and pictures the many scenes of worship, festivity, war, and love that the bust may have gazed upon. It is one of the most ambitious and poetic of recent American orchestral works. His "Vagrom Ballad" is a wild and bohemian orchestral suite, the idealization of tramp-life. His most recent "Tam O'Shanter" is a rollicking setting of Burns's celebrated poem as an orchestral picture and is appropriately both Scottish and bacchanalian.

Henry K. Hadley's recent symphonic works show great advance and may take place in the standard·repertoire. Edgar S. Kelley's " New England Symphony" is another important orchestral work.

Arthur Shepherd, born at Paris, Idaho, February 19, 1880, is composing some sterling works, his piano sonata being a striking one in the modern style of free composition. Charles Wakefield Cadman has composed some charming songs founded on Indian melodies and has also a very good sonata (piano) to his credit. He also belongs to the younger composers, having been born in Johnstown, Pennsylvania, December 24, 1881. Henry F. B. Gilbert is beginning to do excellent work in the native school. His Comedy Overture on Negro Themes and other orchestral pieces have a good, spicy, and unstrained style.

Edward Burlingame Hill, who has done much in musical literature, is also active in composition, even in the large orchestral forms, and Philip G. Clapp has written a most intricate symphony which had the honor of performance in Boston Symphony concerts. Louis Campbell Tipton is a most poetic composer in the small forms, having something of the elusive grace of Debussy. John Powell, of Richmond, Virginia, has a fine violin concerto to his credit. Rosseter G. Cole has done some good work in the larger forms. Henry Clough-Leiter has produced some very worthy songs. Walter A. Kramer is composing some sterling works in the short forms. The violin and concerted pieces of Arthur M. Curry and of the blind violinist of New York, Edwin Grasse, deserve chronicling. Victor Harris, Arthur Nevin, and G. B. Nevin have brought forth excellent songs. Alexander Hull is decidedly modern in his harmonic treatment, yet he has something to say, and is to be counted among the promising composers. A. W. Lilienthal has created some graceful works which are standard. Arne Oldberg has written much in both large and small forms.

The musical festivals which have been conducted by Mortimer Wiske in the Eastern states are an excellent influence, and Dr. John Frederick Wolle has conducted symphonic festivals and especially great Bach performances on both the Atlantic and Pacific coasts.   Dr. Wolle has done more for the appreciation of Bach in America than any other man.   John Alden Carpenter (born at Park Ridge, Illinois, 1876) is becoming prominent with very genial orchestral compositions.

Another addition to musical endowments must be chronicled. The Cincinnati orchestra has been left a large sum by the will of Miss Martha Cora Dow.   Thus three orchestras have now large endowments : the Boston, the New York, and the Cincinnati.

Among the litterateurs we find a new name of importance, — Daniel Gregory Mason (born Brookline, Massachusetts, November 20, 1873), — and its bearer has written many standard books on music besides composing in the classical forms.   A recent addition to the ranks of eminent American critics, Algernon St. John Brenon, of the *New York Morning Telegraph*, has become famous for most readable and intelligent reviews.   Another eminent litterateur, this time a veteran, has branched out in a new direction.   John C. Freund (editor of " Musical America") has been giving lectures all over the United States, championing the cause of the American composer and teacher.   Rupert Hughes has gone from his musical literary work into novel and play-writing with the most brilliant success. Mr. Leonard Liebling, the brilliant editor of " The Musical Courier," has also won success in some lines of composition.   Among women composers one might mention Gena Branscome (Mrs. John F. Tenney) as an American Chaminade, although by no means as prolific as the French composer.

It is a list which is constantly changing and enlarging, this roster of American composers.   The volume entitled " American Composers " by Rupert Hughes and Arthur Elson gives a much more extended list than the above.   It is difficult to say whether all of these deserve a place in history, yet they are all good workers in an Art that is growing most rapidly among us and may be regarded as among the later crop of pioneers.

SUPPLEMENTARY CHAPTERS TO 1925

By Arthur Elson

CHAPTER I

THE ELDER LEADERS

In the two decades that have passed since this work was first issued many changes have taken place in American music. Composers who were once prominent and active have retired, or passed away; while new men have arisen, to inherit their fame and carry on their work. But some have maintained their position as leaders, and are even better known in 1924 than they were in 1904; and the opening chapter may be fitly devoted to them.

Of the earlier leaders, Chadwick seems to hold his place as well as any. His music still occupies a prominent position on symphonic programs, —not alone because of his conducting ability, or his long directorship of the New England Conservatory, but because of its intrinsic worth. His admirable overtures include one to "Euterpe," in addition to those mentioned in earlier chapters. Among his later symphonic poems are "The Angel of Death" and "Cleopatra," the former treating its subject with due dignity, while the latter is naturally more impassioned in style. Orchestral works of his later years include a Suite in A, the set of Symphonic Sketches (containing the "Vagrom Ballad"), and a Suite Symphonique. His Symphonietta, recently revived, is markedly attractive. In the dramatic field, he has composed the tragedies "Padrona" and "Love's Sacrifice," and written incidental music to "Everywoman."

Chadwick's versatility was well shown by the performance of an all-Chadwick program, which scored a Boston success when given by the People's Symphony Orchestra. There are few among the American composers, past or present, who could stand such a test; but Chadwick is a master of many styles, ranging from the lofty seriousness of his overtures to the plantation flavor of some of his symphonic and string quartet movements, and a true sense of humor that shows in his Symphonic Sketches and other works. It is the last-named quality, and not the second alone, that makes him a representative American composer. This facetious, almost irreverent treatment of life is found in several of his works. This is especially true of the "Vagrom Ballad," a rollicking picture of vagabond life that has suggested the apt quotation,

> "A tale of tramps and railway ties,
>   Of old clay pipes and rum,
>   Of broken heads and blackened eyes,
>   And the 'thirty days' to come."

Music of this sort is as typically American as that of Moussorgsky, for instance, is Russian, or that of Weber German.

That the local or national color is not used to cover any lack of real inspiration may be shown by a quotation from Carl Engel, himself deserving mention as a leading musical writer. According to him, Chadwick is "not dependent upon war-paint or burnt cork"; and the composer's idiom "is not necessarily punctuated by the hiccough of an Indian drum, does not jabber with the twang of a negroid banjo, or fall into the puling of a shopharic saxophone." National styles are effective when well used; but the great composer should be their master, and not their slave.

Horatio W. Parker (d. 1919) brought an honorable career to a close without producing any important new works except the music for the Yale Pageant of 1916. His "Hora Novissima" is still his masterpiece, and many consider it the best single work by any American.

Arthur Foote is another composer who rests his laurels upon his earlier works. Their scholarly classicism is of more worth than his incursion into romantic fields with the "Omar Khayyam" pictures.

Frederick Shepard Converse has continued to hold a position of leadership, and has produced many interesting works. In addition to the symphonic poems already mentioned, his "Night" and "Day," for piano and orchestra, show the expected contrast of style in masterly fashion. "The Mystic Trumpeter" is another successful work, inspired, like the two preceding pieces, by Walt Whitman. "Ave atque Vale," another tone-poem for orchestra, shows a striking dignity of effect. A symphony in C minor is another earnest work, having been inspired by the war. Though not meant as definite program music, the stern character of its opening movement, and the martial, victorious swing of the finale, portray their subject admirably. A recent Concertstück for piano and

orchestra is effective enough, but somewhat fragmentary and modernistic in comparison with the clear beauty of his earlier works. His other
compositions include a violin concerto, two string quartets, the oratorio
"Job," the cantata "The Peace Pipe," the overtures "Youth" and
"Euphrosyne," and a partly completed opera on the subject of Sindbad
the Sailor. Perhaps the lack of a local opera company has made the
composer give precedence to symphonic works.

Henry Kimball Hadley is another active musician who has added
many successes to his list. His third symphony, in B minor (preceding
"North, East, South, and West"), makes a dignified entrance into the
field of pure music. His overtures now include "In Bohemia," "Herod,"
and "Othello," his early work in this form being entitled "Hector and
Andromache." To "Salome" and "The Culprit Fay," which are really
remarkable works, he has added the later symphonic poems "Lucifer"
and "The Sea," the former powerfully dramatic, while the latter gives
a fair amount of the breadth and power of expression demanded by its
subject. Among his other orchestral works are a Symphonic Fantasia,
the Oriental Suite, three Ballet Suites, and a concert piece for 'cello.
His chamber works and songs are now well known, while his compositions
in the larger vocal forms include the choral works "The New Earth"
and "Resurgam," and the shorter prize-winner "In Music's Praise."

In opera, Hadley has been more active than almost any other American.
His oriental "Safie" was well received abroad. "Azora," or "Montezuma's Daughter," received many plaudits in Chicago. Azora loves
Xalca, a visiting prince; but Ramatzin, head of the local army, and
low-voiced villain, loves her also. When she dares at last to show her
preference for Xalca, Ramatzin chooses the pair as a human sacrifice to
Totec; but the coming of the Spanish priests saves them. The score
is too orchestral in style, the voices "tossing on a surge of passionate
polyphony." "The Garden of Allah" is another subject demanding
passionate treatment; but a greater success in this style is "Cleopatra's
Night." This is based on Gautier's story of the handsome young officer
who penetrated the palace privacy to claim Cleopatra's love, and was
given it for a night on condition that he would forfeit his life next morning. He almost arouses her love to the point of saving him; but the
unexpected return of Antony seals his doom. Less tragic and more
lively is "Bianca," a version of "La Locandiera" in which a stilted trans-

lation is somewhat of a handicap. Bianca, the innkeeper, is seen serving two local admirers, when the gruff Cavaliere del Ruggio arrives. As he has said he could put Bianca in her place, she tries her woman's wiles to charm him, with more or less success. Meanwhile her aid, Fabricio, pleads his own love, and finally wins by stopping with his ironing-board a duel between the Cavaliere and one of the local admirers. Her reverie after Fabricio's first declaration, and his later pleading, are charmingly set; and the score as a whole caused the work to be called "the least boresome of American operas." Hadley's other stage works include the comic opera "Nancy Brown," and "The Atonement of Pan," composed for the open-air festival of the San Francisco Bohemian Club.

Edgar Stillman Kelley has not given the world any successor to his graceful "Puritania," though he has continued to write incidental music, such as that for "Prometheus Bound." His miracle play "Pilgrim's Progress" scarcely comes under operatic standards. The New England Symphony has proven rather too serious for frequent repetition; and the composer's fame still rests on his earlier songs and orchestral suites.

Louis Adolph Coerne (d. 1922) added to his renown by composing the ballet "Evadne," the melodrama "Sakuntala," two violin concertos, a six-voiced mass, and other large works. His contrapuntal skill did not prevent him from leaning toward modernism, which consists largely of the use of more involved harmonies than were employed in classical and romantic works. Modernism is therefore largely a matter of individuality, including such diverse effects as the whole-tone scale of Debussy, the system of fourths developed by Scriabine, or the sometimes aimless dissonances of Schoenberg. Coerne's harmonic coloring is richly beautiful, as may be seen from his song "The Sea," among other available bits. In this song the melody flows on smoothly over rich harmonies of a constantly changing, kaleidoscopic beauty. In many cases the modernist composers are merely imitative; but Coerne was original.

Loeffler seems content with the fame of his earlier works, though his Irish Songs with Orchestra have met with success in symphonic programs.

Gustav Strube has a long list of works to his credit. His two symphonies show a modernism that is strong and virile in effect. His attractive symphonic poems include "Lorelei," "Narcissus and Echo," "Longing" and "Fantastic Dance" with viola, and a "Poème Antique" for violin and orchestra. His "Fantastic" overture is admirably worthy of its title, while "Puck" and "The Maid of Orleans" have been well received also. Other works by him include three violin concertos, a 'cello concerto, some worthy chamber music, the choral works "Rhapsody" and a "Hymn to Eros," and the manuscript opera "Ramona."

Van der Stucken, who migrated to European shores, has shown his American tendencies in the march "Louisiana." His other later works include a suite, a number of orchestral pieces, and a "Festival Hymn" for men's voices and orchestra.

Ernest R. Kroeger has continued an active career by composing the overtures "Atala" and "Pittoresque," the suite "Lalla Rookh," a Scherzo, two Marches, and many smaller works.

Rubin Goldmark considers that his recent "Negro Rhapsody" is one of his best works; and its New York success justifies this estimate. Another impressive work of his is the tone-poem "Requiem," inspired by Lincoln's Gettysburg address. A prize-winning string quartet deserves mention as representing much excellent chamber music by this interesting composer.

Henry Schoenefeld has fulfilled his early promise by a second (Spring) symphony, a Festival Overture, two American Rhapsodies, two Indian Legends, a Suite Characteristique, the nocturne "California" for strings, a violin concerto, a piano concerto, the ballet "Wachicanta," and many smaller works. He has in manuscript an opera on an Indian subject.

Henry Holden Huss, who showed his devotion to the letter H by marrying Hildegard Hoffman, numbers among his later works a violin concerto, a "Wald-Idyll" for small orchestra, and several admirable chamber works.

Harry Rowe Shelley is responsible for a "Baden-Baden" suite. But his later works are mostly in the cantata field, including "The Inheritance Divine," "Vexilla Regis," "Death and Life," and "Lochinvar's Ride."

Howard Brockway has continued his activity with a number of works for violin and orchestra, and the cantata "Sir Oluf." He has investigated the songs of the Kentucky mountaineers, which he has published under the title of "Lonesome Tunes."

Adolph M. Foerster has added to his other works a symphonic poem, "Sigrid," an orchestral Ode to Byron, and two suites.

Carl V. Lachmund has written a second overture, an Italian Suite, and several smaller works.

Arthur B. Whiting has enlarged his list of works by a second piano concerto and many shorter compositions. Of late he has devoted himself to reviving the harpsichord and other music of the seventeenth and eighteenth centuries, giving many beautiful programs from the early masters.

George E. Whiting (d. 1923) added to his compositions a number of organ and sacred works.

Harvey Worthington Loomis is now known by his music to plays and pantomimes, as well as melodramas, which he calls "musical backgrounds." He has also written an opera, "The Traitor Mandolin," and a number of operettas. His piano works include "Lyrics of the Red Man," treating aboriginal subjects.

Johann H. Beck numbers among his well-known works the overtures "Romeo and Juliet," "Lara," and "Skirnismal," several orchestral pieces, the cantata "Deucalion," two string sextets, a string quartet, and many examples of the shorter forms.

Silas G. Pratt (d. 1916) was not wholly successful in bringing his large works to public performance, though their grandiose structure once caused Wagner to say to him, "You are the Wagner of America."

Arthur Bird, living abroad, has produced comparatively few new works, resting his fame on the success of his ballet "Rübezahl."

Templeton Strong has been more active, composing cantatas, orchestral works, and various other pieces. Later successes are a humorous string trio, and the choral work "Der Dorfmusikdirektor." Strong has made many four-hand arrangements of Bach's organ works.

W. W. Gilchrist (d. 1916) composed a second symphony, a "Song of Thanksgiving," and the cantatas "Rose" and "An Easter Idyl," with orchestra.

A. J. Goodrich (d. 1920) became known through an overture and other orchestral works, as well as cantatas and chamber music.

CHAPTER II

DRAMATIS PERSONÆ

A CHAPTER on American opera and allied stage forms may strike the average reader as a novelty; but the progress of American music has made it possible. Although we have no outstanding operatic success, it is evident that even in the older musical countries, the composers of really successful operas are few and far between. The periodicals chronicle a long list of stage works being brought out, in the musical centers of Germany, France, or Italy, which for the most part achieve a *succès d'estime* and are then retired to the shelf. American opera can show this much of progress; and even now it includes many works whose music is valuable for its own sake, if not dramatic enough for wide popular success. As yet the American composers have shown themselves almost too earnest for dramatic success, as operatic music needs a striking character of its own, if not actually a little tawdriness.

As regards subjects for librettos, we have a great variety of the best. They include Indian legends, colonial adventures, pioneer events, and historical scenes of great power; and they vary in local color from the Latin-American glamour of the tropics to the icy grandeur of the frozen north. With these advantages, librettists do not need to rush to foreign stories, or resuscitate antiquities. Neither do they need to remain conventional. As an example of the latter defect, one may quote the case of Francisco de Leone's "Alglala," a recent work acclaimed as treating an Indian subject. The plot consists merely of the story of a native girl who is loved by two men, — one white, and the other of her own race. There is a sad lack of novelty about such a story; and putting it where Indian effects can be made, on the stage or in the music, does not really make it an Indian opera worthy of that title, though a good score may win success for it. With the dramatic episodes that abound in the legends, and even the history, of the aborigines, it should not be hard for anyone with literary and dramatic taste to concoct a libretto that should be little inferior to the Wagnerian stories in stage effect.

Reverting to the musical side of opera, it becomes fairly evident that our composers really do need to study for the somewhat cheap but very powerful effects of real operatic music. A certain direct vigor is demanded, — a strength that is not to be developed in the composition courses of "highbrows" on the one hand, nor in the intellectual subtleties of modernism on the other. The Soldiers' Chorus from "Faust," for example, or the Toreador's Song and other popular bits from "Carmen," or the great march and stately choruses of "Aïda," or even many of the Wagnerian melodies, from the Spinning Song to the Ride of the Valkyries, are diatonically very simple; but they have a strength, a "punch," as the slang goes, that "gets them across."

Even the best composers are not always successful in opera; so it is not surprising to find that the American leaders do not excel in this form. "The Pipe of Desire" is too allegorical. "The Sacrifice" has its soldiers' chorus, and other moments of dramatic force, but drags as a whole. "The Scarlet Letter" was made of slow music on a still slower subject. "Judith" can scarcely claim to be more than an animated oratorio. Hadley has shown more directness, but even his operas do not come in for frequent repetitions. Herbert's "Natoma," too, was only a partial success.

Among those who have taken Indian subjects for librettos, Charles Wakefield Cadman (1881–   ) is undoubtedly deserving of first mention. Widely known by the rare beauty of his Four American Indian Songs, in which native tunes (printed along with the composer's settings) are harmonized in richly beautiful fashion, he has also made a name for himself in other fields, by such works as his piano trio and his one-act opera "The Garden of Mystery," treating Hawthorne's story of Rappacini's daughter. Among his compositions are also an excellent song album on texts of various character, the Japanese cycle "Sayonara" (with native melodies), "Three Songs to Odysseus," "Idyls of the South Sea Islands," "The Morning of the Year" (for mixed quartet and piano), the piano suite "Hollywood," and many other beautiful numbers. But his most ambitious works are his two operas on Indian subjects. Of these, "Daoma," or "The Land of Misty Water," is a full three-act affair, with a libretto, based on native legends, by Francis LaFleche and

Nelle Richmond Eberhart, the latter deserving mention for many beautiful texts which Cadman has set. More successful in point of performance is "Shanewis," or "The Robin Woman." This is in two scenes. In the first, a masquerade ball is given at the California home of a Mrs. Everton to honor the return of her daughter Amy from college, and her protégée, Shanewis, from a singing school. Shanewis sings two Indian songs, "The Robin Woman" and an "Ojibway Canoe Song." Lionel Rhodes, who has an understanding with Amy, forgets his duty and becomes violently smitten with the Indian girl. She, not knowing of his relations with Amy, is gradually persuaded to accept him, on condition that he must visit her tribe and see if he still loves her when in her home and native surroundings. The scene then changes to an Indian festival in Oklahoma. Philip, a native who has loved Shanewis, and still hopes she will give up white civilization, is jealous of Lionel. Amy and her mother come, and when Shanewis

FIG. 104.—CHARLES WAKEFIELD CADMAN.

learns of Amy's disappointed love, she refuses Lionel, and Philip then kills him. The music, partly Indian, but largely Cadman, is very beautiful, though not always dramatically powerful. In this plot, as in that of Herbert's "Natoma," the contrast between white cultivation and native barbarism is made to form a strong point, though the heroine rises above her racial surroundings.

Arthur Finley Nevin's "Poia," on another Indian subject, has been well received abroad.

Of the elder composers, Damrosch has followed his "Cyrano" with "The Dove of Peace." He has also written incidental music to Euripides' "Iphigenia in Aulis" and the "Medea" and "Elektra" of Sophokles, all showing dramatic force.

De Koven (d. 1920) entered the field of serious opera with his "Canterbury Pilgrims" and "Rip van Winkle."

Paul Allen has written a number of operas for performance in Italy, — an eminently proper proceeding, in view of the number of Italian operas given here. He is known locally through his piano album and other short works.

Joseph Carl Breil's opera "The Legend," on a Russian subject, was given a successful performance at the Metropolitan Opera House. He has written also several comic operas.

Homer N. Bartlett (d. 1920) wrote the opera "La Vallière," and the operetta "Magic Hours."

Pietro Floridia, of Sicilian birth, composed several operas in Italy, continuing his work in our own country with "Paoletta" and "The Scarlet Letter." He is well known through his songs, and has also written a symphony and an overture.

Albert Mildenberg is responsible for "Michael Angelo," and for the shorter operas "The Wood-Witch," "Rafaello," and "Love's Locksmith."

John Adam Hugo has composed "The Hero of Bysanz" and "The Temple Dancer" (the latter given at the Metropolitan), in addition to a symphony, two piano concertos, and some chamber works.

Jules Jordan is responsible for "Rip van Winkle" and "Nisida," as well as several operettas.

Francis Richter has to his credit "The Grand Nazar."

William J. McCoy has composed the opera "Egypt," as well as two so-called "grove-plays" for the open-air festivals of the San Francisco Bohemian Club. This organization has done much to encourage music by having good composers set some operatic subject for its annual "High-Jinks." McCoy has written also a symphony and the "Yosemite" overture.

For the same organization, Edward Faber Schneider has set "Apollo" and "The Triumph of Bohemia." He has also composed the symphony "In Autumn," and some violin and piano pieces.

Humphrey J. Stewart has composed the grove-plays "Montezuma,"

"The Cremation of Care," and "Gold," as well as the operas (not all serious) "Bluff King Hal," "His Majesty," and "The Conspirators." He has also written the oratorios "The Nativity" and "The Hound of Heaven," three masses, the orchestral suites "Montezuma" and "California Scenes," some incidental music, and shorter works for voice, violin, organ, and piano.

Thomas Carl Whitmer has composed six Mysteries, or sacred music dramas, in addition to a "Syrian Ballet" for orchestra, a "Poem of Youth" for piano and orchestra, a sonata and other works for violin, organ pieces, choruses, and songs.

Henry Bethuel Vincent includes among his compositions the opera "Esperanza," the oratorio "The Prodigal Son," and shorter works for organ and voices.

Frederick Zech is known by a long list of works, including the operas "La Palóma" and "Wa-Kin-Yan" (the latter on an Indian subject), six symphonies, the symphonic poems "St. Agnes' Eve," "Lamia," "The Raven," and "The Wreck of the Hesperus," four piano concertos, a violin concerto, a 'cello concerto, and a large amount of chamber music in various forms.

Earl R. Drake has composed "The Blind Girl of Castel-Cuillé," in addition to a ballet, a Dramatic Prologue, some violin pieces, and the "Gypsy Scenes" for violin and orchestra.

Benjamin Lambord (d. 1915) composed the opera "Woodstock" in collaboration, the choral-orchestral "Verses from Omar," an Introduction and Variations, a piano trio, and several songs and piano pieces.

Harrison Millard is responsible for the sacred opera "Deborah," a mass, some church music, and a very large number of songs.

Willard Patton has composed the opera "Pocahontas," the oratorio "Isaiah," several cantatas, and an orchestral work on national themes.

Florizel von Reuter is responsible for three operas, but is better known by his Rumanian Dances and other violin works.

Bertram Shapleigh is another prolific composer whose operas are not yet well known. Besides several of these, he has composed two symphonies, other large orchestral works, the tone-poem "Mirage," with chorus, many choral works ("The Raven," "Dervish Dance," "Vedic Hymn," etc.), a mass, and many chamber works and shorter pieces.

Among operas to be given an early performance are Ralph Lyford's

"Castle Agrazant," and "The Echo," by Frank Patterson. Timothy M. Spelman has composed "The Sunken City," the pantomime "The Romance of the Rose," and several melodramas. Alexander Hull, a modernist in songs and orchestral works, has in manuscript the operas "Paolo and Francesca" and "Merlin and Vivien." Theodore Stearns is responsible for "The Snowbird." Among many others with operatic manuscripts are Thomas Whitney Surette, Henry B. Pasmore, the violin composer Louis Campbell-Tipton, and W. Franke-Harling. The American Operatic Society, of Chicago, has a list of sixty composers, and can supply ninety-six works in this form.

In the field of comic opera, Dennée has been a prolific composer. Arthur Weld (d. 1914) deserves mention also. Rudolf Friml, coming from Prague, has composed many stage works, including "The Firefly." Alfred G. Robyn, in addition to light operas, has written a symphony, the symphonic poem "Pompeii," a piano concerto, chamber works, and sacred cantatas; while Lucius Hosmer, known also for light operas, has composed overtures, suites, and a "Southern Rhapsody."

Among masque composers, Charles Louis Seeger has written chamber works as well, and the overture "Shadowy Waters"; while George Colburn, another masque and pageant writer, produced the symphonic poem "Spring's Conquest." Howard Talbot has composed many operettas, including "A Chinese Honeymoon." Nathaniel Clifford Page has done good work in this field also. Frederick Fleming Beale has produced "Magic Hours," as well as orchestral dances; while Paul Bliss's "Ghosts of Hilo" has a Hawaiian subject. It may not be amiss to mention here the children's operettas of the late Louis C. Elson ("Dragon-Fly Day," "Prince Puss-in-Boots," "The Rebellion of the Daisies"), which show much melodic freshness.

Melodrama, or music to a spoken text, is well represented by Rosseter G. Cole's "King Robert of Sicily." Cole's other works include the "Pioneer" overture, a Symphonic Prelude, and a ballad with 'cello, as well as the cantata "The Rock of Liberty," written for the Plymouth tercentenary celebration of 1920.

Walter Keller is another composer of melodrama, his "Alaric's Death" being in this form. He is responsible also for the comic opera "The Crumpled Isle." He shows much learning in his canons and other organ works, which include a synchronous prelude and fugue.

John Alden Carpenter (1876–   ) deserves high praise and extensive mention in any list of American composers, because of the marked originality of his works.   He received early instruction from his mother, who had studied singing with Marchesi and Shakespeare.   In piano he was taught by Amy Fay and W. C. Seeboeck.   Carpenter studied farther with Prof. Paine while at Harvard, and also with Bernard Ziehn, besides a short period under Elgar.   Soon after graduation, he entered the

business firm of his father in Chicago, — George B. Carpenter & Co., dealers in railroad and shipping supplies.   In 1909 he became vice-president of the company.   Music is therefore an avocation with him, — a fact which makes his attainments in this field all the more remarkable.

Among Carpenter's early works are a set of eight interesting songs, published in 1912.   This is the group that includes "Bid Me to Live," "Don't Ceare," "Looking-Glass River," etc. But even more strikingly original and beautiful are

FIG. 105. — JOHN ALDEN CARPENTER.

the "Gitanjali," a set of six songs to poetic texts by Rabindranath Tagore.   Originally for piano, they were later arranged for orchestra by the composer.   His early works include also the set entitled "Water Colors," and the very pleasing group of "Improving Songs for Anxious Children."   His violin sonata was another excellent example of this period.

In the orchestral field, the composer made an instant and marked success with his suite "Adventures in a Perambulator."   This is a six-movement affair, with descriptive text for each movement. The first, "En Voiture," forms a good introduction, with its picture of baby, nurse, and "pram." Next comes "The Policeman," whose ponderous steps are depicted in the score with telling humor, while a little flirtation with the nurse adds more drollery. "The Hurdy-Gurdy" is self-explanatory, though one must praise the effective way in which the fragmentary bits of street music are introduced. The xylophone effects deserve to rank in cleverness with those of St. Saëns in the "Danse Macabre." In the fourth movement, "The Lake," comedy is put aside for the moment, and the rippling of wavelets is pictured with much beauty. "Dogs" brings a return of the humorous effects; while "Dreams" forms a dignified conclusion to a delightful work.

Concerning the Concertino, for piano and large orchestra, it may not be deemed inappropriate to quote from a criticism (the last) by Louis C. Elson. According to his review, "There is much antiphonal work between the piano and the orchestra which is interestingly developed. The composer himself defines it as a conversation between piano and orchestra. The gradual intertwining of the two forces is done in a masterly manner. There is real geniality in the work. . . . Some touches of orchestration are beautiful, notably the violoncello and other string passages of the second section. The work is pigment from beginning to end, and its finale works up to a fiery climax, with piccolo shrieks and much percussion."

Carpenter's Symphony No. 1, in C, has for its motto the phrase "Sermons in stones," from the passage in "As You Like It" beginning, "Sweet are the uses of adversity." But the composer does not go into details, merely stating that the mood of the work is one of optimism. The opening movement has the unusual tempo of Largo, though it contains some more animated sections; and it combines a powerful dignity with more impassioned moods. The second movement is a Scherzo, with an Adagio middle part in good contrast to the string pizzicati, the rapid minor passage, and the waltz-like theme of the opening section. The third movement, Moderato, contains also a slow section (Lento), and an Allegro that brings the final climax, with return of themes from the first movement.

As a ballet composer, Carpenter has produced two very successful works. The first is "The Birthday of the Infanta," in which a festival for the young princess includes the advent of children and grown-ups, the bringing of gifts, Spanish dances, juggling, a mimic bull-fight, and the caperings of the dwarf Pedro, who fell in love with the Infanta, but died of surprise and shock when he saw his own image in a mirror. The second ballet, "Krazy Kat," is based on the cartoons of Herriman, and gives a delightful tonal picture of the various adventures of Krazy Kat herself, Ignatz Mouse, Officer Pup, and the rest of the cartoon characters. This is naturally one of the most extremely American of all native works. A third ballet by Carpenter is to be produced soon at Monte Carlo.

Charles Tomlinson Griffes (1884–1920) belongs in the ballet list because of his dance-drama "The Kairn of Koridwen," for celesta, harp, five wind instruments, and piano. He composed also the Japanese mime-play "Schojo." His symphonic poem "The Pleasure Dome of Kubla Khan" gives an admirable picture of the

> "Miracle of rare device,
> A sunny pleasure-dome with caves of ice,"

with suggestions of the sacred river running through caverns to the sunless sea. In good contrast is a middle section giving echoes of the dancing and revelry within the palace. His "Roman Sketches" for piano, orchestrated later on, contain the proudly glowing "Peacock" and the delicate "Clouds." He wrote also a Poem for flute and orchestra, and Three Poems from Fiona Macleod, with piano or orchestra. His other works include Three Songs with Orchestra, two pieces for string quartet, and for piano various sets of Tone Pictures, Tone Images, Fantasy Pieces, etc.

Henry F. Gilbert (1868–   ) has won much success with his ballet "The Dance in Place Congo," a New Orleans story in which a negro girl is loved by two rivals who come from work on the levee. Gilbert first became known by his "Comedy Overture," containing a minimum of comedy, but a good assortment of interesting negro themes. It is supposed to portray the "Uncle Remus" stories. His "Riders to the Sea" is a short but very dramatic prologue to the play of that name by Synge. Other orchestral works by Gilbert include a Legend and Negro Episode, an "Americanesque" on "Old Zip Coon," "Dearest Mae," and "Rosa Lee," a set of American Dances, the soprano Scena "Salammbo's Invocation to Tanith," and four songs. There are also a Hymn to America, and a large number of songs with piano.

Bainbridge Crist is known chiefly as a singing teacher, but he has composed several large works. He is entitled to rank with the ballet composers because of his dance-drama "Le Pied de la Momie." He has composed the suite "Egyptian Impressions," a number of arias with orchestra, the string quartets "Japonaise" and "Clavecin," and a number of piano pieces and songs.

With all these names, in addition to the stage composers among the earlier leaders, it is evident that American opera is a subject that deserves due attention from the musical historians.

CHAPTER III

CERTAIN PEOPLE OF IMPORTANCE

In treating of the work of many men who have become known lately by their orchestral compositions, it will not be possible for the writer to give more than passing mention to many whose works deserve fuller description. The list of names is extensive, and the spread of musical appreciation in our country, no less than the development of excellent music schools in many places, has resulted in a high standard that is reflected in the large number of native orchestral works now available.

Arne Oldberg is a strong candidate for leadership among his contemporaries. A Chicago product, and pupil of Gleason, he studied also with Rheinberger in Munich, under whom he naturally became devoted to the classical forms. His first symphony received a National Federation prize, while his second has been prominent on various programs. Among his other orchestral works are the overtures "Paolo and Francesca" and "Festival," the rhapsody "June," the fantasy "Night," a set of variations on an original theme, a song cycle, and concertos for piano, for organ, and for horn.

Edward Ballantine is responsible for the symphonic poems "St. Agnes' Eve" and "The Awakening of the Woods," an overture to "The Piper," and incidental music to Hagedorn's "Delectable Forest." Ballantine has won recent fame by his piano setting of "Mary Had a Little Lamb," in the style of ten different composers. The set includes an "Agnelletto" for Mozart, a Beethoven Adagio dedicated to Countess Lämmlein-Plutschsky, a posthumous Chopin nocturne subject to publishers' disputes, a "Musical Half-Moment" by Schubert, a Tchaikowsky "Funeral Waltz," a Sacrificial Scene and Festmahl from the tenth act of a Wagnerian "Lammfell," a Grieg lyric entitled "Mruks Klönh Lmbj," a Macdowell number with a Celtic quatrain, Debussy's "Evening of a Lamb," with weird and wonderfully amusing directions for performance, and a Grand Étude by Liszt for hands, arms, shoulders, back, and hair.

John Powell shows the southern effect of his Richmond birth in such works as his "Negro Rhapsody," for orchestra, his "Virginianesque" violin sonata, and the piano suite "In the South." He has composed also a concerto for piano (his instrument), another violin sonata, three excellent piano sonatas, a set of piano variations with double fugue, and several other good piano works.

FIG. 106. — JOHN POWELL.

Mortimer Wilson, of Atlanta, has composed the large number of five symphonies, besides a "Country Wedding" suite (in apparent rivalry to Goldmark), the prize overture "New Orleans," and works for violin, organ, and piano. The territorial flavor is shown in his "Suwanee Sketches," for violin, and in the piano suites "In Georgia," "Rustica," and "By the Wayside."

Ernest Schelling is another symphonist, having written also a Symphonic Legend, a suite, a violin concerto, and a Fantasie for piano and orchestra, in one movement of which he makes good use of "Dixie" and "The Suwanee River." In his "Impressions of an Artist's Life," he follows Elgar's example, and lets each variation indicate a more or less unexplained person. But the initials affixed to each title give some clue, in addition to tributes to Mahler and Pfitzner. Paderewski, Kreisler, Muck, and many others are here pictured in tones.

Henry Albert Lang is a native of New Orleans; but his works are chiefly of classical rather than pictorial tendencies, except for the some-what suggestive flavor of his Fantastic Dances. He has composed two symphonies, much earnest chamber music, and many lesser pieces.

Arthur Farwell has continued his earlier work on Indian subjects by "The Domain of Hurahan" and a "Navajo War Dance." His other orchestral works include "Dawn" and a "Cornell" overture. Many of his piano pieces use Indian themes.

Charles Sanford Skilton has used the aboriginal flavor in his two "Indian Dances" for orchestra, his three "Indian Scenes" for string quartet, and his three "Indian Sketches" for piano. His other works include the symphonic poem "A Carolina Legend," the overture "Mount Oread," the cantatas "Carmilhan" and "The Witch's Daughter," a 'cello sonata, and various pieces for piano or organ.

Carl Busch, of Danish birth, did not make a shibboleth of Indian tunes and themes, but treated a native subject with orchestral beauty in his symphonic poem "Minnehaha's Vision." He has composed also "The Passing of Arthur," a symphony, several suites, and many prize-winning cantatas, including "The Four Winds," "America," "May," and "The Song of a Star."

David Stanley Smith, Dean of the Yale School of Music, showed the classical vigor of his teacher, Horatio Parker, in a Prelude, Choral, and Fugue for orchestra and organ. His two symphonies have been acclaimed at Norfolk and Chicago; and he has recently finished a Miniature Sym-phony, with parts for soloists instead of instrumental groups. His other orchestral works consist of a Symphonic Ballad, a Concert Overture, the overture "Joyeuse," "L'Allegro and Il Penseroso," an Allegro Giocoso, the suite "Impressions," "A Poem of Youth," and a "Fête Galante" with flute. He now has in manuscript the opera "Merrymount," on a subject full of dramatic possibilities. Among his other vocal works are the oratorio "The Rhapsody of Saint Bernard," some Lyrics for female voices and orchestra, and the prize chorus "The Fallen Star." His piano trio and three string quartets have met with due approval in public performances.

Leo Sowerby is a recent leader, and the first to hold an American *Prix de Rome*. He shows due sense of form, as well as musicianship, in his symphony. "A Set of Four" is less formally ambitious. "Comes Autumn-Time" and "The Sorrows of Mylath" are symphonic poems.

Other orchestral works include a piano concerto, a 'cello concerto, and settings of British folk-tunes. Sowerby's various chamber works, including violin sonatas, a 'cello sonata, and a woodwind quintet, as well as his organ preludes and piano sonatas, all show an excellent blend of learning and originality.

William E. Haesche, another Yale leader, is responsible for a symphony, a symphonietta, a "Wald-Idyll," a fantasy entitled "The South," "Springtime," and the overture "Frithjof and Ingeborg." His two violin suites are entitled "Eyes of the Night" and "Characteristic." He has composed also several piano trios, two piano suites, and a cantata, "The Haunted Oak."

Camille Zeckwer (d. 1924) won favorable notice by his "Jade Butterflies," a set of five pieces entitled "Dance Rhythm," "Silence," "Balance," "Return," and "Motion." These movements, each prefaced by verses from a poem paraphrasing Japanese effects, show remarkable pictorial power and much delicate orchestral beauty. Zeckwer numbered among his other orchestral works the symphonic poem "Sohrab and Rustum," a piano concerto, and a Swedish Fantasy with violin. He wrote also a cantata, "The New Day," an opera, "Jane and Janetta," and much excellent chamber music.

Blair Fairchild, who has elected to live in Paris, is much devoted to oriental subjects. This tendency shows in his symphonic poems, such as "East and West," "Zal," and "Shah Feridoun." A violin concerto, much chamber music, and an organ fugue show his knowledge of the classical forms also. His songs revert to national styles, including Tuscan, Greek, and Persian sets.

Victor Benham, another expatriate, has produced two symphonies, two piano concertos, a violin concerto, and many string quartets.

Max Bendix returned to his ancestral Danish home, after writing a violin concerto and several orchestral works.

Louis Kelterborn has settled in Basel, where he is winning much orchestral renown.

Hugo Kaun is continuing his very successful career in Germany.

Albert Augustus Stanley, who settled in Berlin, is responsible for a symphony entitled "The Soul's Awakening," the symphonic poem "Attis," an orchestral scherzo, five cantatas, incidental music to Greek plays, and "Greek Themes in Modern Settings."

Sigismund Stojowski is a leader among the foreigners who seem settled in America. His long list of compositions, which often show the fiery spirit of his native Poland, includes a symphony, a suite, three piano concertos, a Rhapsody with piano, a 'cello concerto, a Romanza with violin, several chamber works, a number of piano pieces and songs, and the choral works "Le Printemps" and "Prayer for Poland."

Frederick A. Stock, the Chicago conductor, has produced a symphony, some Symphonic Tone-Pictures, a violin concerto, shorter orchestral works, a string quintet, and a string quartet.

Felix Borowski witnessed the performance of his ballet "Boudour," and is responsible also for the symphonic poems "Youth" and "Abelard and Heloise," as well as shorter pieces.

Ernest Bloch, coming from Switzerland, made a strong impression with his "Trois Poëmes Juifs." Like his string quartet and other works, these are powerfully expressive.

Arthur Claassen has composed the symphonic poem "Hohenfried-berg," a suite, and various orchestral and choral works.

Other prominent foreigners, culled from a long list, are Ernest Hutcheson, W. C. Seeboeck, Fritz Stahlberg, Rudolf Ganz, and Lazare Saminsky. Christian Sinding came to the Eastman school at Rochester, but produced no large works to rival his Norwegian compositions.

A leader in the Roman church is Ludwig Bonvin. Coming from Switzerland to Canisius College, he has composed a symphony and many other orchestral pieces, besides masses and choral works.

Nicola Montani is another Catholic composer, who has produced a Missa Solemnis and an orchestral suite.

Pietro A. Yon is another mass composer, while Charles Winfred Douglas has composed masses for the Episcopal church, and Henry G. Thunder is known by a mass and a historical cantata.

John Eliot Trowbridge, still another mass writer, has composed also the oratorio "Emmanuel," and a patriotic cantata.

Returning to the native orchestral leaders, Edward Burlingame Hill deserves high praise for the beauty of his two "Stevensoniana" suites. The first illustrates the "Marching Song," "The Land of Nod," "Where Go the Boats," and "The Unseen Playmate," while the second comprises "Armies in the Fire," "The Dumb Soldier," and "Pirate Story," all from "A Child's Garden of Verses." The various movements are well contrasted and expressive. Hill's other orchestral works include "Lance-lot and Guinevere" and "The Fall of the House of Usher." Among his earlier compositions are several pantomimes. His "Jazz Study" for piano, and a number of his songs, are also widely known.

Arthur Shepherd is one of the more advanced modernists. He has composed three striking overtures, the "Joyeuse," "The Festival of Youth," and "The Nuptials of Attila." Most successful is his "Humoreske" for piano and orchestra, which shows some real humor, and is excellently interwoven into a coherent whole. Shepherd's other works include a suite, and the cantatas "The Song of the Sea Winds" and "The City in the Sea."

Philip Greeley Clapp is now credited with three symphonies; but his extreme modernism makes them into involved rhapsodical affairs rather than the clean-cut, well-balanced form of classical and romantic times. His other works include the prelude "In Summer," and the tone-poems "Norge" and "The Song of Youth."

A less radical symphonist is Edwin Grasse, the blind violinist. He has written a concerto and five sonatas for his instrument in addition to a string quartet and two piano trios. His symphony and orchestral suite show much expressive power.

Eugene Gruenberg is another violinist who has composed a symphony.

Ellsworth C. Phelps has written program symphonies, such as "Hiawatha" and "Emancipation." He is known also for symphonic poems, overtures, two comic operas, and the cantata "David."

Nathan Hale Allen is an earlier writer of cantatas and symphonic pieces.

Daniel Gregory Mason, known by his literary work, has composed some chamber work and many shorter pieces, as well as a symphony and the music for the Cape Cod Pageant.

Frank Edwin Ward is responsible for the symphony "Shakespearian Moods," as well as an "Ocean Rhapsody," the scherzo "Peter Pan," and a host of other orchestral, choral, and chamber works.

Fred Preston Search has produced a Romantic Symphony, an overture, some incidental music, and chamber works.

George Eliot Simpson is another active composer, with two symphonies, four overtures, three suites, and many other works to his credit.

Frederick Jacobi has produced an impressive Assyrian Symphony.

Louis Leslie Loth has written two symphonies and some chamber music.

Edward Shippen Barnes, known for his excellent organ and vocal works, has published a good organ symphony. His other large works include two suites and several sacred cantatas.

Clarence Dickinson, also, has produced an organ symphony, in addition to church work and a couple of light operas.

Not all symphonies are worthwhile. Some composers err by lack of inspiration; while others write with so much modernistic freedom that they might as well call their works tone-poems. But the above-mentioned examples are all of some value, and in many cases show excellent musicianship.

Arthur Mansfield Curry has treated a native subject in his symphonic poem "Atala." He has written also the overtures "Blomidon" and "Elegie," and a "Keltic Legend," with chorus.

Cecil Burleigh, known for his work on Negro spirituals, has composed the tone-poem "Evangeline," three "Mountain Pictures," and two violin concertos, besides lesser works.

Maurice Arnold is responsible for overtures and "Plantation Dances."

W. H. Humiston has written a "Southern Fantasy," in addition to a suite and the overture "Twelfth Night."

Horace Alden Miller has chosen a western subject for "The Wickiup."

Emerson Whithorne, more general in his sources of inspiration, has composed the symphonic poems "Ranza" and "The City of Ys," a Japanese Suite, three string quartets (one entitled Greek and one Oriental), and various worthy violin and piano works.

Patrick O'Sullivan is responsible for the symphonic poem "Heraklius," a "Fantaisie Irlandaise" with piano, an Epithalamium, and piano works and songs of Irish national flavor.

Deems Taylor has scored a marked success with his suite "Through the Looking-Glass," the "Jabberwocky" movement being especially effective and full of humor. Among his other orchestral works are "The Portrait of a Lady" and the prize-winning "Sirens." He has composed large cantatas, such as "The Highwayman" and "The Chambered Nautilus," and incidental music to many modern plays.

Chester Edward Ide has produced the symphonic poem "Pan's Dream of Syrinx," the suites "Winter" and "Idyllic Dances," and incidental music to Mackaye's "Caliban."

John Spencer Camp has composed the overture "Zeitgeist," a "Pilgrim's Progress" suite, several cantatas, and many smaller works.

A. Walter Kramer has written four Sketches, a rhapsody with violin, chamber works, and many deservedly successful pieces for violin, organ, piano, and voice.

Philip James is responsible for the symphonic poem "Aucassin and Nicolette," an overture, several cantatas, and smaller works.

Elliott Schenk has two operas in manuscript, — "Tess of the D'Urbervilles," and "The Children of the Evening Star." His orchestral works include the tone-poems "The Lost Joy" (an Olive Schreiner subject), "The Sorceress" (after Theocritus), and "In a Withered Garden." He has composed also the overture "Perseus and Andromeda," and incidental music to "The Tempest," "The Piper," and "The Arrow-Maker."

Abraham W. Lilienthal has composed orchestral dances and transcriptions. He is well known also because of his chamber works, violin music, and songs.

Among those who have written good overtures, Samuel Bollinger has produced also the suite "Sphinx." Smith Newell Penfield (d. 1920) supplemented his orchestral work by church music. Eric Delamarter composed the overture "The Faun," in addition to chamber works and shorter pieces. Leo R. Lewis, of Tufts, followed his prelude to "The Blot on the 'Scutcheon" by a large cantata. Lindsay Norden worked in the same forms. William H. Oetting, Walter Spry, Winthrop Sterling, and Howard R. Thatcher are other overture composers.

Among those who have written piano concertos, John Carver Alden, Heinrich Bellermann, Walter Ruel Cowles, and E. A. Parsons deserve mention.

Violin concertos worthy of note have been produced by Albert Spalding and Arthur Emil Uhe.

Good suites have been composed by Arthur Olaf Andersen, George Whitfield Andrews, John Hyatt Brewer, Chalmers Clifton, Preston Ware Orem, and Louis Arthur Russell.

Others deserving mention for shorter orchestral works are Stanley R. Avery, James P. Dunn, William J. Kraft, Frank Stuart Mason, Henry Dike Sleeper, Benjamin P. Whelpley, and Paul White.

The many names in this chapter will serve to show that orchestral composition in the United States is surely in a flourishing condition.

CHAPTER IV

MEN AND WOMEN

Place aux dames, as the saying goes ; and the women who have written for orchestra may serve here as a transition to the men who have worked in the shorter forms.

Of the women composers already mentioned, Helen Hopekirk has produced no new orchestral works, but has published some remarkably interesting piano compositions. Her "Iona Memories" are an excellent tribute to the land of her birth. A piano Suite is another excellent work ; while a second Suite (entitled "Serenata") revives early styles and old dances in most charming modern fashion.

Mrs. Beach has devoted much of her working time to large cantatas, such as "The Rose of Avontown," and "The Sea Fairies."

Isabella Beaton displays much classical dignity in her works, which include an orchestral Scherzo, two string quartets, a piano sonata, several fugues, and other piano works.

Clara A. Korn, of German birth, has been even more active, composing a symphony, a piano concerto, and an opera, "The Last War," as well as chamber works, a piano sonata, and various shorter pieces and songs.

Mary Carr Moore, composer of songs, has written also the opera "Narcissa," treating the story of Narcissa Prentiss, who married Marcus Whitman and accompanied him on the ill-fated pioneering expedition to Oregon, which ended in a massacre by the Indians.

Harriet Ware has composed the tone-poem "Undine," which has been arranged as a short opera. Her other works include a piano concerto, the cantata "Sir Oluf," and "The Cross," for violin and orchestra, in addition to many songs and some piano works.

Edith Noyes Porter has composed the Indian opera "Osseo," which contains some interesting music, even if it has not reached the stage.

Her other compositions consist of many pleasing works for violin, piano, or voice.

Gena Branscombe, known by the cycle "A Lute of Jade" and by many other remarkably beautiful songs, has entered the orchestral field with a Festival Prelude.

Margaret Ruthven Lang now has three overtures to her credit, but is still best known by her songs, such as "Tryste Noël," "Northward," "My Lady Jacqueminot," "Eros," and so forth.

Mabel Daniels has continued her career with a Ballad for baritone and orchestra, and the effective orchestral-vocal work "Peace with a Sword," with words based on the Massachusetts state motto.

Fannie Dillon is reputed to have several excellent orchestral works in manuscript.

Marguerite Melville-Liszniewska is known as a composer of chamber music and piano pieces.

Laura Sedgwick Collins, too, has written good chamber works.

Florence Newell Barbour is well known because of her songs and piano pieces, the latter including such suites as "A Day in Arcady," "All in a Garden Fair," "Forest Sketches," and "Nature Pieces."

Patty Stair, pianist and composer of piano works, has excelled also in both serious and humorous songs.

Mrs. C. W. Krogmann and Mrs. L. E. Orth are known for their excellent teaching pieces for piano.

Beatrice Mary Hall and Eva Ruth Spalding are among the most recent piano composers.

Among the song composers, Mary Turner Salter has written "The Cry of Rachel" and other examples of dramatic power. Mary Knight Wood is known by her "Ashes of Roses" and various lyrics. Lily Strickland has shown much grace and daintiness in her work. Among very many names, some that deserve mention are Lola Carrier Worrell, Fay Foster, Fanny Knowlton, Eleanor Freer, Gertrude Sans-Souci, Florence Turner-Maley, Floy Little Bartlett, Harriet P. Sawyer, Anne Stratton, Theodora Dutton, Phyllis Fergus, Ina Rae Seitz, Lalla Ryckoff, Natalie Wollin, Elizabeth Siedoff, Kathleen L. Manning, Beatrice Fenner, Natalie Curtis, Ruth Rapoport, and the hymn composer, Fanny Spencer.

Returning to the men, Homer Norris has entered the orchestral field with his "John the Baptist."

Gerrit Smith (d. 1912) was known as composer of the cantata "David," as well as the "Aquarelles" and other works for piano.

George Balch Nevin, a cousin of Ethelbert and Arthur Nevin, is another cantata composer, who has written also much excellent organ music and many anthems and sacred songs.

Charles Whitney Coombs is another who has specialized in sacred cantatas.

Others who have worked in this field are Harvey B. Gaul, Harry Alexander Matthews, John Sebastian Matthews, Philo Adams Otis, Charles Gilbert Spross, Frederick Stevenson, and Frederick William Schlieder.

Henry Clough-Leighter, working largely in the secular cantata field, deserves especial mention for his melodic gifts. Besides five cantatas, he has composed a vocal suite, "The Day of Beauty," and several Odes, including "Lasca," "Recessional," and "The Christ of the Andes."

Clifford Demarest and Will C. Macfarlane are other cantata composers, while Agide Jacchia, the "pop" conductor, has composed a "Centennial American Hymn," among other choral works.

Nathaniel Dett is the leader of the American Negro composers. His cantatas consist of "The Chariot Jubilee" and "The Death of Moses." His many effective songs include the cycle entitled "The Heart of a Poet." For piano he has composed a sonata, various pieces such as the "Juba Dance," and the suites "The Magnolia" and "In the Bottoms." Dett's music shows the intensity of expression and exotic beauty that one would expect from the descendants of a race originally living in primitive tropical conditions.

Louis Victor Saar has devoted himself largely to chamber music, producing a string quartet, a piano quartet, and other works.

Albert Stoessel has composed a string quintet, a string quartet, and various violin works.

Walter Stockhoff is responsible for several piano trios, as well as other chamber and piano works.

Franklin M. Class, a physician who makes music an avocation, has composed a string quartet and several pieces for 'cello and for flute.

William N. Pommer has written a piano quintet, a piano trio, and a violin sonata.

Edward Baxter Perry became known for a string quartet, in addition to piano pieces.

W. Humphrey Dayas (d. 1903) produced a string suite and a violin sonata, as well as settings of several Psalms.

John Beach has essayed chamber music of a rather advanced and formless character.

Abram Ray Tyler is responsible for a piano trio and a violin sonata, as well as music for Protestant and Jewish services, and several settings for Greek Plays.

Clarence G. Hamilton has also set Greek plays, in addition to writing some choral music.

Wallingford Riegger won a Coolidge prize with "La Belle Dame sans Merci," for voices and several instruments. Incidentally this prize, offered at intervals by the public-spirited Mrs. Coolidge, of Berkshire Festival fame, has done much to encourage local as well as foreign talent, and has brought forth excellent compositions.

Among violin composers, those who deserve mention include Arthur Hartmann, Eddy Brown, Gustav Sänger, Alberto Bachmann, and Samuel Gardner.

Frank LaForge is known for some excellent piano pieces, in addition to his songs.

Herman P. Chelius is responsible for a Grand Prelude and Fugue that deserves high praise.

Frederick Ayres is another fugal writer.

Noble Kreider is a more ambitious piano composer, whose various large works for this instrument show great power.

Leo Ornstein is known as a modernist, such titles as the "Gargoyles" from "Notre Dame" and the "Wild Man's Dance" indicating the style of his music quite clearly.

Georges Antheil, known as an advanced radical, has produced a rather tame "Jazz Sonata." More striking is his "American Symphony," depicting "skyscrapers, machines, subways, electric lights," etc., and scored for bassoon, trumpet, trombone, flute, and violin.

George Gershwin is another composer who has tried to unite jazz and the classical forms.

Other piano composers include Francis Hendriks, Albert Ross Parsons, Alvah Glover Salmon, Aaron Copeland, and Thurlow Lieurance.

Among various organ composers are Everett E. Truette, R. Huntington Woodman, George W. Stebbins, Nicholas Douty, John Winter

Thompson, Ralph Lyman Baldwin, Walter C. Gale, Stanley T. Reiff, and Russell King Miller.

The introduction of carillons into this country has increased the duties of the organists. These carillons are chromatic scales in chimes, upon which much good music can be performed. The history of the subject may be found in a work by William Gorham Rice.

Among those who have written much part-music, both sacred and secular, are Sumner Salter, Peter C. Lutkin, and Frederick Maxson.

Sidney Homer is undoubtedly the leader among our native song-composers. He has far more than mere melodic gifts, for he imparts to his music a most vivid and intense dramatic power. This gives his compositions the same preëminence here that the ballads of Loewe, or the more dramatic of the Schubert songs, have enjoyed in German musical history. Homer's songs show also an almost Wagnerian unity between the sense of the words and the character of the setting. Such powerful bits as "Prospice," "The Pauper's Ride," or "To Russia," are excellent examples of the composer's intense expressive power.

As for the other song-composers of our country, their name is legion. A few of the better-known men who have worked in this field during the last two decades are James Carroll Bartlett, Robert Braine, A. Buzzi-Peccia, Charles H. Dana, William H. Dana, Louis R. Dressler, William Arms Fisher, Hallett Gilbert, Frank S. Hastings, Charles Huerter, Rupert Hughes, Herbert Johnson, William Spencer Johnson, John A. Loud, H. C. MacDougall, A. A. Mack, Malcolm D. McMillan, H. R. Palmer, Bernard Rogers, Winthrop L. Rogers, Walter Morse Rummel, Arthur Ryder, Alexander Steinert, R. M. Stults, A. W. Thayer, Everett H. Titcomb, Stephen Townsend, R. S. Willis, G. D. Wilson, and H. Wintter-Watts. Those who wish may find hundreds of other composers in the review columns of the musical periodicals.

The large number of names mentioned in this and the preceding chapters will show that composition is now in a flourishing condition in our country. Perhaps not all of the men listed here will win any large amount of permanent future fame; but it may be claimed with safety that all of them have done work of a high standard.

The question as to whether we have a national school is one that the present writer would answer in the negative. We have many excellent and well-known composers; but their music is cosmopolitan rather than national.   This is by no means a reproach; for Tchaikowsky and Rubinstein were accused of being too cosmopolitan, this accusation coming from the Balakireff group, whose members were more national, but more limited in their styles of composition.

If folk-song is to be the basis of a national school, then our country is too large to have a unified style; and different sections of it have different schools of folk-music.

The attempt to popularize Indian melodies is no doubt praiseworthy, but will hardly result in a national style.   MacDowell's Indian Suite is still somewhat of an interesting curiosity.   Cadman's rich harmonies are still his own, whether wreathed around aboriginal themes or used to describe Odysseus or other gentlemen of the white persuasion.   Farwell, Lieurance, and the others who have used Indian themes, could have invented just as good material of their own, if they had so desired.   And no matter how well a composer may use these Indian motives, they do not clearly show their character to those hearers who are not musically educated; and this wide appeal is just what real folk-music should have.

The negro melodies are more widely known, and more easily recognizable in such works as those of Chadwick, or in Dvořák's beautiful "New World" symphony.   But only the simpler styles of this school are well known; and the trend of modernism has been to draw away from a simplicity that is not always combined with strength or dignity.   In other words, the plantation style, interesting as it is, may sometimes grow too cloying in its sameness.

There are a number of schools of folk-music in America that are scarcely known to the composers, to say nothing of the general public.   In spite of Brockway's researches, for example, few know of the songs of the Kentucky and Appalachian mountaineers.   Fewer still are familiar with the cowboy songs, described by John Lomax and others; yet "The Old Chisholm Trail" and other cowboy ballads are effective enough in their way.   Very few indeed are aware that the lumbermen of Maine and other sections have folk-ballads, unknown to the general musical public.   Even the sailors' chanteys, so varied and well known in the American sailing days, are almost wholly unfamiliar to composers; though their frequent harmonic crudenesses would hardly make them available for extended treatment.

American popular music, even more than that of the European countries, is a thing apart, and not well suited to the composer's uses, Hill's "Jazz Study" to the contrary notwithstanding. The popular school has run through many phases, changing from the plantation sentiment of Foster to the ragtime of fifteen years ago, the "blues" that started as harmonic settings, and the jazz that in its best form is free counterpoint. The syncopated ragtime was probably named from the so-called rent rags of the negroes, which were festivities intended to raise money for the landlord; though many think that the name refers to ragged rhythm. Blues have degenerated into jumbled settings of popular dances. Jazz has become a privilege of the saxophone. If jazz is merely the weaving of a free contrapuntal part about a known composition, then it may be, and sometimes is, a most attractive affair; but in most cases it has become a brazen blatance that had better be left unsaid, or at least unplayed.

The European war brought out many popular songs that still have some vogue, besides leading the composers to produce many works of real musical merit. Less well known are the trench songs of the American Expeditionary Force, though all who took part in the service are familiar with them. In most cases they were merely set to some well-known tune, such as "The Old Gray Mare." There were songs for the Engineers, the Artillery, the Cavalry, the M. P.'s, and others. There was a doleful jingle for the private who had to sweep out the barracks because no one else would. Best known of all, however, because of the numbers singing it, was the refrain of the foot-soldiers, running as follows : —

> "The infantry, the infantry, with dirt behind their ears,
> The infantry, the infantry, they lap up all the beers;
> But the cavalry, the artillery, and the grimy engineers,
> They couldn't lick the infantry in a hundred thousand years."

Songs developing under conditions like those of the war have a good chance to become real folk-music; but the cosmopolitan character of our personnel probably prevented any original tunes from arising.

As indicated before, the trend of modernism has had a paramount influence on American composers. Modernism implies a free use of advanced and intricate harmonic designs. These are well suited to more or less definite tone-pictures, and have made program music, which illustrates a subject or tells a story printed on the program, the most important school of the present. Arousing much opposition at first, the modernists have now won their case; and one may be pardoned for quoting the often-told remark of Rimsky-Korsakoff. When that famous leader heard Stravinsky perform selections from his "Oiseau de Feu," he remarked, "Don't play that stuff any more, or I shall begin to like it." Yet even though the public has long since begun to understand the modern harmonic freedom, there is still a need for composers to show a sense of balance, contrast, and proportion, and a proper amount of real inspiration. While the United States has had no wild pioneers of the Schoenberg or Malipiero type, it has many composers who have done admirable work in this school. Therefore it must be fairly admitted that American music has justified itself. Though we have no classical masters to look back upon, and no operatic background of the Gounod-Verdi type, it is none the less true that our present-day composers have placed us fully abreast of the most recent developments in music.

The great spread of musical education in our country is bound to improve the standard that has already been attained. Music schools are springing up in profusion; college after college has created a music department; symphony orchestras are more numerous than ever; even small towns are taking steps toward municipal education in music; and in the large cities, millionaires of the Juillard type are beginning to establish musical foundations. With all these points to consider, we may look forward to a constant increase in the spread of musical taste, and to the advent of even more and better composers than those who have already won personal fame and given us national prestige by their many excellent compositions.

GENERAL BIBLIOGRAPHY

Bay Psalm Book. Boston, 1646.

BILLINGS. New England Psalm Singer. Boston, 1770.

BAKER. Biographical Dictionary of Musicians. New York, 1900.

BAKER. Ueber die Musik der Nord-Amerikanischen Wilden. Leipsic, 1882.

BOISE. Harmony made Practical.

BROOKS. Olden-time Music. Boston, 1888.

Boston Almanacs of 18th Century. Boston.

Boston Gazette. 18th Century. Boston.

CUMMINGS. "God save the King." London, 1903.

Columbian Musical Miscellany. Northampton, 1798.

Dwight's Journal of Music. Boston, 1852–1854.

ELSON, ARTHUR, and RUPERT HUGHES. American Composers. Boston, 1915.

ELSON, L. C. Curiosities of Music. Boston, 1890.

—— Our National Music and its Sources. Boston, 1900.

ELSON, ARTHUR. A Critical History of Opera. Boston, 1901.

—— Woman in Music. Boston, 1903.

FINCK. Songs and Song-writers. New York, 1900.

—— The Wagner Trilogy. Cincinnati, 1903.

FILLMORE. History of Pianoforte Music. New York, 1883.

FLETCHER. A Study of Omaha Indian Music. Cambridge, 1893.

FISKE. The American Revolution. Boston, 1891.

GROVE. A Dictionary of Music and Musicians. London, 1879–1890.

GOULD. History of Church Music in America. Boston, 1853.

GOODRICH. Complete Musical Analysis. Cincinnati, 1889.

GOLDSTEIN. Die Oeffentliche Musikpflege in den Vereinigten Staaten von Nord-
Amerika. Leipsic, 1880.

HENDERSON. The Story of Music. New York, 1889.

HOLYOKE. Harmonia Americana. Boston, 1791.

HUGHES. Contemporary American Composers. Revised by Arthur Elson. Boston,
1914.

—— The Musical Guide. New York, 1903.

HOOD. History of Music in New England. Boston, 1846.

HOWE, DE WOLFE. The Boston Symphony Orchestra. Boston, 1914.

KREHBIEL. Notes on the Cultivation of Choral Music in New York. New York, 1893.

—— The Philharmonic Society of New York. A Memorial. London, 1892.

—— Review of the New York Musical Season. New York, 1886–1890.

LAHEE. Great Pianists. Boston, 1901.

—— Great Singers. Boston, 1898.

—— The Organ and its Masters. Boston, 1903.

The Musical Times. London, 1902.

MADEIRA. Annals of Music in Philadelphia. Philadelphia, 1896.

MATHEWS. One Hundred Years of Music in America. Chicago, 1889.
—— The Great in Music. Chicago, 1900.
Musical Courier. National Edition. New York, 1898.
Music Teachers' National Association. Annual Records, 1890–1914.
MOORE. Encyclopædia of Music. Boston, 1875.
NASON. Our National Song. Albany, 1869.
PERKINS and DWIGHT. History of the Handel and Haydn Society. Boston, 1886–1893.
PREBLE. History of the Flag of the United States. Boston, 1880.
Post-boy. 18th Century Files. Boston.
Programmes (analytical) of Philharmonic Society. New York.
—— Philadelphia Symphony Orchestra. Philadelphia.
Programmes of Cincinnati Orchestra. Cincinnati.
—— Boston Symphony Orchestra. Boston.
RITTER. Music in America. New York, 1890.
SACHSE. The Music of the Ephrata Cloister. Lancaster, 1903.
SEWALL. Diary of Judge Samuel Sewall. Boston, 1878.
Scharff and Westcott's History of Philadelphia. Philadelphia.
Stoughton Musical Society's Centennial Collection. Boston, 1878.
SONNECK. Early Opera in America. New York, 1915.
—— Francis Hopkinson and James Lyon. Washington, 1905.
—— The Star-spangled Banner. Washington, 1914.
—— Early Concert-life in America. Leipzig, 1907.
—— Early Secular American Music. Washington, 1905.
SEIDL, ANTON. A Memorial. New York.
UPTON. Standard Oratorios. Chicago, 1888.
—— Standard Symphonies. Chicago, 1896.
—— Standard Cantatas. Chicago, 1889.
WALLATSCHEK. Primitive Music. London, 1893.
WINSOR. Memorial History of Boston. 1880.
WILSON. Musical Year-books of America. Boston, 1890–1892.
WHITE. National Hymns; how they are written and how they are not written. New York, 1861.

My Days Have Been so Wondrous Free

(THE FIRST AMERICAN COMPOSITION)

FRANCIS HOPKINSON (1759)

INDEX

Abbey, Henry E., 115.

Abbott, Emma, 310.

Academy of Music, Boston, 52; influence in many states, 80; founded public school music in United States, 80; orchestra, 52.

Academy of Music, New York, 109, 115.

Academy of Sacred Music, 74.

"Adams and Liberty," 151, 154.

Adams, Charles R., 309; as Whitney's choir-boy, 269.

Adams, Mrs. Mehitable, 314.

Adams, Suzanne, 310.

Advertisements, of ancient music (*see* List of Illustrations); early music-teacher's, 42.

Aldrich, Richard, 320.

Allen, Charles N. (taught Hadley), 191.

Alves, Mrs. Carl, 301.

"America" (new tune to words), 147; first performance, 147.

American fingering derived from England, 41.

American opera, prize offered for, 109.

American symphony ("From the New World"), 348.

American teachers for American pupils, 343.

American trilogy, An, 239.

"Anacreon in Heaven" ("Star-spangled Banner"), 150.

Anacreontics of London, The, 150.

Ancient American instrument, like that of Nineveh, 124.

Andrews, G., 274.

"Angel of Peace," American hymn by Keller, 163.

Anschütz, Carl, 109–110.

Anti-Federalists in 1798, 148.

Apollo Club, Boston, 81 (*see* also Lang, B. J.); Cincinnati, 82 (*see* also Foley, B. W.).

Apollo Musical Club, Chicago, 329.

Apthorp, William F., 323 *et seq.*; analytical programmes, 326; taught Clayton Johns, 247.

Archer, Frederick, led Pittsburg Orchestra, 66; organist, 92; concert in Boston, 262; city concerts in Pittsburg, 274.

Arditi, Luigi, 115.

Arens, F. X., 71.

Arion Society, New York, 76; made trip to Europe, 192. (*See* also Ritter; Damrosch.)

Arnold, Dr. Samuel, music to "Star-spangled Banner," 150.

Associations, musical, *see* Academy of Music, Boston; American College of Musicians; Harvard Musical Association; Musical Fund Society, Philadelphia; Music Teachers' National Association; Manuscript Society, New York; Manuscript Society, Chicago; also Dwight; Mason.

Astor Place Opera House, 107.

Atlantic Monthly, Apthorp, music critic of, 323; Ticknor, assistant editor, 326; "music in public schools" (footnote), 348.

Austrian national hymn, 140.

"Azara," opera by Paine, 169.

Baermann, Professor Carl, 287 *et seq.*; taught Converse, 204; C. H. Morse, 273; Mrs. Beach, 289, 297; death, 289.

Baker, Theodore, Dr. (work on Indian music), 332.

Balatka, Hans, 328.

Baldwin, Samuel A. (organist at World's Fair), 274.

Baltimore American (first prints "Star-spangled Banner"), 154.

Baltzell, W. J., 326.

Band mobbed for playing classical music, 44.

Band music, early New England, 42; West Point (footnote), 42.

Banjo more advanced than Indian instruments, 133.

Barnum, P. T., tour with Jenny Lind, 108.

Barrell, Edgar A., 274.

Bartlett, Homer N., 256.

Bates, Arlo, poem set by Johns, 248.

Baton, first use in conducting, 51.

"Battle-cry of Freedom," 162.

Baur, Miss Clara, Cincinnati Conservatory, 347.

"Bay Psalm Book," 3–4.

Beach, Dr., Whitney's choir-boy, 269; marries Amy M. Cheney, 298.

INDEX TO SUPPLEMENTARY CHAPTERS